MONEY
WELL
SPENT?

MICHAEL GRABELL

MONEY WELL SPENT?

THE TRUTH BEHIND THE
TRILLION-DOLLAR STIMULUS,
THE BIGGEST ECONOMIC RECOVERY
PLAN IN HISTORY

PUBLICAFFAIRS
New York

PublicAffairs books are available at special discounts for bulk purchases in the
U.S. by corporations, institutions, and other organizations. For more information,
please contact the Special Markets Department at the Perseus Books Group,
2300 Chestnut Street, Suite 200, Philadelphia, PA 19103, call (800) 810-4145,
ext. 5000, or e-mail special.markets@perseusbooks.com.

Library of Congress Cataloging-in-Publication Data
Grabell, Michael.
Money well spent?: the truth behind the trillion-dollar stimulus, the biggest
economic recovery plan in history / Michael Grabell. — 1st ed.
  p. cm.
Includes bibliographical references and index.
ISBN 978-1-61039-009-5 (hbk.) — ISBN 978-1-61039-010-1 (electronic)
 1. United States—Economic policy—2009— 2. United States—Economic
conditions—2009– 3. Job creation—United States. 4. Economic development
projects—United States. 5. Economic stabilization—United States. 6. Federal
aid—United States. 7. Recessions—United States. I. Title.
HC106.84.G73   2012
330.973—dc23
2011040969

Editorial production by *Marrathon* Production Services. www.marrathon.net
Book design by Jane Raese
Text set in 12-point Dante

FIRST EDITION

10 9 8 7 6 5 4 3 2 1

TO LAURA

CONTENTS

INTRODUCTION

THE AMERICAN RECOVERY AND REINVESTMENT ACT was the largest economic recovery plan in history. Better known as "the stimulus," the $825 billion package passed in February 2009 included a mixture of tax cuts, safety net spending, and long-term investments in renewable energy, education, and infrastructure. Adjusted for inflation, it was nearly five times more expensive than the Works Progress Administration (WPA), credited with easing if not helping to end the Great Depression. The stimulus cost more than it did to fight the Iraq War from 2003 to 2010. It was bigger than the Louisiana Purchase, the Manhattan Project, the moon race, and the Marshall Plan to rebuild Europe after World War II. When the various extensions of stimulus provisions are taken into account, the recovery program cost well over a trillion dollars.

Seventy-five years from now, historians will still be debating the effect the federal stimulus package had in ameliorating the Great Recession, just as they do now with the New Deal. Economists and nonpartisan forecasting firms estimate that the Recovery Act created and saved 2 million to 3 million jobs. Without it, they say, the unemployment rate would have reached 12 percent and lingered in the double digits until 2012. When the last dime is spent, more than 41,000 miles of roads will be paved, widened, and improved; 600,000 low-income homes weatherized and made more energy-efficient; over 3,000 rural schools connected to high-speed Internet. A relatively small pot of education grants goaded thirty-two states to enact major reforms, such as tying teacher pay to student performance or lifting caps on charter schools. At least thirty states liberalized unemployment laws, such as opening up benefits to part-time workers, those in job training, or people who left the workforce to care for a sick relative. The stimulus created an unprecedented buzz around clean energy, popularizing the term "green jobs," and turning attention to solar panels, wind turbines, electric cars, weatherization, biofuels, smart energy meters, and high-speed rail.

The Obama administration kept its own stable of superlatives on hand to describe the Recovery Act in speeches. The largest investment in education in American history. The largest investment in clean energy in American history. The most progressive tax cuts in American history. The biggest public works plan since Eisenhower approved the Interstate Highway System in the 1950s. The largest boost to biomedical research in history. The new Department of Homeland Security headquarters was the largest federal building project since the Pentagon.

Despite all these honorifics, the Recovery Act did not bring about a strong, sustainable recovery. More than four years since the start of the recession, the economy remained horrendous. Businesses were reluctant to hire. Foreclosed homes sat empty. Infrastructure was still crumbling. With nearly all the money spent, the unemployment rate was 9 percent. Including those who had settled for part-time jobs or given up, it was more than 16 percent. The middle class and the working poor were increasingly unable to make ends meet. And nothing political leaders tried seemed to get us out of the ditch.

For all its promise, the federal stimulus package became one of the most reviled pieces of legislation in recent memory. Conservatives branded it a flop and a porkfest, a radical takeover of the economy that discouraged businesses from investing and that would saddle our grandchildren with crippling debt. Liberals cried that the stimulus was too small, a flimsy and visionless cave-in to Republicans as part of a foolish foray for bipartisan support. With such polar polemics dominating the TV, radio, and Twitter, it's been difficult for ordinary Americans to know what to make of what the government did with the taxpayers' dime. Where did all the money go? Was the stimulus too big or too small? Did it pull us back from the brink or push us deeper into the abyss? Somewhere in between these simplified extremes lies the truth.

The stimulus was designed in three parts. First, a flood of money in tax cuts, food stamps, and unemployment checks would get consumers spending. An even greater deluge of education and health care money would stop the bleeding in state budgets. Then, a wave of "shovel-ready" infrastructure projects would kick in, creating new jobs repaving roads and making homes more energy efficient. As the economy got churning again, new investments in wind farms, solar panel factories, electric cars, broadband, and high-speed rail would lead America out of the recession and into a twenty-first-century economy competitive with the rest of the world.

But it didn't happen like that. The White House's economists, like nearly every forecaster, misread the recession. The state assistance wasn't enough to plug the budget holes and, in many cases, the school aid merely delayed rather than prevented teacher layoffs. Infrastructure projects took months longer to break ground than the public had been led to believe. Such recovery as there was seemed weak, and investments in new technologies were decades away from rebuilding a manufacturing base for working Americans.

With these disappointments, the stimulus left a lasting impression on politics. Already seething from the bank bailout, the rush of public spending pushed small-government supporters over the edge, leading to Tea Party protests across the country. The early activism allowed like-minded people to find each other, organize the tax-day rallies, and coalesce into a movement that acquired more momentum as it confronted the health care reform bill in the summer and fall of 2009. In the midterm elections, Republican and Democratic shoo-ins became pariahs. Suddenly, the time-honored distinction of bringing money back to the home district became a liability. And an era of federal spending on America's greatest challenges seemed to come to an end.

A common theme in the news coverage was that the White House bungled the message on the stimulus. This is partly true. The emphasis on shovel-ready infrastructure inspired visions of the New Deal and created the impression that the stimulus was largely a public works package. It wasn't. But the administration spent little time showing off the areas where more money was spent: the teacher whose job was saved, the middle-class family whose taxes were cut. Since the stimulus passed, Obama administration officials have gone on more than four hundred trips to attend groundbreakings, announce funding, and otherwise promote the stimulus. Each time, they told the story of a president who put Americans to work, pulled the country back from the brink, and invested in the future. The Obama team had a far better narrative, but the Republicans had better talking points. And in a world where more and more Americans got their news in 140-character chunks and in the extremes of cable TV and blogs, the story didn't matter. It was the uppercut that counted.

The bigger problem was that so much of the stimulus was invisible. More than half of the package was in tax cuts and safety net programs. The largest single item in the Recovery Act was a $116 billion tax credit for the middle class. Rather than handing out checks, the economic team felt people were more likely to spend it if they didn't notice it. So instead, it was spread out in paychecks at about $10 a week. It worked. People didn't notice it. It was also difficult to imagine the world that might have been if there had been no stimulus. If a teacher was in the classroom, no one gave the administration any credit. Money for Medicaid, unemployment checks, and food stamps meant that somewhere down the line, a nurse and a grocery clerk kept their jobs. But it was hard to see the connection.

Of the parts that were visible, it often seemed that the stimulus was providing money for everything. Instead of investing in a few marquee projects, Congress tried to make the stimulus a cure-all. There was money for every one of society's ills, from cancer to cogongrass, from ailing infrastructure like bridges and rails to invasive species like Asian carp and Russian olive trees.

Critics seized upon the stimulus for silly-sounding projects: turtle tunnels, electric fish displays, and research involving monkeys and cocaine. But Earl Devaney, the burly inspector general brought in to investigate the stimulus, told me that ultimately very little of the money was lost to fraud, waste, and abuse.

In reading about the New Deal, I couldn't help but notice the similarities. Lost to the popular myth is the fact that the WPA was feverishly mocked during its day. Critics said the initials stood for "We Piddle Around." Louis Armstrong recorded a song called "WPA" with lines that went "Sleep while you work, rest while you play / Lean on your shovel to pass the time away." One of the many jokes at the time told the story of a man whose brother had been trying to get into the WPA.

"What's he doing now?" another man asked.

"Nothing," he said. "He got the job."

The right wing at the time called the WPA a breeding ground for socialism, and at a hearing on the Federal Emergency Relief Administration in 1935, a crafts instructor told of teaching men how to make "boon doggles," giving birth to the word applied to many stimulus projects today.[1]

The New Deal has been glorified over time. As the story goes, Franklin D. Roosevelt put the down-and-out to work building enduring feats of engineering like the Hoover Dam and brought about an end to the Depression. In truth, it took four years for the unemployment rate, which peaked at 25 percent in 1933, to come down to 14 percent. It didn't return to normal until after World War II. The Hoover Dam took five years to build after taking more than two years to break ground. The project was actually authorized by Congress in 1928, before the stock market crash, during the administration of President Calvin Coolidge. It was constructed by the Bureau of Reclamation and the Public Works Administration, not the WPA. While the WPA had its wonders, New York's LaGuardia Airport and San Francisco's Cow Palace among them, most of its projects were minor jobs building monuments, painting murals, and paving roads.

What has changed is the scale of government. In building a modern system, we have developed a process and procedure for everything. Construction projects can't simply be doled out to untrained workers and begun tomorrow. To protect taxpayers, we've developed a process of competitive bidding, whereby any qualified contractor is given a fair shot to win the project. We've enacted environmental rules to ensure a project doesn't pollute streams or kill off wildlife. The U.S. Department of Transportation funds highway projects through a formula, in which the federal government picks up 80 percent of the cost. The Department of Education contributes billions of dollars every year for special education and disadvantaged students.

When measured as a percentage of the federal budget, the Recovery Act equaled a little more than 25 percent of the $3 trillion in regular government spending in 2009, including Social Security and Medicare. In contrast, the Public Works Administration, which cost $3.3 billion, was more than 70 percent of the federal budget in 1933. The $11 billion for the WPA was more than what the government typically spent in three years.[2] In today's terms, it would be as if Congress passed a $2 trillion stimulus package in 2009 and followed up with another one worth $8 trillion a few years later. So while the New Deal probably felt like going to from zero to sixty miles per hour, the Recovery Act was more like going from thirty-five to fifty.

I got the idea to write this book after watching a speech that Vice President Joe Biden gave at the Brookings Institution in September 2009. The vice president, who had been appointed by President Obama to oversee the stimulus, was giving a progress report on the program. As he concluded the speech, Biden said that because of the Recovery Act, people he visited were now describing their towns differently. Instead of pointing out landmarks and saying "that used to be," they were now showing off factories and boasting "this is going to be." Could this be the time in history, I wondered, when the United States finally reversed its long industrial and middle-class decline?

In researching this book, I have traveled to fifteen states to visit stimulus projects, interviewed hundreds of people, and read through tens of thousands of pages of government documents and project reports. Still, witnessing everything was impossible. Any event I didn't observe firsthand was reported out with interviews, video, transcripts, White House pool reports, and notes taken by sources.

My goals were to follow the money and to focus on the ground level, on the construction workers, teachers, and solar engineers who received jobs from the stimulus, on the auto workers who didn't, and on the families who lost their homes and struggled when help didn't come.

I have tried to tell the stories of three very different cities. Elkhart, Indiana, one of the hardest hit places of this recession, saw its unemployment rate rise from 4 percent to 20 percent when the recreational vehicle plants closed in the fall of 2008. Aiken, South Carolina, became one of the biggest winners of the stimulus when the Department of Energy awarded $1.6 billion to clean up a Cold War nuclear plant in this deep-red Republican region. In Fremont, California, on the edge of Silicon Valley, I visited a company that received a $500 million loan guarantee from the stimulus to build a new factory making rod-shaped solar panels. The groundbreaking came on the heels of news that Fremont's largest employer, the NUMMI automobile plant, was shutting its doors and laying off 4,700 people. Despite the brief hope the solar panel factory provided, it too closed down as the company filed for bankruptcy and ended up in an FBI investigation looking into the government loan.

These stories help answer the questions that have surrounded the stimulus from the beginning. And they document a unique period in American history, when the election of a dynamic president made anything seem possible to a time when, overwhelmed by infighting in Congress, the country nearly defaulted on its debt and everything suddenly became impossible.

Let America be America again.

Let it be the dream it used to be.

—Langston Hughes

PART 1

RECESSION

ONE

FILE YOUR UNEMPLOYMENT ELECTRONICALLY

The principal supporting business now is rage.
Hatred of the various grays . . .
—Richard Hugo, "Degrees of Gray in Phillipsburg"

MARCH 2009

The Monaco Coach RV factory in Wakarusa, Indiana, is a low-slung beige complex surrounded by a gigantic parking lot and a chain-link fence topped with three strands of outward-slanted barbed wire. With the exception of a trimmed lawn and scattered trees in front, its utilitarian structure implies nothing about the beauties that workers make, or rather used to make, inside. Day in and day out for decades, they came here to recreate the luxuries of home for the open road. One of Monaco's models was the Diplomat, which was about the size of a motorized sperm whale, furnished with floral-print sofas, hardwood cabinets, built-in flat-screen TVs, a refrigerator, a microwave, a king bed, and a ceramic-tile kitchen, all balanced on six wheels and complete with safety features like antilock brakes.

All of this required skilled workers. Mechanics to build the chassis. Seamstresses to sew the seat fabrics. Electricians. Graphic designers. Woodworkers to saw and mold the cabinets. People like Ed Neufeldt.

On July 17, 2008, a Thursday, Neufeldt woke up at 4:00 A.M. as he always did to fit in a two- to three-mile run before his shift. He drove

3

his white Chevy S-10 pickup to the plant and pulled into the parking lot. His wife, Marianne, didn't like him jogging on the road in the dark, now that they had seven kids. So he ran the perimeter of the parking lot. Rumors had been flying around the plant for weeks that a group of Monaco executives from Oregon were coming to Wakarusa today for a big meeting. Gas prices had been stuck at $4 a gallon for months and it was no secret that people weren't buying RVs.

Would it be a layoff? A cutback in production? Neufeldt wondered as he jogged in the dark before sunrise. Like many companies in the RV industry, Monaco had always experienced swings in production, laying off a couple hundred employees one year, hiring a couple hundred the next. In 2007, Monaco shuttered its Elkhart plant and workers like Neufeldt were moved to Wakarusa. By the spring, other RV companies in the area, Travel Supreme, Newmar, Coachmen, all had announced layoffs, cut shifts, or consolidated operations. Neufeldt had been laid off before for a couple of months in 1978 and managed to get by until orders picked back up and he was called back to work. But now he was sixty-two. If he could just tough it out a few more years, he'd have it made. *Nah,* he thought. He'd had the same boss for he didn't know how long. Plus, he hadn't missed a day of work in twenty-seven years.

After the run, Neufeldt went up to the break room and fixed himself a cup of coffee and ate a Little Debbie Nutty Bar as he read through some psalms in his Bible as he always did. The shift started at 6:00 A.M., and Neufeldt headed to the mill room where he operated the saws cutting wood for cabinets. It was almost break time when the foreman was called into a meeting. The meeting didn't last very long. But when he came out, Neufeldt noticed he had tears in his eyes.

The foreman called the fifty to sixty workers together. Then, he shook his head.

"It's not a layoff," he told them. "We're closing the doors."

Up to this point in his life, Neufeldt seemed to be living the American dream. Despite having only three years of college, he had worked in the RV industry for thirty-six years, earning $21 an hour, roughly $40,000 a year. It wasn't easy street, but it was enough.

After workers asked some questions, which the foreman didn't have answers to, they were dismissed for the day. By now, the heat had reached the mid eighties and was heading for a near record ninety-one degrees. Neufeldt got back in his Chevy S-10 and drove home on County Road 42. After a few miles, he turned right on County Road 1, driving past the corn and soybean fields where his father-in-law had settled generations ago, past the pond where he and Marianne had started out in a trailer, past the one-story modular home they moved into next, and pulled into the driveway of the white farmhouse with the big front porch they had built fifteen years ago and got ready to break the news to his wife.

$ $ $

Signs of the recession were everywhere as I drove through Elkhart in March 2009. The one above the mechanic's shop read ELKHART, LET US HELP. 10–15% OFF REPAIRS. At the insurance company: COBRA TOO EX-PENSIVE? CALL OR STOP IN FOR A FREE QUOTE. The Salvation Army: WE HAVE NEW MATTRESSES. Hopman Jewelers: BUYING OLD JEWELRY. On the billboard over the Cock-A-Doodle Café, a new church had a website for the times: WWW.MYSPIRITUALSTIMULUS.COM. Residents buzzed about the woman in nearby South Bend who robbed a Long John Silver's, apologizing tearfully, "If I wasn't down and out, I wouldn't be doing this."[1] Martin's grocery advertised Manwich on sale, ten cans for $10. The library was almost all out of home-repair manuals. The GED books had a waiting list. Amid the sundries and secondhand furniture at the You Never Know Flea Market, the store sold a T-shirt that read I WANT A BAIL-OUT FOR ME!!! Even the welcome plaque in the civic plaza downtown called to visitors: CITY OF ELKHART. THE CITY WITH A HEART. FILE YOUR UNEMPLOYMENT ELECTRONICALLY.

Residents came and went from the unemployment office. The maintenance worker. The parking lot paver. The secretary for the RV manufacturer laid off after twenty years. They lined up in the dark well before the office opened at 7:00 A.M., drinking coffee and reading the local newspaper named simply *The Truth*.

They shared a similar drama. Laid off on Friday. Been out for six weeks. Every place I go says they're not accepting applications. It's just been a long haul. I worked for the company for twenty years in the RV industry and it's completely down. I was laid off five months ago. Unemployed nine weeks. I've been out since October. Too old to start a new career but too young to retire. There are no jobs here.

Elkhart itself had become a sign of the downturn. With an unemployment rate that had quadrupled to just over 20 percent since the recession began, by March 2009, Elkhart had lost jobs faster than any other county in the country. The *New York Times* called it "the white hot center of the meltdown." A British tabloid labeled it "Joblessville, USA." It's where Barack Obama made his first trip as president to launch the Recovery Act at a town hall meeting; he tried to put a face on the dire statistics, promising that the stimulus would lift not just Elkhart but countless other hard-hit cities toward recovery. But a month after the president's visit, the picture remained bleak. The first infrastructure project hadn't begun, and many residents doubted the stimulus would help much at all.

$ $ $

Elkhart began as many small Midwestern cities did with the arrival of the railroad. More than a hundred trains still pass through every day, punctuating conversations with whistles and freezing traffic at all but the three crossings in town with an overpass. The city of 52,000 has a small downtown of squat brick buildings from the turn of the century, the grander Queen Anne homes now boarded up, the opera house with a statue of the Muse of Tragedy torn down for a parking lot. A British journalist described the district's current visage as "a mouthful of broken teeth." Surrounding the downtown is a ring of middle-class homes and, beyond that, flatlands that stretch for miles.

Elkhart is home to the largest maker of high school band instruments in the United States. For many years, it was where Alka-Seltzer was made. But Elkhart's largest industry started when Wilbur Schult saw a trailer display at the 1933 Chicago World's Fair and, with an entrepreneurial gumption that residents say typifies the town, started selling trailers outside his father's clothing store. Trailer manufacturers, dealers, and suppliers popped up everywhere. Elkhart became the Detroit of the motor home industry, the "RV Capital of the World."

About 75 percent of all recreational vehicles in the United States are made in Elkhart. About one in four jobs here are tied to the industry. This time of year, the streets were usually filled with RVs, families touring factories and browsing dealerships for the spring camping season.

Empty buildings filled the streets instead.

Monaco Coach. Closed. Hart City RV dealership. Closed. Flytraps bar and grill, Alley Oops diner. Both closed. A Laundromat-slash-tanning salon. Closed. Elkhart Centre—Revitalizing Our Downtown. Closed.

Elkhart's problems began in late 2007, when the unemployment rate was 5 percent. As gas prices climbed above $4 a gallon, fewer people wanted to buy a vehicle that could cost $600 to fill up. Then, as gas prices began to slide, a credit clampdown made it hard for buyers to finance RV purchases.

On Nappanee Street, the withering lifeline of the RV industry, a road once lined with dealerships, there were only four. A graveyard blended into an RV lot, making the white towable trailers look like tombstones. Then, as I drove down Main Street past the downtown and over the Norfolk Southern railroad tracks, I noticed a sign erected in someone's yard:

GOVERNMENT BAILOUTS DON'T WORK.

FORECLOSED.

WE LOST THIS HOME.

FAMILY WITH 9 CHILDREN PUT OUT.

Inside the old brick house at the corner of Prairie Street, Terry and Desiree Gonyon were heating up some frozen thin-crust pizzas for dinner. Some of their boys were taking a bath while the girls brushed their hair. The littlest ones watched Elmo movies, falling asleep on a gray couch next to a pile of Cheetos.

Terry, thirty-eight, wore a sweatshirt, baseball cap, and jeans and had a thin goatee and mustache. He was an independent contractor and, with Elkhart's recreational vehicle workers racing to meet America's desire for the open road, Terry had been pulling in $1,500 to $2,000 a week, hanging drywall, pouring foundations, wiring, painting, and fixing broken furnaces and broken water pipes.

When Terry was in high school, he wanted to be an auto mechanic, so the career center placed him in a job at a gas station "basically fixing tires and stuff like that," he told me once. One of the customers who came in a lot had a wife who worked at a store that sold car stereos. Like many young guys, Terry wanted a good radio, so he bought some equipment from him. A week later, he lost his job.

"I called the guy and told him I didn't have any money to pay him for the stuff I owned," Terry said. "Turns out he was a construction worker and was a drywall hanger, so he called me up."

The man introduced him to his boss and got him a job. He started out at $3.50 an hour learning how to finish sheetrock.

"I was like greener than broccoli," Terry said. "The guy basically gave me a chance and I worked for him for fourteen years. All because I owed a guy money."

In 2001, Terry and Desiree met over the Internet. Desiree was living with her mother in Paris, Texas, and one night as a joke her mother signed her up for an online dating website. Terry didn't know it at the time, but for the first week, he was actually chatting with Desiree's mom. Desiree eventually warmed to the idea and after about six months of talking on the computer late at night, she felt a strong connection to Terry.

"It just got to the point where I really felt that there was something there," she said. "I mean love at first sight but we hadn't even seen each other, you know?"

Terry came down to visit for the weekend. Then Desiree went to Indiana. They traveled back and forth for several more months. He bought her a cell phone and they didn't go a night without talking. They eventually decided to get married and Desiree moved up to Elkhart for good.

The Gonyons (rhymes with "onions") bought the house for $129,000 in 2006. They had been living in a two-bedroom house with Terry's children from a previous marriage and Desiree's children, and then they had some children together. Soon, they needed a bigger place, and with construction jobs steadily rolling in for Terry, they took a chance on a foreclosed Italianate house behind a vacuum cleaner store just south of the railroad tracks.

But when the recession swallowed the town in the fall of 2008, plant after plant shut down. The RV workers lost their jobs, and they stopped hiring Terry to paint their walls and build additions to their homes. His earnings dropped below $500 a week. The Gonyons fell behind on their mortgage. In January, the bank foreclosed.

"I tried to reason with them," Terry said. "You know work's down. I'm not working. We really didn't make enough to save up through winter. I tried setting up some kind of deal where they would drop the interest rate or drop the payments."

But nothing worked. Fed up with begging the bank for a lower rate, Terry got some metal and some wood and erected the sign. It was his way of expressing the desperation that whipped through this city two hours east of Chicago.

Among the nine children are Crystal, eighteen; Allison, sixteen; Breana, nine; Michael, nine; Aedily, seven; Tylar, seven; Kyle, six; Zachary, six; and Haylee, twenty-three months. The Gonyons's second floor was piled with garbage bags full of aluminum cans. They used to take the few dollars they made from collecting cans and deposit it in their children's bank accounts. Now they used it to pay their bills. With money tight, Desiree's mother moved in from Colorado to watch the kids so Desiree could get a minimum-wage job at Subway. But it wasn't enough.

Since the house was foreclosed on and sold at a sheriff's sale, Terry and Desiree had been talking to anyone who would help. They tried to rent apartments and houses, called Habitat for Humanity, homeless shelters, 1-800-Hope-Now, responded to every card or flyer left on their door, and tried several foreclosure counselors, but they wanted 20 percent of the loan balance just to get started.

"Where are you going to go with nine children?" Desiree asked. "We just can't find anyone to work with us. We can't find anyone who would even allow us to stay for a minimum time until we could find something bigger. Right now we're just kind of in limbo. We don't know what we're going to do. It's a waiting game. Every day, we've got to wait and see if we got an eviction notice on the door or if the sheriff's going to come banging on the door and tell us we all got to get out."

$ $ $

After being laid off from Monaco, Ed Neufeldt spent his days volunteering at the Faith Mission, a soup kitchen and shelter off Martin Luther King Jr. Drive. It's a place filled with irony. The former home of the Recreational Vehicle/Motor Home Heritage Foundation, the mission was now a mausoleum of the RV industry, a place where laid-off workers came for a meal, a bed, or an odd job to keep their hands and minds occupied.

When I visited, Neufeldt and other former RV workers were busy converting the old Cobb Funeral Home next door to the mission into rooms for unwed mothers. The inside was dark and smelled of fresh paint and sawdust as a wooden skeleton outlined where apartments and hallways would be. The workers had spent the morning painting rooms and hanging drywall and now took a break to smoke and shoot the breeze.

The late-morning sun slanted through the heavy clouds. It was cold and the workers' breath quickly turned into gray vapor. They stood on a patch of yellow grass behind the funeral home, with their hands tucked into hooded sweatshirts looking down. If Jean-Francois Millet had painted RV workers instead of peasant farmers, the scene would be his modern-day *Angelus*.

Neufeldt walked across the road and parking lot to the Faith Mission. He took off his dust mask and work gloves. The plainspoken father of seven had a thin layer of gray hair often hidden by a baseball cap. He had earnest eyes, ruddy cheeks and a ruddy chin, and a tendency to see the positive in a world of negatives. Dave Engbrecht, his pastor at the Nappanee Missionary Church called him "Mr. Middle America." "He just is always warm, friendly, gregarious," he said. "What you see is what you get." Five or six times, he described Neufeldt as "the real deal," before reminding me as we hung up, "Hey, I do want you to know: Ed Neufeldt's the real deal, man."

Neufeldt's faith could be traced back to a car accident in 1968 which left him lying on the side of the road, bleeding, spinning in and out of consciousness. A passenger in the car, Neufeldt was thrown onto the steel pipe of a guardrail, which missed his spine by a quarter of an inch. Growing up in Nashville, Neufeldt went to Baptist church but wasn't very serious about it. He was more into sports and wanted to be a physical education teacher. Then, one day in church, his pastor stopped him. "Hey, Eddie," he said. "The Lord really did something for you. You could have died. You could have lost your life in that accident. I want you to get up and tell your testimony." Neufeldt looked at him and told him he wasn't going to do it. He didn't want to do it. He ran out of the church and got into his car and drove over to the community center. "I started playing some basketball and they said it's time to clear the gym out," Neufeldt recalled. "They cleared the gym out, and here came these paraplegics coming in to play basketball. At that time, it's like God just spoke to me and he said, 'Eddie that could have been you.'"

At that moment, Neufeldt decided to dedicate his life to God. It wasn't long after that, dropping off his sister at church, he noticed two blondes in the parking lot and rolled down his window to flirt with them. They had just moved to town from Wakarusa, coming to Nashville because they loved gospel music. One was named Rita, and her sister was Marianne. A few years later, Neufeldt and Marianne moved back to Indiana and got married. And Neufeldt took a job in the RV industry. Over the years, he and his wife had taken in seventy foster children. They'd adopted several, and some had followed him into the RV business. In the recession, two of his daughters and two of his sons-in-law were laid off as well.

Neufeldt introduced President Obama when he came to Elkhart in February to sell his economic recovery package. But a month later, Neufeldt had his doubts that it would mean much for Elkhart.

"They're going to come through with the stimulus plan, but I don't think that's going to help the RV workers much," he said when I met him at the Faith Mission. "What's a man like me going to do when I worked in the mill room or saw room? How am I going to get a job in road construction or any of my buddies?"

It was lunchtime, and Neufeldt walked through the soup kitchen carrying a tray of sloppy joes and vegetables to a table where his buddies—he never calls them coworkers—were already sitting. Pete Swathwood spent seventeen years in the woodshop for Monaco.

Donnie Gaut, whose son married one of Neufeldt's daughters, did maintenance at Travel Supreme since the early 1970s. Buster Coleman also used to work for Monaco.

"Them places aren't going to hire people off the street," Coleman said of road construction companies. "They're going to hire all the people they laid off before. Well, this guy worked for him this many years. He's got a buddy that needs a job. So where's that going to put us?"

"That Dick Moore, the mayor of Elkhart," Neufeldt chimed in. "He made the statement that this would open up jobs for us, and the middle class would start to buy RVs again. I don't think it's going to open up for any of us."

"Probably going to contract it out of state like everything else," said Coleman.

"You've got a lot of union people sitting on the bench, too," added Gaut. "These road jobs are usually union. And they're not going to want a lot of nonunion scabbers out there. That's what we would be. Scabs."

$ $ $

When Obama announced the stimulus package, Mayor Moore and other city officials drafted a $92 million list of projects they estimated could create 2,300 jobs. The list included a $34 million railroad overpass on Prairie Street, $5.5 million to repave Runway 9-27 at the municipal airport, and $17 million to renovate the neoclassical Lerner Theatre, one of the city's last vestiges of the vaudeville days.

"They are projects that we must do, have to do," Moore said in his State of the City address. "No pie in the sky and no pork."

The day after Obama was sworn in, Moore and other city officials flew to Washington, DC, to make the pitch for Elkhart. Moore hired a lobbyist and created a team of administrators to comb through the piles of paperwork for any money Elkhart could get its hands on.

In his office at the municipal building, Moore was finishing up an interview with a German television crew. It was nothing unusual. Since becoming known as the capital of the recession, Moore had received calls from reporters as far away as Iraq and Japan. Just that past week, MSNBC.com announced that it would adopt Elkhart, stationing four reporters in the newsroom of the *Elkhart Truth*, perhaps even buying a house, to chronicle the city's struggle to recovery. Also that week, former presidential candidate and Fox News host Mike Huckabee visited to shoot a TV special called "Save This Town."

Standing outside the RV/MH Hall of Fame, the former Arkansas governor held a camp meeting of sorts, where he praised Elkhart for its "strong work ethic," "excellent business climate," and "very hospitable people." He interviewed business owners who were growing, building electronic amplifiers and energy-efficient RVs. And he toured the hall of fame, where he saw the 1931 Chevrolet House Car that Mae West used to . . . well, Huckabee, a former Baptist pastor, declined to find out.

Huckabee closed his show with a message for Obama: The people of Elkhart didn't need any "spending orgy bills" from "Uncle Sugar" to save their town. They just needed lower taxes to unfetter their entrepreneurial spirit.

Mayor Moore, seventy-four, is an unabashed promoter of Elkhart. Elected in November 2007 just as the first signs of the downturn surfaced, he said there was no other place he'd rather be than behind the captain's wheel. A former streets commissioner, Moore can remember his father working for the Works Progress Administration during the Great Depression, manning the WPA store for the workers building the town's sewer system and the stone walls that still line the St. Joseph River running through downtown.

He said he had two answers for the RV workers who don't think the stimulus will help them. "For one thing, don't sell yourself short," he said. "You come off an assembly line process where you worked. You pulled some wires. You did some plumbing. You did some carpenter work. You did some welding. You did all kinds of things. You have all kinds of skill levels coming out of there. It wouldn't take any college training to put them on a construction job." Second, creating jobs in Elkhart and elsewhere will get the economy moving, he said. More jobs mean people will have more money to buy RVs.

"This isn't an Elkhart, Indiana, stimulus plan," he said. "This isn't a state of Indiana stimulus plan. This is a nationwide stimulus program. Once we put people back to work, the impact is going to be felt in many areas of the country as everything starts picking up again. The guy that wanted to buy that nice RV fifteen months ago hasn't lost his desire to do that. We get the stimulus money, we're going to put a bunch of people to work, and that same person is going to go out and buy that RV."

Still, that didn't mean that Moore didn't think Elkhart deserved special treatment.

"The true intent of the stimulus was to send the money to places in this country that are most economically distressed," he said. "If that's true, then aren't we right up there on the top of the list?"

Elkhart and the surrounding area had been promised about $25 million so far. Projects included $11 million to build a median along U.S. 33, a crumbling stretch of road leading to a shopping mall southeast of town; $4.2 million to repave the airport runway; $2.25 million to board up, demolish, and renovate vacant homes. According to Education Department estimates, Elkhart schools would receive about $2.8 million to help teach economically disadvantaged students. The county was due $3 million to remove lead paint in public housing. Heart City Health Center would receive $200,000 for low-income patients, and police would get $170,000 for lights and sirens.

Though intended for the auto industry, $2 billion for research into lithium ion batteries could also help the RV industry, and a sales tax credit for new vehicles was also opened to RVs, thanks to the lobbying of Indiana senator Evan Bayh. Laid-off employees who opt for temporary COBRA health insurance would have 65 percent of it paid for by the government. Elkhart's unemployed, like anyone who loses their job, would get $25 extra a week and their checks would be exempt from income tax.

Elkhart had been here before. When gas prices rose over a dollar a gallon in the late 1970s, the RV industry stayed in a slump for several years. Thousands of Elkhart workers lost their jobs. But as the crisis subsided and motorists got used to the higher prices, the industry and the city returned. In one month in 1983, there were thirty-nine new companies registered in Elkhart, according to the chamber of commerce. But the 2008 recession was somewhat different, Moore said.

"In previous times, when we had downturns, our companies were owned by local people," he explained. "They struggled more to hold on to their employees. They were loyal to their employees. Their employees were loyal to them."

Not so anymore. Now the companies are owned by large conglomerates. It's nothing for a company to leave the city and never come back.

$ $ $

The knock the Gonyons had been waiting for arrived on March 24. A man from the bank came and informed them they would be evicted by the end of the month. They started packing their things in boxes.

When I was at their house two days before, I had asked them if they thought the stimulus would help any.

"I don't think it will," they said in unison.

"Nothing has even started," Desiree said. "No construction crews. Nothing. I really don't think that anything is going to come out of it. I think it was more of a show for 'Look, I'm in office. I'm going to tell you I'm going to do all this stuff for you.'"

By choosing Elkhart for his first trip as president, Obama had set the scales for judging whether or not the stimulus had worked. The president seemed to have a special attachment to the city. He had visited it twice before on the campaign trail, making a promise he would help it recover. The Gonyons were like millions of homeowners who lost their homes in the recession. And Neufeldt was a breed of worker becoming ever more rare in the United States. He worked for the same company nearly all his life and it had provided well for him. He was an archetype of the blue-collar middle class that Obama described in his political memoir *The Audacity of Hope* and over and over again on the campaign trail. For the stimulus to work, Elkhart would have to be lifted up as well.

One day while putting together a scrapbook for her father, Neufeldt's daughter Lisa, an aspiring songwriter scribbled some lyrics on the back of an envelope:

He wakes up at 4 A.M.
Goes to work today again.
Hasn't missed a day in almost thirty years
but today he tries to hold back tears.
He punches in for the last time
but he works, his head held high.
Guy who would have thought after all of this time,
he'd have to leave it all behind.

The sheriff's deputies arrived at the old brick house on Main Street on March 31. It was time for the Gonyons to go. They were in the middle of transporting furniture to their new place, and when they returned, the deputies had already kicked in the door.

Frightened, their cat scattered and hid in the basement. The Gonyons were allowed one more trip inside the house to pick up the cat and whatever was left. They loaded the last of their stuff into Terry's pickup.

Then, they said goodbye to their dream home and moved into a single-wide trailer on the outskirts of town.

TWO

THE DITCH

THE ENERGY IN CHICAGO'S GRANT PARK on the unseasonably warm night of November 4, 2008, was electric. More than 125,000 people had gathered under a crescent moon to see Barack Obama, just five years ago a little-known state senator from Illinois, or in his own words, "a skinny kid with a funny name," become America's first black president. More than that, though, he had campaigned on a message of hope and change, and the ecstatic sea of supporters was breathless with expectation.

Around 11:00 P.M., Obama strode onto the stage. It had been set up so that, when closely cropped for television, it appeared that he was speaking against a pitch-dark sky, a mythic fog swirling around him. Behind him stood a row of American flags gently fluttering in the southerly wind. To his left lay Lake Michigan, to his right the Chicago skyline. Lights from cell phones and digital cameras twinkled in the crowd. With tears in their eyes and a flurry of mini-American flags in their hands, some in the crowd rose up in cheers that dissolved into the familiar chant "Yes, we can! Yes, we can! Yes, we can . . ."

All around Obama, the economy was cratering. That very morning, a headline in *USA Today* asked, "Is This Another Great Depression?" Financial titans were crashing one by one like piles of poker chips that had been stacked too high. The Big Three automakers, once a symbol of American industrial might, were on their knees. Already, more than 2 million people had lost their jobs.

When Obama formally announced his candidacy in early 2007, the unemployment rate stood at 4.5 percent, the second-lowest month since before the September 11 attacks. At the time, the going theory was that the greatest challenges for the next president would be immigration reform and the war in Iraq. But the housing bubble that artificially supported the economic prosperity deflated over the next several months under the weight of subprime mortgages. Gas prices began their seemingly endless climb toward $4 a gallon.

President George W. Bush first tried to stimulate the economy in early 2008. Speaking in the White House's Roosevelt Room, where his administration a few years back had taken down a portrait of FDR, he proposed a series of tax incentives to encourage business owners to make investments and create jobs, and rebate checks to spur consumer spending. But he was vague on the details, saying the package needed to be "big enough to make a difference in an economy as large and dynamic as ours, which means it should be about 1 percent of GDP." One thing he was clear about, though, spending money on things like public works projects, education, and food stamps was not the answer.

"This growth package must be built on broad-based tax relief that will directly affect economic growth, and not the kind of spending projects that would have little immediate impact on our economy," he said.

Speaking later that afternoon at a lawnmower factory in Frederick, Maryland, Bush stood on a yellow commercial mower and assured reporters that if Congress passed the tax plan, "we're going to be just fine." With that, he bid the company's CEO to "crank this sucker up" and performed a zero-radius turn while waving at the cameras.

The leading Democratic presidential candidates were much more specific with their proposals. The week before, Hillary Clinton had called for a $70 billion spending package that included an "emergency housing crisis fund," assistance to help low-income families pay their heating bills, extended unemployment checks, and $5 billion for alternative energy programs. She also proposed a tax rebate if the economy weakened. Obama upped her a few days later with a $120 billion plan that included a tax credit for workers and $10 billion each to boost state and local governments facing budget crises, extend unemployment benefits, and help homeowners refinance their mortgages. Like Clinton, Obama also included a rainy-day fund if things got worse.

One of the first people to call for a stimulus package was Larry Summers, the former Treasury secretary and Harvard president who would go on to become Obama's chief economic adviser. Writing in the *Financial Times* in November 2007, Summers predicted a recession and advocated for an "immediate temporary stimulus through spending or tax benefits for low- and middle-income families if the situation worsens."[1]

At a Joint Economic Committee hearing two days before Bush unveiled his package, Summers outlined a three-prong test for an effective stimulus plan. First, a stimulus should be *timely*, focusing on measures that can inject money into the economy quickly. Second, a stimulus should be *targeted*, channeling money to people who need it most and are likely to spend it fast. Third, a stimulus must be *tempo rary*, felt within the first year, or it will sacrifice credibility and lead to inflation and high interest rates. Such guidelines supported tax refunds for the poor and middle class and increases in food stamps and unemployment benefits. Summers argued against cutting business taxes or designing new programs that would only transfer money to federal agencies or state and local governments to spend gradually. But overall, the message of the influential Summers was that the time for stimulus was now. "The risks here of 'too little, too late' are far, far, far greater than the risk of 'too much, too soon,'" he told the committee.

Bush, however, was optimistic, or at least he presented it that way. In his New Year's Day message, he wrote, "The underpinnings of our economy have proven strong, competitive, and resilient enough to overcome the challenges we face." His underlying message to

Congress in speech after speech was that they should act to extend
the sweeping tax cuts passed during his administration. The looming
expiration date of 2010, he said, was a significant source of uncertainty in the economy.

Meanwhile, the Democratic and Republican leaders in the House
of Representatives, Speaker Nancy Pelosi of California and Representative John Boehner of Ohio, moved forward with Treasury secretary
Henry Paulson to hammer out a stimulus bill they all could agree on.
The Economic Stimulus Act of 2008, signed by Bush on February 13,
included $600 tax rebates to middle-class workers and smaller pay-
ments for seniors, disabled veterans, and workers who didn't earn
enough to pay taxes. It allowed businesses to write off taxes on new
plants and equipment and increased the maximum home value to
qualify for a federally insured housing loan. With the unemployment
rate still relatively low at 4.9 percent, there was little effort to tie the
stimulus to creating jobs. Ideas floated by other policymakers during
negotiations—extending unemployment checks, expanding food
stamps and Medicaid, investing in infrastructure and renewable
energy—would all have to wait.

As soon as the ink on the $168 billion act dried, the drumbeat for a
second stimulus began. The next day, Senate Democrats proposed a
bill to stem home foreclosures. A newly formed coalition of governors and mayors named Building America's Future called for a major
federal investment in infrastructure, like roads and bridges, water and
sewer systems, airports, public transit, and dams.

Bush's streak of fifty-two straight months of job growth had come
to an end in January 2008. Nearly 1.3 million workers had been out of
work for more than six months, meaning they had run out of the
twenty-six weeks of benefits allowed by law. According to the National Employment Law Project, that was almost twice the number
of the long-term jobless than at the start of the previous recessions of
1990 and 2001.

Larry Summers minced no words when asked to speak at Stanford
University's annual economic summit in March.

"We are facing the most serious combination of macroeconomic
and financial stresses that the United States has faced in at least a gen-

eration and possibly much longer," Summers told the audience of economists and academics. He said the federal government should start preparing for a second stimulus to deal with rising foreclosures and tightening credit.[2]

Such dire warnings were beginning to seep into Obama's speech-making on the campaign trail. Speaking at a town hall meeting at a community college near Pittsburgh in March, Obama said bluntly, "Our economy is in shambles . . . This economy is contracting, it is heading toward recession. We probably already are in one." A few weeks later in Fort Wayne, Indiana, upon hearing the latest unemployment numbers, Obama released a statement that would serve as the music sheet he would sing from for the rest of the campaign:

> Instead of doing nothing for out-of-work Americans, we need a second stimulus that extends unemployment insurance and helps communities that have been hit hard by this recession. Instead of tolerating decades of rising inequality, we need to grow the middle class by investing in millions of new green jobs and rebuilding our crumbling infrastructure. And after decades of flawed trade agreements and tax breaks that ship jobs overseas, we need to invest in companies that create jobs right here at home.

As Obama revved up his economic message, Bush seemed ever more out of touch. He continued to play Pollyanna, saying that the American economy had just hit a "rough patch" and that if Congress waited for the stimulus checks to take effect, things would bounce back by the summer.

In a speech at the Economic Club of New York, surrounded by bankers in the epicenter of the financial crisis, Bush said it was important not to "do anything foolish." "In a free market, there's going to be good times and bad times. That's how markets work," he said. "The market is in the process of correcting itself; markets must have time to correct . . . I guess the best way to describe government policy is like a person trying to drive a car on a rough patch. If you ever get stuck in a situation like that, you know full well it's important not to overcorrect—because when you overcorrect, you end up in the ditch."

$ $ $

In the summer of 2008, Bush's stimulus checks kicked in and for a time consumer spending rose. But they did little to stop the disaster that was spinning offshore and about to make landfall. Much of the money was saved and used to pay down debt. And much of it was guzzled up by gas prices, which by now had exceeded $4 a gallon.

The presidential campaigns spent their time debating who was more out of touch with working-class America: Obama, the glittering celebrity who seemed to denigrate blue-collar workers as bitter cynics who "cling to guns or religion," or John McCain, the glowering maverick whose top economic adviser, former Texas senator Phil Gramm, called America "a nation of whiners."

As his running mate, Obama chose Joe Biden, a veteran senator from Delaware with the political and policy chops to balance his new-kid image. Biden was elected to the Senate in 1972 at the age of twenty-nine, when Obama was eleven years old and living with his grandparents in Hawaii. In addition to lending his foreign policy experience and Washington know-how, Biden gave Obama the working-class appeal he so desperately lacked. Where Obama could fire up a stadium, Biden had a folksy charm and an affable glow that allowed him to connect with real people. The public knew his hardships well. A month after being elected to the Senate, Biden's wife and baby daughter were killed when their station wagon was hit by a tractor-trailer. Then in 1988, he suffered an aneurysm and was even given his last rites before recovering.[3] Because of the automobile accident, Biden started taking the train from Wilmington each day so he could be with his two sons at night. He commuted throughout his decades in the Senate, becoming friendly with the conductors and earning the nickname "Amtrak Joe."

Biden has a face built for a caricature artist. It is anchored by a megawatt smile that causes his cheeks to stand out and his eyes to crinkle. When he speaks of serious matters, the wrinkles and veins in his forehead seem choreographed to his points as his eyebrows rise and fall with the tone. He talks in a rough, unfeigned dialect, often beginning sentences with "folks" or "look." By doing this, he holds fast to what he has described as his Grandpop Finnegan's first principle: "Tell them what you really think, Joey. Let the chips fall where they may."[4] Prone to rambling, Biden often veers from prepared remarks to tell a story, share some family wisdom, or slip in a line of poetry gleaned from his years reciting verse in the mirror to overcome a stuttering habit. Biden's tendency to interrupt himself to say hello to a friend in the crowd was so memorable that it was spoofed by *Saturday Night Live*: "Hey, Phil! How ya doin', Phil? It's Phil Malloy, head of the Local Workers Steel!"

He had a wealth of personal economic stories to draw from. He grew up in an Irish Catholic family in Scranton, Pennsylvania, a coal and steel town that had seen better days. As a kid, his father couldn't find work and moved the family to Delaware for a new job. Describing it later, Biden said, "The longest walk in America is a father or mother walking up a short flight of stairs to their kid's bedroom to say, 'Honey, I'm sorry, I lost my job.' Or, 'Honey, we're not going to be able to stay in this house, you're not going to be able to be in that ball club next year. Everything is going to be okay.' My father made that walk, like maybe your father did, back when I was a kid in the '50s and said, 'When I get a job in Wilmington, I'll come back up and we'll get you all, we'll move from Scranton.' Too damn many people have had to make that walk." Another Biden gem was when he cited his grandfather's expression on economic reality: "When the guy from Throop is out of work, it's an economic slowdown. When your brother-in-law is out of work, it's a recession. When you're out of work, it's a depression." Those anecdotes would serve Biden well in speeches when Obama appointed him to be his point man on the recovery plan.

$ $ $

By the end of the summer, the unemployment rate stood at 6.1 percent and the downturn had reached state budgets. Home foreclosures caused tax revenues to plummet. At the same time, more people sought Medicaid and food stamps to survive the recession. Facing billion-dollar deficits, states cut programs and laid off workers. In Rhode Island, the state cut funding for health care, early education, and affordable housing. In Nevada, the governor capped the number of patients allowed into its children's health insurance program. In California, the fund to pay jobless workers their benefits was about to run out of money.[5]

Meanwhile, the bones of an economic stimulus package were starting to be put into place. In June, at a campaign stop at the North Carolina State Fairgrounds, Obama called for a $50 billion stimulus that included money for states to avoid cuts, help for homeowners to refinance their mortgages, and another round of tax rebates. Later that month, Congress passed an extension of unemployment checks, as part of bill to fund the wars in Iraq and Afghanistan. In July, Democratic leaders in Congress met with economic advisers, including Summers, to craft a $50 billion plan. In addition to the proposals laid out by Obama, ideas bouncing around the Capitol included increases in food stamps, more Medicaid money for states, spending on schools, investments in renewable energy, and more than anything, money for infrastructure, especially road and bridge projects.

The planning stalled in August with the congressional recess and party conventions. But the pop-pop-pop collapses of Lehman Brothers, Merrill Lynch, and AIG on September 15 and 16 provided whatever momentum the Democrats needed.

On September 26, the House passed a $61 billion stimulus bill. But the hope that relief was on its way quickly evaporated. That same day, a companion bill failed in the Senate. The bills had little in common. The House version focused on infrastructure and social services. The Senate version included those too, but in smaller amounts to make room for a wish list of items members of the appropriations committee had been trying to get passed for years. Either way, the bills had little hope of becoming law. Bush promised to veto them. Lawmakers were consumed with passing the bank bailout. And Congress was set to recess in October for the final stretch of the campaign.

As the economy darkened, House Speaker Nancy Pelosi raised her pitch for a stimulus, now calling for a $150 billion plan and scheduling congressional hearings for the weeks before the election. On October 13, Pelosi held a two-hour summit with leading liberal economists, some of whom would become Obama advisers. All provided essentially the same advice: the economy needed a comprehensive recovery plan, as large as $300 billion, not just for the short-term but with a vision for rebuilding America.

$ $ $

Obama could hardly have been more different from the president he would succeed.

He had attended college with the help of student loans, which he struggled to pay off until his forties. As a community organizer in the 1980s on Chicago's South Side, he witnessed a neighborhood devastated by the shutdown of the local steel plant.

After becoming a U.S. senator and probing his presidential ambitions, he translated that worldview into a policy agenda in the 2006 book *The Audacity of Hope*. America is going through a "fundamental economic transformation," Obama wrote. The blue-collar factory jobs that once made for a strong middle class across the Rust Belt were being automated and sent offshore as globalization runs its course. The problem was nothing new, he wrote, but it had been neglected for decades.

In the book, he spread the blame among Republicans and Democrats, corporations and labor unions. But he saved his sharpest rebuke for the "Ownership Society," a phrase used by Bush to describe his belief that people should have more control over their choice of health care, education, and retirement investments. In truth, Obama wrote, it was laissez-faire economics taken to the extreme—a strategy of doing nothing.

In his speech accepting the Democratic presidential nomination, Obama distilled his critique. "In Washington, they call this the Ownership Society, but what it really means is 'you're on your own.' Out of work? Tough luck. No health care? The market will fix it. Born into poverty? Pull yourself up by your own bootstraps—even if you don't have boots. You're on your own."

In turn, Obama mustered his greatest praise for FDR's social compact. About halfway through the book, in a chapter titled "Opportunity," Obama outlined a reading of American history in which in times of great economic challenge, the government had taken an activist role.

"The Hoover Dam, the Tennessee Valley Authority, the interstate highway system, the Internet, the Human Genome Project—time and again, government investment has helped pave the way for an explosion of private economic activity," Obama wrote.[6]

The way to stop the loss of jobs overseas and rebuild the economy was a large-scale government investment in education, science, and alternative energy.

"Investments in these three key areas would go a long way in making America more competitive," he wrote. "If we act boldly, then our economy will be less vulnerable to economic disruption, our trade balance will improve, the pace of U.S. technological innovation will accelerate, and the American worker will be in a stronger position to adapt to the global economy."[7]

It was a strategy conceived long before anyone had heard of the Great Recession, subprime mortgages, credit-default swaps, or the growing need for an economic stimulus package.

$ $ $

The intoxication that followed Obama's victory on Tuesday, November 4, was about to get a cold shower. On that Friday, the Labor Department released latest unemployment numbers that showed 10 million people were now unemployed. It was the highest number since the fall of 1983.

Obama was in Chicago meeting with his economic advisers at the downtown Hilton, a hotel that overlooked the park where just days before Obama had accepted the presidency. The meeting was attended by a pantheon of economic sages and political gurus, many of whom were veterans of the Clinton White House. Warren Buffett, the second-richest man in the world, known as the "Oracle of Omaha," participated by speakerphone. And, of course, there was Larry Summers.

The experts talked about how the financial crisis was spreading to other sectors of the economy, including small businesses. They discussed the budget crises confronting state and municipal governments. They listened to the latest news about troubles in the auto industry. And they spoke urgently about designing a rescue plan, centered around Obama's campaign promises: clean energy, health care, education, and tax cuts for the middle class.

At 3:00 P.M., Obama entered a hotel ballroom for his first press conference since becoming president-elect. With his brain trust, a row of American flags, and a blue curtain behind him, he approached the lectern and looked out at the press corps.

"Oh, wow," he said.

Obama began by addressing the horrible unemployment news and reminding everyone that he wasn't president and wouldn't be for another two and a half months. Despite that, he pressed Congress to get moving.

"A fiscal stimulus plan that will jump-start economic growth is long overdue," he said. "We should get it done."

The government needed to stop the spread of the crisis, which was becoming increasingly global. Obama expressed little confidence that Congress would pass a stimulus package during the lame-duck session, but still, as he met with President Bush and toured the White House the following Monday, he pressed him to try to achieve one before the inauguration.[8]

Appearing on ABC's *This Week*, Rahm Emanuel, the savvy power-broker whom Obama had recently named as his chief of staff, was asked whether the economy had caused Obama to postpone his other domestic priorities. Emanuel responded that rather than getting in the way, the crisis provided an opportunity for the administration to get them done. Many issues that were usually thought of as long term were now immediate and had to be tackled.[9] It was something Obama had said before and would say again Saturday in his weekly radio address. But Emanuel had a knack for sound bites, intentional or not. Speaking again at a *Wall Street Journal* conference for CEOs, he said, "You never want a serious crisis to go to waste."

The comment kindled one of the Republicans' first resentments—that Obama was exploiting the plight of the unemployed worker to force through a liberal agenda. But the comment also reflected a new reading of the downturn. Economists were starting to realize that this was a big one and a quick infusion of cash wasn't going to do the job. There was a growing consensus in Democratic circles that the slowdown wasn't just the symptom of a housing bubble or a greedy Wall Street but instead the consequence of inaction over decades. The energy crisis of the early 1970s, the failure of health care reform in the 1990s, the lack of financial regulation after the savings and loan crisis and then the Internet bubble, the stagnant wages of the middle class all had contributed to the crash. The goal was no longer to simply stimulate the economy but instead to rebuild it. Speaking at the same conference, Larry Summers rattled off a new rubric for a recovery plan. Instead of "timely, temporary, and targeted," the test was now "speedy, substantial, and sustained."

$ $ $

The announcement of a nascent recovery plan didn't come in a grand oration in a Rust Belt gymnasium so commonplace on the campaign trail. It came on November 22 in a weekly radio and YouTube address. Sitting in a dimly lit office at his transition headquarters, an American flag on his right, a potted plant and framed picture of his family on his left, Obama read into a camera. He said that he had directed his economic team to develop a plan to create two and a half million jobs over two years. It was not just a plan for the immediate crisis but "an early down payment" on the promises he made during the campaign.

"We'll put people back to work rebuilding our crumbling roads and bridges, modernizing schools that are failing our children, and building wind farms and solar panels, fuel-efficient cars, and the alternative energy technologies that can free us from our dependence on foreign oil and keep our economy competitive in the years ahead."

The plan was based on a theory laid out by British economist John Maynard Keynes, who in the 1930s promoted government intervention and public spending as the antidote for economic downturns. Widely respected in the decades that followed, Keynes's ideas fell out of favor in the 1970s and 1980s as "stagflation," the rising of unemployment and inflation at the same time, led to the prominence of supply-side economics. Even though Keynesian economics advocated tax cuts to stimulate demand, by the time Obama's team picked it up, it had become synonymous with big government. Its revival was sure to be controversial.

The biggest and best-known example of public spending in a downturn was the alphabet soup of programs created by FDR during the Great Depression. The Works Progress Administration put 8 million people to work building roads and monuments. While the Depression didn't end until World War II, the vast defense buildup was itself a form of stimulus, as was the Interstate Highway System and the space race during the 1958 recession. To recover from the 1960–61 recession, President Kennedy signed bills to retrain workers displaced by technology and to provide grants and loans for businesses in low-income areas to hire workers and build new plants. President Nixon expanded these programs with the Comprehensive Employment and Training Act of 1973. Throughout the 1970s, Congress distributed billions of dollars to local governments and nonprofits to create jobs for the poor and unemployed. But as Keynes's influence ebbed, America soured on such ambitious stimulus efforts. A relatively modest $16 billion stimulus proposed by President Bill Clinton in 1993 disintegrated in a partisan standoff in the Senate. During the presidency of George W. Bush, stimulus took the form of tax rebate checks in 2001 and then again in 2008. By the time Obama announced his plan, the modern example of a public works stimulus was Japan, which had languished for two decades despite trillions of dollars in stimulus packages.

The Monday after announcing his recovery plan, Obama was back in the ballroom at the Hilton Chicago, to introduce the first members of his economic team. Timothy Geithner, the head of the New York Fed, would serve as Treasury secretary. Melody Barnes, domestic policy adviser during the campaign, would play the same role in the White House. To lead the Council of Economic Advisers, he chose Christina Romer, a professor at the University of California, Berkeley. And as his chief economic adviser, he picked Larry Summers.

Romer was a scholar of the Great Depression, having spent much of her life studying the New Deal and the economic expansion after World War II. She argued that FDR's deficit spending plan was right. But it ultimately was too small to counteract a large tax increase at the end of the Hoover administration or the cuts enacted by state and local governments to balance their budgets. Romer's interest in recessions was also personal. She later recalled how in the aftermath of the

1981–82 recession, her father lost his job at a chemical plant, telling her that he had "been sacked." That same year, her mother found out that her teaching job was in danger. In Obama, Romer saw a president she wholeheartedly believed in. On election night, after celebrating with a glass of champagne with some friends, Romer and her husband got in their car and drove to downtown Oakland where people were rowdily honking their horns. "There we were," she recalled later. "Two middle-aged economists dancing in the street with the Oakland teenagers." Standing at the press conference, with her fingers clasped in front of her, Romer seemed to be trying to stifle a giggle. She looked cherubic and bashful. It was almost as if she couldn't believe she was there.

Summers, in contrast, looked dour and unfazed by the honor. Summers was a no-brainer for the captain of Obama's economic recovery team. The son of two economists, the nephew of two Nobel Prize–winning economists, a boy who entertained himself with math problems and developed a model to predict a baseball team's performance, Summers was one of the most intellectual economic minds of the generation.[10] As a key official at Treasury under Clinton, he was credited with engineering the policies that led to the prosperity of the 1990s. But Summers could also be blunt and dominating, arrogant and brash.

Not satisfied to quietly build his team and prepare his agenda, Obama was perhaps more present as president-elect than Bush was in his final weeks as president. On Tuesday Obama was back in the Hilton Chicago ballroom for another press conference to announce that Peter Orszag, the congressional budget director would be his White House budget director. On Wednesday, he was in the ballroom once more, the same lectern, the same row of American flags, the same blue curtain. This time, it was to appoint Paul Volcker and Austan Goolsbee to lead a new independent panel known as the President's Economic Recovery Advisory Board.

On December 1 came the official word. The National Bureau of Economic Research announced that the United States was in a recession and had been since December 2007. The coronation came as a surprise to no one. More than 30 million people were now on food stamps, the most in history. That same day, Governor Arnold Schwarzenegger declared a fiscal emergency in California, as an $11 billion budget deficit threatened to grow, giving the state two months before running out of cash.

But Obama's economic advisers didn't have to look that far to realize the desperation. The next day, just five miles up the Chicago River from transition headquarters, the workers at the Republic Windows and Doors factory found out that the plant would close in three days and all 250 of them would lose their jobs. They would not get severance pay or any compensation for their accrued vacation days despite a federal law requiring that workers get sixty days' notice before a significant layoff. Instead of going quietly, Armando Robles and other leaders of the United Electrical, Radio and Machine Workers of America Local 1110 organized a sit-in of the metal factory building on Goose Island. For six days, the workers occupied the plant in rotating shifts until negotiating a deal with the banks that had caused the crisis by pulling a line of credit. The workers had entered the factory helpless and exited as heroes. However, they still did not have jobs.

Obama's economic team was scrambling to hear from every constituency. Emanuel and other aides were dispatched to the halls of Congress, where they met with the heads of every committee. At Philadelphia's Independence Hall, Obama met with the nation's governors, who wanted $136 billion for ready-to-go infrastructure projects and $40 billion to buttress their Medicaid programs.[11] The list of their priorities, Emanuel told reporters, included roads and bridges, high-speed rail, water-treatment systems, schools, public transit, broadband Internet, electronic medical records, and "green" technology.[12]

Obama met with Tom Brokaw on *Meet the Press*, where Brokaw asked him the question on everyone's minds: "How quickly will it mean jobs out there across America and how much is it going to cost and who's going to pay for it?"

Obama didn't answer directly. He talked about how governors had infrastructure projects lined up to begin, how his economic team was working on the price, and how the public shouldn't worry about how to pay for it.

"We've got to provide a blood infusion to the patient right now to make sure the patient is stabilized," he said. "We can't worry short-term about the deficit. We've got to make sure that the economic stimulus plan is large enough to get the economy moving."[13]

But how much should a recovery plan cost?

It was a question Obama's economic advisers had been wrestling with for weeks. Go too high and it might not get through Congress. Go too low and it might appear to have failed, gumming up any chance of a second bite at the apple.

Romer and Summers had been dialing up economists of every stripe asking for advice. Martin Feldstein, president of the National Bureau of Economic Research, which officially calls recessions, recommended $800 billion divided over two years.[14] In Stockholm, Sweden, to accept the Nobel Prize, Princeton economist and *New York Times* columnist Paul Krugman said it should be north of $600 billion. Another Nobel economist, Joseph Stiglitz, suggested between $600 billion and $1 trillion. Robert Reich, Clinton's Labor secretary, was one of the highest. When asked for advice by Romer, he said $600 billion. "For one year?" Romer asked. "Six hundred billion for each of two years," he replied. On the other side was John Taylor, an adviser to both President Bushes, who said it should all be in the form of lower taxes.

When Romer flew out for her first meeting with Obama in mid-November, he got immediately to the point. The Fed is largely out of bullets, he said. They needed to start thinking of some sort of fiscal stimulus. Ever since, Romer had been running models to see what would happen to the economy with $400 billion, $600 billion, $800 billion, and $1.2 trillion. The analysis indicated that given the path the economy was taking, a $1.2 trillion stimulus plan was needed to get the unemployment rate back to normal quickly. But the aides had decided that the T-word would never make it in Congress. Being new to government, Romer chose not to fight rather than seem like she didn't understand the realities of Washington. She had already convinced the economic team to raise the price to $800 billion. So in a bit of internal censoring, Summers suggested they take the $1.2 trillion figure out of the first draft, and Romer agreed. Obama would never see it. In the thick report that Summers presented to the president-elect, there was no mention of the trillion-dollar plan.

$ $ $

On December 16, the economic advisers flew out to Chicago for what Romer called their "Outward Bound experience." With the transition team on a tight budget, they flew coach and ended up with the middle seats of the last four rows of the plane. Little did the other passengers know, but the fate of the American economy rested on the plane landing safely at O'Hare. "If this plane goes down, the entire economic team goes down," Romer remembered thinking.

In Chicago, it was a frigid winter's day. A high of twenty-two degrees, a low of nine. The snow fell steadily for ten hours, blanketing the streets in white. Inside transition headquarters, Obama met with his economic advisers to hash out a cost for the recovery plan. He was getting ready to leave for a two-week family vacation in Hawaii. But first he wanted to hear what they had learned.

In addition to Summers, Romer, Emanuel, and Orszag, around the table were Treasury secretary Tim Geithner, Vice President Biden, Melody Barnes, climate and energy adviser Carol Browner, the vice president's economic adviser Jared Bernstein, and David Axelrod, Obama's longtime confidant.

Romer opened the meeting by describing an imminent slump of the size and severity not seen since the Great Depression. Without immediate action, the economy could lose another 3 million to 4 million jobs in the next year.

"The economy is very weak and deteriorating fast," she began. "David just told us the American people hadn't had their 'holy-shit moment.' Well, Mr. President, this is your 'holy-shit moment.' This recession is very bad and we need to hit it with everything we can."

Surprised at what the seemingly sweet Romer had just said, Obama replied, "Did she just say shit?"

Romer then took on the role of professor, running through a series of charts and graphs on PowerPoint, explaining the baseline forecast and the concept of fiscal multipliers. She then talked about the two big risks facing the administration. In one, the economy went into a deflationary spiral leading to a second financial panic. In the other, America would end up like Japan, where the economy stops falling but struggles with ten years of anemic growth.

Over the course of four hours, as snow continued to fall to a record of five inches, Obama heard from all his aides. Geithner talked about the credit crisis, how the lockdown on lending threatened to pull the economy into a downward spiral. Orszag, who turned forty that day, closed the meeting with a dismal report on the deficit.

"It was an unforgettable series of presentations," Obama would recall later.

The recovery plan was divided into three parts. A third of it would go to tax cuts to help the middle class and encourage businesses to invest. Another third would assist those hurt by the recession, pouring money into food stamps, health care for the poor, and state budgets to prevent layoffs. The final third would be dedicated to investments to lay the groundwork for Obama's priorities of energy, education, and infrastructure.

Throughout the meeting, there was a constant tension of wanting programs that would hit the economy quickly and wanting to do a "moonshot." Why for example couldn't they build an entire high-speed rail system? Why couldn't they modernize the electricity grid, bringing in high-voltage lines to move wind energy from the Dakotas to the population centers of the Midwest?

On the latter question, the answer proved to be much more difficult than pouring a bunch of money into it. To build the "smart grid," the federal government would need the cooperation of state and local regulators across the country or face a fight over eminent domain. Summers, Orszag, and Browner said it would take too long for the money to get into the economy. But Biden was animated. This was surely something that he and Obama could solve if they could get all the governors in a room. The trio was assigned to go back to Washington and see if it could be done. But it couldn't. Orszag met with experts who had worked on electricity issues. "It just wasn't feasible," he said. "The initial indications from the Hill were, 'Are you crazy?'"

As the meeting broke up, the aides gathered at the far end of the conference room. Emanuel took charge. They would present a plan of $675 billion to $775 billion, with the expectation that it would only grow.

With the snow clogging Chicago's streets, the aides hopped on the El train thinking they'd have a better chance of getting to the airport. Flights were delayed for hours and, stuck at O'Hare, they had plenty of time to bond. It was Browner's birthday that day too. So they celebrated at one of the many nondescript airport restaurants.

With the snow cleared and the planes now thoroughly deiced, they boarded their flights and took off into the dark night back to the nation's capital.

They would call the proposal the American Recovery and Reinvestment Plan.

Now all they had to do was get it through Congress.

THREE

LET'S MAKE A DEAL

"In politics," John Kennedy used to say, *"nobody gets everything, nobody gets nothing, and everybody gets something."*
—Senator Arlen Specter, *Washington Post*, February 9, 2009

IN THE BASEMENT of the Capitol building, dozens of congressional aides crowded into a tiny conference room to hear about the recovery plan the Obama transition team was proposing. It was December 18, the Thursday before Christmas, and they had been given only hours notice of the meeting, scheduled to begin at 4:30 P.M. Yet more than forty staffers showed up, packing into a room with a table meant for fifteen people. It was standing room only as Obama economic adviser Jason Furman and congressional liaison Phil Schiliro laid out a framework for the recovery plan. Rather than dictating specific proposals, however, Obama's emissaries were there to provide guiding principles and to solicit ideas from the top aides of each committee that would be writing the bill.

That day, Senate majority leader Harry Reid's office had sent an e-mail to top Democratic aides urging them to begin drafting the bill as soon as the new Congress took over on January 6, with the goal of sending it to the president to sign by Inauguration Day two weeks later. Many people in the room that evening acknowledged that, even with the extraordinary Democratic gains in the election, that fast a turnaround for a major piece of legislation was unrealistic. Furman and Schiliro went around the room asking each committee what projects they could invest in that would efficiently and effectively create jobs.

One of the most prepared was the House transportation committee, which nearly a year before had put together a $15 billion infra-
structure proposal called Rebuild America. The revised plan, now
estimated at $85 billion, included $30 billion for highways and bridges,
$12 billion each for public transit and sewage systems, $10 billion for
federal buildings, and $3.4 billion to start an American high-speed rail
network. The plan also included a "use it or lose it" provision, requiring that half the funds for highways and bridges be under contract
within ninety days. If the states missed the deadline, they would have
to return the money. Earlier that afternoon, committee chairman Jim
Oberstar held a lengthy conference call with fourteen state transportation secretaries and transit chiefs, who assured him that they
had billions of dollars in projects ready to go. Once the contracts
were awarded, the plan said, work could begin within thirty days.
Then, in bold, underlined font it stated, "In this way, the Rebuild
America proposal can 'put shovels in the ground' within 90 days of
enactment."

As congressional aides worked on the bill, states and cities scrambled to put together their wish lists. The most prominent project list
floating around was one put forward by the U.S. Conference of Mayors. At more than 1,500 pages long, it contained 15,000 projects totaling $96 billion. The vast majority of projects on the list were needed
infrastructure projects or civic programs in danger of being cut. But
Republicans and the media found a number of questionable proposals. Durham, St. Cloud, and San Bernardino wanted skateboard parks.
Austin, Texas, wanted to build a Frisbee golf course. Providence suggested a polar bear exhibit at the Roger Williams Zoo. Las Vegas
mayor Oscar Goodman proposed a museum dedicated to the mob.

Almost every interest group had a plan for how to spend the
money. The National Association of Realtors wanted a tax credit for
new home buyers. The National Automobile Dealers Association
pushed for a "cash for clunkers" program, in which consumers could
get a tax credit for trading in old cars and trucks. The steel lobby
wanted a "Buy American" clause. Even the American Apparel &
Footwear Association got into the mix, urging Congress to eliminate
a tariff on shoes.

Columnists spoofed Obama's refrain of creating a package not for Wall Street but for Main Street by saying it was really a package for K Street, the gilded avenue lined with lobbying firms in Washington, DC. The charge that the stimulus was turning into a porkfest led Democratic leaders and the transition team to agree that the bill would contain no earmarks.

"I know it's the Christmas season but President-elect Obama and I are absolutely determined that this economic recovery package will not become a Christmas tree," Vice President Biden said at a meeting with economic advisers.

While the influence peddlers badgered Congress, Biden did his best to lobby moderate Senate Republicans who might support the stimulus. The landslide election left the Democrats with their biggest majority since 1980. Getting the bill through the House, where the split was now 257–178, would be a piece of cake. The Senate was a different matter. Even though they now had fifty-eight members in the Democratic caucus, the Senate leadership would need sixty to defeat a filibuster. Minnesota was still recounting the ballots in the election between Al Franken and Norm Coleman. Senator Ted Kennedy of Massachusetts was ailing from a malignant brain tumor and was rarely seen in the Capitol. Even with those complications, Obama had campaigned on a promise to end politics as usual and establish an era of bipartisanship.

Now, Biden's years in the Senate would come in handy as he worked to get his former colleagues on board. Right around the holidays, Senator Mel Martinez was at home in Florida when he received a call from Biden. The incoming White House wanted to work with him and hear some of his ideas, Biden told him. What, for example, did he think of smart grid? Biden asked. "He talked about that type of thing being the kinds of investments we needed to be making," Martinez told me. "I know I told him that I was really excited that he had called and excited to try to get something going." Senator Susan Collins of Maine got her call as she drove alone to her parents' home in Caribou, Maine, just before Christmas. As she headed toward the remote tip near the Canadian border, her cell phone kept dropping the call. But Biden tried again and again. "I was very impressed with his persistence," Collins told the *Washington Post*.[1] Biden also reached out to Maine's other senator, Olympia Snowe, giving her his home number in Delaware so she could call him on the weekends. Like other senators courted by Obama and Biden, she was surprised by the genuine interest and attention from the new administration. "I had an infinite number of ideas, because they had been stored up," Snowe told *Time*. "Now somebody was listening."[2] Biden's efforts continued as lawmakers returned to Washington in January. He kept a locker in the Senate gym and used the time to bend the ear of any member he ran into while exercising.[3]

The prospect of bipartisanship didn't seem that outlandish as the new Congress was installed. Speaking on the Senate floor, Republican leader Mitch McConnell of Kentucky echoed Obama's conciliatory tone. He said "the two parties in Washington are in broad agreement" about the need for a stimulus and promised to work with Obama. "The president-elect has promised leadership that sees beyond the politics of division," he said to his colleagues. "But that responsibility does not rest with the president alone. It rests with all of us."

$ $ $

Christina Romer had been working since before Christmas on an internal report that would allow the administration to explain more clearly what effect the stimulus would have on jobs. The plan had been receiving flak about whether the focus on infrastructure meant that women would be left out, and there was interest in analyzing what types of jobs would be created and who would get them. Without the resources of a White House, the transition team was spread thin. "Much of this was me and my laptop," Romer recalled.

Joining her on the report was Jared Bernstein, who was appointed to the newly created position of economic adviser to the vice president. Romer and Bernstein were economists of a different stripe than the more fiscally conservative advisers who came out of the Brookings Institution's Hamilton Project and now made up Obama's inner circle. The Hamilton Project was created in 2006 by Robert Rubin, Clinton's former Treasury secretary who went on to serve as a director and then chairman of Citigroup. The think tank advocated public

investment in education and infrastructure and a social safety net—
but always with an ear to the business world and a watchful eye on
the deficit. The first director was Peter Orszag, followed by Jason
Furman. Obama, then a senator, spoke at the inaugural forum. Other
economists in this camp included Larry Summers and Tim Geithner,
who had served with Rubin at Treasury.

If that wing of Obama's economic team could be seen as the disci-
ples of Rubin, Bernstein and Romer could be viewed as coming from
the line of Robert Reich. As Clinton's Labor secretary, Reich helped
expand the safety net with the Family and Medical Leave Act and an
increase in the minimum wage. During the debate over Clinton's
mini-stimulus, Reich advocated for a Rooseveltian investment in job
training and infrastructure. Like Reich, Romer taught at the University of California, Berkeley. Bernstein served as deputy chief economist for Labor under Reich and was now at the Economic Policy
Institute, a labor-oriented think tank in Washington. Bernstein was a
gray-haired economist in his early fifties, a former Harlem social
worker and jazz player, who appeared regularly on CNBC and NPR.
In 2008, he wrote a layman's book explaining why middle-class wages
shrank despite the seeming prosperity of the 2000s. Called *Crunch:
Why Do I Feel So Squeezed? (And Other Unsolved Economic Mysteries)*, the
book is filled with simple analogies and boiled-down "crunchpoints"
and haikus, such as "The economy grows. / Yet my resources fail / to
reach my needs."[4] A professor for more than twenty years, Romer
also had a knack for distilling complicated economic principles for her
young students. Among the pantheon of advisers on the transition
team, Romer and Bernstein were perhaps the best suited to explain
the stimulus to the American public.

In doing their research, the pair concluded that a stimulus package
of about $775 billion, with the types of spending and tax cuts being
discussed, would create somewhere between 3.3 million and 4.1 million jobs by the end of 2010. More than 90 percent of the new jobs
would be in the private sector. While more than a million jobs would
be created in construction and manufacturing, the state aid would save
jobs for teachers and nurses and the middle-class tax cut would result
in retail jobs. Romer and Bernstein concluded that without the stimu-

lus, the unemployment rate by the end of 2010 would be about two percentage points higher than if one was passed, potentially reaching 9 percent. The estimate was in line with what other forecasters were anticipating but far more optimistic than the widely quoted Moody's economist Mark Zandi, who predicted that if no action were taken, unemployment could reach 11 percent.

Romer presented the paper to the economic team, which decided that the fourteen-page report should be posted online. Aides throughout the transition read it over, and at the last minute someone said the report would look better if it had a visual. "I thought, Great! Here, I can make this picture quickly on Excel," Romer told me. "It was not thought about at all." The graph showed that if Congress passed the recovery plan, the unemployment rate would never go over 8 percent. As the report neared publication, Romer asked her husband, also an esteemed economist, if he would read it over.

"Now you know you're breaking an implicit rule," he told her. "You don't put down a number like the unemployment rate because it's easy to turn out to be wrong."

"Listen," she told him. "If the unemployment rate is 10 percent, we have much bigger problems than that I didn't predict it correctly."

It was a line graph that would live in infamy.

By the time the stimulus passed in February, unemployment was already over 8 percent. From then on, Republicans would use the chart to prove that the stimulus had failed. Romer and Bernstein had relied on the best numbers available at the time, the gross domestic product from the third quarter of 2008. But by January 10, when the report was released, the economy had deteriorated further. In the last four months of the year, the economy lost 2.4 million jobs, making 2008 the worst year for job creation since World War II. Looking back, Romer said that if she could turn back time, she would have emphasized the uncertainty of such an analysis. The report had mentioned this only briefly, noting that the estimates were subject to "significant margins of error." "Furthermore," the authors wrote, "the uncertainty is surely higher than normal now because the current recession is unusual both in its fundamental causes and its severity."

While the economic analysis turned out to be far more rosy than
what actually happened, it's easy to forget how abysmal 9 percent
unemployment seemed at the time. Obama didn't hold back. Two
days earlier in a speech at George Mason University in Fairfax, Virginia, Obama summed up the dire spiral into which America was
heading.

"If nothing is done, this recession could linger for years," he told
the audience, which was dead silent. "We could lose a generation of
potential and promise, as more young Americans are forced to forgo
dreams of college or the chance to train for the jobs of the future.
And our nation could lose the competitive edge that has served as a
foundation for our strength and our standing in the world."

After laying out the goals of the plan, Obama concluded: "I urge
Congress to move as quickly as possible on behalf of the American
people. For every day we wait or point fingers or drag our feet, more
Americans will lose their jobs. More families will lose their savings.
More dreams will be deferred and denied. And our nation will sink
deeper into a crisis that, at some point, we may not be able to reverse."

$ $ $

The architect of the stimulus bill, now called the American Recovery
and Reinvestment Act, was an old liberal bull named David Obey. A
congressman from Wausau, Wisconsin, and chairman of the powerful House Appropriations Committee, Obey had come to Washington in 1969 in the wake of President Lyndon Johnson's Great Society
programs. A dyed-in-the-wool progressive, an advocate for organized
labor, someone not afraid to tussle with a president from his own
party, Obey is often described with words like "prickly," "cantanker-
ous," "brusque," and "blustery."

Obey privately groused that Obama's stimulus plan was too small.
In conversations with the administration and Democratic leaders,
Obey pushed hard for a package of $1.4 trillion. But the administra-
tion balked; so he trimmed it to $1.2 trillion.

"Geez," Chief of Staff Rahm Emanuel said to him, according to
the *Fiscal Times*. "Do you really think we can afford to come in with a
package that big; isn't it going to scare people?"

"Rahm, you will need that shock value so that people understand how serious the problem is," Obey replied.[5]

Inside the transition, aides viewed it as liberal David Obey just pushing to spend money.

"It was never going to work in the Senate," one adviser told me. "So it was nice that it was a proposal, but he was off in la-la land in terms of getting it through the Senate."

With that in mind, the message was clear. "People got afraid of doing anything over a trillion dollars," recalled Congressman James Clyburn, who had also been pushing for a $1.2 trillion package. "Whatever we approved in the House had to be under a trillion."

Obama's budget director, Peter Orszag, met with Obey to discuss the package in early January, along with his deputy director, Rob Nabors, who had been staff director of the Appropriations Committee. The transition team and Obey were in broad agreement on many items in the nascent bill. But Obey wanted money for special education and schools in poor neighborhoods while Obama's advisers were pushing for education reform.

The transition team clashed with congressional Democrats over several proposals. While giving a presentation on the stimulus at a caucus meeting on January 9, Larry Summers expressed his concerns that a heavy investment in infrastructure would take too long to get out the door. Representative Jim Oberstar was in the back of the room and grabbed a microphone. Summers just didn't get it, Oberstar said. Transit agencies wouldn't need to go through the time-consuming process of awarding new contracts. They already had billions of dollars in pending options for new buses and railcars. They just needed money to exercise them. In a follow-up letter, Oberstar wrote that he met with the leadership of the New Flyer bus company, which had plants in his home state of Minnesota. With new funding, transit agencies could exercise their options in a matter of days, creating jobs not just at the bus and rail plants but also at steel mills and other suppliers.

An Obama proposal to offer businesses a $3,000 tax credit to hire new workers was rejected. Lawmakers argued that employers would be rewarded for people they would have hired anyway. And it didn't address the lack of demand, which they viewed as the real reason companies were reluctant to hire. Instead, congressional Democrats wanted more tax breaks for renewable energy companies to build wind and solar farms.

A middle-class tax cut for 95 percent of American workers, dubbed "Making Work Pay," was also criticized. The economic team believed that Bush's tax rebate checks of 2001 and 2008 had failed to stimulate consumer demand because most people saw them as a one-time bonus rather than an increase in income that would encourage them to spend. Instead, the team believed the tax cut should be spread out over two years, in tiny increases in their paychecks that people wouldn't notice. While that might have worked if the tax cuts were substantial, congressional Democrats argued that $10 a week wouldn't be enough to counteract the prevailing fear of losing a job, a home, and years of retirement savings. The criticism was ultimately proved right. Even the people who did spend the extra money didn't notice it. Obama lost not just political credit but also the boost in consumer sentiment a large check might have provided.

One of Obama's key olive branches to Republicans was the promise of almost $300 billion in tax cuts in the plan. Romer and Bernstein had concluded that while tax cuts wouldn't create that many jobs, they could be implemented quickly. While nearly half of that was tagged for his campaign promise of the Making Work Pay credit, the inclusion of such a substantial portion for tax relief was an attempt to make the plan seem balanced and collaborative. Senator Dick Durbin of Illinois saw that as one of the biggest political errors of the stimulus: "Our belief was that that would bring the Republicans to the table. Well, it turned out that it didn't." Obama received no goodwill for the tax cuts, as Republicans lambasted the plan as a spending bill that would result in increased taxes later. By offering the tax cuts at the outset instead of having Republicans demand them, Obama gave up a critical bargaining chip that might have made the stimulus seem a more bipartisan effort.

"If that money had been spent in visible changes—to make an example, school construction—if we started putting insulation and fuel efficiency in schools across America, it would have been a much more visible expenditure that people would have seen in communities large and small," Durbin said. "We learned the hard way that the tax cuts that were supposed to bring on Republicans didn't bring them on and might not have been the most effective way to instill consumer confidence."

Senator Mel Martinez was struck by the lack of involvement from the transition team in crafting the bill. The Bush administration often came to Congress with its own proposal and assigned top aides to shepherd it on the Hill. For weeks there remained a question of whether Obama would put forth his own proposal. But short staffed and stretched thin, the transition team had little capacity to create a major piece of legislation. Obama's advisers also rationalized that the bill would get more support if members of Congress wrote it themselves. "It's damned if you do it, damned if you don't," Durbin said.

Obama had decided to trust Speaker Nancy Pelosi and to trust that Republicans and Democrats could trust each other enough to reach a compromise. It was a rookie mistake. While many Republicans genuinely believed in Obama's overtures, they were skeptical of Pelosi and Obey.

When Obey unveiled the bill on January 15, it seemed that the only one not getting a handout was *Hustler* magazine publisher Larry Flynt, who had recently proposed a bailout for the porn industry.[6] With projects ranging from improving computer technology at the Farm Service Agency to cleaning up lead paint in public housing to installing explosive detectors in airports, the $825 billion package read like the miniature version of the federal budget. The plan included $275 billion in tax cuts along with major spending for energy efficiency, highway construction, computerized medical records, and modernized schools. There was also money for unemployment and food stamp benefits and for states to avoid laying off police, firefighters, and teachers.

However polarizing the stimulus would become, the plan received strong public support at the time. An Associated Press-GfK poll found that 58 percent believed it would significantly improve the economy.[7] And according to a *Wall Street Journal*/NBC News poll, people supported government spending over tax cuts by a margin of two to one.[8]

$ $ $

Having missed the original Inauguration Day deadline, Congress got to work the next day in the House Appropriations Committee. In glasses and a salt-and-pepper beard, Obey presided over the meeting with a stubborn impatience. Anytime Republicans offered an amendment or suggested slowing deliberations, Obey rebuked them. He said he had asked Republican leaders for input but got none. "This is an extraordinary circumstance," he said, gesturing with a pencil. "Every day that we delay, ten thousand more people at least lose their jobs."

The stimulus bill sailed through committees on partisan lines. Unable to get their amendments passed, Republican leaders vowed to take their proposals directly to the president. On January 23, at a meeting with congressional leaders from both parties, they presented him with a plan that relied solely on tax cuts. The main provision would drop the lowest income tax brackets to 5 percent and 10 percent. They also called for tax breaks for small businesses and new home buyers and the suspension of the income tax on unemployment benefits. Obama tried to emphasize the common ground and signaled that he was open to compromise on some ideas. But he rejected the effort to tilt the package in favor of tax cuts. Obama acknowledged the differences in opinion but told them he was president and thus would prevail. "I won," he reminded them.

Republicans amplified their criticisms. The bill gave money to the National Endowment for the Arts, they complained. It would plant grass on the National Mall and turn the Lincoln Memorial reflecting pool into an ice skating rink. The bill included taxpayer funding for contraceptives through a change to the Medicaid rules regarding family planning services. Billions of dollars could go to ACORN, the community action group reviled by conservatives as a front for voter fraud. College students would be forbidden from praying in dorms. Millions would be spent on honeybee insurance. And, Mitch McConnell pointed out, if you had spent $1 million a day since Jesus was born, it still would not add up to the price tag of the stimulus package.

While some of the criticisms, such as the money for birth control and the math about Jesus, were true, many were outright ludicrous. One of the first myths to make the rounds was that of salt marsh harvest mouse. The adorable little critter was portrayed as a cause célèbre for Nancy Pelosi, who was said to have snuck an earmark into the stimulus for it. Republicans flooded inboxes with the story of the salt marsh harvest mouse. They blasted it on cable TV. One congressman even gave a presentation about the mouse on the House floor with a blown-up picture of the creature. But the mouse was nowhere in the bill and never championed during the debate. Instead, it was on a list of several animals native to Bay Area wetlands that could benefit from a $30 million fund for habitat restoration. However untrue some of the sound bites were, Republicans painted Pelosi as the divider and forced Obama into the role of mediator, placing the burden on him to follow through with his pledge of bipartisanship.

For the most part, Obama did keep his promise. On January 27, as snow fell across Washington, he took the extraordinarily rare move to meet privately with House and Senate Republicans on their own turf on Capitol Hill. For more than an hour with each caucus, Obama led an in-depth discussion on the stimulus, fielded questions, and listened to their complaints that Democrats had shut them out of the process. Several members passed envelopes with ideas to the president and Larry Summers, who was by his side. Obama was receptive and indicated his willingness to consider their ideas, such as a $70 billion proposal by Senator Charles Grassley of Iowa (also favored by some Democrats) to adjust the alternative minimum tax so that upper-middle-class earners wouldn't get stuck with higher tax bills. The president asked each member to evaluate the plan not through a political lens but by considering what works economically. The meeting eventually returned to a common philosophical roadblock about whether low-wage workers who don't make enough to pay income taxes should receive a "tax cut." Obama asked the room how many members had a picture of Ronald Reagan in their office. Many raised their hands and nodded their heads. Obama used the survey to make the point that Reagan had also supported tax credits for low-income families when he expanded the Earned Income Tax Credit in the 1980s. Many Republicans left impressed with Obama, and some even stopped to ask for pictures with the new president.

On the eve of the House vote, the White House continued its last-minute lobbying. Obama called Representative Henry Waxman, a

California Democrat, and persuaded him to strip the family planning funds from the bill. House Democrats also dropped the $200 million for National Mall renovations. Several Republicans who appeared to be on the fence were invited to the White House that night for a meeting with Rahm Emanuel. Obama planned to host a cocktail party for leaders of both parties after the vote.

Speaking to reporters at the White House press briefing, spokesman Robert Gibbs was confident. "I think we will have Republican support for this bill," he said.

But unbeknownst to Gibbs, hours before the Capitol session with Obama, House Republicans held a closed-door meeting, in which party leaders John Boehner of Ohio and Eric Cantor of Virginia told them they wanted "100 percent" opposition to the bill.[9]

Sure enough, when the votes were tallied the following day, not a single Republican had voted for the stimulus.

$ $ $

The Senate version of the stimulus bill had grown to nearly $900 billion. That didn't sit well with Senator Susan Collins of Maine who felt the bill was far too expensive and bloated. Many of the provisions were worthwhile, she thought, but didn't belong in a bill whose sole purpose was to create jobs quickly. Senator Ben Nelson, a moderate Democrat from Nebraska, felt the same way. On January 29, as they voted on a children's health insurance bill on the Senate floor, Collins and Nelson discussed their concerns and agreed to work together to come up with a better plan. The next day, they met in Nelson's office along with Nebraska's other senator, Republican Mike Johanns, to lay out a game plan.

When word of the side negotiations reached the administration and Democratic leadership, they were angry and aggravated.

"Are you trying to torpedo the administration?" Rahm Emanuel demanded.

"You don't have sixty votes," Nelson replied.

Nelson promised to keep them all informed. Senate Majority Leader Harry Reid had only one rule: no surprises.

On Sunday, February 1, Nelson and Collins appeared on CNN's

State of the Union with John King. The stimulus had become a vehicle for Democrats to push money into their favorite programs, they said. Instead of programs like comparative health research and antismoking campaigns, the bill needed more funding for infrastructure.[10] Obama appeared to be getting the message, telling Matt Lauer in a White House interview taped later that day, "We're going to be trimming out things that are not relevant to putting people back to work right now."[11]

That night Obama prepared to host a group of Democratic and Republican lawmakers for a Super Bowl party at the White House. The Pittsburgh Steelers were playing the Arizona Cardinals, and the guest list included representatives from their home states, including Senator Arlen Specter of Pennsylvania. Specter had been taking some heat from Democratic senators who told him that if he wouldn't promise to vote for the bill, they weren't going to support the additional $10 billion that Specter wanted for the National Institutes of Health. Senator Durbin was at the party too, and as the Steelers rallied to win, he tried to smooth things over.

Sitting down next to him, he said, "Arlen, as far as I can tell in this business, a person is as good as his word. I promised you that I would vote for this. I didn't condition it on your voting for final passage. And I'm going to keep my word."

"Well," Specter replied. "I appreciate that."

While Durbin again didn't ask for a commitment, the conversation would be pivotal in winning Specter's support. On Tuesday, February 3, Specter got his wish. Joined by Durbin, he introduced the amendment on the Senate floor.

That same day, Senator Mel Martinez hosted a meeting in his office with a group of Republican senators. They knocked around some ideas trying to come up with their own proposal. What became clear was that there were two camps of Republicans: those who wanted a viable alternative and those who just wanted to have a counterproposal knowing full well it would fail. The first group coalesced with Martinez, Collins, Specter, George Voinovich of Ohio, and Lisa Murkowski of Alaska. The other group was led by Obama's presidential opponent John McCain and included Lindsey Graham of South

Carolina, Johnny Isakson of Georgia, and John Cornyn of Texas. Mc-Cain drafted a $400 billion plan focused on tax cuts and military equipment. It was quickly rejected on the Senate floor.

Meanwhile, the compromise group moved forward with the staffs of Nelson and Collins leading bipartisan meetings until four or five in the morning, crossing things out and shuffling the money around, trying to condense the bill.

When the president got word that Nelson, Collins, and Snowe weren't just offering suggestions but in the process of drafting a substitute bill, he summoned each of them to a private meeting at the White House. All three expressed surprise to find Obama alone in the Oval Office with no staff. They were one on one with the president.

Snowe and Collins each gave the president a list of items they thought should be cut from the stimulus package. Among them were $870 million to prepare for a pandemic flu and $14 million for cyber security. Collins was initially looking for a package of around $650 billion. But Obama made the case for a compromise in the neighborhood of $800 billion. The package needed to be sufficient to jolt the economy or it would all be a waste, Obama said, convincing Collins that the bill should be larger.

On her way out of the meeting, Collins ran into Nelson, who had just arrived for his time with the president.

"I guess we're here to deliver the one-two punch," she joked.

"Depends on how many you threw," Nelson fired back.

The president started his meeting with Nelson with some light banter, trying to find out what the senator was up to, what was his goal. Like the others, Nelson told him he thought the bill was too large and had a list of things he wanted to change. Unlike meetings Nelson had had with President Bush, there was no arm-twisting from Obama, just a genuine interest in hearing him out.

While Obama was trying to lure moderate senators with honey, the Democratic political operatives were splashing them with vinegar. MoveOn.org, American United for Change, and several unions sponsored television commercials targeting the centrist lawmakers. "Tell Senators Collins and Snowe: Support the Obama plan for jobs, not the failed policies of the past," the ad in Maine ended. Americans United for Change also released ads directed at Specter, Voinovich, and Murkowski. The ad against Martinez highlighted the state's high rate of foreclosures.

Privately, some Republicans fumed at what they saw as a continuation of the attack ads from the campaign. "They only make you angry and they only make you less willing to work together," Martinez said.

To be sure, the Republican leadership had stopped playing ball at this point. Despite his pledge to work with the president, Senate majority leader Mitch McConnell was working hard to ensure that his party remained united against the bill. As Specter recalled later, the message was that if Republicans could break Obama on the stimulus, it would be his "Waterloo."

Also not helping was the growing disagreement among aides who were working on the bill. In a late-night session that one aide described as "an absolute shit show," Democratic staffers rushed through the bill cutting and tallying, cutting and tallying rather than going through it line by line. The aides went around the room asking others what their senators had to have in the bill.

But leading up to a bipartisan Senate meeting on Thursday, February 5, it appeared that as many as ten Republicans might support the bill. Martinez was optimistic, declaring, "There's a great desire by a number of us to move pretty quickly."[12] That morning, at ten-thirty, a group of about twenty Republican and Democratic senators gathered in a hearing room in the Dirksen Senate Office Building to hash out a compromise. Taking their seats around the table, the senators had only pens and paper. To another aide in the room, it felt romantic, as if they had traveled back in time to an "old school" legislative meeting of seventy-five to eighty years ago, where the senators literally sat down to resolve their differences. Outside, dozens of reporters and cameramen camped out, as if awaiting a puff of white or black smoke to come steaming out of the room.

Sometime in the afternoon, the bipartisan support began to fray. Specter insisted repeatedly that his vote hinged on the inclusion of the NIH funding. He was also adamant that he wouldn't be the lone Republican. "I don't want to go to the dance without the Maine sisters," he said at one point, according to sources. Each senator took a turn saying what they needed in the bill. When one senator expressed concern that her proposal didn't make it, another assured her that she would get it back in conference. That way she could look like a hero.

Martinez was getting antsy. Leaning back, he whispered to an aide, "This is making my stomach turn."

"It was essentially about going around the table and instead of talking about the merits of the bill, it was what goodies they could get, what pet projects and the value and the price of it," Martinez told me later.

By the next day, he was out, declaring that he would not support the bill. So were Murkowski and Voinovich.

The prospect of a deal came to depend on the final four: Nelson, Collins, Specter, and Snowe. As the senators went to work, the Labor Department announced that—following a string of layoffs at Caterpillar, Microsoft, General Motors, Home Depot, Pfizer, and Macy's—the nation had shed 598,000 jobs in January, raising unemployment to 7.6 percent.

It was a day of shuttle diplomacy between the group of four and the Senate leadership, between the White House and Congress, between the Senate and the House. Aides scrambled back and forth across the Capitol with marked-up drafts of various sections of the bill. Lawmakers ducked into back rooms to share their frustrations and ease their tensions. Phones rang repeatedly from the White House to check how things were going.

Vice President Biden had been trying for two days to reach Specter in hopes of persuading him to raise his ceiling for the recovery package. But the fiercely independent senator wouldn't return his calls. Finally, Reid got Specter in a room in a meeting with White House aides and the compromise senators.

"My impression was he was not going to go a cent over $800 billion, just was not," Orszag, the White House budget director, recalled. "It was not going to happen."

The talks lasted into the late afternoon with various offers flying back and forth. Publicly, they appeared hopeful about a compromise. But inside the negotiations, things were not looking promising. At one meeting in Reid's office, the majority leader presented Collins with a plan that cut just $63 billion off the Senate bill, bringing the total to $837 billion. She was ready to throw in the towel.

The compromise senators had been looking at a measure in the $720–$730 billion range, and now after days of work, they were still $110 billion apart. Specter urged Collins to take a break and pulled her into his Capitol hideaway. There, the senators and their aides combed through the counteroffer looking for some way to salvage the deal. Eight hundred thirty-seven billion? It was such a weird and arbitrary number. But in it, some aides thought they saw a latent signal from Senate leadership—a willingness to compromise. Halfway between their offer and the one from Reid was the nice, round number of $780 billion. In reality, there was no calculation behind the number other than the serendipity that subtraction offered. But after days of intense negotiations and little sleep, they decided to give it one more try. Reid called Emanuel to come up to the Hill to try to hammer out a final agreement. Also joining him was Senator Joe Lieberman of Connecticut, an independent senator who was close to Collins from their work on the Homeland Security committee. Collins debated whether it was worth going, expecting a ridiculous counteroffer.[13] But Reid and Emanuel agreed on the $780 billion proposal and, in a subsequent meeting with the Democratic caucus, urged their colleagues to vote in favor of it.

Speaking triumphantly as the Senate debate began Friday night, Nelson said, "We trimmed the fat, fried the bacon, and milked the sacred cows."

The White House had worked hard to preserve many of its landmark investments, such as $20 billion for electronic health records, which several of the centrist senators wanted to cut. To get to yes, however, they slashed $40 billion to stabilize state education budgets and $20 billion for school construction.

A hundred and fifty miles away at the Kingsmill Resort in Williamsburg, Virginia, Nancy Pelosi was fuming. The changes "do violence to what we are trying to do for the future," she told reporters at the House Democratic retreat. "The cuts are very damaging."[14]

Back in Washington, Collins refused to budge. If the items she viewed as wasteful were put back in during conference negotiations between the Senate and the House, she wouldn't vote for it.

Specter, speaking on the Senate floor that night, summed up the uneasiness that, despite the agreement, still hung over Obama's stimulus package.

"There are reasons to argue that this is a bad bill," he said. "But I do not believe that there is any doubt that the economy would be enormously worse off without it. That's the kind of choice we have to make."

After the speech, Specter, who facing reelection in 2010 had taken a huge political risk, walked back into the Republican cloakroom and ran into a senior colleague.

"Arlen, I'm proud of you," the unidentified senator said.

"Will you join with me?" Specter asked.

"No, I couldn't do that," came the reply. "Might cost me a primary."

With his first big initiative in doubt, a package of reforms that would lay the groundwork for everything else he wanted to accomplish, Obama switched from defense to offense. He sharpened his rhetoric, criticizing Republicans who blasted the stimulus as a spending bill: "What do you think a stimulus is? That's the whole point!" He localized the pain, releasing a specific but dubious breakdown of the number of stimulus jobs that would be created in each congressional district. And he returned to the campaign trail. On Monday, February 9, Obama was going to Elkhart.

$ $ $

Ed Neufeldt had just returned from church that Sunday when his phone rang.

"Neufeldts!" he answered cheerily, picking up the receiver. His face immediately turned white. His wife, Marianne, thought it was bad news involving one of his relatives in Tennessee. After he hung up, she asked what happened.

It was Stephanie from the White House. They had seen him talk about his layoff on ABC News. Obama was coming to Elkhart and they wanted him to introduce the president.

Neufeldt was a lifelong Republican who had voted for McCain, and with the exception of telling his accident story in church, he wasn't much for public speaking. But in Obama, he saw the hope that he had always tried to keep. He had seen so many people down and out from the recession. Now here was a president with a plan for putting people back to work.

The night before the president's visit, Neufeldt's hands were sweating and he couldn't sleep. He called his pastor, Dave Engbrecht, who almost everyone calls Pastor Dave, and asked if he would come over the house and pray with him. Pastor Dave asked the Lord to give him wisdom and clarity of mind, to just be honest, and to believe that God would give him the strength. He left him with a passage from Joshua 1:9: "Have I not commanded you? Be strong and courageous. Do not be terrified; do not be discouraged, for the Lord your God will be with you wherever you go."

The next morning, Neufeldt couldn't fit into his suit and had to borrow his brother-in-law's for the occasion. He drove over to the Concord High School gymnasium where Obama would hold the town hall meeting and he went backstage.

Neufeldt paced back and forth. Obama came over to introduce himself. "I'm going to talk for about three to four minutes and then we'll let Ed talk for about twelve," he said. Obama's joke helped to calm his nerves.

As the crowd of 2,500 filled the gym, it was time for Neufeldt to take the stage.

"Ed, go ahead," Obama said. But he couldn't do it. "Ed, go ahead," he repeated. Still he couldn't move. Finally, the third time, Obama said, "Ed! Gooooo a-head."

"And I just looked up and felt this peace," Neufeldt recalled. "I felt this strength and this energy."

Neufeldt told his story about being laid off, about seeing his daughters and sons-in-law lose their jobs, about his hope that Obama and the leaders in Washington could get the economy moving again. Then he recited from typed notes that read, "It is my honor to introduce to you the president of the United States, President Barack Obama."

Back in Washington, the Senate continued to debate the compromise bill over the weekend and into Monday morning. Obama's advisers flooded the Sunday shows with the talking point that the House and Senate measures had 90 percent in common. But an agreement was still uncertain.

"We can't afford to wait," Obama said. "We can't wait and see and hope for the best. We can't posture and bicker and resort to the same failed ideas that got us into this mess in the first place."

Obama said his plan would cut taxes for 95 percent of workers and create or save 3 million to 4 million jobs over the next two years, 90 percent of them in the private sector. It would help 76,000 "Hoosier families" send their kids to college and rebuild roads like U.S. 31 that "Hoosiers can count on."

"Now, I know that some of you might be thinking, well, that all sounds good, but when are we going to see any of this here in Elkhart?" The answer wasn't weeks or months, but quickly, as soon as Congress could agree on a bill and send it to his desk. "Endless delay or paralysis in Washington in the face of this crisis will only bring deepening disaster," he said. "I can tell you that doing nothing is not an option."

After taking questions from the crowd he departed not to a rock song as he did on the campaign trail but instead to "Hail to the Chief."

Backstage, Obama turned to Neufeldt and made a promise: "We'll get you back to work, Ed."

$ $ $

After a prime-time news conference at the White House, the next stop on Obama's recession road trip was Fort Myers, Florida, a palm-tree-dotted city that had been battered by the foreclosure crisis. While the stimulus package was getting little Republican support in Washington, there were four Republican governors who said their states desperately needed it. The trip to Fort Myers underscored that, as Obama was introduced, and embraced, by Governor Charlie Crist.

It was a hug that would come back to haunt Crist in the Republican primary for Senate when the public mood had soured on the stimulus.

About midway through the town hall meeting, as Obama fielded a question about tax cuts, an aide handed him a message.

"I just want to announce that the Senate just passed our recovery and reinvestment plan," Obama told the crowd to applause.

Still the bill had to be reconciled with the House. With competing priorities and no room to grow, Orszag and Emanuel were again dispatched to be the fixers in the Capitol. While many of the disagreements were bridged by simply splitting the difference in cost, others led to marathon deal-making that lasted until midnight Tuesday in Pelosi's office and started again Wednesday morning.

Susan Collins had major concerns about the school construction grants and the fund to shore up education budgets, worried that they gave the federal government too much power over what had historically been state and local issues. Collins wanted to give more discretion over education spending to the governor. But Representative Clyburn of South Carolina wanted a provision for state legislatures to bypass the governor because, in his state, Governor Mark Sanford had vowed to turn down the money. After a shouting match with Obey, Clyburn got his way.

At one point, Senator Collins read the latest draft and felt betrayed.

"You guys told me the House was going to conform to my wishes," she berated White House aides. "This is ridiculous."

The aides hustled back to the House to try again. The drama was so high that Harry Reid was now over on the House side and told Orszag to find Collins immediately to see if the changes would be amenable. Collins was in a committee hearing with Joe Lieberman, and both stepped into the anteroom to hear from Orszag. Collins said she could live with it. But she wanted to make sure that the business community was on board and requested additional money for businesses to claim "bonus depreciation" on equipment purchases. Orszag agreed to try to include the provision in the next year's federal budget.

"We had to constantly check back with Reid because in a sense we were sort of making deals that we needed to make sure wouldn't lose some other vote," Orszag said. "He was at this point, 'Basically, just go do it. Whatever you need, just do it.'"

All along there was an underlying fear by members of the House that they were going to get steamrolled by the Senate. As a way to make room for the lawmakers' priorities, the White House agreed to scale back their middle-class tax cut from $500 per person to $400. Emanuel also had a special request from the president: $8 billion to begin building a high-speed rail system. The last-minute proposal surprised some in the transportation community who had fought for more rail money early on but were denied. The House bill provided just $300 million for high-speed rail while the Senate version included $2 billion. When Republicans learned of the stunning increase, they painted it as a back-door money grab by Reid to pay for a train from Las Vegas to Anaheim. In truth, Reid did advocate for the rail money, his spokesman Jim Manley told me, but there were no guarantees that Nevada would get the funding. At the time, the route wasn't even one of the federally designated rail corridors.

The final battle of the stimulus emerged over an obscure formula used to distribute $87 billion in Medicaid funding to the states. The formula delivered extra money for states with high unemployment. But that didn't sit well with Senator Ben Nelson of Nebraska, where unemployment was just 4 percent. He wanted to shift the formula to send more money to rural states.

An $800 billion bill was held up over a $10 million quibble.

Nelson backed down, and a few months later a regulatory change was made steering more money to rural and community hospitals in Nebraska.

Around 3:00 P.M., the senators emerged from their meeting and announced they had struck a deal.

"Like any negotiation, this involved give-and-take and, if you don't mind my saying so, that's an understatement," Reid said.

But as they got ready to sign the agreement in the ornately decorated Lyndon B. Johnson Room, no House members showed up. There was one last flare-up, as Pelosi and other House leaders realized that a line item for school construction was gone.

Reid went over to Pelosi's office, where several committee chairs were sitting around a conference table grumbling about the Senate news conference.

"I don't have the votes for it," Reid told them. "It's as simple as that."

$ $ $

On Friday, February 13, the House passed the American Recovery and Reinvestment Act by a vote of 246–183, with every Republican and seven Democrats voting "nay." That night, after holding the vote open for several hours to allow Senator Sherrod Brown to return from his mother's memorial service in Ohio, the Senate passed the bill, 60–38.

With all the changes, the $787 billion recovery plan totaled 1,071 pages, making a loud thump when House Republican leader John Boehner dropped it on the floor for effect. It contained money for roads and bridges, levees and dams, airport runways, city buses, shipyards, fire stations, public housing, rural community centers, food stamps, food banks, crop insurance, farm loans, job training, unemployment benefits, child care, Social Security checks, community service programs, economic development grants, teachers, police officers, police equipment, enhanced gun and drug patrols on the Mexican border, violence against women prevention, Indian jails, crime victim support groups, child pornography stings, small business loans, summer jobs for teenagers, special education, Head Start, Early Head Start, Pell grants, education data systems, energy efficient buildings, weatherization, the electricity grid, lithium ion car batteries, carbon capture and storage, wind farms, solar panels, biofuels, hybrid government vehicles, community health clinics, computerized medical records, renovations to the National Institutes of Health, a new headquarters for the Department of Homeland Security, anti-obesity and anti-smoking programs, research into prescription drugs and medical procedures, independent living centers, services for the blind, the 2010 Census, digital television converter boxes, art exhibits and theater performances, AmeriCorps, climate change research, space exploration, high-speed Internet, high-speed rail, Veterans Affairs claims processors, watershed rehabilitation, military base renovations, environmental cleanup, federal courthouses, border stations, radios for immigration agents, explosive detection machines for airports, port security, trail restoration, abandoned mines, national parks, wildlife refuges, wildfire prevention, fish hatcheries, historically black colleges, stream gauges, leaking gas tanks, water treatment plants, sewage pipes, diesel emission reduction, lead-paint removal, the Smithsonian, and computers for the Social Security Administration.

Passing by the press pool that Friday afternoon, Obama gave a thumbs-up. Then, after weeks of stressing that every day of bickering meant thousands of more people would lose their jobs, he boarded Air Force One and headed to Chicago to spend the long President Day's weekend at home. Rather than sign the bill immediately, Obama chose politics over the imperative, waiting for four days until a formal ceremony could be arranged at the Denver Museum of Nature & Science.

On February 17, after touring the museum's solar panel installation, Obama declared, "We have begun the essential work of keeping the American dream alive in our time."

Obama's economic team gambled that the recovery plan would only grow in Congress, and it was right, though not as high as it hoped. But the increase wasn't only the result of spendthrift Democrats. Ironically, it was the acceptance of ideas from Senate Republicans who didn't vote for the bill that pushed the bill north of $900 billion and made the centrists willing to stomach a package of just under $800 billion.

All of that, though, would be little remembered as the Recovery Act took effect. It was the Democrats' stimulus now. More important, it was Obama's. And thus began the political struggle to define "The Stimulus." The grand vision versus the flopping "porkulus."

FOUR

FOLLOW THE MONEY

We're in the money, come on, my honey.
Let's lend it, spend it, send it rolling along!
—lyrics by Al Dubin, *Gold Diggers of 1933*

THE CONSTRUCTION WORKERS in orange vests and hardhats and the highway commissioners in suits and overcoats gathered at the foot of the rusty Depression-era truss bridge on the dirt banks of the Osage River. It was February 17, 2009, and they had come to Tuscumbia, Missouri, a rural village in the center of the state, to break ground on the first project funded by the American Recovery and Reinvestment Act. Minutes after President Obama signed the stimulus bill in Denver, the commissioners banged the gavel at a makeshift meeting and approved the bridge replacement. Sparks flew on the old steel bridge, as a backhoe, already in place, began digging a hole for the supports of a new one. Fifty years earlier, Missouri became the first state in the nation to break ground on the Interstate Highway System. Now, the Show Me State claimed the fame again in what many believed would be a historic event.

Across the country were stories of the Recovery Act's initial impact. In Columbus, Ohio, twenty-five police cadets who had been laid off after training were reinstated thanks to stimulus money and sworn in at a ceremony at the Aladdin Shrine Auditorium. The University of Virginia lowered a planned tuition hike and the state restored funding for children's mental health facilities. SolarCity, one of the biggest solar installers in the country, ended a hiring freeze and planned to add sixteen work crews.[1] The expected influx of funding for education and Medicaid allowed governors and legislatures to balance their budgets and avoid painful cuts. The stimulus saved the jobs of 700 state workers in Maryland, 3,800 school employees in Alabama, and 2,000 elementary school teachers in Los Angeles. Within weeks came other projects: a trail in the San Bernardino National Forest, an electrical transmission line along Oregon's Columbia River, the repaving of New Hampshire Avenue in Silver Spring, Maryland.

One of the Recovery Act's first big successes came at the Chicago windows factory, where in December workers had staged a sit-in after learning that the plant was closing. Watching the protest unfold on TV, Kevin Surace, the chief executive officer of a green building company called Serious Materials, decided to buy the plant. With the Obama administration planning to pour billions into energy efficiency, the Sunnyvale, California, company saw an opportunity to expand by buying abandoned factories in America's industrial belts. One of them was the Kensington Windows factory in Vandergrift, Pennsylvania, a city that used to be home to one of the largest sheet steel mills in the world. The other was on Goose Island in the "stormy, husky, brawling City of the Big Shoulders." A few days before Christmas, Armando Robles, the worker who organized the sit-in, was in the union hall when he received a call from Surace wanting to know how to buy the plant. On December 28, the union leaders met with Surace at a hotel at O'Hare, and the next day, they toured the factory where Surace marveled at the machinery.

"You know what," Robles told him. "You buy this factory, and it's going to be my birthday present."

"Why's that?" Surace asked.

"Because today is my birthday," said Robles, who just turned thirty-nine.

Nine days after the stimulus was signed, Serious Materials purchased the factory out of bankruptcy court and promised to reopen the plant and give their workers their jobs back. A maintenance worker, Robles was one of the first seven employees called back to work. For years, he worked second shift, but now his days started at

6:00 A.M., as he cleaned out garbage and old furniture to prepare for production. A few months later in June, the workers punched and welded a frame, installed the glass, and completed their first window as employees of Serious Materials. As a symbol of their revival, they displayed the window in the cafeteria for the whole first year.

"I was feeling like the company is my company and my coworkers' company," Robles recalled. "I was feeling real, real satisfied. It was like a dream, like a dream that came true."

But despite these few bright spots, overall, the economy was sinking. In March, the Labor Department announced that the unemployment rate ticked up to 8.1 percent in February, already eclipsing the White House's forecast of what would happen to the economy if the stimulus were passed. About 12.5 million people were now out of work. The economy had lost more than 600,000 jobs for the third month in a row, the first time that had happened since record-keeping began in 1939. When the markets reopened that Monday, the Dow Jones Industrial Average hit its lowest point in more than a decade, closing at 6,547, less than half its mark at the start of the recession.

$ $ $

As Americans learned of the first projects funded by the Recovery Act, they also discovered programs that seemed to have little to do with job creation. There was $650 million to ensure that people with rabbit-ear TVs wouldn't have snowy screens when the country switched from analog to digital broadcasting in June 2009. The stimulus created the Council for Comparative Effectiveness Research, which would review research and make recommendations on the use of drugs and medical procedures. The Alcohol, Tobacco, and Firearms Bureau received $10 million to prevent gunrunning on the Mexican border. And at the behest of Senate appropriations chairman Daniel Inouye of Hawaii, the stimulus included $200 million for long-sought reparations for Filipino World War II veterans, many of whom didn't live in the United States.

Inouye admitted the compensation wasn't about stimulating the economy. The matter was more one of fulfilling a moral obligation made generations ago. In 1941, President Franklin Roosevelt enlisted about 470,000 residents of the Philippines, at the time a U.S. common-wealth, to fight the Japanese. Many were captured or killed in the war, including in the Bataan Death March. The president promised compensation, but Congress reneged in 1946. Since then, Filipino vet-erans, now in their late eighties and nineties, had fought to restore it, and Inouye was a big supporter. "The nation made a solemn promise, and with hardly a hearing, we revoked it," he said in a statement. "This is not the America I know and love." Under the stimulus, Fil-ipino vets who were U.S. citizens would receive $15,000; noncitizens would get $9,000.

In theory and publicity, the stimulus package was free of ear-marks, the specific items that lawmakers attach to bills to funnel money back to their home districts. Congress was still smarting from the Jack Abramoff scandal, in which a lobbyist provided gifts and free trips to lawmakers in exchange for political favors benefiting his clients. America had blanched over outrageous earmarks, such as a teapot museum in North Carolina and the infamous "Bridge to Nowhere" which would have connected the residents of Ketchikan, Alaska, across an inlet to their airport. While the stimulus may not have contained any pet projects officially, it certainly contained pet is-sues. Members of Congress and their aides knew the formulas, under-standing that an extra billion here or there could mean the difference between funding a project in their districts or not. Add more money for transit, for example, and New York City might finally be able to build the Second Avenue subway.

By far the bulk of the stimulus spending was doled out through agencies like the Department of Transportation using existing formu-las, and decisions about which projects would get funding were made on the basis of merit by expert grant reviewers and state and local of-ficials. But throughout the bill were dozens of narrowly defined pro-grams that sent money to specific areas or catered to special interests. The package included an insurance exemption—but only for compa-nies that work on recreational boats longer than sixty-five feet. An-other provision lifted a Medicare regulation affecting only three long-term care hospitals in the country. There was also language re-quiring the Transportation Security Administration (TSA) to buy

100,000 uniforms from U.S. apparel makers, inserted by a congressman from a North Carolina district home to many textile mills.

Project supporters insisted that the criticism was unwarranted. Their projects not only saved or created jobs, they said, but in some cases corrected oversights in previous legislation. No doubt the yacht repair yards in Representative Debbie Wasserman Schultz's district in South Florida benefited from her amendment. Until then, the law required them to hold additional longshoreman's insurance because workers on bigger boats and ships faced greater dangers. But since then, yachts have gotten longer and owners were skipping to Mexico, Canada, and the Caribbean for cheaper repairs, creating a hardship for small businesses in South Florida, Seattle, New England, and the Great Lakes.

"It's not the Flamingo Hall of Fame," her spokesman Jonathan Beeton said in exasperation. "This is if you are a carpet installer. . . . In order for you to go in as a small business owner and step foot on that boat, you have to have longshoreman insurance for your employees."

"The economic impact on these areas is pretty high."

Representative Larry Kissell made a similar argument when he offered the amendment for TSA uniforms, which were made from fabric from North Carolina but sewn together in Mexico and Honduras. Working in the local textile industry for twenty-seven years, Kissell had witnessed plant closings as more and more jobs fled overseas.

"The immediate impact would be to bring the assembly work to the U.S., which would create jobs," said Lloyd Wood of the American Manufacturing Trade Action Coalition, an industry group that had lobbied for the provision for five years. But there was also a political bonus for Kissell, who as a freshman Democrat could gain an early victory that his Republican predecessor had been unable to secure.

The Medicare provision for three hospitals demonstrated how easily complexity got lost in the political wrangling. The amendment was inserted by Representative Pete Stark, a Democrat from California, in the House Ways and Means Committee. The three hospitals that would receive additional funding as a result were in or near the districts of two other congressmen who sat on the committee. The president of a Connecticut hospital benefiting was also the president of the National Association of Long Term Hospitals, which had lobbied for the change. Republicans on the committee insisted that the provision be labeled an earmark in the bill. But Stark said the measure simply fixed a mistake in a previous law that unintentionally excluded the three hospitals.

Stark also drew scrutiny for another provision, first reported by the Associated Press,[2] that would reverse a $134 million Medicare cut for hospice care. The National Hospice and Palliative Care Organization had fought against the reduction, spending $1 million in 2008 and employing ten outside lobbyists, according to public records compiled by the nonpartisan Center for Responsive Politics. One of those lobbyists was once a top aide to Stark and the Ways and Means Committee. While the hospice organization confirmed that the former aide worked on the provision, Stark's office said neither the congressman nor the committee had contact with him.

"I don't think there was undue influence—this provision has been vetted and studied," Jon Keyserling, the organization's vice president for public policy told me. "Someone has to step up and speak for patients and families who are going to be denied services if this rate cut was allowed to go into effect."

Fear of having their handiwork labeled an "earmark" led some drafters to some awkward circumlocutions. Take this wording from the section of the Senate Appropriations Committee report on $2 billion for the Army Corps of Engineers:

> The committee has granted extraordinary discretion to the administration in determining how the funds provided in this act should be expended. . . . The committee is not recommending funding for specific projects in this act. However, the committee has had extensive consultation with the Corps concerning how the funds provided under this heading could be used in broad program categories.

Such cryptic language spawned a Washington parlor game to find the hidden projects. The initial House bill included $50 million for "restoration and mitigation of National Aeronautics and Space Administration owned infrastructure and facilities related to the consequences of hurricanes, floods, and other natural disasters occurring during 2008 for which the president declared a major disaster under title IV of the Robert T. Stafford Disaster Relief and Emergency Assistance Act of 1974." Could that be the Johnson Space Center in Houston, whose roof was damaged by Hurricane Ike? The final version of the Recovery Act was far less specific, listing it only as $50 million for "cross agency support." But sure enough, NASA announced in June that the money would indeed help repair the Johnson Space Center.

Two million dollars for "one or more near-zero emissions power plant(s) designed to capture and sequester a high percentage of carbon dioxide"? Google "near zero emissions power plant" and the first thing that popped up was FutureGen, billed as "the first-of-its-kind coal-fueled, near-zero emissions power plant." FutureGen was a government project started in the Bush administration to demonstrate a new technology that could "clean coal" by converting carbon emissions into a liquid, which would then be injected into the ground. The FutureGen Industrial Alliance, a group of the biggest coal companies, had studied the proposals and chosen a site in Mattoon, Illinois. But shortly after the announcement was made, the Bush administration killed the plant in 2008, saying it had become too expensive, and opted instead for several smaller test sites. That led to an intense lobbying effort by members of Illinois's congressional delegation, who now filled many slots in the Obama administration, including the president himself.

As Congress drafted the Recovery Act, Senator Dick Durbin of Illinois helped craft a line item for more than $1 billion for clean-coal technology in hopes of securing funding for FutureGen. Durbin told me in an interview that he had no guarantee FutureGen would get the money and that it would have to be formally vetted by the Energy Department. But at the time it was the only "shovel-ready" project that fit the description. Senator Tom Coburn of Oklahoma, a Republican critic of the stimulus obsessed with rooting out waste, called it the biggest earmark in history. Facing criticism, Durbin told the bill writers to make the language as generic as they wanted and he would try to sell it to the administration. So in the end, the line item was boiled down to "fossil energy research and development." And in June, the Energy Department committed $1 billion to the project.

"This was not a matter of an earmark as something that no one had ever heard of; that it was just the favorite of one senator," Durbin told me. "It had been subject to a previous administration's creation, competition, and selection. So I think that distinguishes it from other types of earmarks."

$ $ $

To stop embarrassing projects before they started, Obama appointed Vice President Biden to serve as "the sheriff" of the stimulus package. It was more than an honorary title, as the stimulus would consume much of the vice president's time. In a speech, Biden recalled a conversation he had with the president in the Oval Office, saying, "You know, if we do everything right, if we do it with absolute certainty, we stand up there and we make really tough decisions, there's still a 30-percent chance we're going to get it wrong."

Fraud has been a part of American infrastructure projects since at least the early 1800s when stone-breakers working on the National Road sold the same pile of stones over and over again.[3] There was little in the government's recent history to suggest the stimulus would pass without some major scandals. The reconstruction in Iraq had been plagued by rampant corruption and allegations of political favoritism. A report that January by the special inspector general detailed case after case of bribery, extortion, fraud, and money laundering. The response to Hurricane Katrina was similarly doomed with much of the work awarded in no-bid contracts. There were the stories of unused trailers sitting at an airport in Arkansas and ice trucks driving aimlessly around the country instead of reaching those in need. The bank bailout of 2008 was mired in controversy as the Treasury Department refused to release details of who received money or require that banks tell the public how they spent it.

Heightening the risk was the reality that the Recovery Act was pouring money into tiny government programs, whose skeleton crews had never dealt with so much money, which they now were being told to spend fast. The best example of this was the $5 billion weatherization program, in which contractors would insulate low-income homes, caulking leaky windows and replacing energy-sapping appliances. This represented a dramatic increase from the program's annual budget. The Obama administration set a goal of weatherizing one million homes a year, seven times the number of homes done normally. States saw their budgets go up ten, twenty, even sixty times. On top of that was a dispersive funding mechanism in which money would flow from the federal government to a state agency to a community nonprofit to a local contractor.

The setup prompted Senator Claire McCaskill, a former Missouri state auditor, to call out the program during a Senate hearing, noting that the Urban League of St. Louis had gone from handling $1 million in grants to $15 million. She predicted "ugly stories," such as an agency "giving a second cousin, who has a pickup truck and two friends, a bunch of money to go weatherizing homes" only to find out that all they did was glue some weather-stripping to the front door.

Another program that saw its budget balloon was the Rural Utilities Service, an Agriculture Department bureau started during the New Deal to bring electricity to the South. The agency managed the government's broadband program, which in 2008 had a lending authority of $300 million. Now, it would administer grants and loans worth $2.5 billion in one of the Obama administration's marquee projects to expand high-speed Internet to underserved areas. The broadband program did not have a good history. In 2005, the Agriculture Department's inspector general found problems with a quarter of the funds the program had received in its first four years. The bureau had used $45 million to wire nineteen affluent subdivisions in the Houston suburbs. One of those, the Sienna Plantation, was built around a golf course within five miles of the city limits. Another, River Park West, was just outside Sugar Land, which has a median household income of $95,000. Shortly after the stimulus passed, auditors warned that things hadn't improved. Since the 2005 report, more than 90 percent of the loan applications the agency had approved went to areas that already had broadband service.

Several reports in the spring of 2009 spotted high-risk areas for stimulus spending. Critical to the Recovery Act's investment in solar panel factories, wind farms, and electric cars were a couple of loan programs run by the Department of Energy. But even though the programs had existed for two years, the department hadn't approved a single proposal. Much of the federal government was a bureaucratic morass and spending money quickly *and* responsibly was not its forte. The Association of Certified Fraud Examiners estimates that U.S. organizations lose 7 percent of their annual revenues to fraud. Against the $787 billion budget for the stimulus plan, that meant the potentially whopping figure of $55 billion.

The Obama administration attempted to get in front of the problems by incorporating a series of accountability and transparency measures. The act allocated $350 million for oversight, or about $1 for every $2,250 in the plan. Lawmakers prohibited funding for casinos, aquariums, zoos, golf courses, and swimming pools. In the weeks after the stimulus was signed, Vice President Biden met with governors, mayors, and county officials warning them of the stakes should the money be misspent.

"If the verdict on this effort is that we've wasted the money, we built things that were unnecessary, or we've done things that are legal but make no sense, then, folks, don't look for any help from the federal government for a long while," Biden told a room of state officials.

When local officials came to the White House for their meeting the following week, Biden asked them to think about what it would be like if the project was splashed across the front page of their hometown newspaper.

"The president and I can't stop you from doing some things, but I'll show up in your city and say, 'This is a stupid idea,'" Biden warned them. "Do you think I'm kidding? This is the only part the president was right about—'Don't mess with Joe'—because I mean it. I'm serious, guys. I'm serious. I'm absolutely serious."

$ $ $

The centerpiece of the administration's oversight plan was Recovery .gov, a government website that would track every project, reporting to the public who got the contract, how much money was spent, and how many jobs it created. It was based on USASpending.gov, an open-government site created by a bill Obama sponsored during his time in the Senate. Recovery.gov was an ambitious endeavor, requiring tens of thousands of stimulus recipients to file quarterly reports with one hundred pieces of information. By doing this, the administration hoped to encourage John Q. Public in Anywhere, USA, to visit his local project and check if it was actually done or if the contractor was the mayor's brother-in-law. The transparency should have provided a political advantage as well, as anyone who doubted the stimulus was working could go online and see how their community was benefiting.

"Instead of politicians doling out money beyond a veil of secrecy, decisions about where we invest will be made transparently," Obama said in announcing the plan. "Every American will be able to hold Washington accountable for these decisions by going online to see how and where their taxpayer dollars are spent."

The website would be overseen by a new oversight board devoted to rooting out waste, fraud, and abuse before it occurred. The panel was named the Recovery Accountability and Transparency Board, which almost everyone quickly abbreviated to the "RAT board." To head it, Obama recruited a veteran government watchdog named Earl Devaney. Up until then, some members of Congress had complained that the board would interfere with investigations, jeopardizing the independence given to agency watchdogs. But the concerns were instantly quieted by Devaney's name.

Devaney was best known for helping to take down the lobbyist Jack Abramoff while he was inspector general for the Interior Department. He had also exposed sex, cocaine, and corruption in the government program handling oil and gas royalties. And he famously once caught an Interior official accepting a bribe by using a camera hidden in the mouth of a motorized alligator's head. For years, he prominently displayed the alligator's head in his office as a memento and to spook the department's midlevel managers.

But with thirty-nine years working for the federal government behind him, in 2009 he was ready to retire. The Friday after the stimulus was signed, Devaney received a call from Biden, saying that he wanted him to come in Monday to talk about a position overseeing the stimulus money. Devaney was hesitant but agreed.

"I didn't tell my wife about this. This was a big mistake," Devaney told me in his trademark gravelly voice, which retained a wisp of his

Massachusetts accent. "So I practiced all weekend in the mirror saying no—'No, thank you, Mr. Vice President.' 'I'm honored, but I can't do this, Mr. Vice President'—because I had told my wife about six months earlier that this being my fortieth year in government, it would be a nice round number to end with, and so we were going to retire, I was going to retire. 'Great,' she says. So I go in Monday morning and he was being very nice and complimentary about why they wanted me to do it and I was kind of hesitating and hedging a little bit. I wasn't saying no and he says, 'Well, let's go see the president.' So we did. And here's the problem: I hadn't practiced saying no to a president."

Devaney agreed.

"When would you be making the announcement, sir?" he asked.

Obama looked at his watch.

"In about ten minutes," he said.

With that, Devaney was on TV as the new inspector general in charge of the Recovery Act.

To ensure Devaney's independence, the president appointed another veteran government official to manage the Recovery Act from within the White House. Ed DeSeve was put in charge of coordinating all the federal agencies, clearing roadblocks, and fielding daily calls from state and local officials. He had worked in city, state, and federal government before joining President Clinton's budget office, where he managed the government's effort to upgrade computers for Y2K. While DeSeve was rarely mentioned in news accounts, he played an important behind-the-scenes role in trying to prove, through the stimulus, that the government could work efficiently and effectively in a crisis.

When I visited DeSeve a year and a half later, his office was still very much that of a makeshift operation. The Recovery Act implementation team had been crammed into a tiny surplus office on the second floor of the Eisenhower Executive Office Building next to the White House. Staffers' desks filled a narrow waiting room and the few windows overlooked construction scaffolding. There was little time to decorate, and among the few adornments in DeSeve's office were several torn pieces of paper taped to a white wall. Closest to his desk was one that read:

What We Do

Get the Money Out
Get Money Under Contract
Support Infrastructure Development
Promote Performance
Maintain Support

Recovery.gov launched with much expectation. Early on, in March 2009, the website was getting 3,900 hits per second. "All of this is very transparent," Transportation secretary Ray LaHood said in a town hall meeting in St. Cloud, Minnesota. "Any of you as taxpayers could go on Recovery.gov right now, any time, today, tonight, 24/7, and find out where the money's being spent."

Despite his exuberance, there was little on the site save for a general flowchart breaking the bill into chunks worth tens of billions of dollars. It would be months before the public could see where the money was going in their communities. And the first weekly reports from agencies were full of impenetrable acronyms. The Commerce Department, for example, noted that it was spending $650 million on "NTIA DTACBP."[4] For the layman, that stood for the National Telecommunications and Information Administration's digital-to-analog converter box program, or rather the money being spent to remind the public that their TVs wouldn't work if they didn't buy a special piece of equipment by June.

Speaking to mayors in February, Vice President Biden made a serendipitous slip, calling the website Recovery.com.[5] The address directed people to another website set up by a private research firm to help companies get government contracts. The firm, Onvia, had been tracking bid solicitations for more than a decade and at the time had a much better stimulus website than Recovery.gov.

$ $ $

President Obama had campaigned on a pledge to beat back the influence of special interests in Washington, but the stimulus package was red meat to lobbyists. In an effort to curtail the backstage conversations, the administration came up with an extreme solution. No registered lobbyist could talk to any agency official about any stimulus project. Instead, they would have to put their communication in writing and it would be posted on the Internet.

The rules drew outcries from groups ranging from the American League of Lobbyists to the Citizens for Responsibility and Ethics in Washington. Not only did the rules violate the ban on free speech, they complained, but they shut out the little guy while doing nothing to stop phone calls from savvy corporate executives. The stimulus was a confusing jumble of programs to many small municipalities. Matt Dunn, chief of the volunteer fire department in Readfield, Maine, told me that he had trouble finding a source of money for a long-sought addition to the firehouse. So he contacted state and local officials, who found that they had to navigate thirty different government websites to learn about all the funding the town of 2,500 people might be eligible for. But lobbyists soon found a way around the rules. If the administration didn't want "registered" lobbyists, then they would simply deregister, limiting their activity to avoid the threshold for disclosure. Other lobbyists outfoxed the administration by coaching their clients to contact the decision makers and tout their projects themselves.

The results were stunning. While more than eight hundred lobbyists filed reports with Congress disclosing work on the stimulus, only twelve of those lobbyists showed up in the filings posted on agency websites.

"Nobody's losing business on the stimulus," said Dave Wenhold, president of the American League of Lobbyists.[6]

The stimulus did little to stop the flow of government contracts to big businesses that were well connected in Washington. As a senator, Obama criticized the Federal Emergency Management Agency for awarding four $100 million no-bid contracts to Bechtel, Fluor, the Shaw Group, and CH2M Hill in the wake of Hurricane Katrina.

"Rather than use the reconstruction process to help those companies and those workers in the affected regions," Obama said in a 2005 news release, "we are seeing many of the large prime contracts go to some of the biggest contractors in the country."

Just three months into the Recovery Act, those same four contractors, or joint ventures in which they were partners, had received $2.2 billion in stimulus projects, nearly two-thirds of the federal contracting money to date. Other early winners included IBM, General Electric, URS, and Jacobs Engineering. Much of that money was tacked on to existing contracts that had been openly competed. But in an effort to get the money out the door quickly, the Pentagon awarded nearly $250 million in no-bid contracts, more than one quarter of its spending in the first five months.[7]

In addition, the federal government awarded millions of dollars to big contractors that had violated environmental, safety, and other regulations. One of them, CACI International, came under fire in a 2004 Army investigation, which found that interrogators it provided for the Abu Ghraib prison in Iraq had dragged a handcuffed prisoner along the ground and placed a prisoner in an "unauthorized stress position." The investigation found that the company had an insufficient screening process and hired employees who "lacked sufficient background and training." Under the stimulus, it won three contracts worth $1.5 million to provide contracting specialists to the Forest Service.[8] The first two stimulus contracts awarded by the Army Corps of Engineers division in New Orleans went to Manson Construction and Great Lakes Dredge & Dock—for a $10 million project dredging the Mississippi River ship entrance. The two companies had worked side by side before, and both paid settlements to the Environmental Protection Agency in 2003 and 2004 after their leaky barges spilled dredging waste into a national marine sanctuary near Richmond, California. In 2002, Great Lakes also paid $1 million in damages for dragging a dredge pipe across the bottom of Florida Bay, causing a thirteen-mile-long scar and destroying nearly 200,000 square feet of sea grass, which the area's fish, manatees, and turtles depended on for food.

No program better encompassed all the fears of the stimulus spending than the $6 billion devoted to clean up Cold War nuclear weapons sites. The Energy Department had enough radioactive waste in its landfills to fill the Louisiana Superdome. And it had 2 million acres of land—the size of Rhode Island and Delaware combined—dotted with abandoned reactor buildings and other hulking relics that needed to be decommissioned or demolished for fear of contamination.

The monumental nuclear cleanup had fallen years behind schedule and gone billions of dollars over budget with some projects not planned for completion until 2050. The Government Accountability Office, the investigative arm of Congress, said the Energy Department had a "record of inadequate management and oversight" of its contractors and designated the program as a "high risk for waste, fraud, abuse, and mismanagement." Now, the stimulus money would try to make a dent in the work. The Energy Department allocated $750 million to demolish buildings at Tennessee's Oak Ridge reservation, which enriched the uranium for the atomic bomb dropped on Hiroshima. And it gave $2 billion to remediate soil and groundwater at Washington's Hanford complex, which produced the plutonium for the bomb dropped on Nagasaki. There was additional money to remove uranium mill residue away from the Colorado River in Moab, Utah, and to accelerate waste shipments to a repository carved out of a salt formation near Carlsbad, New Mexico.

Much of the stimulus work had been awarded to joint ventures of the biggest construction and engineering firms, a rotating cast of Bechtel, CH2M Hill, Fluor, URS, Jacobs Engineering, and others, depending on the site. Many of those contractors were the same ones responsible for the accidents, cost overruns, and delays. At Oak Ridge, workers for Bechtel Jacobs were demolishing a 1940s building in 2006 when a worker fell through the weakened floor. The accident prompted a safety review, which found that the building was far more contaminated and deteriorated than originally thought. Work was halted for months, and as officials reevaluated the site conditions, costs to clean up the reservation increased $1.2 billion and the expected completion date was extended nine years. Washington Closure Hanford, the company responsible for cleaning up the nuclear waste along the Columbia River, had been fined $1.1 million in 2007 for failing to properly dispose of waste in the landfill and falsifying records about it. The year before, the company breached an old pipeline, spilling a chemical containing chromium that potentially threatened workers and the river. Speaking at a congressional hearing, Representative Marion

Berry of Arkansas summed up the history of the nuclear cleanup efforts: "I think this is where the definition of 'snafu' came from."

In an effort to accelerate the cleanup, the stimulus funding nearly doubled the program's annual budget. The line item was pushed by Washington senator Patty Murray, whose state includes Hanford, and was protected in negotiations by South Carolina's representative Jim Clyburn, whose district neighbored the Savannah River Site. In the run-up to the 2010 elections when the prudishness over pork-barrel projects had faded, Clyburn boasted to a reporter about his handiwork.

"I brought $1.6 billion to SRS in one fell swoop," he said. "I earmarked it."[9]

$ $ $

The Savannah River nuclear site was one of the first true Cold War bomb plants. While Oak Ridge, Hanford, and Los Alamos were built to develop an atomic bomb during World War II, Savannah River was born out of fear that the Soviets would produce the hydrogen bomb first. Since construction began in 1951, the plant processed more than 40 percent of the plutonium in the U.S. nuclear weapons stockpile—and 90 percent after 1970.[10] The plutonium necessary to power the deep-space program was processed at Savannah River. Even after the reactors were shut down in 1988, the plant continued to process tritium, a radioactive isotope necessary to maintain the stockpile.

The Savannah River Site is located on a 310-square-mile swath of rolling sandhills and pine forest in central South Carolina. It is almost in the dead center of the river basin that forms the Georgia state line, just far enough from the Lowcountry beaches and the Appalachian foothills to mean that there is neither an ocean nor a mountain breeze. The sun shines down on you like a heat lamp. To get to Savannah River, drive down Whiskey Road, a street that sounds like a Willie Nelson song and makes for thought-provoking intersections like the corner of Whiskey and Grace. It is a journey through the many faces of the modern South. The road starts in Aiken, once a winter colony for the wealthy, in a charming downtown furbished with fountains, antique clocks, and streetlamps. Blue banners hanging from poles on

Park Avenue read CHARACTER, SINCERITY, RESPECT, SELF-CONTROL, RE-
SPONSIBILITY, ATTENTIVENESS, LOYALTY, COURAGE, CITIZENSHIP, TRUTHFUL-
NESS, PATIENCE, COMPASSION, FORGIVENESS COMES FIRST IN AIKEN. Leaving
the business district, the road turns into an avenue lined with pink-
flowering crape myrtles and magnolias as you pass the old estates
with stables and polo grounds and signs that still warn you to yield to
horses in the intersection. The area soon morphs into chain-restau-
rant suburbia as you drive past Applebee's, O'Charleys, Chick Fil-A,
Pizza Hut, Hardee's, Captain D's, and countless other fast-food drive-
throughs. As the road slips into New Ellenton, you enter almost a
movie set version of the rural South, the red-dirt roads and water-
melon stands and rusted cars from the 1950s and 1960s on the front
lawns. On one street, past Ralph's Meat Market ("Open for 2010 Deer
Season"), next to the Talatha water tower, stands (barely) a gray
weathered farmhouse straight out of *Children of the Corn*. A little far-
ther and Whiskey Road dead-ends at the guard station where without
a security badge, the rest of the road is off limits.

The construction of the Savannah River Plant, as it was originally
named, fits snugly into the Obama narrative of American history, in
which government investment spawned a stronger private industry.
The $1.1 billion startup cost (about $9 billion today) brought scientists
and engineers with advanced degrees to a poor area of tenant farmers
and textile workers. More than 30,000 laborers came to build the plant,
setting up trailer cities on the outskirts. By 1955, 87,000 employees had
been hired for the project.[11] It was an investment that would change
the character of the economy forever. "It is as if Scarlett O'Hara had
come home from the ball, wriggled out of her satin gown, and put on
a space suit," the journalist Dorothy Kilgallen commented.[12]

In the memory of many local residents, however, Savannah River
was not a model of government spending but a feat of private sector
ingenuity. The plant had been constructed and operated by DuPont,
the American icon that began as a gunpowder maker in 1802, expanded into explosives for mining, invented nylon and neoprene, and
became one of the largest chemical companies in the world. Many
people I interviewed pointed out that the plant took only five years to
go from farmland to fission. "If you tried to build that today, you

wouldn't get through the regulatory process in twice the five years," one Savannah River worker mused.

As the Great Recession darkened in the spring of 2009, South Carolina had one of the highest jobless rates in the country, and Aiken County wasn't spared. While better off than most, unemployment more than doubled since the year before, hitting 10.2 percent in June. The Savannah River Site had employed 25,000 people in the early 1990s but, with the change in mission and recent job cuts, the workforce was down to 11,000. The city of Aiken weathered the transition as retirees discovered the community in the late 1990s and 2000s, saving it from the common industrial devolution. But the surrounding areas hadn't fared so well and consisted of some of the most depressed areas of the country. Allendale, on the southeastern edge of the site, never really recovered when the interstate was built, leaving behind roadside motels on Highway 301. With a median household income of $25,000 and an unemployment rate of more than 20 percent, Allendale was one of the poorest places in the country.

More recently, the town of Graniteville to the west saw its economy collapse when Avondale Mills shut down and laid off nearly 2,000 employees in 2006 following a train crash and chlorine spill that killed nine people. Even before the tragedy, the region's textile industry had been devastated, dropping from 31,000 jobs in 1997 to just 8,000 by 2005. Avondale Mills used to be one the largest textile plants in the antebellum South, a company that made uniforms for the Confederacy. Now, on a rainy, gray afternoon the abandoned redbrick mill loomed in the valley next to the canal and railroad tracks that cut through the center of town.

The Recovery Act promised to save and create 3,000 jobs at the Savannah River Site with $1.6 billion in new funding. The announcement was so significant that the next day, the *Aiken Standard* ran the story underneath a Pearl Harbor–style headline. About $1.4 billion of that would go to Savannah River Nuclear Solutions, making it the biggest contractor of the stimulus program. A partnership between Fluor, Northrop Grumman, and Honeywell, the company took over management of the site in 2008. Now, with the infusion of money from the Energy Department it needed workers to dismantle reactor buildings and fill them with concrete to seal off the radiation. It needed more workers to dig out contaminated equipment that had been buried in culverts underground. It needed others to repackage that waste so it could be shipped to the depository in the New Mexican desert. The goal was to reduce the footprint of the site by 40 percent and save money on maintenance, environmental monitoring, and security.

To find workers, Savannah River held a series of job fairs in South Carolina and Georgia. Thousands showed up to each one, lining up before the events started. Video of the Augusta job fair, shot by the Energy Department, shows the floor of the James Brown Arena filled with job seekers seated in blue chairs. One woman told of losing her job due to state budget cuts. A man said he'd worked in an industrial plant in Savannah for twenty-one years and needed a job to put his daughter through college. Another had been working in Kuwait and was trying to come back home to his wife and three daughters. In all, 13,500 people attended the five job fairs.

"One man came down from Michigan, drove down with his daughter because he heard we were having a job fair. We had two homeless girls show up that were living in their cars. It really hit you in the face," said Paivi Nettamo, a public affairs specialist for Savannah River Nuclear Solutions. "At least it gives them some hope to know that there are some jobs out there."

The spring of 2009 was full of anticipation and aggravation. Not since the Great Depression had the government held out so much promise for so many who needed it. America expected a lot from the Recovery Act. The recession was going to come to an end. Millions of jobs would be created and saved. The unemployed and the uninsured would get the help they needed. We were going to build bridges, wind turbines, and schools of the future. We were going to finally get serious about clean energy, reducing our dependence on foreign oil and creating whole new industries. We were going to stop losing jobs to China. We were going to reform our schools. We were going to do it fast. We were going to make lasting investments. And we were going to do it transparently so there would be little if any waste, fraud, and abuse.

President Obama and Federal Reserve chairman Ben Bernanke were already talking about "glimmers of hope" and "green shoots" of recovery. But to Americans on the front lines (a.k.a. the unemployment lines), the economy seemed to only worsen. Obama had ridden to the White House on a promise to change the ways of Washington. Yet on his first major piece of legislation, the ways of Washington won. He promised bipartisanship, but only three Republicans voted for the stimulus. He promised no backroom deals, but his aides made them out of necessity. He promised no pet projects, but they were scattered throughout the bill. He promised to crack down on special interests, but lobbyists maneuvered around his rules. He promised transparency, but so far his website had little information. Americans were scraping every penny, but Washington was spending. While tested and respected, to the layman, Keynesian economics seemed contrary to common sense. As one person said to me, "If I just lost my job, and my wife suggested we fix up the house, I'd say she was crazy."

To make matters worse, the $787 billion stimulus package was the North Star in a constellation of expensive bills at the time. It came on the heels of the $700 billion bank bailout, was followed by a $400 billion leftover spending bill, and passed weeks before the White House unveiled a $3.6 trillion budget proposal. To top it all off, some of the same banks that had caused the financial crisis were now paying gigantic bonuses. The negative perceptions would linger, setting the tone for Obama's first term. Just as the plan sold to help homeowners became a bailout for banks, the stimulus was sold as an infrastructure plan but turned out to spend money in nearly every government program. People were angry.

FIVE

NO, THANK YOU

They knew that government "help" to business is just as disastrous
as government persecution, and that the only way a government can
be of service to national prosperity is by keeping its hands off.
—Ayn Rand, *Capitalism: The Unknown Ideal*

ON JANUARY 25, 2009, as the stimulus bill was winding its way through Congress, a Seattle blogger named "Liberty Belle" logged on to her laptop and sent a missive into the ether. She spoke about being a closet conservative in "a mecca of radical liberalism." Frustrated by what she saw as out-of-control spending and big government embodied by President Obama, she wondered out loud if there were others out there who felt alone in their opinions. Conservatives weren't strange or "dinosaurs who need to progress." They were just as passionate about the country as the grassroots movement that rallied behind Obama. The only problem was conservatives weren't organized enough to have their own "revolution." "We need to find our voices, and we need to use them!!" she wrote.

"So what if we picked a day to all 'come out?'" she asked. "If you read this post, let me know what you think of this idea. It is just one idea to try to bring us together as a cohesive group, and to stand up against those that use our silence to spread lies."

The simple blog post would be one of the origins of the Tea Party movement that would soon sweep across the nation and reshuffle the deck of national politics. With few readers outside her family, Liberty Belle began posting videos on YouTube. One showed a montage of sweet-looking children set to gentle guitar strums. In captions, it read, "The American Recovery and Reinvestment Act, also known as 'the stimulus,' will leave our children with trillions of dollars in debt, creating a new generation of indentured servants. Right now Congress is voting to steal your child's future, to spend on wasteful programs they are forcing through without debate, without your voice, without your children's voice. . . . Tell your senator to vote NO."

With the stimulus, which she called "the most frightening bill on Earth," now having passed both houses of Congress, she decided to stage a "porkulus" protest in downtown Seattle. "Unlike the melodramatic lefties, I do not want to get arrested," she wrote on her blog. "I do however want to take a page from their playbook and be loud, obnoxious, and in their faces. If I don't do something, I might just lie around totally depressed. Who's with me??"

The woman behind the blog was Keli Carender, a twenty-nine-year-old adult education teacher who fit the stereotype of an Obama youth, not a Tea Party member. She had long curly hair, hipster glasses, three tattoos, and piercings in her nose and the cartilage of her inner ear. She was born in El Paso and moved to Colorado and then Seattle, where she lived in a rental home in a nontraditional family where her mom worked and her dad stayed at home with the kids. Her parents were involved in the civil rights movement and gave their daughters names with eccentric spellings. When Carender was a child, she loved Jesse Jackson so much that her dad took her out of school to see him speak. After college, she spent her twenties bumming around the world, picking up a teaching degree at Oxford, working as a waitress in Ireland, and moving to Australia and New Zealand. Now, she worked at a nonprofit teaching basic math to welfare recipients and lived in a neighborhood full of immigrant businesses.

When I met Carender on the July Fourth weekend of 2010, she was performing in an improv comedy show called *Inferno: Sinners, Demons, and Drag Queens.* The black-box theater was in a neighborhood of vegan restaurants and head shops (yes, plural) near the University of Washington. Before the show, I grabbed a beer with her and the troupe at the Rat and Raven pub, which had a Jagermeister machine and Pabst Blue Ribbon on tap. Carender ordered a Manny's IPA and the fish tacos. The premise of the show, she explained, was that audience members would write down on a slip of paper something they regret, a sin they committed, or a little white lie. The troupe would then act out the sin and its extreme consequences as the players received their punishment in hell, or rather a "hellish" place (to accommodate different beliefs). The show starred a drag queen in a blond wig and her demon sidekick, who did parkour, a type of street gymnastics that involved a lot of back flips. At intermission, a cabaret performer stripped to a thong and lit a match off her nipple.

I caught up with Carender the next day so that she could explain how in the world she had helped start a political movement often associated with red-faced retirees. Her parents were conservative Democrats who felt the party had left them during the Clinton years, she said. But she wasn't any sort of political junkie. She doesn't own a TV and she doesn't listen to talk radio. Like many young people, Carender was inspired to become active in politics by the enthusiasm surrounding Obama, only in a different direction. She saw Obama as a far-left-wing candidate who was pretending to be a pragmatic centrist. Throughout the campaign, she felt a constant tension hanging out with her liberal theater friends while keeping her conservative views to herself. Nowhere is this dichotomy better displayed than the list of favorite books posted on her blog: *Pride and Prejudice*, the Constitution, *Anna Karenina*, *Liberal Fascism*.

"I started reading books, started reading blogs, and really started to get into it," Carender told me. "The first one I read was *Basic Economics* by Thomas Sowell, and I'm a ginormous Thomas Sowell fan. He's like one of my heroes. I think he's one of the most brilliant people on the face of this earth. And I want to meet him. I wrote the Hoover Institute and actually was like, 'Is Thomas Sowell going to be in Seattle anytime?' I was like stalking Thomas Sowell. And I started reading *National Review*. I wanted an intellectual basis for what I was thinking."

Carender cried on Inauguration Day, but they weren't tears of joy. She was talking about politics all the time by then. Her fiancé, Conor, who was apolitical and voted for Obama, was tired of hearing about it and suggested she start a blog. What set her off was the combination of the bailout and the stimulus.

"Eight hundred billion dollars," she said. "I mean $800 billion! And we didn't have the money and I just thought it was going to turn into a slush fund for favorites. It was going to be a bunch of crony capitalism."

She tried calling her congressman and senators to complain, but their voicemails were full for days leading up to the vote. She decided that she could sit around and mope or she could follow the lead of the antiwar and World Trade Organization protesters she had seen in Seattle and *make* the politicians listen. With her improv background, she knew a thing or two about using theatrics to drum up media attention.

"I just saw over the eight years of Bush how protesters created a narrative," she said. "In every news cycle, every news story, it was a protest here, a protest there. And you see the signs and you see interviews with people and you see what they're saying and so it becomes part of the everyday story. And so I just thought, 'Well, we can do the same thing, but with our message.'"

So Carender decided to hold a rally on February 16, the day before Obama was to sign the stimulus. She named it the porkulus protest after seeing the word on conservative columnist Michelle Malkin's blog. "I've never done this before," Carender recalled feeling. "How do you do this? I was total geek about it. . . . I thought it was just going to be me and Conor and my family." Carender started contacting every conservative she knew: the Young Republicans, local economists, a friend in college whose dad was active in the Republican Party. A conservative radio host let her go on his show. But it didn't get a lot of attention until she e-mailed Malkin, who posted the event on her blog. About 120 people showed up at Westlake Park in downtown Seattle. They held homemade signs, played patriotic music, and chanted. Malkin even bought them two giant pans of pulled pork for the protest, which they later donated to a homeless shelter. Carender took another page from the Obama playbook, collecting e-mail addresses at every event so she could begin building an action network.

That morning, she had written a prescient blog post. "Make no mistake," she told her growing list of followers. "The President will be signing that bill tomorrow. I have no illusions that he will actually listen to us. BUT, maybe, just maybe, we can start a movement that will snowball across the nation and get people out of their homes, meeting each other and working together to redirect this country towards its truly radical founding principles of individual liberty and freedom."

Her blog was getting national attention. People wrote in from Georgia and northern Michigan. One commenter promised to support the Seattle protesters from the California state capitol in Sacramento where he would hold a sign saying HONK IF YOU HATE THE STIMULUS! Malkin challenged others to speak up about the stimulus. The day Obama signed the bill in Denver, more than five hundred people showed up, some with rubber snouts and homemade signs, and ate a whole roasted pig on the steps of the capitol. The next day in Mesa, Arizona, where Obama announced a plan to help homeowners facing foreclosures, hundreds more protested.

If a new movement of Republicans, conservatives, and libertarians was afoot, what would it call itself? Carender wondered on her blog. Conserpublitarian? Liberservlican? Repervatarian?

On February 19, CNBC reporter Rick Santelli supplied the answer. In what became the rant heard 'round the world, Santelli expressed outrage with the stimulus and the housing plan, adding that the founding fathers would be rolling over in their graves.

"This is America," he said gesturing to a room full of futures traders at the Chicago Mercantile Exchange. "How many of you people want to pay for your neighbor's mortgage that has an extra bathroom and can't pay their bills?" Then, to cheers and whistles, he told the CNBC hosts, "We're thinking of having a Chicago tea party."[1]

"Yes! Yes! Yes! You tell 'em Rick!!!!!" Carender wrote on her blog.

Through Twitter, some of the earliest Tea Party activists arranged a conference call to organize a nationwide protest on February 27. There were websites and Facebook pages now. Carender returned to Westlake Park, this time with three hundred people. The protesters brought hundreds of tea bags. Some hung them from their fishing hats, and others held the historical flags reading DON'T TREAD ON ME. At one point, they called Democratic senator Patty Murray and collectively booed on her answering machine. Nationwide, thousands of people showed up to tea parties in Atlanta, St. Louis, Los Angeles, and elsewhere. An anonymous commenter wrote into Carender's blog: "Success is yours, the Obamunists are on the run."

When we met, I couldn't help but ask Carender about her tattoos. She has a blue spiral, an Irish symbol she got when she turned eighteen, on her bicep and a chain of elephants on her ankle, which she swore wasn't a Republican symbol but a design she saw on a girl at college and wanted herself. On her wrist she has a scarlet pimpernel taken from a BBC movie version of a book she and her sister loved as kids. Carender saw parallels between the Scarlet Pimpernel character invented by Baroness Orczy, who tries to rescue people from French Revolution guillotines, and the Tea Party movement. It's trying to save people from the wrong kind of revolution led by radical progressives, she explained, and steering them toward a revolution that upholds freedom.

"I think next time I'm going to get my favorite amendments tattooed on me," she said. "Let's see, I like the First, the Second, the Tenth, the Fourteenth."

$ $ $

As the grassroots movement grew, largely ignored by the mainstream press, a more prominent fight between the White House and Republican governors was playing out on cable TV. Several governors vowed to reject certain parts of the stimulus that they saw as a federal intrusion. The dispute centered on a $7 billion unemployment modernization fund. The Recovery Act promised generous grants to states that expanded unemployment benefits to cover part-time workers, those in job training, or people who left the workforce to care for a sick relative or because of domestic violence. In many states, especially in the South, only a fraction of unemployed workers received jobless benefits. But the governors complained the short-term fix would leave them with a long-term budget hole when the stimulus money ran out. As unemployment trust funds dried up with all the new people seeking benefits, states would be forced to raise taxes on businesses to sustain it.

Onto the national stage came South Carolina governor Mark Sanford, a former congressman known for sleeping on a futon in his office to save money and for carrying two squealing piglets into the state legislature to make a point about pork-barrel spending. The chairman of the Republican Governors Association, Sanford was depicted by critics as trying to raise his profile for the 2012 election. But his stance on the stimulus remained true to a fiscally conservative philosophy he had promoted for years.

While Sanford was still in high school, his father was diagnosed with Lou Gehrig's disease, and so at a young age he stepped in to manage the family farm, known as Coosaw, near Beaufort, South Carolina. "When his father fell ill, Mark felt responsible to his father and his family," his ex-wife, Jenny Sanford, wrote in her memoir. "After his father died, the tough decisions Mark had to make to save Coosaw made him the embodiment of someone who had lived through an experience like the Great Depression, almost like someone from another time. This was the heart of his deep-seated frugality."[2] Sanford was also relentlessly ambitious, once asking Jenny to bring on a date a list of her lifetime goals to discuss over dinner. Sanford went into real estate. He told me that he dreamed of being the "Sam Zell of the Southeast," referring to the Chicago real estate magnate. But as he learned the business, he became frustrated with how his investments were affected by policies in Washington. "Federal borrowing to cover the deficit and national debt was competing with the capital available for the private sector, which consequently made it tougher for me to earn a living," he wrote in a hard-to-find book published in 2000.[3]

Sanford was swept into Congress in the 1994 Republican wave on the platform known as the Contract with America. In the 2000 book, Sanford described showing up at a ceremony in Charleston in his beat-up Honda as South Carolina's senators arrived from Washington via a Gulfstream III private jet. Compounding his discomfort with the extravagance, he wrote, Senator Strom Thurmond wanted his lemonade without ice, and "a battery of full colonels . . . leapt into action, straining lemonade with their fingers" as it sluiced down their shirt-sleeves.[4] During his time in Congress, Sanford was among a small group of fiscal conservatives, including Ron Paul, who reliably voted against federal spending. After keeping his commitment to serve only three terms, Sanford ran for governor and won, clashing often with both Democrats and Republicans in the legislature as he tried to rein in government.

Sanford relished the media attention not only on himself but also on the issue that for years got him up in the morning. He was one of the first governors to oppose federal aid to help states balance their budgets. The "bailout" as he termed it would allow states to kick the can down the road and punish other states that had saved money when times were good. "We've already unloaded truckloads of sugar in a vain attempt to sweeten a lake," he wrote in an op-ed for the *Wall Street Journal*. "Tossing in a Twinkie will not make the difference."[5] He compared the stimulus to Joseph Stalin's Soviet grain quotas.[6] And he said it would turn the American economy into that of Zimbabwe, which has had to print trillion-dollar notes because of spiraling inflation.[7]

Joining Sanford and Louisiana's Bobby Jindal in opposing the stimulus were governors Rick Perry of Texas, Haley Barbour of Mississippi, Bob Riley of Alabama, C. L. "Butch" Otter of Idaho, and Sarah Palin of Alaska. Nearly all of them readily accepted the infrastructure funding, but they promised to refuse any part that had too many strings attached.

Inside the White House, the governors' refusal to take stimulus money was viewed as an opportunity. Here they were, Republican leaders who were more interested in scoring political points than helping those hurt by the recession. "It was a winning argument to say, 'Really, you're going to deny X, Y, Z to your population because of some misguided thought that you have,'" one adviser told me.

Sanford opened the battle with the White House in March, when he asked Peter Orszag for permission to use the $700 million allocated to the state for education and other services to instead pay down debt. Orszag promptly rejected the proposal. Jim Clyburn, a congressman for South Carolina, expected Sanford would be a problem and had inserted a provision in the stimulus bill allowing state legislatures to go around their governors if they wouldn't request the money. South Carolina lawmakers introduced a resolution to accept the funds themselves. But congressional researchers questioned the constitutionality of the provision. Allowing a legislature to override the governor, they concluded, would likely violate the separation of powers clause and the Tenth Amendment, which prevents the federal government from meddling in the affairs of a state. The Sanford standoff was destined for the courts.

In Alaska, Governor Palin was preparing for a showdown of her own. Many of the provisions in the Recovery Act were tangled with government strings. Palin's issue was a $29 million grant to the state to promote renewable energy and make buildings more energy efficient. Palin insisted that taking the money required the state to adopt universal building codes, dictating what kind of lightbulbs residents could have, the thickness of their windows, and the color of their roofs. Such a "one-size-fits-all" policy didn't make sense in a state where tens of thousands lived in villages on remote islands or the Arctic tundra. In her memoirs, Palin described her opposition to the stimulus.

"What is most dangerous about these power grabs is that they're usually done in the name of a good cause—insuring the uninsured, for example—and have a big wad of cash attached to them," she wrote in *America by Heart*. "The Obama administration's mammoth $787 billion stimulus package is a good example of this tactic of bribing states to surrender their rights."[8]

In *Going Rogue*, Palin describes a conversation she had with her daughter Bristol after picking her up from her job as a coffee shop barista. Palin was frustrated with the Democrats' economic policies, and the conversation turned to Bristol's goal of opening her own coffee shop one day. Starting a business in this climate was a terrible idea, Palin advised, because the Democratic government would dictate everything through regulations.

"In fact, don't do this until this administration understands government's role in private business," Palin told her daughter. "Or wait until they're out of office."

"What do you mean 'don't do it'?" Bristol bristled. "Business owners are smarter than politicians give them credit for, and President Obama is wrong to think more government control is the answer. Pay attention to the tea parties, Mom. You're not alone in this."[9]

$ $ $

By the time of the tax-day protests on April 15, 2009, the Tea Party fervor had crystallized into a national political movement. In Washington State alone, there were Tea Parties in Anacortes, Bellevue, Bellingham, Bremerton, Colfax, Colville, Everett, Friday Harbor, Grays Harbor, Issaquah, Monroe, Moses Lake, Mount Vernon, Oak Harbor, Olympia, Okanogan, Port Angeles, Port Orchard, Pullman, Redmond, Richland, Shelton, Spokane, Tacoma, Vancouver, Yakima, Wenatchee, and Walla Walla.

In Seattle, more than one thousand people showed up at a protest organized by Keli Carender, who dressed as Alice in Wonderland. But the news media couldn't figure out her costume. "I was Little Bo Peep, Swiss Miss, all these things," she told me. "I was like, 'It's a Tea Party! Alice in Wonderland? Going down the rabbit hole? Like, hello?' I thought it was very witty, but apparently most people didn't get it."

While counts differed, nationwide as many as 500,000 people rallied in 750 cities to protest the expansion of the federal government and future tax increases expected as a result of the stimulus. In Sioux Falls, South Dakota, children held signs reading KEEP YOUR HANDS OUT OF MY PIGGY BANK as men dressed as colonists dumped boxes labeled STIMULUS and PORK into the local lake. In Austin, Texas, Governor Perry stoked supporters with suggestions that Texans could secede "if Washington continues to thumb their nose at the American people." At the White House, someone threw a box of tea over the fence, prompting the Secret Service to deploy a bomb robot. And in Montgomery, Alabama, a radio talk show host compared the events to the solitary protest of Rosa Parks refusing to give up her seat.[10]

Despite the lofty claims to history, many in Washington dismissed the Tea Party protests. "It's not really a grassroots movement," House Speaker Nancy Pelosi told a TV reporter. "It's AstroTurf by some of the wealthiest people in America to keep the focus on tax cuts for the rich instead of for the great middle class."[11]

Pelosi had a point. The Tea Party movement was heavily aided by Americans for Prosperity and FreedomWorks, two nonprofits started and funded by David Koch, a billionaire who co-owns the oil, chemical, and paper conglomerate, Koch Industries. The chairman of FreedomWorks is Dick Armey, the former House majority leader who helped engineer the 1994 Republican takeover that ushered conservatives such as Mark Sanford into office. Some of the first protesters against the stimulus came from the nonprofits' local chapters. FreedomWorks provided activist training, and in early 2009, sent an e-mail to members encouraging them to protest the stimulus.[12] Fox News promoted the rallies. But Pelosi was wrong to cavalierly put down the masses. Many people who attended the protests were part of the "great middle class" she spoke of, but felt squeezed by tax and social policies that either benefited the very rich (like the bank bailout) or the very poor (like welfare). The Tea Party was rife with contradictions, but its supporters were true believers who had felt ignored for decades as American industry, which once provided a middle class for blue-collar workers, had slowly faded away. Now the expansion of social networking through Twitter and Facebook made it easier to connect, spread alternative ideas, and organize.

The rise of the Tea Party should have come as a surprise to no one. It mirrored the anti-elite and anti-coastal populist movements that have followed every major recession in recent American history. The Panic of 1873 brought the Greenback Party, made up mainly of farmers who opposed the national banking system. The Panic of 1893 fueled the People's Party, which pitted white farmers in the South and Midwest against the banks and railroads. The Great Depression saw tax revolts. Father Coughlin used the radio to unite lower middle-class workers in his suburban Detroit parish and elsewhere against FDR, international bankers, and the world court. With Barry Goldwater, populism shifted right, joining the anti-elite, small-government, and anticommunist factions of the conservative movement. In the 1970s, Proposition 13 in California cut property taxes, leading to similar protests and petitions around the country. The early 1990s saw the grassroots presidential campaign of Ross Perot, who campaigned to reduce the deficit and opposed free trade agreements as a danger to American jobs. Anger over taxes and big government was evident in the 2008 election with the popularity of Ron Paul and the late-October focus on Joe the Plumber, the everyman who worried that Obama's policies would raise his taxes.

Antipathy toward taxes is a sentiment as old as the Bible, where in the Gospel of Luke, the people of Jericho express outrage that Jesus would visit the home of a tax collector, who immediately repents for his sins. The first Tea Partiers I met were Kathleen Virnig and Jim Rugg in St. Cloud, Minnesota, in the congressional district of Representative Michele Bachmann. We met at a traditional German restaurant, where every now and then, the owner would come over and inquire, "Zo far, zo gut?"

Virnig, sixty-five, owned a Catholic bookstore in town that had to cut employee hours because of the recession. One of the few items selling well was the St. Joseph real estate kit, a small statue that religious homeowners bury upside down in their yards in hopes that it will make their homes sell. Rugg, seventy-six, ran an air-conditioning business before retiring. Before dinner, he handed me a blue folder he said would help me understand everything I needed to know. The Great Recession was a planned downturn, he explained, orchestrated by elements seeking to create a "Single World Order" to control banking, health care, education, and ultimately the individual.

Over a dinner of sauerbraten and spaetzle, Virnig and Rugg argued that the stimulus package was yet another attempt by the government to intrude on people's lives. The two helped organize St. Cloud's April 15 protest against government policies like the stimulus that they feared would lead to higher taxes.

"To me, it's a bunch of money that we don't have that is being thrown around to cull favor," Virnig said.

"It's a political move," Rugg added, "but it has a mission to degrade the free-market system."

The $8 billion in the stimulus for public transit? An unnecessary subsidy for a system that should sustain itself. The plan to bring high-speed Internet to rural communities? A grab for big telecom. Grants for "smart meters"? An attempt to dictate how much electricity people can use.

"The impression I have of Obama is that he hates America," Virnig said to the background sound of lively German music.

$ $ $

The seething soon reached local officials who held the power of the purse. While rare, some county boards and agencies refused their share of stimulus money. The housing authority of North Platte, Nebraska, turned down $588,000 to repair sidewalks and install security cameras.[13] In Warren County, Ohio, northeast of Cincinnati, commissioners rejected $373,000 to buy three new transit buses and make other upgrades to their fleet. "I'll let Warren County go broke before taking any of Obama's filthy money," Commissioner Mike Kilburn told a reporter.[14]

Meanwhile, the showdown between the governors and the Obama administration continued to flare. The day after the Tea Party protests, a high school student sued the state of South Carolina to force Sanford to spend the allotment for education. The governor was taking heat from all sides. Teachers, parents, mayors, university presidents, Republican legislators, and state officials all urged him to take the money. They pointed to the plight of the jobless, the run on food banks, the rural school that Obama highlighted in a speech that shook every time a train passed. If Sanford didn't spend the money, teachers would be laid off, college tuition would rise, prisons would be closed, and criminals freed. The Democratic National Committee ran television ads accusing Sanford of playing politics instead of doing what's right. Adding some history to the dispute was a group that built a tent city in a park near the governor's mansion and erected a sign reading WELCOME TO SANFORDVILLE.

"He is saying to children in these schools that need to be fixed, that I am so concerned you are going to have to pay this back twenty-five years down the road that I'm going to deny you a solid education that will prepare you to pay it back," Congressman Clyburn told reporters. "You tell me how that makes sense?"[15]

Sanford was bothered by the criticism that he was heartless, didn't care, or was just an ideologue. In his mind, he was acting in the best interests of the students by thinking about long-term improvements in education, such as consolidating rural districts and turning over the state school bus system to local control. The stimulus, he thought, was allowing legislators to avoid making tough decisions that would have meant more money for education in the long run.

In late April, the South Carolina legislature approved a measure directing Sanford to take the stimulus money. A few weeks later, the governor vetoed it, and the legislature overrode his veto. That set up a court battle. Sanford sued the state attorney general to prevent him from enforcing the legislature's action. Another student, this one in law school, sued the state, with the opposite intent. Sanford himself was sued by the state association of school administrators. On June 4, the South Carolina Supreme Court ruled against Sanford, finding that the power to appropriate money rested with the legislature and that the governor had a duty to follow their direction. A few days later, Sanford signed the papers formally requesting the stimulus funding.

"When you lose, you lose in politics," Sanford told me. "You can go back and fight yesterday's battle if you like, but I think at that point you're being belligerent just for belligerency's sake."

Beaten and blistered locally, Sanford's star was rising on the national stage. For months, he was Obama's chief opponent on the stimulus, appearing day after day on cable television and in the opinion pages of national newspapers. The 2012 election was three and a half years away but with Sanford in his final term as governor, buzz followed wherever he went about what he would do next. Appearing on MSNBC, Sanford was lauded by host and former congressman Joe Scarborough. "I want you to run for president," Scarborough said. "That's all I'm going to say. I think you need to run for president. Republicans need you."[16]

But all along, Sanford held a secret. Shortly after losing the stimulus battle, his wife told him to leave. It had been nearly five months since she discovered a series of love letters between him and a woman from Argentina. Sanford's professional life seemed to be building unstoppably, but behind the scenes, his personal life was crumbling. For forty-eight hours that June, the nation wondered, where was Mark Sanford? Officially, he was taking time off to recharge from the stimulus fight by hiking on the Appalachian Trail. But when a reporter from the *State* newspaper met him coming off a plane at the Atlanta airport, the alibi fell apart. Sanford admitted he had flown to Argentina to see the woman with whom he was having an affair. The newspaper published a set of steamy, gushing e-mails Sanford sent to the woman he called his "soul mate." In one Sanford wrote, "I could digress and say that you have the ability to give magnificently gentle kisses, or that I love your tan lines or that I love the curves of your hips, the erotic beauty of you holding yourself (or two magnificent parts of yourself) in the faded glow of night's light—but hey, that would be going into the sexual details we spoke of at the steakhouse at dinner."[17]

Suddenly, Sanford's presidential prospects, if not his political future, were over. He was no longer a viable voice challenging Obama's economic policies.

$ $ $

On July 3, Sarah Palin stepped down as governor of Alaska. Within weeks, Alaska lawmakers called a special session and overrode her veto of the stimulus energy funds. Officially, Palin resigned because "obstructionists" had made it too distracting for her to serve Alaskans effectively. Or in the words of her father: "Sarah's not retreating, she's reloading!"[18] Either way, at least for now, she was out of the picture.

Suddenly it seemed that all of Obama's opponents on the stimulus were falling away. First Jindal, who had bombed his first national speech, then Sanford, and now Palin. Obama got his break into national politics under similar circumstances when every major contender for the Illinois senate seat decided not to run or withdrew from the race. But despite the fortunate chain of events, Obama was losing ground because of his own mistakes. For months, a president whose own election testified to the power of grassroots activism through social networking ignored the rising voice of the Tea Party. He underestimated Fox News personality Glenn Beck who portrayed the stimulus as the blueprint for a socialist takeover. By the summer, the Tea Party had coalesced into a movement with the power to challenge the health care bill and reshape electoral politics.

PART 2

RECOVERY?

SIX

SHOVEL-READY

Should I give up or should I just keep chasing pavements?
—Adele, "Chasing Pavements"

WHEN CONSTRUCTION BEGAN on the first Recovery Act project, America's infrastructure was in terrible shape. A report card issued by the American Society of Civil Engineers graded it a D. One in four bridges was either structurally deficient or functionally obsolete. A third of major roads were in poor or mediocre condition while nearly half of urban highways were congested, leading Americans to waste 4.2 billion hours stuck in traffic every year. Mass transit and subway stations deteriorated with rust and peeling paint. More than 1,800 dams were classified as unsafe and likely to cause fatalities if they failed. Leaking pipes lost about 7 billion gallons of clean drinking water a day. Aging sewage systems discharged billions of gallons of untreated wastewater into rivers and streams every year. Thousands of toxic waste sites sat untouched in cities across the country, as funding shrank to the lowest level since 1986. The National Park Service faced a $7 billion maintenance backlog on trails and visitor centers. Freight trains were plagued by bottlenecks, and Amtrak fell years behind the bullet trains running in Europe and Asia. Air traffic controllers continued to use radar to track planes when satellite-based navigation was already available for every American car. An electricity grid using technology from Thomas Edison's time strained under increased usage, making it prone to blackouts on hot summer days.

In total, America needed a five-year investment of $2.2 trillion to bring its infrastructure into good repair. "Years of delayed maintenance and lack of modernization have left Americans with an outdated and failing infrastructure that cannot meet our needs," the ASCE concluded. From the New York City blackout to Hurricane Katrina, from the Minneapolis bridge collapse to the Midwest floods, year after year, man-made failures pointed to the growing problem.

"Shovel-ready" became the buzzword of the day, signifying a project that had received all its permits and was ready to go once funding became available. The term originated in the late 1990s as a way to attract development for industrial sites and was adopted by several governors. But the idea of "shovel-ready projects" didn't become popular until Governor Ed Rendell of Pennsylvania used it in early 2008 to promote a state economic program. Rendell went on to become chairman of the National Governors Association and, as founder of a group called Building America's Future, was actively promoting a national infrastructure plan when talk of a stimulus bill began on Capitol Hill. After Governor David Paterson of New York used it in a congressional hearing in October 2008, "shovel-ready" quickly became the bar for federal stimulus projects. Testifying at the same hearing, Jared Bernstein, who went on to become the vice president's economic adviser said, "I believe that you craft a package where eligibility requirements are contingent upon shovel-readiness." By the time Obama used it on *Meet the Press* in December, the word was on everyone's lips.

President Obama billed the Recovery Act as a program that would "immediately jumpstart job creation" with "shovel-ready" projects to rebuild "our crumbling infrastructure." Such rhetoric deliberately conjured New Deal images of blue-collar workers heading out to the heartland with sledgehammers and pickaxes over their shoulders. His advisers hammered the message home on cable talk shows. Asked by CNN's Wolf Blitzer how soon the public would feel the results, Larry Summers said, "You'll see the effects begin almost immediately."[1] Speaking the next week on Fox News Sunday, David Axelrod said, "I think that there'll be signs of activity very quickly. . . All over the country, you're gonna see shovels in the ground, you're going to see construction projects under way."[2]

No industry had been hit harder than construction. The housing bust followed by the frozen bond market and the decline in investments and tax revenue meant that neither the private nor the public sector was building. By the spring of 2009, more than 21 percent of construction workers were out of work. Despite the publicity about shovel-ready projects, only about $80 billion, one-tenth of the Recovery Act, was devoted to infrastructure, as economists like Summers warned the money would take too long to get into the economy. Billions would go to passenger rail, public transit, water and sewer systems, airports, environmental cleanup, and the Army Corps of Engineers. But the largest part of the infrastructure funding by far, $27 billion, was reserved for roads and bridges.

As a term to describe the infrastructure projects under the Recovery Act though, "shovel-ready" was fairly misleading. Under the law, states had to get half their road money approved by the U.S. Department of Transportation within 120 days. But once a project was given the green light by DOT, it could still be months before any shovel hit the ground. States had to advertise the project to allow contractors to submit bids. They needed to review those bids and sign the contracts. When that was done, they had to go back to DOT for the final okay. Then the contractor had to marshal equipment and hire workers. While some projects such as the bridge replacement in Tuscumbia, Missouri, broke ground right away, many more were like the bridge over the Conodoguinet Creek in central Pennsylvania. Vice President Biden used the project as the exemplar of stimulus money translating quickly into jobs. But local officials pushed construction back several months to the summer to avoid detouring school buses that depended on the bridge for their routes.[3]

Despite this reality, the Obama administration continued to tell the public that the Recovery Act was ahead of schedule, pointing out that all the states met their 120-day deadline. While paper pushers were indeed getting projects approved faster than usual, the incongruent boosterism when contrasted with actual construction made the wait for jobs only feel even longer. By the end of July 2009, only 20 percent of projects had started, according to Transportation Department data. The timing of the stimulus was poor to bring about the flood of construction projects everyone expected in the first year. By the time officials and contractors had jumped through all the required hoops, it was already late in the construction season, and many projects would have to wait until 2010. It appeared that what "shovel-ready" really meant was ready for politicians to pose with a shovel for a photo op.

One of Obama's chief stimulus pitchmen was ironically a former Republican congressman, whom he had appointed as Transportation secretary. Ray LaHood represented Peoria, Illinois, for fourteen years, having won the seat in the same year as Mark Sanford and others elected in the Republican takeover. While he presided over the vote to impeach President Clinton, LaHood developed a reputation for reaching across the aisle and tempering the partisan tones of Congress. He was also known as an unabashed earmarker, occasionally steering money to campaign donors. His biggest contributor, the construction equipment giant Caterpillar, based in his district, now stood to gain substantially from tens of billions of dollars in transportation projects.

Despite the criticism tossed at the stimulus by his fellow Republicans, LaHood played the role of an ebullient traveling salesman, crisscrossing the country to promote the stimulus plan, standing at a podium in front of a Phoenix light-rail line, speaking at the airport in Pittsburgh, posing with a backhoe behind him in New Hampshire. LaHood was everywhere. He even had a blog, which he wasn't shy about using to refute reports that questioned the department's stimulus spending. In his entries, the Recovery Act was moving swiftly, improving safety, easing congestion, creating jobs, and making the lives of commuters easier. Touting the two thousandth project to receive funding, the widening of an interchange near Kalamazoo, Michigan, LaHood wrote, "That's what 'reinvestment' and 'recovery' mean, and **that's what DOT has delivered** [emphasis his]."

One of the points that LaHood underscored frequently was that construction bids were coming in far below estimates, allowing states to fund more projects and put more people to work. The downturn in the construction industry meant that asphalt, steel, and other building materials were extremely cheap. Lack of work also made for fierce competition among contractors, who were willing to take a far lower profit margin than usual. The trade group the Associated General Contractors of America surveyed its membership in early 2010 and found that 90 percent had lowered bids to stay competitive. Some contractors said they were even underbidding the cost of the project, essentially "buying work" to keep their crews employed. State transportation departments saw three to four times the usual number of bidders. Nationwide, states saved $7.5 billion in total, allowing the Department of Transportation to fund an additional 2,500 projects.

But the practicality of "shovel-ready" often conflicted with the ambitious goal of rebuilding the nation's infrastructure. To get the money out the door fast, many states opted for short-term paving projects instead of addressing their critical needs. The list of projects ranged widely from cleaning and painting steel supports on the Kuwaikahi Bridge in Hawaii to repaving a stretch of interstate in Mattamiscontis, Maine. Costs ranged from $261 million to reconstruct a tangle of highways in the Dallas–Fort Worth suburbs to $1,117 to repave a road in Opelika, Alabama. About 67 percent of the road and bridge money was spent repaving and widening roads. Less than 12 percent went toward bridges. As another measure of how small scale much of the work was, 92 percent of the projects cost less than $5 million.

Officials often spoke of how the stimulus would rebuild our roads, bridges, and schools, but they forgot to mention another thing the stimulus would rebuild: our bathrooms. Among the federal project reports were ones to demolish the sauna at Grand Forks Air Force Base and to buy twenty-two precast concrete toilets for the Mark Twain National Forest in Missouri. No doubt Twain would have had a field day with that one. It's hard to imagine anyone reminiscing wistfully about their daddy repaving a road or installing a toilet during the Great Recession in the same way Mayor Moore of Elkhart remembered his father's work for the WPA. In retrospect, the New Deal seemed bold and efficient compared to the Recovery Act, even though in reality, it suffered the same tensions. One of the New Deal's first programs, the Public Works Administration, was tasked with building large-scale infrastructure projects. But by the fall of 1933, with spending and job creation sluggish, Roosevelt raided its funds to form the WPA, which would focus on short-term projects of less significance.[4]

$ $ $

A good example of this tension between the timely and the transformative was the stimulus funding for airport projects. Before the Recovery Act passed, aviation groups lobbied heavily for an investment in NextGen, a long-awaited plan to overhaul the national airspace system by converting from radar to satellite-based air traffic control. Every year, tens of millions of flights are delayed not because of weather but because of volume. A move to GPS technology would allow planes to fly closer together on more direct routes, reducing delays, cutting carbon emissions, and saving airlines money. It was exactly the type of public investment spurring private industry that Obama often discussed. But the stimulus provided only $150 million toward this multibillion-dollar project.

The bulk of the aviation money was contained in a $1.1 billion grant program to rebuild runways and make other improvements at the nation's airports. Most people would have expected that money to go to the busiest airports, such as Chicago O'Hare or Hartsfield-Jackson in Atlanta. But among the airports receiving the maximum grant were Kahului in Hawaii and Akiachak and Ouzinkie in Alaska. In fact, more than $100 million went to airports that have fewer than one flight an hour: airports that cater to recreational fliers, corporate jets, or far-flung places.

The village of Ouzinkie is one of the remotest outposts in the United States, home to a mere 167 people on an island off another island off the coast of Alaska. There are no stores, no gas stations, and no stoplights. Yet the village received a new $15 million airport thanks to the stimulus. Officials said the airport would provide a critical link for the Alutiiq natives and the descendants of Russian otter hunters who live there and depend on small planes to get groceries from Kodiak. But investigators from the Department of Transportation inspector general's office noted that the village already had a gravel airstrip, a landing area for sea planes, and access to cargo barges.

By contrast, major hubs such as Newark and Las Vegas didn't get any stimulus money. Atlanta, the busiest airport in the world, received nothing in the first round of grants, getting funding only when savings from lower bids opened the door for additional projects.

Ouzinkie's largess was the result of the complex set of rules laid out by the Recovery Act. To qualify for stimulus money, airports were required to have a project ready to start in thirty days. Awards were limited to $15 million per project, and no airport board could receive more than $20 million. That meant the Port Authority of New York and New Jersey—which operates the Newark, LaGuardia, and John F. Kennedy airports—couldn't get any more money than the airport authority in Mott, North Dakota, population 692. Projects also weren't eligible if they had already received money from federal, state, or local governments, or from private sources such as landing fees. Because runways at major airports cost far more than the $15 million maximum, that ruled out many bigger, busier airports.

"We tried to target the ones that have the most urgent needs," Federal Aviation Administration spokeswoman Laura Brown told me. "It was designed to fund projects that otherwise might not have been funded . . . For some airports, this is probably a unique opportunity."

So it was at the Standing Rock Sioux Reservation in North and South Dakota, where unemployment is 45 percent in the summer and tribal funds are limited.

"You need to devote as much of the money as you can to taking care of the social needs," said the tribal chairman, Ron His Horse Is Thunder.

Under the stimulus package, the Standing Rock Airport, about sixty miles south of Bismarck, received $1 million to repave the runway, install lights, and build a fence. The airport has about two hundred takeoffs and landings a year, roughly the traffic Atlanta has every hour and a half. But the upgrades might help the reservation attract new wind energy business or defense contracts, His Horse Is Thunder told me. Most important, it will improve the chances of getting air ambulance service for emergencies, he said.

To select airports for stimulus funding, the FAA relied on its National Priority Rating system, which scores projects on a scale of 0 to 100, based on safety, security, and capacity needs. Typically, airports must score a 40 or higher to be approved. In the stimulus, the FAA raised the threshold to 62 to be certain worthy projects would be funded. Yet the FAA chose more than fifty projects below that mark, "raising concerns about whether the agency's process resulted in funding the highest priority ARRA projects," the inspector general said. Ouzinkie, for example, had a score of 40. One reason the FAA selected low-priority projects was to ensure that every state got at least one airport project. By doing that, the FAA engaged in what Robert Puentes, an infrastructure expert at the Brookings Institution, calls "the peanut butter approach" in which scarce dollars are spread thinly instead of targeted to critical projects.

Funding for little-used airports was a focus for Republican critics of the stimulus, who singled out a regional airport in Johnstown, Pennsylvania, that bears the name of former Democratic congressman John Murtha, whose generous earmarking was under FBI scrutiny at the time. The *Washington Post* reported that the airport had received $200 million in federal funds in the past decade, including $800,000 in stimulus money.[5] That prompted the National Republican Congressional Committee to dub it the "Airport for No One."

But large chunks of stimulus money went to airports that were closer to major cities and got far less use than Murtha's. One such recipient was the Williamson Flying Club. The group of roughly two hundred hobbyists who fly Pipers and Cessnas owns and operates the Williamson-Sodus Airport about thirty miles east of Rochester, New York. The private club received $385,000 to resurface its runway. While the airport is considered a "reliever" runway for Greater Rochester International, 90 percent of its flights were by local recreational or business aircraft. During one week, almost half the takeoffs and landings recorded on air traffic websites were by the flying club or one of its officers.

Then there was the Purdue University Airport in West Lafayette, Indiana. The airfield was closed to commercial flights more than seven years ago and is mainly used by students in the aviation technology program, the football and basketball teams, and senior administrators. Under the stimulus package, it received $660,000 to raise its fence from eight feet to twelve feet and add a barrier to prevent animals from burrowing underneath. The FAA recommended the project several years ago to meet new safety standards, Purdue airport director Betty Stansbury told me. "I said, 'We'd be happy to do it if you provide funding for it because we don't have the resources,'" she said. At the time of the stimulus, Purdue was proposing a 5 percent tuition increase for in-state students. The taller fence and barriers would prevent wildlife from getting in the way of planes. But since 1990, the airport had reported only one incident of a plane striking a burrowing animal, when the propeller of a Piper Cherokee hit a skunk.

Whether the stimulus money was being spent on the most critical projects was a common theme in almost every infrastructure program. The Associated Press analyzed bridge projects and found that stimulus funding would fix less than 1 percent of the more than 150,000 bridges considered deficient or obsolete. Nearly half the bridges receiving money were already in good shape but getting more work because it could be done quickly. As an example of project that would have to wait, the reporters cited a wooden bridge in West Virginia that was built in 1900 and now had holes, corroded railings, and missing steel poles. A seventy-five-year-old drawbridge in Seattle, they said, scored a 3 out of 100 for structural sufficiency and had "cracked concrete foundations" and "widespread corrosion" in its steel beams. It too wasn't funded, as the Department of Transportation prioritized quick-fix projects like paving roads.[6]

Even the roads that were resurfaced weren't the ones most in need of fixing. *USA Today* reported that highway money had "largely bypassed dozens of metropolitan areas where roads are in the worst shape," such as in Detroit and the Bronx.[7] In response, LaHood used his blog to take swipes at experienced reporters with cheap shots such as, "Most people know that numbers and reporters don't mix." The secretary never provided an answer as to why cities with unacceptable roads weren't given priority, asserting, "The fact is our Federal Highway Administration is one of the stars of the Recovery Act."

The Associated Press also looked at the $720 million allocated to modernize border stations, where trucks and travelers enter the United States. Rather than steering the money to heavily trafficked checkpoints on the Mexican border, the government was spending hundreds of millions of dollars on little-used posts along the Canadian border. The station in Whitetail, Montana, which saw about five cars a day, received $15 million; the crossing in Laredo, Texas, which handled more than 55,000 travelers and rated among the highest priorities, got nothing. The Associated Press said the Whitetail project benefited from the political pressure of Montana senators Max Baucus and Jon Tester.[8]

Homeland Security secretary Janet Napolitano dismissed the reports, but after facing criticism halted new construction to conduct an independent review. The disparity seemed to mainly result from a decision by Congress to spend more money on the northern border, which was ill equipped to handle concerns about terrorism after 9/11. Some of the posts were built before World War II. The report noted that the Whitetail facility was the size of a small gas station. The bathroom floor had been scraped away to its plywood base. There was mold and asbestos. The water wasn't drinkable. The building had no holding facilities if a terrorist were caught there, and the lighting and cameras were so poor that officers couldn't take accurate pictures of license plates if a driver decided to speed past the checkpoint. The deficiencies would be comical if not for the terrorist threat. At another station in Morses Line, Vermont, built in 1934, the only detention option was to handcuff a suspect to a bench. Space was so limited that once when officers tried to detain a family, most of the family members successfully escaped back to Canada on foot.

The review concluded that there was no political interference in the selection of projects. But it also presented an interesting timeline that it failed to explain in detail. Up until the House and Senate leaders met in conference committee, all previous versions of the stimulus bill included more money for the agency that handles the majority of stations on the Mexican border. But in the conference committee, which included Baucus, the funding was tipped toward the agency with more stations on the Canadian border. The questions over little-used border stations returned a year later when Canada announced that it would close its side of the Whitetail crossing. By then, Homeland Security had spent more than $1 million on design and initial site work, such as building foundations and installing utilities.

$ $ $

The reality was that much of the project money wasn't going to communities that were hit hardest by the Great Recession. Stimulus spending was all over the map with some battered counties hauling in large amounts while others that were just as bad off received little. South Dakota, where unemployment barely cracked 5 percent, received $1,952 per person, not including tax cuts, according to an analysis my colleagues and I did at ProPublica. That was twice as much as Florida, which had 12 percent unemployment but received less money per capita than any other state. Nevada and Michigan, which competed for worst jobless rate, both breaking 14 percent, also weren't given any special preference. They received $1,139 and $1,348 per person, respectively.

What seemed like an unfair distribution of money was the result of a hodgepodge of government funding formulas written years before the recession. Road and bridge money was based on such factors as the number of federal highway miles in a state. Education money was distributed by a combination of population and the number of school-age children. Lawmakers tried to steer some money to hard-hit places by directing states to prioritize highway projects in economically distressed areas and allocating 10 percent of rural development funds to counties with persistent poverty. But in the end, Congress mostly stayed with the existing formulas to avoid a political tug-of-war that could have dragged on for months.

The social safety net programs, such as food stamps and unemployment insurance, were of course geared to people who were out of work or needed groceries to feed their families. But the reliance on old formulas left the White House with little discretion over how to spend the bulk of the money. Many of those decisions rested with state officials. When Obama administration officials could target assistance, they did, awarding advanced battery grants to Rust Belt

communities with auto plants and sending money to hire police officers to cities with increased crime and budgetary problems.

Despite such efforts, analysis after analysis found no relationship
between where projects were funded and unemployment and
poverty. Some counties with high unemployment got a windfall while
others that were just as bad off got scraps. Trigg County, Kentucky,
on the Tennessee border northwest of Nashville, saw its unemployment reach 16 percent when its largest manufacturer, which made car
seat frames, closed in March 2009. The county of 13,000 people received $41 million in project money, about $3,100 per person. Right on
the heels of the plant shutdown came a $30 million grant to widen
U.S. Highway 68, about $2 million to clean up a park devastated by an
ice storm, $1.5 million to improve its water and sewage system, and $1
million for a facility to convert wood chips to fuel to heat a local
hospital.

Despite having a higher unemployment rate, peaking at 21 percent, LaGrange County, Indiana, didn't fare so well. Like its neighbor-
ing county Elkhart, LaGrange saw its economy crater when RV plants
closed their doors in the fall of 2008. But LaGrange received just $8
million, about $213 per resident. The government provided little more
than the education and rural housing money that every county received. The county had several needed transportation and infrastructure projects, economic development director Keith Gillenwater told
me. "It's frustrating," he said. "To me there's a lot of disparity that
should be reexamined and taken into consideration."

While hard-hit counties struggled to get help, some of the richest
places in the country received stimulus money. The city of Fairfax and
Arlington and Loudoun counties in Virginia each got more than
$1,000 per person thanks to their proximity to Washington, DC, and
being home to a major airport, a university, government offices, and
contractors.

One of the biggest winners, at nearly $21,000 per resident, was
Thomas County, an area of 583 people in the Nebraska Sandhills. Unemployment there was about half the national rate, but the county
fared well because of its small population and a few million-dollar
road projects. Still, many residents thought the main stimulus project,

a $7 million viaduct over the railroad tracks, was a waste of money, Judy Taylor, chairwoman of the Thedford village board, told me. "Out here, there seems to be plenty of work for people," said Janice Hodges, whose family owns a gas station near the viaduct. "It probably could have been better used somewhere else."

The biggest determining factor separating the winners and losers was whether a county had a huge project relative to the size of its population. Hyde County, South Dakota, did well because the Interior Department was building a new $37 million school for the Crow Creek Sioux Tribe. Norton County, Kansas, benefited from a $100 million broadband plan; Bristol Bay, Alaska, and Esmeralda County, Nevada, from geothermal projects. Thanks to the massive cleanup of the Savannah River nuclear plant, Aiken, South Carolina, received three times as much money as Charlotte.

Unable to control all the money, the Obama administration was left to defend the disparity.

"We put recovery projects where they're needed, regardless of a state's unemployment rate," Jared Bernstein, the vice president's economic adviser, wrote on the White House blog. "To put this point in historical context, think back to the New Deal. One of the most memorable and lasting projects from that era was the Hoover Dam. This project was built in a region where the unemployment rate was probably around zero, because it was in the middle of the uninhabited Nevada desert!"

LaHood and the Department of Transportation repeatedly noted that the physical location of a project didn't mean that the economic impact was isolated to that area. When the Akron transit authority bought nineteen buses, for example, it created work at local rubber suppliers but also at factories that made the buses in Kansas, North Dakota, and California. Moreover, construction workers would drive wherever they could find work. To make its point, the department highlighted the case of Willie Fort. The thirty-two-year-old Mississippi construction worker was about to lose his job when he found work on a stimulus project four hours away in Shreveport. So he left his wife and four young children back home and temporarily relocated for the prospect of two years of steady work. He visited his family once every two weeks, and the money allowed them to move ahead with their plans to buy a house in Mississippi.

$ $ $

As the dreary summer of 2009 wore on, the soothsayers on Wall Street and the bloviators in Washington tried their darndest to divine the direction of the economy. Consumer confidence increased but consumer spending didn't. The Institute for Supply Management's manufacturing index had its best showing in a year but the sector continued to bleed tens of thousands of jobs a month. Every new figure brought a new storyline. If the unemployment rate got worse, Republicans branded the stimulus a failure while Democrats said it wasn't enough and called for another. If the situation improved, the Democrats hailed the stimulus as a success while the Republicans said the rest of it wasn't needed and should be repealed. Whatever the verdict, it always leaned toward the extremes. It's moving too slowly. It'll ramp up any day now. The stimulus has failed. We need another one. The economy is improving. The worst is yet to come.

On the hundredth day of the stimulus, Vice President Biden released a report highlighting a hundred projects that were making a difference. It told the story of Joe Jamiel, owner of Jamiel's Shoe World, who said a loan backed by the Small Business Administration "gave us a second chance at saving our family business." In Pearl, Mississippi, a health clinic received a grant to open three new locations serving another 9,000 low-income patients. Anderson Windows of Bayport, Minnesota, called back nearly half the 560 workers it had let go, thanks to tax credits for first-time home buyers and energy-efficient improvements. "Across America, recovery is under way," Biden said in a note accompanying the report. The stimulus, he wrote, had already created 150,000 jobs.

The figure was based on economic assumptions about the impact of government spending rather than any hard data. The media was skeptical. Such proclamations of ballpark predictions as facts made the public doubt the administration's figures later on when they *were* backed by sound economic data. Whatever effect the stimulus was having on employment didn't change the horrid litany of job losses that arrived from the Labor Department on the first Friday of every month.

In June, Labor announced that Americans had lost another 345,000 jobs in May. That followed 539,000 in April. It was better than the first quarter of the year, when the economy was losing 700,000 jobs a month, but it was still worse than anyone had seen in twenty-five years. The unemployment rate, in just a few short months, had leaped from 7.2 percent to 7.6 to 8.1 to 8.5 to 8.9 to 9.4.

At the first Recovery Act implementation meeting back in February, Biden, with the smudged cross of Ash Wednesday still on his forehead, declared that the stimulus would "drop-kick us out of the recession." Now he was urging America to be patient. The administration delivered platitudes like "we didn't get into this overnight and we're not going to get out it of it overnight" or "things are going to get worse before they get better." The inability to show concrete progress made the early argument that "every day Congress delayed passing the bill more people would lose their jobs" seem disingenuous. As one reporter pointed out at a White House press briefing, "The message seems to be, well, just wait, it's coming, it's coming."

On June 8, the vice president responded to the worsening job market by announcing the "Roadmap to Recovery," a plan to ramp up stimulus spending over the summer in the program's second hundred days. Sitting at a rectangular table decorated with ferns in the White House's state dining room, Biden delivered the plan to the president. "What we're talking about here is putting some pace on the ball here, Mr. President," Biden said as Obama fiddled with a pencil.

The plan had ten major initiatives. They included creating 125,000 summer jobs for teenagers, starting work on 1,500 highway projects, and putting 5,000 police officers on the streets. By the end of the summer, Biden said, the administration would create or save another 600,000 jobs. But the White House was simply announcing projects that were already in the works and expected to happen regardless of any extraordinary effort by the administration.

The bigger news of the day came when Biden's economic adviser, Jared Bernstein, walked reporters through a PowerPoint of maps explaining the plan during the White House press briefing. Asked about his January report that predicted unemployment wouldn't rise above 8 percent if a stimulus package were passed, Bernstein acknowledged that the economy was far worse than they knew at the time. "Now, looking back," he said, "it was clearly too optimistic."

The admission was amplified when Biden said in a television interview in Iraq, "The truth is, we and everyone else misread the economy."[9] Even though few economists had predicted 10 percent unemployment, the admission that the president's top economic advisers had "misread" the situation generated new doubts about the stimulus.

"If the diagnosis was wrong, how can you be sure that the prescription, the stimulus package, was right?" ABC News correspondent Jake Tapper asked Obama during the president's trip to Russia.

"There's nothing we would have done differently," Obama replied.[10]

The stimulus prevented doomsday scenarios for state budgets. Everywhere officials could point to jobs that were saved and valuable programs that weren't cut. As the unemployment figures showed a steep rise in the private sector, employment for government workers remained fairly flat. But even with those achievements, the funds for state budgets weren't enough to prevent some painful cuts, tax increases, and worker furloughs that essentially served as a pay cut. The reduction in spending by the states somewhat negated the effect the federal stimulus package was having.

In July, the Labor Department reported that the economy lost 467,000 jobs the month before. It was worse than forecasters expected and it reversed a positive trend of declining job losses. The unemployment rate ticked up to 9.5 percent. For the first time since the Great Depression, the downturn canceled out all the jobs created during the period of growth, according to the Economic Policy Institute. The darkening picture gave rise to the prospect of a jobless recovery, in which the economy bounces back even as workers can't find jobs or have to settle for ones with lower pay. Such a situation followed the last two recessions in 1990–91 and in 2001. Many wondered if America was in store for even bigger jobless recovery, as the country transitioned from a manufacturing economy into one more reliant on the service sector, just as the Depression had marked a final shift from agriculture to manufacturing.

If the administration's original outlook was overly optimistic, it was now staring reality in the face. Obama announced at a news conference that it was clear the unemployment would go over 10 percent by the end of the year. As the sobering numbers made it to the White House economic team, so came another troubling set for the political team. Obama's poll numbers were falling. Fewer and fewer Americans had faith in the stimulus and in the administration's ability to bring about recovery.

Liberal economists led by Nobel laureate and *New York Times* columnist Paul Krugman and outside White House adviser Laura Tyson were now calling for another stimulus package. While still early in the game, the woes exposed the Recovery Act's flaws and made it the butt of numerous jokes. Warren Buffett described the stimulus as "like taking half a tablet of Viagra and then having also a bunch of candy mixed in."[11]

At the same time, Republicans, defeated miserably less than a year before, were now hitting their stride. Led by House leaders John Boehner of Ohio and Eric Cantor of Virginia, they branded the Recovery Act a failure and a flop. They repeated and repeated the rosy 8 percent unemployment forecast and how the country had already surpassed that. Boehner released a tongue-in-cheek video featuring a bloodhound named Ellie Mae on the hunt for stimulus jobs.

"We went to AIG where the stimulus meant big bonuses for big executives but no new jobs," said the narrator, a Georgia congressman with a down-home accent. "In Wisconsin, the stimulus paid for a bridge to a bar called Rusty's Backwater Saloon. They've got great burgers but no new jobs. Finally the dog tracked down something. In North Carolina, they used stimulus money to hire one new state worker. His job? Apply for more stimulus funds from the taxpayers by the way of the federal government."

"After five months and billions in debt on our kids and grandkids, where are the jobs?" the narrator asked. While the examples were selective and exaggerated, the messaging was effective. By simply repeating the question—Where are the jobs? Where are the jobs?

Where are the jobs?—the Republicans could remind people of the pain and the promise in four simple words while the White House tinkered with a narrative built around the idea of a "New Foundation."

In truth, it wouldn't have been hard for the GOP to find people hired for stimulus projects. The Obama administration issued a press release virtually every time someone got a job. The Recovery Act team, led by Ed DeSeve and working out of a cramped office in the Eisenhower Executive Office Building, daily sent reporters a list of positive press clippings titled "Recovery in Action." The Department of Transportation produced videos of construction workers called "Voices of the Recovery Act." The economic advisers, Summers, Orszag, and Romer, fanned out to think tanks across the Beltway to give speeches, where they said the stimulus and other measures had pulled the economy back from "the brink of disaster." And the White House took aim at its critics. Speaking at a community college near Richmond in Cantor's congressional district, Biden noted that while the Republican leader was criticizing the stimulus package, he was also asking for stimulus money to bring high-speed rail to his constituents.

As July turned to August, the administration got a reprieve. The Federal Reserve's "beige book," a report on the economic conditions around the country, noted that things were beginning to stabilize. The Commerce Department reported that gross domestic product shrank at an annual rate of only 1 percent, a tremendous improvement largely due to the stimulus money flowing into the economy. Then came the big number, the only one that seemed to seep into the American mindset: the unemployment rate. The Labor Department reported that in July the economy lost 247,000 jobs. It would have been a devastating number if not for the fact that just months before America was losing three times as many jobs. And for the first time in more than a year, the unemployment rate, tentatively reported at 9.4 percent, was going in a different direction.

Shortly after 1:00 P.M. on that day, August 7, Obama stepped out to the White House Rose Garden and looked out at a rope line of reporters against a clear blue sky. After months of batting away criticism and hedging his remarks, he could now speak with conviction. "While we've rescued our economy from catastrophe, we've also begun to build a new foundation for growth," he said. "I am convinced that we can see a light at the end of the tunnel."

The stock market was rallying out of its hole, with the Dow Jones Industrial Average having risen nearly 3,000 points since March. In some corners, it felt like people were popping champagne bottles, clinking glasses, and striking up the band in a chorus of "Happy Days Are Here Again." Responding to the unemployment numbers, the investment bank Barclays Capital sent a note to its clients declaring, "The recession is dead; long live the recovery."[12]

All the happy talk didn't mask the larger reality that in almost every other corner but Wall Street, people were suffering. As long as the economy was losing hundreds of thousands of jobs a month, it was hard for the administration to claim success. White House aides were careful to speak in measured tones. Obama's press secretary, Robert Gibbs, called it "the least bad report that we've had in a year." It was a confusing time to read the economy. For liberals hoping for more money for clean energy, social services, and high-speed rail, the short-term positive would turn into a negative in the long term, as the calls for another big stimulus package, arguably needed, began to die down.

Officially, the stimulus was slightly ahead of schedule. But if credit for the economy were due to the Recovery Act, it was difficult for the public to see. Almost all the spending thus far was for Medicaid, tax cuts, and saving teacher jobs. Very few of the promised "shovel-ready" projects had broken ground. The Associated General Contractors of America said construction was "disappointingly slow." And a USA Today/Gallup poll conducted in August found that 57 percent of Americans felt the stimulus was having no effect or making things worse.

At a congressional hearing at the end of the summer, LaHood gave a glowing assessment of the stimulus. "When you look at our portion of the economic recovery, a lot of people are working around America," he testified. "Look at the orange cones. Look at the orange barrels. Go fly into any airport I've flown into. They're all resurfacing their runways." But spending numbers released that day told a different story. The nonpartisan Congressional Budget Office had originally estimated the Department of Transportation would spend about $5 billion by the end of the first fiscal year. But LaHood said that only $3.4 billion had been spent, about a third less than expected.

Testifying at the same hearing was Jeff Taylor, the transportation manager in Elkhart County, Indiana. Taylor said the county had struggled to get stimulus money for roads and been bogged down in paperwork for projects that were shovel-ready. Because of the delays, the county wouldn't be able to bid projects until November, meaning that work wouldn't begin until April 2010.

"It was my understanding, along with millions of other Americans, that the ARRA was a jobs creation and jobs retention bill," Taylor said. "If it is true we are in an economic crisis, we should expedite the paperwork process, and target those areas hardest hit by the economic downturn."

SEVEN

RECOVERY INACTION

On the street
Slung on his shoulder is a handle half way across,
Tied in a big knot on the scoop of cast iron
Are the overalls faded from sun and rain in the ditches;
Spatter of dry clay sticking yellow on his left sleeve
And a flimsy shirt open at the throat,
I know him for a shovel man . . .
　　　　—Carl Sandburg, "The Shovel Man"

ALBERTVILLE, MINNESOTA. Exit 205. The bright orange traffic sign on the side of the road said it all: for the next forty-nine miles, I would be driving on a road being repaired by the American Recovery and Reinvestment Act. Here was the work I envisioned when I began covering the economic recovery, American laborers digging and building and given new hope. But as I drove past the barns and silos that dot Interstate 94 on my way to St. Cloud, the sign was the only visible indication of any construction work. St. Cloud's experience was like that of many American cities—still waiting for the promise of stimulus money and wondering when the wave was going to come in.

"We were hopeful that from transportation to wastewater to cops, those things would be almost immediate," Mayor Dave Kleis told me, "and we haven't seen that." When I interviewed him in the summer of 2009, St. Cloud's main stimulus road project hadn't started yet. Nor had the stimulus upgrade of the veterans' hospital heating and cooling system, the $1.6 million project to rehabilitate foreclosed homes, the weatherization job at city hall, or the new jet bridge at St. Cloud Regional Airport. Wherever I went, whenever I picked up the phone the first year of the Recovery Act, it seemed the stimulus was yet to arrive.

One of the reasons that projects were slow to get off the ground was the pile of red tape tucked into the bill. The provisions had noble intentions as all bureaucratic hurdles do: to give everyone a fair shot at the contract, prevent waste, protect the environment, preserve history, pay a decent wage, and avoid sending jobs overseas by ensuring materials are American made. But they also delayed the Recovery Act's impact and may have even prevented more workers from being hired. Some projects in public housing, waterworks, and home insulation remained paralyzed for six months to a year as short-staffed agencies reviewed waiver requests and calculated prevailing wages for every county in America.

Pushed by unions and the steel lobby, the authors of the bill included a "Buy American" clause, requiring that all iron, steel, and other goods used in public works projects be manufactured in the United States. The measure reached deep into American sinew and soul as an industry that once made cities and magnates and named football teams had been decimated in the face of cheaper imports from China and India. American workers were hurting. So why should stimulus money create jobs in factories overseas? The business community said that the argument was shortsighted given the global market and supply chain on which American companies depended. Higher costs meant fewer projects would be funded. And the losses from copycat measures by other countries could outweigh the jobs created. Early on, the clause threatened to set off a trade war or, at a minimum, spur retaliation, such as "Buy Canadian" provisions in cities and provinces on the northern border. Some economists said Congress was repeating the mistakes of the Smoot-Hawley Tariff Act of 1930, which raised duties to historic highs, invited backlash, and potentially hastened the Great Depression. The tensions ultimately eased after repeated diplomatic assurances and slipped-in language that the measure would comply with international trade agreements.

The more visible effect that Buy American had on the recovery was in stalling projects that were otherwise ready to go. Contractors could be granted a waiver from the rules if they could show that the material or equipment was not produced satisfactorily in the United States or would add more than 25 percent to the cost of the project. If nothing else, the clause exposed how much America's infrastructure relies on foreign-made projects.

Water and wastewater treatment plants, for example, are heavily dependent on foreign suppliers, with some specialized pieces of equipment unavailable in the United States. A waiver request from Frederick County, Maryland, was illustrative, seeking approval to buy a membrane system from Canada, air dryers from the United Kingdom, and vacuum ejectors from Sweden. Mike Welch of BRB Contractors told of his roadblock on a wastewater project the firm was doing in Overland Park, Kansas. The original plan called for a cogeneration unit that would take methane from the wastewater and produce electricity for the plant, having the side benefit of cutting the carbon footprint. But the $2 million unit was made by a General Electric subsidiary in Austria. Buying one from a U.S. manufacturer would cost 30 percent more. "We're having problems getting any of the people in the line of command to make a decision on whether or not this is okay for us to go ahead and buy this thing," Welch said. The Environmental Protection Agency ultimately granted nearly ninety waivers in a process that lasted into the fall of 2011.

"The result of the Buy American provisions has been a paperwork nightmare," Ron Collins, the president of a family-owned Texas pipe-fitting company, said in comments attached to a U.S. Chamber of Commerce report. "Every part, even a $10 one, requires certification, paperwork and proof that it fulfills the 'Made in the U.S.' requirements," he said. "Waivers are difficult to obtain and are rarely granted. In sum, the provision is causing huge delays, and the confusion regarding the provision is stalling otherwise viable projects."

A Homeland Security project to install more baggage screening machines in airports had to wait for a waiver after the contractor discovered that American-made components wouldn't integrate with an airport's security systems. Similar delays were reported for public housing projects because of confusion about whether the Buy American requirement applied. The U.S. Department of Housing and

Urban Development eventually determined that it did, but only for projects costing more than $100,000. In some cases, that forced housing agencies to find new vendors and contractors.

Historic preservation rules, while important, were bogging down projects to improve the security of train stations and make federal office buildings more energy efficient. In Michigan, human services officials estimated that 90 percent of the homes in line for weatherization work would need a historic preservation review. But as of late fall 2009, the office responsible had only two employees.

Weatherization was the low-hanging fruit of Obama's green jobs plan, or as Energy secretary Steven Chu liked to say, it was "fruit on the ground." It didn't require a college degree or any advanced technical training. It didn't require a new building or breakthrough technology. It simply required a caulking gun. "When you think about the emerging green economy, don't think of George Jetson with a jet pack," Van Jones, the activist turned White House adviser, wrote in *The Green Collar Economy*. "Think of Joe Sixpack with a hard hat and lunch bucket, sleeves rolled up, going off to fix America."[1] The idea was that by increasing funding, contractors could hire an army of low-income people who had been historically shut out of the economy, train them with new skills, and set them out in their own neighborhoods sealing leaky windows and installing insulation. It was a win-win-win. Do it enough times and utilities could save entire coal plants worth of greenhouse gas emissions. Homeowners would see lower heating bills. Thousands would get jobs. Best of all, the jobs couldn't be outsourced because a worker in China couldn't weatherstrip a door in Cleveland. And it wouldn't take nearly as long as building a wind farm or developing a mass-market electric car.

But all that wishful thinking (and speech making) didn't take into account an obscure Depression-era law that would stop states from spending their weatherization money for months. The Davis-Bacon Act required that contractors on federal construction projects pay workers the local prevailing wage, usually the union rate. It was passed by Congress in 1931 after stories that a contractor in New York had shipped in cheaper African American laborers from Alabama. The intent was to encourage the hiring of local workers. But the law had never applied to weatherization work, and so the Labor Department had to conduct extensive wage surveys to determine the going rate for weatherization for every county in the country.

The Department of Energy encouraged states and the nonprofits that administered the program to start anyway and worry about the difference later. But many were reluctant to do so. Congressional auditors from the Government Accountability Office found that half the states in their review had decided to wait to avoid forcing contractors to pay back wages. Iowa officials told auditors that back pay would be especially burdensome on smaller contractors. Officials in California said that Davis-Bacon would hinder the goal of workforce development because contractors wouldn't pay prevailing wages to inexperienced, entry-level workers. The rates were eventually set between $9 and $27 per hour depending on location and the type of work performed.

In theory, the weatherization money should have provided jobs for out-of-work home builders and renovators like Terry Gonyon, the Elkhart contractor with nine children who lost his home. But the jobs were few and far between. By the end of 2009, only 9,100 homes had been weatherized nationwide out of a goal of nearly 600,000 in three years. New York had planned to renovate 45,000 homes and apartments in that time, but had completed just 280. Texas hadn't repaired any. In California, where the construction industry has lost a third of jobs since the start of the recession, the grand total of homes it had weatherized was 12.

The pace would dramatically speed up in 2010 and 2011 but the new rules delayed the weatherization program's impact and created the impression that green jobs were a far-off goal. In previous national emergencies, such as Hurricanes Andrew and Katrina and the 1970s inflation crisis, the presidents, albeit Republicans, had suspended Davis-Bacon. The Great Recession was a far more dire crisis. Basic math shows that paying a worker $9 an hour instead of $18 an hour would have meant twice as many jobs created, far more homes renovated, and significantly more energy saved.

I posed this dilemma to Van Jones, who popularized the term "green jobs" in his book before joining the White House Council on

Environmental Quality. "You can go fast and create a bunch of crappy jobs that don't pay well and aren't done well, and then you're going to get criticized for having gone too fast and having done shoddy work and having trained people too poorly," he told me. "You have to pick the problem you want to have. I think it's better to have the problem, but you also have the opportunity, to have some of these fights that you're going to have in building the green economy anyway. . . . There's always an excuse to rush past all that. We were in an emergency situation and we wanted to move as quickly as possible. But I think it would have been a worse mistake to set precedent that these jobs can just be crappy."

Whatever the long-term impact, the slow pace of weatherization meant that most of the workers who staged the historic sit-in at the Chicago windows factory in 2008 were still waiting to return to work. Their protest had already become lore in the labor movement, and the quick purchase and reopening of the factory by Serious Materials in California was an oft-repeated story of the stimulus bill's success. Vice President Biden had visited the plant, to much fanfare in April, when he had spoken of the palpable optimism that a recovery was taking root: "This is the story of how a new economy predicated on innovation and efficiency is not only helping us today but inspiring a better tomorrow."

The story of the protesters returning to work had become part of the Obama team's narrative. But in truth, by the end of the year, only 20 of the 250 employees had been called back to work. One who hadn't was Ron Bender, a fifty-seven-year-old machine operator from the South Side who had worked at the plant for fourteen years. Now, he joined the ranks of the long-term unemployed, making do with odd jobs and his wife's employment as a woodworker making musical harps. They cut down on going out to eat and grilled outdoors to save money on the electric and gas. Bender didn't turn on the air conditioning until the temperature reached ninety-three degrees. "I thought it would be going a lot better than it is," he told me. "But I understand it. Hey, you can't call people back if you don't have no work for 'em."

It seemed that every project Biden touched was doomed to face delays. Promoting faster stimulus spending in the summer of 2009, he visited highway projects in Kansas and Kalamazoo. But the first trip was marred by news that a nearby project would be delayed because it conflicted with the cleanup of a hazardous waste site. Construction on the latter project had to wait until spring 2010 because a shipment of steel would have shifted the work schedule into the cold Michigan winter.[2] Biden later visited Cincinnati's old American Can Building, a blighted factory being turned into apartments and stores with the help of stimulus money. But it would be eight months before the city issued the first construction permit for the site.[3]

Perhaps the starkest example of how stimulus hopes floundered against a tougher reality was the experience of the New Flyer bus company in St. Cloud, Minnesota. The blue-and-gray New Flyer factory sits on the southeast edge of the city in an isolated business park near crop fields and the city's sewage treatment plant. Visiting it is a disorienting experience. A snake of a transit bus emblazoned with transitchicago.com on its side passes a bus marked SEPTA, the transit system of Philadelphia. Then comes a Rochester bus and one belonging to Blacksburg Transit in southwest Virginia. It's as if you were waiting at a bus depot in the twilight zone. This is where many of the transit buses that grunt and hulk and crawl the streets of America's inner cities roll off the assembly line.

New Flyer started in Winnipeg, Canada, in 1930, and opened its St. Cloud plant in 1999. Since then, it had become one of the city's largest private employers, with roughly 700 workers. The company seemed poised to win big from the $8.4 billion in public transit money tucked into the stimulus package. The individual grants weren't big enough to build new rail lines, and initially transit authorities couldn't spend the money on operational costs. So instead many agencies plowed the money into buying hybrid buses. New Flyer was the largest manufacturer of heavy-duty transit buses in North America. And it had taken initiative in going green.

Before the stimulus kicked in, New Flyer, which produces roughly 2,500 buses a year, had a backlog of orders and options for 9,800 buses. More than three-quarters were for hybrid or natural gas vehicles. Despite the economic downturn, the company had added 230 employees in the past two years, as rising gas prices and greater environmental awareness led to a record number of public bus riders.

Biden heralded New Flyer at a town hall meeting at the St. Cloud factory shortly after the Recovery Act passed. The vice president portrayed the company as a symbol of the new middle-class economy built on green manufacturing, for which the administration hoped the stimulus would lay the foundation. Federal transit officials predicted 4,000 new buses and transit vehicles would be ordered by the fall of 2009. But the transit money took longer to get out the door because every grant had to be reviewed by the Labor Department to ensure that they wouldn't have a negative impact on transit unions.

By the summer of 2009, New Flyer, with 40 percent of the U.S. market, had yet to hire anybody because of the stimulus. Then in August, the Chicago Transit Authority postponed an order of 140 buses indefinitely because it couldn't secure state funding. New Flyer announced that it would lay off more than 300 employees. The CEO Paul Soubry told Congress that things would have been much worse without the stimulus package. By the fall, it had received orders for 600 buses and transit vehicles. But because buses are engineered to unique customer specifications, the production schedule couldn't be easily rearranged to replace the Chicago order. Once a symbol of the Recovery Act's potential, New Flyer now exemplified a large-scale problem: cutbacks by states were canceling out the effects of the federal stimulus.

$ $ $

As I traveled through St. Cloud, I came across the city's annual arts festival, which is always capped by an evening symphony concert and the mayor's lemonade toast. Vendors hawked pottery and windsocks and beaded glassware and goat's milk soap. One sold ink drawings of bygone train stations. The blistering afternoon sun was now sinking, and a light breeze rustled the trees. Somewhere nearby a guitar and harmonica player drove to the chorus of "The Times They Are a-Changin'."

The chords transported me back to election night, to the energy that pervaded Obama's acceptance speech less than a year before when so much seemed so possible. Now the irony was startling. Despite the visions that danced in Americans' heads of bipartisanship, the New Deal, the jobless going to work, across the country so little seemed to be a-changin'.

Jobs were so few and far between that the St. Cloud regional workforce board had an old cowbell missing its clanger that they rang with a drumstick anytime one of their clients secured a job. One of the few tangible signs of Obama's promise to put America to work in year one was a program giving summer jobs to teenagers and young adults. More than 300,000 low-income youths, ages fourteen to twenty-four, got jobs creating fish habitats, helping the elderly, and cleaning classrooms for the next school year.

The number far exceeded Biden's goal of 125,000 summer jobs. In 2009, the unemployment rate among sixteen- to nineteen-year-olds was 24 percent. It also took a page straight out of history. In 1933, President Franklin Roosevelt put hundreds of thousands of young men to work through the Civilian Conservation Corps, building trails in forests and planting trees. Creating summer jobs for low-income teenagers became an annual priority for the federal government when President Lyndon Johnson launched the War on Poverty in the 1960s. But the dedicated program ended in 1999, replaced with more marginal efforts until the Recovery Act revived it.

All the politicking over the stimulus was far above the dozen teenagers who on a boiling hot day raked wood chips and added rocks to the shoreline at St. Cloud's Lake George park. Abdiaziz Ali, Marissa Parmar, Hutton Tomporowski—they were just happy to have jobs for the summer.

Martell Burson, sixteen, had moved to St. Cloud from Chicago a few years ago and was living with his mother, a certified nursing assistant for the elderly. He had been applying for jobs all spring at Burger King, McDonald's, and other fast-food restaurants, but no one ever called him back.

"I was looking all over St. Cloud, and this was the only opportunity I got," said Burson, his face dripping with sweat.

For four weeks, the 192 young people in the summer job programs would paint buildings, clear trails, pick up trash, distribute posters for an epilepsy walk, and make hats for cancer patients. Those that succeeded earned $980, minimum wage plus bonuses.

While many of the stimulus jobs had yet to come, here was at least something: an assembly line of four teens lifting football-size stones from a pile, passing them down, and dropping them into the back of a utility vehicle for a ride down to the lakeshore. Lifting and passing. Lifting and passing. Across the country, both employers and participants felt the summer jobs program was a success, and many states exceeded the number of youths they hoped to serve, congressional auditors reported. About 345,000 people participated nationwide, and program officials found jobs for 91 percent of them, according to a Labor Department report. A girl in Weatherford, Texas, who wanted to be a veterinarian, for example, was assigned to work in an animal shelter.

But the program was not without problems. California found jobs for only 42 percent of the youths it served, the auditors said. In Detroit, some teenagers waited in the rain for four hours to get their paychecks, and on several occasions police had to be called to control the crowds. A key goal of the program was to train young people in "green jobs," such as developing biofuels and retrofitting homes to make them more energy efficient. But in Columbus, Ohio, two youths assigned to a company designing alternative-fuel vehicles spent most of their time clearing brush and painting a fence.

$ $ $

For all its flaws, when the infrastructure part of the Recovery Act did finally get up and running, in the fall of 2009 and more prominently in 2010, it set a floor for the construction industry. The census data on construction spending were stunning. Nearly every construction sector, private and public, residential and nonresidential, hotels, offices, factories, power, health care, and schools had seen the bottom drop out since the start of the recession. But highways and streets, where the stimulus provided $27 billion, remained fairly steady. Representatives of asphalt, gravel, and road construction companies said the stimulus was the only bright spot in an otherwise bleak economy, allowing them to keep their crews intact.

"In state after state, we're seeing a meaningful impact on jobs," La-Hood insisted in a speech on the recovery. "The Maryland Department of Transportation has recalled all of its laid-off employees back to work. A private contractor in Massachusetts has brought back nearly its entire workforce—more than 300 people. In Missouri, Texas, Colorado, Georgia, and elsewhere, this story is being repeated. I have personally met with workers around the country who would not be getting paid this week without stimulus-funded transportation jobs. And because they are working, they can support their families, pay their bills, and pump some dollars back into their local economy."

A typical project was the replacement of two Route 46 bridges over the Saddle River and Main Street in Lodi, New Jersey. Built in 1936, the bridges showed signs of wear and tear and erosion on the center pier. When it rained hard, the river overflowed its banks and flooded the street. "We've had several instances in the little over a year that we've been here where there's cars floating under this bridge when the river comes up," said Sean Desmet, the project engineer for the contractor Creamer-Sanzari. The project called for improving drainage, raising the bridges, and widening the highway, a high-volume route used by buses shuttling commuters into Manhattan. Originally slated at $48 million, the winning bid came in at $31 million.

The construction site in Lodi (pronounced *LOW-die*) was located in a blue-collar area outside the Meadowlands not far from the go-go bar where *The Sopranos* filmed scenes for the fictional strip club, the Bada Bing! Surrounding the bridges were a Dunkin' Donuts, working-class homes, used-car lots, Dinette City, a kickboxing studio, and a new ShopRite. When I visited in the summer of 2010, Creamer-Sanzari had just completed the new eastbound lanes of the bridge and demolished the old westbound side.

To the outsider the scene appeared chaotic with activity. About thirty to forty men from the local laborers', ironworkers', dockworkers', and carpenters' unions hustled about in hardhats and yellow mesh safety vests as everything seemed covered in orange dust.

Cars honked as trucks backed up beeping and rumbling. A Caterpillar carried a bucket full of gravel. A backhoe scraped the sloping dirt.

Desmet guided me through the site. Here, in four-foot-deep bunkers, workers secured a lattice of crisscrossed rebar by tying coil wire around the intersections. The rebar would add strength to the bridge when tomorrow the crew poured the concrete for the footings. Here was the oil-filled tube where they rerouted the electrical lines. Here the parapets with mint-green epoxy-coated rebar to prevent corrosion from the road salt in winter. Here the piles of plastic pipes, sand, and gravel awaiting their functions.

The crews had been working on the bridge for nearly a year, often working overtime from 7:00 A.M. to 5:30 P.M. on weekdays and Saturdays. The plan called for completion in the fall of 2012, but the project was actually finished in 2011. At its peak, the bridge replacement provided jobs for the equivalent of 66 full-time employees. But by the time the project was done, about 250 construction workers and suppliers had found at least part-time jobs at the site.

Derrick McRae, a thirty-four-year-old carpenter from Paterson, took a break to tell me what the work meant to him. He pulled off the black Arctic sunglasses that shaded his eyes and took a sip from a bottle of water. McRae had a thin black mustache and goatee and wore a maroon shirt, dirt-caked jeans, and tan work boots. Around his waist was a tool belt, dangling with everything he needed: a wrench, hammer, pliers, etc. On his head he wore a black do-rag underneath a red hardhat with an American flag sticker reading UNITED WE STAND. A journeyman for the local Brotherhood of Carpenters, McRae had been out of work six months before finding this job in the newspaper.

"It was rough," he said. "I had just a bought a house two weeks, three weeks prior to being laid off, so I had to really budget my unemployment check because I had spent my savings on buying the house."

McRae made do with the $1,180 every two weeks in unemployment paying for the mortgage and bills. His girlfriend of eight years helped him out with her job at a pocketbook distributor. McRae now worked full time at the site, earning $39.54 an hour, building wood for the decks and helping out wherever needed.

"This job helped save my house basically," he said. "If I would have stayed on unemployment, right now I'd probably be homeless."

There were stories like McRae's all across America. Serious questions hung over the stimulus about whether there should have been more money for infrastructure or whether the funds moved fast enough. But "there's no doubt that a lot more workers would be out of work today without the stimulus," Ken Simonson, chief economist for the Associated General Contractors of America, told me. While estimates vary, stimulus funding for road and transit projects created and saved nearly 100,000 direct on-project jobs.

$ $ $

The vast majority of highway projects involved paving roads, and there was a constant sacrifice for the speedy over the spectacular. But the notion that the New Deal built bridges and dams while all the stimulus did was fill potholes isn't entirely true. Generations from now, there will be countless projects that communities can point to as the enduring legacy of the American Recovery and Reinvestment Act. The $80 billion for roads, runways, waterworks, rails, federal buildings, and parks was one of the largest investments in the nation's infrastructure since President Eisenhower established the Interstate Highway System in the 1950s.

The Recovery Act helped build major highways like the $1 billion DFW Connector, clearing a traffic mess in the Dallas–Fort Worth suburbs, and a $650 million elevated truck route easing access to the Port of Tampa. It raised bridges like the new Cleveland Innerbelt Bridge and it drilled tunnels like the fourth bore to the Caldecott Tunnel through the hills separating Oakland and Contra Costa County, California. The Recovery Act invested in new light rail lines in Salt Lake City and Dallas and upgraded tracks to extend Amtrak's Downeaster train to Brunswick, Maine. It built a new eight-story federal courthouse in Austin, Texas, a 500,000-square-foot hospital at Camp Pendleton in California, and a "warriors in transition" complex to help wounded veterans at Fort Bliss in El Paso. And the stimulus money finally replaced a century-old drawbridge over Connecticut's Niantic River that in 2009 got stuck shut, trapping boats for hours.

In some cases, the projects had struggled to find funding for years while in others, the stimulus provided the crucial check to move a project forward. But these massive new icons failed to alter the persuasion that stimulus infrastructure was piddling. One reason is that the projects had been on city planning lists for decades. So once they broke ground, people didn't see them as stimulus but instead as the civic works that were going to happen anyway—someday. Another factor diminishing the public perception of the Recovery Act is simply a symptom of modern government. No longer does the federal government fork over the entire cost of railroads, canals, dams, or nuclear weapons plants. Today, megaprojects are financed by multiple funding sources: a combination of federal and state tax revenue, bond sales, tolls, and private capital. The largest stimulus road project, the DFW Connector, for example, included $250 million from the Recovery Act, but also $667 million from public gas taxes and $107 million in bonds.

One of the most historic stimulus projects was the consolidation of the Department of Homeland Security headquarters, the largest federal building project in the Capital region since the Pentagon was constructed during World War II. Created rapidly after the September 11 attacks, the department was scattered in dozens of offices across the Washington area. The $3.4 billion multiyear project would move most of the employees into an abandoned section of St. Elizabeth mental hospital, a redbrick Victorian, Gothic, and Colonial revival complex originally known as the Government Hospital for the Insane. Over the years it had housed would-be Reagan assassin John Hinckley and the poet Ezra Pound. Located atop a bluff near the confluence of the Anacostia and Potomac Rivers, the campus offered panoramic views of the nation's capital, and local leaders hoped the project would revitalize a blighted neighborhood.

The Recovery Act appropriated $650 million to build the 1.2-million-square-foot Coast Guard headquarters, phase one of the project, and to make other improvements to roads, utilities, and security. The energy-efficient design called for the Coast Guard complex to be built into the hillside in linked, cascading quadrangles with green roofs, making it appear like a high-tech Hanging Gardens of Babylon.

The contract was awarded to Clark Construction Group, one of the largest general contractors in the United States. Construction began in the spring of 2010 with hundreds of people working on site and was expected to be completed by 2013. Federal officials estimate the entire Homeland Security project will eventually provide jobs for 32,000 people by the time it's finished in 2016.

New Deal programs like the Works Progress Administration and the Civilian Conservation Corps are mythologized for building parks and fire stations and schools, for clearing trails and paving roads. The Recovery Act did all these things. And it also refurbished nearly every American icon from sea to shining sea. At Ellis Island, where millions of immigrants first came to America, workers restored the seawall and stabilized the baggage and dormitory building. The Brooklyn Bridge, Hart Crane's "harp and altar," received a fresh coat of tan paint. Five million dollars was spent to repair the leaky and crumbling tower at Philadelphia's Independence Hall, where the Declaration of Independence was written and adopted. Various sections of the Mississippi River were dredged, upgraded, and restored to prevent flooding. Oklahoma rebuilt eight miles of Interstate 40, where some of the concrete hadn't been replaced since the 1960s, when it was still called Route 66, John Steinbeck's "Mother Road." Yellowstone National Park got a new sewage treatment plant. Crews repaired forest trails at the North Rim of the Grand Canyon. California replaced the southern approach to the Golden Gate Bridge to make it safer in the event of an earthquake. And at Mount Hood in Oregon, workers made various improvements to the Timberline Lodge, one of the classic remnants of the WPA.

At the time the Recovery Act was passed, the National Mall in Washington, DC, was in shameful shape. The seawall protecting the domed Jefferson Memorial was sinking into the Tidal Basin, allowing fish and ducks to swim on the sidewalks during high tide. The World War I Memorial was cracking and rotting. The Lincoln Memorial reflecting pool was so fetid that a park ranger described it as "a poisonous-looking green, like something out of an H. P. Lovecraft horror story. The immense blooms of algae and assorted filth create islands of multicolored floating gunk. The odor is indescribable."[4]

The stimulus bill originally included $200 million to renovate the National Mall. While the line item was stripped to quell Republican criticism, the Obama administration found $55 million in a $750 million allocation to the National Park Service to repair the three monuments. With the funding, workers installed caissons and drove deeper pilings to set the Jefferson Memorial on a firmer foundation. They installed a new concrete floor for the Lincoln Memorial reflecting pool to prevent leaks. They cleaned the rainwater stains and calcium deposits from the war memorial and restored its bluestone base.

From bringing water to the farms of California's San Joaquin Valley to installing plumbing in rural Alaskan villages that relied on honey buckets to dispose of waste, the Recovery Act funded historic projects in communities across America, putting it at the level of the New Deal work programs. In some places, it seemed as if the stimulus played a role in every major project on the planning books. New York City was a perfect example. A Second Avenue subway was first proposed in 1929, and although construction began and then stalled indefinitely in the 1970s, it wasn't until 2009 that work got under way, with the help of $79 million from the stimulus. It had been a long time since the Big Apple had seen so much mass transit under construction at one time. The Recovery Act provided $195 million for a long-planned project to connect Long Island Railroad trains to the Grand Central Terminal on the east side of Manhattan. It chipped in $83 million to renovate a Corinthian-columned post office to make way for a grand Amtrak concourse to be named Moynihan Station. It directed $500 million to untangle the labyrinthine caverns of the Fulton Street transit hub. There was $175 million for improvements to the Staten Island Ferry terminal and $77 million to rehabilitate the century-old Atlantic Avenue viaduct, which carries Long Island rail trains into downtown Brooklyn. Outside of public transit, the stimulus provided money to replace broken planks on the Coney Island boardwalk. The city used a special bond created by the Recovery Act to restart the City Point development, an apartment and retail complex on the old site of a discount mall in Brooklyn.

Then there was the magnum opus in New York metropolitan area planning. The stimulus chipped in $130 million for one of the largest infrastructure projects in the country, a $9 billion commuter rail tunnel under the Hudson River. About 170,000 riders commuted to Manhattan from New Jersey every day. The first new river crossing since the 1960s would do wonders for the transportation needs of a suburbia that had grown considerably since the days of "the man in the gray flannel suit."

"This is a day to focus on renewal and hope, a day when New Jersey stands proudly at the center of America's economic recovery," Garden State senator Robert Menendez said when the stimulus funding was announced.

$ $ $

One of the more innovative programs in the Recovery Act was a $1.5 billion discretionary grant program, known as TIGER, which rewarded regional thinking that combined multiple modes of transportation. A key flaw in American transportation policy is that it is segmented into various silos. Funding is designated for highways, airports, transit, and rail. It is distributed to states and authorities, often setting up a bitter fight between cities and rural areas. These policies help explain why it's so difficult to get from the airport to the downtown and why the government spends so much to support little-used airports.

When the deadline passed, the Department of Transportation had received 1,450 applications worth $59 billion, a testament not only to the appetite for stimulus money but also to the pent-up demand for broader strategies. The act had limited proposals to at least $20 million to encourage big projects that could have regional impact. But like many of the other transportation programs, the department loosened the rules by dropping the amount to open the door for smaller cities and regions. Still, the portfolio of winners contained some transformative projects. The top three grants at about $100 million each were devoted to untangling freight rail lines in the Mid-Atlantic, Chicago, and the Southeast. The program funded streetcars, rapid buses, new bridges, and transit stations. Philadelphia received $23 million to complete a 128-mile network of pedestrian and bike trails in the city and surrounding areas.

Another infrastructure program in the Recovery Act was the creation of a new financing tool known as Build America Bonds. The banking crisis had frozen the municipal bond market, forcing local governments to reconsider their capital projects. With Build America Bonds, or "BABs" as they became known, the federal government picked up 35 percent of the interest. That made it cheaper for local governments to borrow money while also providing investors with a less risky path to greater returns. The new rules revived the municipal bond market by broadening the pool of investors. And the renewal of major infrastructure projects put people back to work. When the program ended in December 2010, more than $180 billion of Build America Bonds had been issued.

The bonds allowed the city of Dallas, for example, to move forward with marquee projects that seemed wishful even in boom times. Boards and agencies in Dallas issued $4.5 billion in Build America Bonds, including $680 million for a new public hospital (the largest in the nation built in one phase) and nearly $400 million for a long-planned convention center hotel. In the midst of a historic recession, Dallas like New York City was experiencing a renaissance of mega-projects. The bonds provided funding to expand the light rail to the western suburbs. Meanwhile, transit grants helped open another new line connecting the northwest suburbs and a low-income neighborhood in southeast Dallas to the downtown. The latter project, at twenty-four miles, was "the longest single-day opening of electric light rail in the United States since 1990," according to the federal Department of Transportation. The TIGER grants provided $23 million for a downtown streetcar, and $17 million was used to build an elevated park over a freeway connecting downtown to the city's thriving uptown retail, arts, and residential neighborhood.

The Recovery Act also invested heavily in new technology. The descriptions of some projects read like something out of science fiction: synchrophasors that can sense surges in the power grid and prevent blackouts. Or heliostats that track the sun and reflect its rays onto a boiler to generate steam and ultimately energy. The Fermi national laboratory outside Chicago received $53 million for "Project X," a proposed facility to develop the next generation of particle accelerators.

Meanwhile, the Berkeley and SLAC labs in California got tens of millions of dollars each for some of the most powerful lasers in the world with the potential for advances in energy, security, and medicine. After the Underwear Bomber tried to blow up a plane to Detroit on Christmas Day 2009, the Department of Homeland Security installed dozens of controversial body scanners that could check for explosives hidden under clothing. The Social Security Administration received $500 million to build a new computer center to handle the workload as more and more baby boomers retire.

Then there was the Cray XT5 computing system, known as the "Jaguar." It was located at Oak Ridge National Laboratory in Tennessee, and thanks to a $20 million upgrade paid for by the stimulus, it became the fastest supercomputer in the world, computer science experts announced in November 2009. At 1.759 petaflops, which means it could perform 1.759 quadrillion calculations per second, Jaguar was more than 100,000 times faster than a home computer. Researchers hoped to use it to improve climate change predictions, design fuel-efficient engines, and find advances in clean energy. One company in South Carolina used it to develop aerodynamic eighteen-wheelers with the theoretical potential to save 1.5 billion gallons of diesel fuel and 16 million tons of carbon dioxide if all big rigs in the United States adopted the changes. The supercomputer allowed the company to go from concept to design in eighteen months, less than half the time expected.

While the Recovery Act built, upgraded, and renovated, it also tore down and cleaned up. Across the country are more than a thousand mines, mills, factories, and dumps that have left a toxic legacy from America's industrial boom. The stimulus dedicated $600 million to accelerate the remediation of these sites. Environmental workers dredged a reservoir at the Iron Mountain Mine near Redding, California, disposing of sediment contaminated with acid and cadmium that had flowed from the mine. In New Bedford, Massachusetts—the inspiration for *Moby Dick*—they scrubbed the harbor, which had been polluted by more than a century of whaling, textiles, and electronics, removing the polychlorinated biphenyls (PCBs) that had led to fishing bans in recent decades. They dug up soil from the yards of hundreds

of homes in South Minneapolis, where for decades the wind blew ar-
senic into the neighborhood from a nearby pesticide plant. Through
other programs, they closed abandoned hard-rock mines, demolished
blighted homes, and retrieved fishing nets from the ocean floor.
While the New Deal is engraved in history for building dams, the Recovery Act will be remembered in some parts for tearing them down.
In Washington State, two Elwha River dams, built in the 1900s to provide hydroelectric power for a paper mill, were removed to restore
one of the most productive salmon streams in the Pacific Northwest
and to return flooded sacred sites to the local Klallam Tribe.

In a way, the stimulus was preparing America for a transition from
an old economy to a new economy. Detroit's former mayor even proposed using stimulus money to knock down the hundred-year-old
Michigan Central Depot, a symbol of the Rust Belt's forgotten
grandeur and its enduring decay.[5] The New Deal invested in roads and
bridges, sewers and dams because America didn't have them in the
1930s or they were wholly inadequate for a growing industrial society.
In the twenty-first century, America didn't need more roads, bridges,
and dams. It needed a new class of infrastructure to compete in an increasingly high-tech, globalized economy. Where the New Deal paved
miles of dirt and gravel roads, the Recovery Act would lay the
groundwork for high-speed rail. Where the New Deal brought electricity to rural America, the Recovery Act would wire those same areas with broadband Internet. Where the New Deal invested in the
infrastructure of its era, the Recovery Act would modernize America's energy infrastructure with fields of wind turbines and solar panels and a more efficient power grid.

Despite the historic investments and endless list of projects, the
Recovery Act in the end created not a crater, but a dent in America's
overwhelming infrastructure needs. It replaced or repaired more than
1,000 deficient or obsolete bridges, but America has more than
150,000 bridges in such conditions. Almost as a testament to that reality, officials announced in late 2009 that both the Lake Champlain
Bridge between New York and Vermont and the Bay Bridge connecting Oakland and San Francisco would need to be closed for repairs because they were structurally unsafe.

"ARRA is helping us hold the decline, the deterioration of infrastructure," Ken Simonson of the Associated General Contractors told me. "But I don't think it's a game changer the way the Interstate Highway System was." Referring to the D grade given by the American Society of Civil Engineers on its periodic report card, Simonson said, "If it even puts a plus on the D, I'm not sure."

While the Obama administration could claim a better narrative in the transformation of America, Republicans had better sound bites, and with tens of thousands of projects to choose from, it was easy to point out spending that seemed wasteful to the American public.

EIGHT

ONE MAN'S WASTE

THE TURTLES STARTED SHOWING UP on Highway 27 outside Tallahassee sometime in late 1999. They lay belly up on the less-than-a-
mile-long stretch of the Lake Jackson causeway, their carcasses strewn
about, their flippers and hinds legs flattened, their marble shells
cracked. Matt Aresco, a graduate student in biology at Florida State
University, noticed the massive amount of road kill in February 2000
and began documenting the devastation to make the case for a solution. On one day, he collected ninety turtle carcasses and laid them
out on a blue tarp like so many eggshells. He took photographs of his
finds and posted them on a website with the message: "WARNING:
Road-killed Turtle Images May Not Be Suitable to All Viewers." In
one, a Florida softshell lies on its back, its arms spread out like a
fainted damsel. In another, a yellow-bellied slider is cracked horizon-
tally like a taco. Yet another turtle, this one saved after it climbed over
a temporary fence, crouches low with its head tucked in, a bloody

splotch on the front of its fern green shell. According to Aresco, Highway 27 was "the world's worst turtle-killing highway."

The problem occurred because the roadway was built across the
western tip of Lake Jackson, a 4,000-acre prairie lake that drains
through two sinkholes, the Porter Hole and the Lime Sink, every time
there's a drought. An 1842 entry from a clergyman's notebook, posted
on Aresco's website, told of how the lake dwellers observed "a strong
current setting from all directions toward one or two particular
spots":

> The waters were all greatly agitated, and strong eddies were ob-
> served to be working where the currents met. The level of the water
> rapidly subsided several feet, then suddenly remained stationary for a
> few hours, and then fell again as the same mysterious currents set in
> afresh from every side. This continued until the whole lake, with the
> exception of a few deep places here and there, was drained; and the
> poor fishes and other swimming and crawling things that 'do busi-
> ness in great waters' lay floundering in the mud.[1]

The natives called it Lake Okeeheepkee, meaning "disappearing
waters." When it happens, the turtles and other amphibians engage in
a mass exodus in search of freshwater. The route is especially popular
for pregnant turtles that cross the highway to nest. The lake dry-down
has happened twelve times in the last 168 years, Aresco said. "When
they built the road decades ago, there wasn't much traffic on it," he
told me. "But as the area has developed, there's about 25,000 vehicles
a day that drive on that road." The convergence of four wheels and
fauna led to an unusual hazard for the turtles and drivers alike. "We
have a lot of turtles getting killed, but we were seeing a motorist
safety issue too," said Joshua Boan, natural resources manager for the
Florida Department of Transportation. "When they get hit, they become flying objects."

Aresco worked with the state DOT on a plan to build an "ecopassage," consisting of a polymer wall along the roadside that directs
wildlife to a culvert underneath the highway. A photograph on the

website shows turtles waddling single-file along a fence like a troop of Cub Scouts. Aresco pushed for seven years, raising private money to buy the right-of-way. And now with the federal stimulus package, the Lake Jackson ecopassage was in line for a $3.4 million grant.

A tunnel for turtles seemed strange on the surface, especially when American infrastructure had so many human needs. A *Tallahassee Democrat* columnist noted, "When I mentioned this column to a co-worker, he screwed up his face and said, 'FSU is talking about laying off 200 people and we're protecting turtles.'"[2] The turtle tunnel seemed strange to a lot of people, including Oklahoma senator Tom Coburn, who featured it in a report on "questionable" stimulus projects in June 2009. "Why did the turtle cross the road?" the report asked snarkily. "To get to the other side of a stimulus project." The project went forward and was completed in August 2010, but it remained the most frequently cited example of waste in the stimulus package, repeated and rehashed by Glenn Beck, Mitch McConnell, and Sarah Palin, among others.

Coburn's report came as the Obama administration struggled to manage the public image of the Recovery Act. It mimicked one released by Vice President Biden a few weeks before. But where Biden's report tried to tug at your heartstrings, Coburn's was meant to tug at your nerves.

Biden told the story of Norman and Ida Layne of Cullen, Virginia, who received loans from the stimulus package that would allow them to keep the family dairy and hog farm for another generation. Coburn chronicled the tale of Optima Lake, a 1960s Army Corps of Engineers project to improve the water supply in Oklahoma's panhandle. The lake never reached more than 5 percent of its capacity and sat dry for much of the year. Photographs in the report depicted a boat ramp in the middle of a field and a sign reading CAUTION: TUMBLEWEEDS ON ROADWAY. The Corps' initial project list included $1.2 million to replace the guardrail. "One thing is sure," Coburn's report stated, "if visitors are clever enough to get past the new guardrail, they will not have to worry about falling into the water."

Coburn's report also detailed some unintended effects of the stimulus, such as Social Security checks being sent to dead people and one community's utility rate hike to cover the cost of a stimulus loan. At Indiana University, the report said, a professor was given $356,000 to study how kids perceive foreign accents. The city of Redmond, Washington, received $11 million to build a bridge that would connect two campuses at the headquarters of Microsoft, one of the biggest companies in the United States and whose chairman was the richest person in the world. Illinois was spending $150,000 to post road signs promoting projects paid for with stimulus money. The signs, which were strongly encouraged but not required by federal agencies, would become a recurring target of criticism, with some states like Texas and New York deciding to forgo the signs.

"Will these projects make real improvements in the lives of taxpayers and communities or are they simply pet projects of politicians and lobbyists that never got off the ground because they are a low priority?" Coburn asked.

Senator Coburn was an obstetrician from Muskogee, Oklahoma. He held a strong distaste for the ways of Washington and went home on the weekends to mow his lawn, attend Baptist church on Sundays, and practice medicine on Mondays. A fierce opponent of pork-barrel spending, Coburn had earned the nickname "Dr. No." Amid an otherwise ornate office of paintings and photos of his family was a framed print of the word "NO" in white lettering over a black background, which he said was sent to him by a liberal supporter.

"'No' is a good word," he told me in an interview in his office. "If you have a three-year-old and they're getting ready to go out into the street, what do you tell them? 'No!' If you have a teenager that's getting ready to smoke their first joint, what do you say to them? 'No!' I mean 'No!' Right now, the trouble we're in, that's the word we ought to be embracing."

Thin with gray hair and glasses, Coburn explained to me his opposition to the federal stimulus package, every so often pausing to politely spit tobacco into a paper cup adorned with the seal of the U.S. Senate. He said he agreed that the government had to do a stimulus of some sort. The trouble was that the bill that passed didn't produce anything, and if you don't produce anything, you can't produce growth. Too little was directed for infrastructure; too much to states that could have used the recession to squeeze waste out of their budgets. When officials picked projects, they took things off the shelf that could be done fast. "But the things that were on the shelf were obviously low priorities or the states would have funded them already," he said.

Like South Carolina governor Mark Sanford, Coburn was swept into Congress during the 1994 Contract with America campaign that led to the Republican takeover of Congress. Along with Sanford, he was one of only three Republicans who vowed to serve only three terms and kept their word. After a four-year break, he ran for the Senate and won. Despite their ideological differences, Coburn and Obama were good friends in the Senate. In 2006, they teamed up on a bill to create a website tracking government spending and they often worked together on issues of transparency and accountability. Coburn told me they still talked about once a month.

"When they're beatin' up on him, I call him to encourage him," he said, explaining that "they" referred to Republican leaders Mitch McConnell and John Boehner. "That's the toughest job in the world, and nobody's always wrong, just like nobody's always right."

But Coburn had less favorable things to say about Obama's right-hand man, Vice President Biden. When Obama announced that Biden would be in charge of the stimulus, Coburn said he had a "little silent laugh," thinking "that means nobody's in charge of it." "Look, Joe Biden's a nice guy," he said. "There's never been a spending bill in Congress that he didn't vote for and there wasn't any part of government he didn't want to grow. He is the last guy to be overseeing the spending of scarce tax dollars to get the best economic benefit. It's never been his forte and it's never been his experience or ability."

When Coburn released his first waste report, he set up a battle project-for-project with the White House. Ed DeSeve, the vice president's senior adviser on the stimulus, shot back with his own report. He said Coburn's list was full of inaccuracies and included projects that had been stopped or never approved. Others were "working quite well." The foreign accent study was important research in the field of speech therapy and would benefit children with hearing deficits. The "Microsoft Bridge," which they relabeled "the 36th Street Bridge," was an important local development project supporting a major employment center. When I visited the project, it certainly seemed like a bridge that would mostly be used by Microsoft employees trying to get back and forth between the old campus and the new campus. But Redmond mayor John Marchione told me that other companies, such as Honeywell and Nintendo, are also in that area. Microsoft contributed $17 million in private money to the project, and during rush-hour, traffic backs up a mile and a half because the current bridge was designed in 1998, when Microsoft had far fewer employees. On the sign issue, the White House noted that signage is standard for transportation projects. During the Great Depression, Roosevelt made the blue eagle a ubiquitous symbol of New Deal work programs. In the same way, Obama gave the Recovery Act a logo, a circle divided into three parts: a blue top half with white stars, a red quarter showing the gears of manufacturing, and a green quarter with a plant to symbolize clean energy.

"With 20,000 projects approved, there are bound to be some mistakes," DeSeve said in response to Coburn's report. "When we find them, we have been transparent about it and worked on a bipartisan basis to shut them down immediately."

The Optima Lake guardrail project, for example, was halted a week before the report after Coburn wrote a letter to the Corps of Engineers raising concerns about it. Biden later said that on forty-nine of the projects, Coburn was "just dead-wrong."

$ $ $

Early on, Biden put together a group of advisers led by DeSeve and Ron Klain, the vice president's chief of staff, to head off embarrassing projects before they became scandals. The team had standing orders to respond to any call or e-mail from a local official within twenty-four hours. Biden himself held frequent conference calls with mayors and governors to hear their problems firsthand. From day one, the administration sent the message down the chain: "Don't send us Frisbee parks, don't send us water slides, don't send us golf courses." Obama tried to set an example by turning down stimulus money to modernize the electrical and heating systems in the East Wing of the White House.

But dealing with local supporters required some diplomacy. "We're not saying it's a bad project per se," a senior administration official told me, explaining their approach. "But given the special sensitivity that the president, vice president, the Congress has placed on Recovery Act moneys, you would be better off either not doing the project if you choose to do that or using other funds that you have for that purpose."

Such a situation occurred when the city of Long Beach, California, submitted plans to spend a $620,000 community development grant to upgrade a skateboard park. The city council argued that the park provided recreation for youth in one of Long Beach's poorest neighborhoods. The administration never told the city to scratch the skate park, but officials sent word that the project wasn't appropriate for the stimulus and asked that they find another project that fit. So Long Beach swapped another grant for the skate park and got stimulus money for sidewalks.

In one of the earliest examples of this proactive approach, the Federal Highway Administration revoked $1 million in stimulus funding from a road project in Grays Harbor, Washington, after an investigation revealed that the county road engineer had owned property near the road and profited from the selling the county the right-of-way.[3] There were numerous other cases. After the Ohio Department of Transportation faced criticism for a proposal to spend $57 million on planning studies, federal highway officials persuaded the state to redirect the money to shorter-term projects. The Army Corps of Engineers planned to spend money on a pamphlet updating a community on the cleanup of Onondaga Lake, a polluted body of water near Syracuse. That was until Senators Charles Schumer and Kirsten Gillibrand of New York sent a letter to the Corps, prompting officials to spend the money on other projects. A request for an economic development grant for a new factory in Columbus, Georgia, was characterized by Ohio politicians as stealing jobs as the NCR Corporation, a manufacturer of ATMs, moved its headquarters from the hard-hit city of Dayton. But the Commerce Department denied the application for stimulus money.

The Office of Management and Budget also helped forestall snafus. Once, Transportation secretary Ray LaHood was flying out to

Arizona to announce stimulus funding for a light rail project. His communications staff had already drafted the press release when the budget office spotted a problem: the project due to get stimulus money had already been completed. He would have to cancel the news conference. LaHood called Emanuel, who asked the budget office if they could find something else that LaHood could announce in the general vicinity. The staff scrambled and finally at midnight came across another project for the next morning's news conference.

Perhaps the greatest example of the administration's deftness at defusing potential scandals came when Senator Pat Roberts of Kansas sent a letter to Biden pointing out a timing conflict. Highway crews would use stimulus money to resurface a road. Immediately after that, potentially even at the same time, heavy trucks would need the road to haul hazardous waste from another stimulus project cleaning up old mines. After so much use, crews would likely have to pave the road again. Klain and DeSeve were already on it. They called the Department of Transportation, which called their area office, which called the state DOT, which quickly agreed to delay the repaving so that it came after the environmental cleanup. Shortly after Biden found out about it, Klain and DeSeve had a resolution. The very next day, Roberts, a Republican, was on the Senate floor applauding the White House. "I want to personally thank Vice President Biden, the man charged with overseeing all the stimulus spending, with taking action to correct this abuse after I contacted him," Roberts said.

Biden had promised government officials that he was going to be "a bit of a pain in the neck." And to some, he kept his promise. Rick Rice, the recovery task force director in California, told me that his office frequently scrambled to put together briefings for Governor Arnold Schwarzenegger on education, transportation, or whatever it was the vice president wanted to talk about on short notice. Once, the state was chastised for spending highway projects too slowly when the federal DOT had approved the multiyear projects, something Rice felt Biden should have known about from his own staff. "They were rattling our cage unnecessarily and it just created havoc here," Rice said. "Quite frankly, I was getting rather tired of the threat of calls from the vice president."

$ $ $

Despite the success his office had in arresting embarrassing projects, Biden failed to follow through on another promise: that he would show up in towns and call out "stupid" projects. In truth, the administration had difficulty defining what it meant when it talked about preventing waste.

The White House provided some insight on what types of projects didn't meet its standards when it announced that it had stopped or altered 170 proposals. On the list were projects to straighten headstones, freeze fish sperm, and steam-clean bird droppings from buildings. But when the stimulus oversight board released its first batch of project reports in October 2009, I found other stimulus recipients had funded the exact same types of projects—to reset headstones, freeze fish sperm, and power-wash bird droppings from bridges. The administration's list of red-flagged projects included nine to renovate athletic facilities such as basketball and tennis courts. But the reports of approved projects included at least six basketball courts and two tennis courts. The White House said it shot down an Agriculture Department proposal to buy Taser stun guns for sheriffs' deputies. But law enforcement agencies around the country used stimulus money buy hundreds of Tasers. The administration didn't explain why the 170 projects it flagged were troublesome.

Very early on, Biden declared his team's waste-fighting efforts a success by referring to the Sherlock Holmes story "Silver Blaze," in which one of the clues was that the dog didn't bark. Everywhere he went, Biden was talking about the dog that didn't bark or the dog that didn't bite. "What could have derailed this in the beginning were those stories: millions of dollars wasted on polar bear tanks," he said in one speech. "But in the first hundred days this was the dog that didn't bite."

Biden's example was an interesting choice. While the administration wasn't spending money on polar bear tanks, I found that it was spending millions on lion and tiger dens at the National Zoo. The Recovery Act explicitly banned state and local governments from spending stimulus money on zoos. But it made no mention of zoos run by the federal government, such as the National Zoo in Washington,

DC. While the zoo certainly had projects that needed repairs, created jobs, educated children, and raised environmental awareness, so did nearly every other zoo across the country.

Coburn called it a classic example of Washington saying, "Do as we say, not as we do." "The question is whether or not the National Zoo is a priority right now given our economic times and the problems that we face," he told me. "Building a new place to house lions? Is that more important than building a new bridge?"

Biden's frequent allusion to the dog that didn't bark prompted Glenn Beck to use his Fox News program one night to bark like a rabid Rottweiler. "The dog hasn't barked?! It's like a pack of wild Cujos ripping up the flesh of the American people!" Beck said, referring to the Stephen King thriller. Beck felt that there were plenty of examples of wasteful projects, and so did a lot of other people. In September 2010, Congressman Darrell Issa, the ranking Republican on the House Oversight Committee, sent a letter to stimulus watchdog Earl Devaney, listing several projects that appeared to violate the law's ban on stimulus spending on zoos, casinos, golf courses, and swimming pools. In addition to the National Zoo, Issa noted that stimulus money had been spent at an Oregon golf course for a school's physical education class and for a program training Native American youth in jobs at the Fortune Bay Casino.

While many of these projects were worthy on their own, they all had to be weighed against other priorities. At a time when factory workers like Ed Neufeldt struggled to find a job, the Corps of Engineers spent $92,000 on costumes for mascots like Bobber the Water Safety Dog. At a time when Serious Materials struggled to rehire employees and New Flyer was going through layoffs, the National Institutes of Health paid a Syracuse psychologist $219,000 to study the hookups of college coeds.

Waste, of course, is always in the eye of the beholder. And many projects that sounded silly on first blush were actually worthwhile. Among the hundreds of thousands of stimulus expenditures were dozens of iPods, toilets, and trips to resort hotels. But according to the reports, those purchases were used to enhance technology in the classroom, make bathrooms accessible to the disabled, and train special education teachers. A contract for "canned pork" in a bill being derided as the "porkulus" made for irresistible snickering without the context that it was supplying food banks that had been struggling to feed hungry families. A health center in northeastern Oklahoma used stimulus money to rent a snow cone and cotton candy machine. But the sugary treats helped lure low-income families to a new clinic, where they took tours and learned about services for the uninsured.

Keynes, the economist, noted that the Treasury could do a pretty good job by filling old bottles with banknotes, burying them in coalmines, and then allowing the private sector to dig them up. "Public works even of doubtful utility may pay for themselves over and over again at a time of severe unemployment," he wrote.[4] Illustrating his point to a fellow economist at the Mayflower Hotel in Washington, DC, Keynes knocked over a stack of towels, arguing that it would stimulate the economy better than taking just one.[5] Even the New Deal project that popularized the term "boondoggle" was valuable to some of the men learning to make cheap leather belts and sleeping bags at a time when money was scarce.

$ $ $

Perhaps the award for most unusual stimulus project would go to Malcolm MacIver, a neurobiology and engineering professor at Northwestern University. MacIver received a $1.25 million grant to study how electric fish from the Amazon use sensory information to make sudden movements when hunting for prey. MacIver felt the research could help in the development of underwater robots to find the source of toxic leaks. Further in the future, he said, it could lead to more agile prosthetics.

Most National Science Foundation grants contain a public outreach component, such as giving a lecture to a high school class. But MacIver had an innovative approach that he thought would be much more powerful and engaging than traditional outreach efforts. MacIver's idea was an interactive art exhibit. Sixteen species of electric fish would be arranged in sculpted fish tanks. The tanks would be connected to an amplifier that could convert the different frequencies that the fish emit into sounds. Using a hacked controller from the

Nintendo Wii video game system, visitors would be able to turn the tanks' amplifiers on and off, essentially conducting an orchestra of electric fish. The species even had names that sounded like rock bands: black ghost knifefish, glass knifefish, and aba aba.

"It's a competitive necessity for our country to increase the level of science literacy," he told me. "To help crack the nut of disinterest in science, it helps to engage people with material which they can relate to and which they find interesting and fun."

MacIver, in his forties, had blond hair and glasses, and wore a gray collared shirt, jeans, and a hip pair of sneakers with several straps. He has served as a science consultant on movies and television shows, such as the sequel to *Tron* and the prequel to *Battlestar Galactica*. On his wall was a picture of a fish fossil believed to be the first animal to have crawled onto land, and he was prone to saying things like, "I've got a theory about why we became conscious as animals."

MacIver's theory goes a little something like this: If you think about driving in the fog and you come across something in the road, you have a limited "pallet of behaviors." You could brake. You could swerve. But you don't have much time to react or display any fore-thought. On the other hand, if you're driving on a clear day, you can see signs and plan when to get gas, when to stop for lunch, and so on. You do this based on what MacIver calls "sensory longing." Eons ago, animals' motor and sensory skills were almost the same impulse, hence the anecdote of driving in the fog. But when animals came onto land, the visibility stretched for miles. Now there was space not just to react but to be aware of the environs and to survey and plan. An animal with a larger sensory space had selective advantages in hunting prey.

$ $ $

Inside MacIver's lab was a Rube Goldberg setup of fish tanks, an ultra-violet filter, and a distribution system made of PVC pipe. The black ghost knifefish huddled in tubes placed in the tanks, emitting a weak electric field. It was their way of feeling secure in the environment, MacIver said. True to their name, the fish looked like tapered knives with a single black fin that fluttered like a chiffon prom dress on a breezy day. To demonstrate how the fish's electric fields could be turned into sounds, he dangled a pair of red and white cables into the water. Suddenly, the attached speaker began to screech with the static of a bullhorn. MacIver explained how a fish, when it senses food with its electric field, can reverse direction in a split second to capture the prey. By studying how the fish's brain translates sensory stimuli into such agile movement so quickly, MacIver hoped to model it on a computer to unlock the mystery of how humans respond to sights, smells, and sounds. In another part of his lab was a fish robot, consisting of a white tube with thirty-two independently controllable fin rays made out of ballet dancers' Lycra, which apparently has the same mechanical properties as the fish's fin. Connected to a computer, the robot could be made to swim in an agricultural tub to mimic the movement of the electric fish.

MacIver came to the electric fish in an odd way, as most people who study electric fish do. He was pursuing a dual PhD in philosophy and cognitive science and decided he wanted to study things at the brain level. So he switched to the University of Illinois at Urbana-Champaign, where he met a scientist who showed him his research into electric fish. *Who cares?* MacIver thought. He could study human brains, and he had plans of going into cognitive neuroscience, where he could perform fMRIs to see how brain areas light up when people thought about different things.

"It takes awhile to see its importance, just like it takes awhile to realize the importance of studying fruit fly genetics," MacIver said. "We can basically understand everything we want to know about genes by looking at fruit flies. So similar with fish, fish have all our circuits except the neocortex. If you want to understand the brain, it's better to look at a creature that has in some sense a simpler brain but still has a circuit of interest."

MacIver's research made a list of wasteful spending put out by Republicans on the first anniversary of the stimulus in February 2010. Congressman Issa later included the project in his letter to Devaney because MacIver had originally proposed doing the electric fish orchestra as an exhibit at an aquarium. Aquariums, along with zoos and golf courses, were banned from receiving stimulus money.

$ $ $

Scientific research provided an abundant source of material for critics seeking to attack the Recovery Act. The stimulus provided $10 billion to the National Institutes of Health and $3 billion to the National Science Foundation, funding thousands of projects. Young adults in Buffalo were paid to answer their cell phones and report on their use of malt liquor and marijuana under a $783,000 grant to study why they're often used together. The *New York Post* reported that the stimulus was paying for "a bacchanalia of behavioral sex research."[6] There was funding to study pollen in Viking Age Iceland, the impact of integral yoga on hot flashes, and the history of civil litigation in colonial Peru. At times, it seemed that some Republicans displayed an utter ignorance for the basics of scientific research, as in the midterm elections when Senate candidate Sharron Angle criticized cocaine addiction research using primate subjects as money for "coked-up stimulus monkeys."

Also taking a beating was the $50 million allocated to the National Endowment for the Arts. Funding for theater, art, music, and creative writing has always been a flashpoint in the debate over government spending, and the stimulus was no different. Fox News quickly found a trove of ripe material. The channel reported on stimulus money going to a San Francisco film society that had recently screened *Thundercrack*, described as the "the world's only underground kinky art porno horror film, complete with four men, three women, and a gorilla." It reported on a dance company that performed in the nude, professing that "in the sharing of a central axis, spine, mouth, genitals, face, and anus reveal their interconnectedness and centrality in embodied experience."[7] The official project reports were far less provocative as agencies sought to avoid having their work ridiculed by using the generic project description, "to support the preservation of jobs that are threatened by declines in philanthropic and other support during the current economic downturn."

During the Great Depression, the WPA provided historic support for the arts, helping to launch the careers of many of America's best-known actors, writers, and artists, including Orson Welles, Arthur

Miller, John Steinbeck, and Jackson Pollock. But unlike the New Deal, the Recovery Act provided very little money to support individual artists. The National Endowment for the Arts funding barely made it in the bill. Critics argued that during a recession, building infrastructure was far more important than frivolous things like the arts. Artists were forced to defend themselves, noting that they also had mortgages to pay and families to feed. The Senate version of the bill included nothing for the arts, but supporters such as Speaker Nancy Pelosi managed to restore funding during final negotiations. Even so, grants were limited to tiny amounts of $25,000 to $50,000 apiece, barely enough to produce an exhibit or a single play.

The Lincoln Center in New York was able to bring in jazz musician Pablo Aslan for a "tango salon." The stimulus saved the jobs of three actors in the Chicago Shakespeare Theater's performance of *Richard III* and the designer of the Cézanne exhibit at the Montclair Art Museum in New Jersey. Nearby at the Paper Mill Playhouse in Millburn, New Jersey, the city-owned theater was able to add six preview performances of *Little House on the Prairie: The Musical*, starring Melissa Gilbert, who played Laura Ingalls in the television series. The stimulus money, along with a private donation, allowed the theater to pay for an additional week of the cast's salaries and fine-tune the production based on the audience's feedback.

If the Recovery Act is to have any effect on the arts world like the New Deal did, it will be through a little-known public buildings program called Art in Architecture. The program, funded by one-half of 1 percent of construction costs, commissions artists to create sculptures and paintings for the entrances and atriums of federal buildings across the country. Through the stimulus, seven artists mostly living in Brooklyn received hundreds of thousands of dollars each to provide artworks for federal buildings in Boston and Houston, a border station in Maine, and the Coast Guard headquarters in Washington, DC.

The WPA arts programs were dogged as purveyors of propaganda and their rolls were said to be rife with communists. Similarly, the stimulus was criticized by Senator Coburn for funding "anti-capitalist, socially conscious puppet shows." As evidence, he pointed to a $25,000 grant that was given to In the Heart of the Beast Puppet and

Mask Theatre. The Minneapolis group takes its name from a quote popularized by Che Guevara and performs at the annual Mayday parade, and features artists who have spoken out against "free market fundamentalism."

Coburn led the charge against arts funding in the stimulus bill. But his efforts, which seemed anti-art in principle, masked a family connection: his daughter, Sarah Coburn, is an acclaimed soprano, who since 2009 has performed with two opera companies that each received $50,000 in stimulus money.

"Dr. Coburn has long argued that stimulus dollars should have been directed to vital infrastructure repairs and improvements and necessary military purchases," his spokesman John Hart responded when I asked about it. "Everything else was lower priority."

$ $ $

While the politicians debated waste, the Recovery Accountability and Transparency Board occupied itself with preventing fraud before it happened. The federal board, charged with monitoring stimulus money, set up shop in a nondescript office building down the street from the White House. Inside, they built a war room of sorts: work stations with three computer monitors each, flat screens overhead displaying maps of hotspots where fraud has occurred in the past. Investigators with backgrounds in economics, mathematics, and engineering spent their days analyzing data looking for nonobvious relationships, such as a business owner with a bad reputation setting up a new company in a relative's name.

The Recovery Board set up a tip line and received thousands of complaints, which they referred to inspectors general for further investigation. With all the eyes on the money, Earl Devaney, the man in charge of stimulus oversight, told me someone would have to be pretty foolish to go after stimulus funds. "If I was a self-respecting crook, I'd go steal some other money," he said.

The constant monitoring and analytical techniques allowed investigators to uncover troublesome contractors and recover millions of dollars, according to an internal memo that detailed a number of cases. In one, a Connecticut nanotechnology company called Inframat received a $150,000 research grant despite being banned from receiving federal contracts. As a result of the board's work, the government was able to recoup $50,000. In another case, a firm called Crestline Construction won a contract set aside for businesses located in economically distressed areas. Investigators found that because of a change in ownership, the company didn't qualify for the program, and federal officials rescinded the $1 million contract. In other cases, the Recovery Board wasn't able to get the stimulus money back but its work helped bar the company from future contracts. Platinum One Contracting, for example, was able to secure twelve roofing projects, worth $2.2 million, at Andrews Air Force Base in Maryland. The board found that the firm was a pass-through to obtain special contracts designated for companies in blighted neighborhoods, and the company paid $200,000 to settle claims that they made false statements to obtain the contracts. But despite its efforts, the Recovery Board was too late to stop one of the biggest cases of stimulus money going to a contractor suspected of fraud.

Craig Jackson was a successful Southern California businessman who had taken over a small heating and air conditioning company in 1981 and transformed it into what some said was the largest African American–owned mechanical contractor in the United States. He had won awards from the U.S. Small Business Administration and was seen as a hero to other black entrepreneurs. But according to documents from a Department of Defense investigation, Jackson took advantage of the program, amassing a portfolio of construction companies in the names of relatives and friends to falsely obtain contracts intended for fledgling minority firms. Over the years, nineteen companies controlled by Jackson received more than $700 million in government contracts through the set-aside program, the government said.

The Defense Department began investigating Jackson in the summer of 2008, but the government didn't suspend the firms from receiving contracts until the fall of 2009. As a result, the air force and the army awarded the companies nearly $30 million for 112 stimulus projects at U.S. military bases across the country. The work included repairing hangars and installing energy-efficient windows at Andrews Air Force Base in Maryland, replacing fencing and renovating the dining hall at Wright-Patterson Air Force Base in Ohio, renovating a child-development center at Fort Knox in Kentucky, repairing the air-field electrical system at Moody Air Force Base in Georgia, and stabilizing a landslide area in Colorado Springs. By the time the Recovery Board discovered this, work had already begun, making it difficult for the military to cancel the contracts.

The blatant example of the left hand not knowing what the right is doing aggravated Senator Coburn. "Where's the notification so you don't give additional contracts to folks who are under investigation?" he said. "If somebody fixed your garage door and they defrauded you—or rather, you thought they defrauded you—would you give them more business? Nobody else in the country would do that."

One of the companies at the center of the alleged scheme was APM LLC, a small construction firm owned by the Cape Fox Tlingit natives of southeast Alaska. The Tlingits had wrested a subsistence life from the harsh coasts for thousands of years, only to see their villages destroyed, their resources exploited, and their population wiped out by disease when white settlers came in the nineteenth century. To right the historic wrongs suffered by all Alaska natives, and pave the way for the Alaska oil pipeline, Congress established native corporations in 1971 and later gave them special privileges to obtain no-bid contracts worth hundreds of millions of dollars. The Alaska natives didn't need to perform the work themselves, and most relied on outside managers like the Cape Fox Tlingit did when they hired Craig Jackson.

The Tlingit native village of Saxman sits on the south end of Revillagigedo Island. It is a world away from APM's headquarters in Yorba Linda, California, located on a thin strip bordered by an inlet filled with salmon and sawtooth peaks carpeted with cedar and spruce. The village is a few miles down the road from Ketchikan, site of the infamous "Bridge to Nowhere." During the summer, cruise ships tower over downtown Ketchikan as tourists flock to the canned-salmon shops and attractions such as the Great Alaskan Lumberjack Show. But beyond the totem poles that lure visitors seeking the native culture is a neighborhood of federally subsidized homes with street names such as Eagle, Raven, and Killer Whale Avenues. When the

Census Bureau last surveyed Saxman in 2000, unemployment was 26 percent and only 9 percent of residents had bachelor's degrees.

While APM looked good on paper, booking tens of millions in revenue year after year, the contracts brought few jobs, no increase in dividends, and a mountain of debt. Meanwhile, Jackson and his companies charged the natives with $16 million in fees, according to a lawsuit filed by the Cape Fox corporation.

Jackson wouldn't talk to me. But in a response to the Defense Department investigation, a lawyer for his engineering firm said the government had always known of the close relationships between the various companies. He added that the Small Business Administration had encouraged Jackson to share his expertise with other minority firms.

In a telling example, though, the Defense Department looked closely at a marketing agreement APM had with a firm that was supposedly run by Jackson's sister, an elementary school principal in Virginia. When investigators interviewed her, she told them she just deposited checks and forwarded the mail to her brother.

"All I know is I am the president and I think Craig is the vice president. I must say I am not completely sure if Craig is the vice president," she said, according to an interview transcript. "I do not really know what the company does or has done."

$ $ $

In December 2009, Senator Coburn released his second report on wasteful and silly stimulus projects, this time joined by Senator John McCain. It was every bit as titillating and as troubling as the first. Nearly $800,000 for Martha's Vineyard residents to buy General Electric appliances that can be controlled remotely by a computer to limit energy usage. St. Joseph, Missouri, was spending $100,000 on a Brazilian steakhouse and a martini bar.[8] The University of Arizona and Arizona State University received nearly $1 million to study ants.

"I had no idea that so much expertise concerning ants resided in the major universities in my state," McCain quipped at a news conference. "In my state, real unemployment is 17 percent. We rank second in homes underwater as far as home-loan mortgages being less of value than the mortgage payments, and serious economic problems, and we're going to spend money on ants."

Rather than rebut the report point by point, as it did with Coburn's first report, the Obama administration simply said that the critics were focusing on a tiny percentage of projects while the overall package was working well. Many of the targeted recipients defended their work as important, as the Republicans talked about priorities. Round and round the whirligig of waste spun, as it would do for the next two years, and as it will continue to do for decades to come.

Even now, after journalists and politicians have combed through the reports, it is easy to find new projects that sound silly and, to many people, even wasteful in a time of crisis. The Guam Council on the Arts and Humanities Agency used part of $25,000 grant to make coconut candy for a traditional dance festival. The city of Cocoa, Florida, received a $162,000 grant for a program often billed as putting police officers on the street. But instead the city spent the money on jewelry-making classes, a Christian rap concert, lemonade stands, a casino night to raise money for the Police Athletic League, an Orlando Magic basketball game, and a field trip for cheerleaders to go to a competition in Daytona Beach.

Total jobs the city reported creating or saving? One.

The list went on and on and on.

While some of the examples may have been overblown, the ability that Coburn and others had to make the stimulus seem ridiculous exposed a central weakness in its design. With money spread so thinly and going to so many different places, it was difficult for the public to grasp what the stimulus was about. But it was easy for small projects to capture the media coverage day after day and overwhelm the narrative the administration was desperately trying to reclaim.

NINE

CASH FOR CLUNKERS

*Listen to the motor. Listen to the wheels. Listen with your ears and
with your hands on the steering wheel; listen with the palm of your
hand on the gear-shift lever; listen with your feet on the floor boards.
Listen to the pounding old jalopy with all your senses . . .*
—John Steinbeck, *The Grapes of Wrath*

FOR ALL THE RECOVERY ACT was doing for infrastructure and education, scientific research and the social safety net, very little of the
money was dedicated to the two of the biggest victims of the Great
Recession: the housing market and the automobile industry. The
Obama administration dealt with housing and autos mainly with left-
over money from the bank bailout. Team Auto, as the task force became known, spent about $80 billion restructuring General Motors
and Chrysler through bankruptcy while also lending money to suppliers and the automakers' financing arms. The administration committed $50 billion to help homeowners avoid foreclosure and more than
$100 billion to rescue the federally sponsored mortgage companies
Fannie Mae and Freddie Mac.

The stimulus package contained a series of less prominent programs: rural housing loans, money to help military families relocate
because of base closures, a program for cities to fix up and sell abandoned and foreclosed homes to stabilize hard-hit neighborhoods. In
autos, the government spent $300 million upgrading its fleet with
fuel-efficient cars. Consumers received a sales tax deduction if they

bought a new car and up to a $7,500 credit if they purchased a plug-in hybrid or electric vehicle.

But through the initial bill and subsequent trims, the Recovery Act also provided money for two of the most popular programs during the recession: the Cash for Clunkers vehicle trade-in program and an $8,000 tax credit for first-time home buyers. Praised by Democrats and Republicans alike, the incentives arrived at a critical time for the country's economic psyche. With Americans discouraged by a stimulus plan that couldn't seem to get off the ground, Cash for Clunkers and the home-buyer credit provided the first glimpse of a horizon and a palpable end to the Great Recession.

The idea for a trade-in program to get gas guzzlers off the road was proposed by Princeton University economist Alan Blinder in a July 2008 *New York Times* column. The former Clinton adviser and vice chairman of the Federal Reserve argued that Cash for Clunkers would be a "public policy trifecta." It would stimulate the economy by luring consumers into deserted showrooms. It would improve the environment because old cars and trucks pollute more than new ones with higher emissions standards. And it would help the poor because low-income people are more likely to drive older-model vehicles.[1]

As the stimulus package developed, the idea also got a big push from the environmental community. Van Jones, the short-lived Obama energy adviser, called for a program dubbed "hoopties for hybrids."

Testifying to its broad appeal, in one week in November 2008, an incentive for car buyers was backed by both conservative economists in the *Wall Street Journal* and by the liberal Center for American Progress Action Fund in a policy memo circulated on Capitol Hill. Cash for Clunkers wasn't a brand new idea. Back in the early 1990s, the elder President George Bush started a "cash for clunkers" program, allowing states and industries to buy old, high-polluting cars and apply the environmental benefits to meet the government's clean air standards. In more recent years, trade-in vouchers were tried in states varying from California to Texas.

By January 2009, auto sales had fallen to their lowest monthly level since 1982. With the Recovery Act being debated in Congress, lobbyists for the automakers and their dealerships pushed the program hard. A bipartisan group of senators led by Dianne Feinstein of California introduced a separate bill for the program in January and worked to include it in the stimulus package. But the various interest groups couldn't agree on how many miles per gallon the new cars should get and whether the program should be limited to American cars. As negotiations turned to reducing the overall cost of the stimulus, Cash for Clunkers was left on the shelf.

Inside the White House, the rescue of the auto industry continued. On the eve of Obama's announcement of his plan, Team Auto gathered in the Oval Office as the president made his courtesy calls. Larry Summers and other advisers consulted members of Congress with interest in the auto industry and realized they had been missing something. "We'd been thinking too much like wonks—obsessively dwelling on financial restructuring and doing too little to promote a broad auto industry recovery," Steven Rattner, leader of the White House auto task force, recalled in *Overhaul*, his memoir on the crisis.[2] A young staffer named Brian Deese brought up the Cash for Clunkers idea. A similar program in Germany had proven successful. According to one economic adviser, Summers was skeptical. He thought it was too gimmicky and made a bet with Deese that it wouldn't do anything to spur auto sales. But despite the doubts, the team agreed, and Deese worked late into the night so the president could include it in his speech the next day.

On March 30, 2009, flanked by his auto advisers in the White House Grand Foyer, Obama unveiled his recovery plan for the industry. He expressed his support for fleet modernization proposals that were pending in Congress and said he wanted to find parts of the Recovery Act that could be trimmed to make room for the program.

The most prominent of the various iterations was a bill sponsored by Congresswoman Betty Sutton, a Democrat and labor lawyer who represented a stretch of northeast Ohio that had seen its share of auto plant closings. Sutton's bill called for a rebate of $3,500 if car buyers traded in a vehicle getting less than eighteen miles per gallon for a car getting more than twenty-two miles per gallon. It offered $4,500 for bigger jumps in fuel economy.

The $4 billion bill had the backing of many Midwest lawmakers, the automobile industry, and the United Auto Workers union. But environmental groups argued that the bill was designed simply to clear Detroit's unsold inventory, noting that even a Hummer H3T would qualify. An alternative plan by Senator Feinstein required increases of at least seven miles per gallon for cars and three miles per gallon for large trucks. The most lucrative rebates were saved for drivers getting thirteen miles more per gallon than their trade-in. Large pickups and SUVs would be eligible only if they got more than seventeen miles per gallon.

Sutton's version ultimately won after it passed easily in the House with 298 votes and the Feinstein bill struggled to gain the necessary support in the Senate. Congress came to a weakened compromise of $1 billion and attached it to a must-pass bill to fund the wars in Iraq and Afghanistan. The Cash for Clunkers bill was signed into law in June 2009. Officially called the Car Allowance Rebate System, the program offered hefty incentives to buy a new car:

$3,500 for

- cars getting better than twenty-two miles per gallon with a trade-in getting less than eighteen miles per gallon,
- light pickups and SUVs getting better than eighteen miles per gallon with a trade-in getting less than sixteen miles per gallon,
- large pickups and SUVs getting better than fifteen miles per gallon with a trade-in getting less than fourteen miles per gallon

or $4,500 for

- cars getting at least ten miles per gallon higher than their trade-in,
- pickups and SUVs getting at least fives miles per gallon higher,
- large trucks getting at least two miles per gallon higher.

Combined with other federal and state incentives, the vouchers could result in significant savings for consumers. But the other two legs of the "public policy trifecta," curbing pollution and reducing income inequality, were greatly diminished. Consumers could get the rebate for vehicles worth up to $45,000, not exactly the kind of car a poor family could afford. The program also penalized environmentally conscious drivers who decided to buy fuel-efficient cars years ago; their vehicles didn't qualify for an upgrade.

$ $ $

When the program took effect in late July, it set off a frenzy at car dealerships across the country. Dealers took out full-page ads in newspapers and ran TV ads featuring animated car crushing, stadium voices, flying dollar bills, and CASH FOR CLUNKERS in bright block letters with as many exclamation points as they could fit on the screen. A number of dealerships, including the Springfield Auto Mart in Vermont, planted a junk car in a Dumpster to attract attention. The first weekend, prospective buyers swamped their lots and showrooms. "The reason that I came in was the program, there's no question about that," Paul Hester, a retired engineer, told a *Chicago Tribune* reporter at Gregory Hyundai in Highland Park, Illinois.[3] Gone were the Broncos and Bravadas, the Windstars and Astros, the Dakotas and DeVilles. Off went new Elantras and Impalas, Focuses and Priuses, Versas and Jettas.

Customers lined up outside dealerships at dawn and were still browsing showrooms at 3:00 A.M. Kitty Van Bortel, who owned Ford and Subaru dealerships outside Rochester, New York, told the Associated Press that she sold more than a hundred cars and trucks, double the usual pace. "Everybody is just panicked that they're not going to get the deal because the money is going to be gone," she said.[4]

Sales teams stayed late scanning documents and typing in vehicle identification numbers into the government computer system. But the program to track payments had structural flaws and was quickly overwhelmed. The website hung up and timed out. Dealers were locked out of the system. "It was sort of like trying to buy U2 tickets in the first five minutes they go on sale," Chris Lemley, president of Sentry Auto Group in the Boston suburbs, told the *Wall Street Journal*.[5]

The U.S. Department of Transportation brought in hundreds of employees to handle phone calls and its contractor, Oracle, repeatedly upgraded its capacity. The White House technology office sent a bunch of crash teams to the DOT to troubleshoot. No one expected Cash for Clunkers to result in so many sales so fast. In the first four days, more than 250,000 cars were sold. Originally intended to last until November, Cash for Clunkers ran out of money in just one week.

President Obama said the program would end if Congress didn't extend it. Bombarded by car dealers and customers who hoped to take advantage of the rebates, the House quickly passed legislation to pour $2 billion from the Recovery Act into the program. The money was sliced from a $6 billion loan program to support clean energy startups like solar panel factories and wind farms. By shifting the funds, Congress hit on a key tension of Obama's economic recovery plan. The energy loans, while slow moving, were considered a critical investment in America's future. But Cash for Clunkers, despite its questionable long-term benefits, was a populist hit right now. The measure passed with nearly 75 percent of the House supporting it, including all the Republicans from Michigan, half from Ohio,[6] and all but one from Indiana. Despite a push for steeper gas mileage requirements, the Senate followed suit and extended the program. Clunkermania continued.

When the program ended in late August 2009, nearly 680,000 cars and trucks had been sold. Cash for Clunkers pushed consumer spending to its highest monthly level in nearly eight years. Automakers had their best sales results of the year with Ford reporting its first monthly increase since 2007. With their inventories wiped out, shuttered and sleepy manufacturing plants came to life again. General Motors increased production by 60,000 vehicles and recalled 1,350 employees to its assembly lines in Lordstown, Ohio, and Ontario, Canada. At plants in Michigan and Indiana, GM added overtime and reversed temporary shutdowns. Ford boosted production by 10,000 vehicles to meet the demand for its fuel-efficient Focuses. Chrysler added overtime and brought back 850 employees at its plant in Belvidere, Illinois, to build more Dodge Calibers. The sales were also good news for autoworkers at foreign-owned plants. Hyundai hired back more than 3,000 workers at its plant in Montgomery, Alabama, while Honda increased production in Lincoln, Alabama, and in East Liberty and Marysville, Ohio.

As a result of the rebound, Michigan's unemployment rate dipped for the first time in nearly two years, beginning a gradual recovery. The White House Council of Economic Advisers estimated the program created or saved 70,000 jobs in the second half of 2009.

Cash for Clunkers was apparently so alluring that some drivers junked used luxury cars that were worth far more than the $4,500 rebate, including Maseratis, an Aurora Shelby Cobra replica, and a 1997 Aston Martin DB7 Volante, originally priced at $140,000, now selling used for $45,000 online. All the publicity had a residual effect as well. Even though their trade-ins didn't qualify for the incentives, many customers visited showrooms and drove off in new cars anyway. To avoid a flaw in Germany's program, in which gas guzzlers were resold in Eastern Europe and Africa, the U.S. Department of Transportation established strict protocol to ensure the clunkers would never pollute again. After draining the motor oil, mechanics filled the engine with a sodium silicate solution. By running the vehicle for a few seconds, the solution would spread through the engine, turning glasslike, and abrade the bearings. The rules created a run on the chemical. Junkyards sold car batteries, scrap metal, and other parts. Bank employees handled thousands of loans.

Transportation secretary Ray LaHood declared it "wildly successful." "It has stimulated the economy, generated jobs, and helped consumers dump their gas guzzlers," he wrote on his blog. "And it's taken toxic greenhouse gases out of the air to improve the environment."

At a time when the White House was sustaining a fusillade of criticism over the pace of shovel-ready projects, Cash for Clunkers provided the first visible proof that Obama's recovery plan was working. In a matter of weeks, the program did what all the PUTTING AMERICA TO WORK signs could not. It provided the Obama administration with something it needed: photo ops. The images of crowded showrooms and clunkers in Dumpsters stayed in people's minds. And it reassured the public that good ol' consumer demand was alive and well. The American economy hadn't fundamentally changed.

"All of us, I think, were a little surprised by what happened with Cash for Clunkers," Obama would say later. "We're trying to figure out, 'Man, how did that thing just blow up the way it did?' It seems obvious in retrospect, but I'm not sure everybody thought about it earlier. Essentially, all the auto companies did the marketing. They did the advertising in a way the government just can't do it and, frankly, even if we did it, people wouldn't listen."

$ $ $

Cash for Clunkers became a model for other Recovery Act programs to follow. In the spring of 2010, states began offering rebates for dishwashers, refrigerators, boilers, and other appliances. More than 70 percent of home energy use is for such items, and the Obama administration hoped the $300 million program, which some called "Dollars for Dishwashers," would encourage homeowners to swap their old appliances for new energy-efficient models.

In many states, where the rebate was a generous $100 to $250, the rebates went like hotcakes. Texas opened its website and phone lines at 7:00 A.M. and handed out the last of its $20 million lot by 2:30 P.M. Minnesota burned through 25,000 rebates in a day. Iowa's disappeared in eight hours. Like Cash for Clunkers, the appliance rebate program had its problems, such as websites crashing under the demand and sporadic attempts to game the system. In one incident reported by investigators, a landlord in Georgia bought multiple hot water heaters, returned them to the store, and then used the receipts to claim the rebates.

A USA Today analysis questioned the environmental gains after finding that very little of the money had been spent on water heaters, one of the biggest energy hogs in a home.[7] By June 2011, consumers had bought 1.4 million appliances, 166,000 heating and air conditioning units, and 30,000 water heaters. With most of the money spent, the program had generated $1.9 billion in sales, saving more than a trillion BTUs a year. On a visit to General Electric's Appliance Park campus in Louisville, Vice President Biden noted that sales of dishwashers had increased by 20 percent because of the rebates. Sales of clothes washers had more than doubled, causing GE to hire 137 employees to meet the demand.

A similar effect happened in housing. The first-time homebuyer tax credit offered $8,000 to anyone who hadn't owned a home in the past three years and made less than $75,000 (or $150,000 for couples). The program was a far more lucrative version of a 2008 tax credit, which offered a $7,500 interest-free loan that had to be paid back over fifteen years. The new program provided cash in hand. With home prices and mortgage rates at their lowest levels in years, there was no better time to buy a home. From south Florida to southern California, the credit prodded families that had been sitting on the fence to make their move. In all, nearly 2 million people claimed the credit by the stimulus deadline, pushing home sales to their highest level since before the recession. The sales generated further economic activity, as new homeowners also spent money on moving vans, realtor commissions, and furnishings.

But the various versions of the home-buyer credit led to confusion for many taxpayers. And the program was rife with dubious claims. The Internal Revenue Service didn't require proof before issuing the credits and allowed people to claim them with the promise that they would buy a home later that year. Auditors examined more than 100,000 cases and referred hundreds for criminal investigation. In one example, 67 people listed the same home to claim the credit. Other purported home buyers included 1,300 prison inmates, 1,300 dead people, and 600 children, including one who was only four years old.

Also dubious were the economic benefits of the credit. So many people took advantage of the credit that the program cost billions more than expected. The Obama administration pointed out homeowners who said the credit was key to their decision and it found families moving from public housing into their own slice of the American dream. According to economists, though, those stories were few and far between. The National Association of Realtors estimated that the credit led to an additional 350,000 sales that wouldn't have happened without it. Moreover, the industry group said it helped stabilize home prices, saving homeowners from going underwater on their mortgages and preventing foreclosures. But the nonpartisan Congressional Research Service concluded the number of additional sales was much lower, between 43,000 and 128,000 homes. The low home prices and mortgage rates were far more important factors in the stabilization of the housing market, it said. Many economists noted that even the industry's numbers showed the government was spending tens of thousands of dollars to spur just one sale, providing little bang for the buck.

Dean Baker, a prominent liberal economist who recognized the housing bubble way back in 2002, told me the credit was perhaps the worst part of the Recovery Act. The credit merely propped up the housing market when prices needed to deflate, he said, because the majority of the homes would have been bought anyway. Baker did however take advantage of the credit himself. He was already looking, but the incentive created some urgency. "I was happy to get the money, but I don't think it was good policy," he told me. "I just don't see any benefit for the government to sustain the bubble a little longer."

$ $ $

Cash for Clunkers was similarly buffeted with questions about whether it truly stimulated car buying or just moved up sales that would have occurred in the near future. The frenzy of July and August was followed by the freeze of September as car sales slowed significantly. The scene at Gene Butman Ford in Ypsilanti, Michigan, was typical of the hangover that panged showrooms when the deals were done. There were more salesmen than customers and the pickings were slim. "We're getting some traffic, but my business is a long way from healthy," one salesman told a reporter from the Associated Press. "We suspect it's going to be ninety days before we get back to any kind of normalcy."[8]

On the two extremes of this debate were Edmunds.com, the publisher of car-shopping guides, and Maritz, a research firm that advises auto manufacturers and dealers. Edmunds analysts concluded that only 125,000 sales were attributable to the rebates. The rest of the customers would have bought cars anyway without trading in an old vehicle. But Edmunds left out an important aspect: the increase in sales that didn't qualify for the rebates because customers, caught up in the excitement, swarmed showrooms and bought cars anyway. Analyzing both trends by surveying new-car and -truck buyers, Maritz found the opposite, calculating 765,000 new vehicle sales as a result of Cash for Clunkers. The firm's researchers discovered that most buyers were long-term car owners who drive their cars until the engine dies. And they also concluded the residual effects on car sales were greatly underestimated.

In its own assessment, the White House Council of Economic Advisers acknowledged that at least some "pull-forward" effect occurred. It concluded that about half of the nearly 700,000 car sales would have happened anyway. But that's not necessarily a bad thing. "Such time-shifting is valuable in a recession, when the economy has an abundance of unemployed resources that can be put to work at low net economic cost," the council said in its report.

The White House advisers noted that many buyers were typically people in the market for used cars and probably wouldn't have bought brand new vehicles without the incentives. But the junking of hundreds of thousands of still-running cars was poison to the used-car market, critics said. The scarcity of used cars would raise prices on the poor who depended on them and had put their faith in the Obama administration. While used car prices were already on a steep climb before Cash for Clunkers, some charged that by destroying a product before the end of its useful life, the program was the modern equivalent of FDR slaughtering pigs to stabilize the farm industry during the Great Depression.

Perhaps the deepest analysis of economic effects of the Cash for Clunkers program was conducted for the National Bureau of Economic Research by economists Atif Mian of the University of California, Berkeley, and Amir Sufi of the University of Chicago. The two economists compared sales in metropolitan areas that had few clunkers before the program started with areas that had a lot of clunkers. By doing this, they hoped to come as close as they could to an alternate universe in which there was no Cash for Clunkers program, a control necessary for such scientific research. After looking at the data from different regions, Mian and Sufi agreed with the White House's estimate that about half the cars sold in the program were real additional purchases. But they noted that nearly all the sales would have happened in the ensuing months. By March 2010, seven months after the rebates ended, the effect on car sales was almost completely canceled out.

Even Alan Blinder, the Princeton professor who first pitched the Cash for Clunkers idea, was disappointed in how the Obama administration handled it. Blinder was baffled as to the short duration of the incentives, noting that he had envisioned a one-year to two-year program. Asked by a reporter whether the money was wasted as stimulus, Blinder replied, "Yeah, mostly. It provided a lift to GDP, but it was so fleeting."[9]

Also questionable were the long-term environmental benefits of the program. On the surface, Cash for Clunkers appeared to be a green success. Consumers traded in vehicles averaging 15.8 miles per gallon and drove off in new cars and trucks getting 24.9 miles per gallon, a gain of nearly 60 percent. Over several years, that could translate to hundreds of gallons saved per driver and millions of tons of carbon dioxide removed from the atmosphere. While that sounds impressive, the gains are tiny compared to how much is emitted by vehicles and factories every day. Others have noted a common effect that greater energy efficiency often leads to greater use, in this case more miles driven, canceling out the benefits. And encouraging consumers to buy cars earlier than necessary increases emissions at auto plants that have to produce new vehicles to keep up with demand.

By opting for the program backed by the industry and unions over the version advanced by environmentalists, Congress created a counterintuitive outcome. The most popular trade was an old gas-guzzling pickup for a new gas-guzzling pickup.[10] Ford F-150 drivers were seventeen times more likely to buy a new F-150 than a Toyota Prius, the Associated Press found. One of the best-selling vehicles in the program was a Chevrolet Silverado, getting a combined fuel economy of just seventeen miles per gallon.

By far though, the biggest winners of the Cash for Clunkers program were Japanese automakers. Consumers traded in Fords, Chevys, and Dodges and drove home in Toyotas and Hondas. The number one dealer was Longo Toyota of El Monte, California, making more than twice as much as any other dealer. The top-selling vehicle was the Toyota Corolla.

But despite the demand for the Corolla, it wasn't enough to save the American auto plant that manufactured them. Just days after Cash for Clunkers ended, Toyota announced that it was closing the New United Motor Manufacturing Inc. plant, better known as NUMMI, in Fremont, California. Nearly 4,700 workers would lose their jobs. One step toward recovery was followed by two steps back.

$ $ $

The NUMMI automobile plant is located near the southeast tip of the San Francisco Bay between the high-tech corridor of Silicon Valley and the soft golden hills of the Mission Ridge. Spanning eighty-eight football fields, the complex measures eight-tenths of a mile end to end.

Ironically, NUMMI was born out of the last great recession in the early 1980s, a solution to the ravages that globalization had wrought on the American automobile industry. Technological advances, cheaper labor, and more fuel-efficient cars from Japan had eaten away at the dominance of Ford, Chrysler, and General Motors. Chrysler teetered on bankruptcy while GM closed plants across the country, including the one in Fremont. Despite their gains, Japanese automakers feared protectionist sentiment—workers in one protest smashed a Toyota with sledgehammers—and began opening plants in the United States. The New United Motor Manufacturing Inc. plant at the site of GM's old Fremont factory would be a joint venture between GM and Toyota. GM would learn Toyota's highly efficient production system while Toyota would try to replicate its lean model with a unionized workforce. The deal was signed on February 17, 1983, exactly twenty-six years before Obama signed the American Recovery and Reinvestment Act.

"At the heart of the NUMMI experiment was a compact," Berkeley professor and labor expert Harley Shaiken said in a 2010 report. "The company committed to job security, and the UAW pledged a flexible workplace and world-class performance."

The enterprise transformed the plant from one of GM's worst to one of its best. NUMMI rose with America's growing love for compact cars, churning out Chevy Prizms, Pontiac Vibes, and Toyota Corollas. In the mid-1990s, they added a truck line for the Toyota Tacoma, which quickly became one of the top-rated pickups in its class. The popularity of Corollas and Tacomas was key to Toyota's surpassing GM as the world's largest automaker in 2008.

Maryo Mendez went to work at NUMMI in 1991, egged on by his father who worked there and had worked at the GM plant before that. Two of his brothers also worked at NUMMI, as did his uncles and cousins. Even his daughter would work there as a summer hire years later.

"It was good," Mendez said in an interview at his house after the plant closed. "It *was* good. You got good pay. It had good benefits. The hours were all right."

A young father, he had been working at a plastics factory ten to twelve hours a day, often on weekends. "My dad kept trying to get me in there," recalled Mendez, now fifty-four. "He was telling me you only have to work eight hours a day. Then go home. You're done. If you want to work overtime, you can, and if you don't, you just go, you know. So I go, 'Sounds good. I'm tired of all these years, sixteen years, of working somewhere and thinking all the overtime that I put in. It's time.'"

At NUMMI, Mendez began working his way up, starting on nights, then days. Underbody. The door line. The trim line. For five or six years, he installed gas pedals. His last job was in conveyance, driving a tugger of dollies stacked with brake pedals, heaters, lug nuts, whatever was needed, to the different stations of the assembly line. The entire time he'd been there, never once did he call in sick. He notched seventeen years of perfect attendance, missing the company's "hero" program only because he took bereavement when his mother and brothers passed away.

NUMMI provided a good life for the Mendez family. A few years ago, they had moved into a housing development called the Meadowlands on the outskirts of San Jose. The streets had names like Grand Meadow, Royal Meadow, Spring Meadow, and Rolling Meadow. And the homes were adorned with Spanish-tile roofs and wildly shaped shrubs like something out of Dr. Seuss.

Mendez was energetic and wiry with gray-and-black hair and sideburns, black-rimmed glasses, and an earnestly quirky sense of humor. He had three kids: two daughters, twenty-nine and sixteen, and a son, eleven.

Mendez always hated foreign cars. He was a Dodge man. When I met him, he was wearing a Dodge Scat Pack T-shirt and he had a 1969 Dodge Dart parked in his driveway. But Toyota grew on him. In 1987, he took over his brother's payments on a Toyota truck and he ended up keeping it for twenty years.

"I couldn't believe how the thing ran and ran and ran," Mendez said. "Our Toyotas were more American than a Cadillac or a Lincoln Continental. It was kind of cool thinking that. These are red, white, and blue American-made cars."

Working at NUMMI was something special. In 1998, his daughter came home from high school and flipped open her history textbook. There was a picture of NUMMI with a caption calling it the first joint venture between an American and a foreign car company.

"That always stuck in my head," Mendez said. "I always thought, you know, no matter what happens, that's something I can say. I'm proud to work here and I'm proud that our company will always be known in the history book. So it's like we'll never be forgotten."

The last few years, Corollas had been selling like crazy, and overtime was easy to come by. So Mendez and other employees felt safe when GM filed for bankruptcy and announced in June 2009 that it was pulling out of the joint venture.

"Everybody was thinking, 'Oh yeah, Toyota's going to buy this place now. Toyota's going to take over,'" he said.

Then one morning in August, NUMMI called its employees into the auditorium and announced they were shutting down. With GM out and the supply chain in the Midwest, a plant in California no longer made sense. They would move the Tacoma production to a newer, nonunion plant in San Antonio and assemble the Corolla in Ontario, Canada. All 4,700 employees at NUMMI would lose their jobs. As many as 25,000 jobs that the plant supported in California would also be at risk. Many NUMMI employees were like Mendez. The average length of service was thirteen and a half years, Shaiken wrote, but many had worked there for seventeen to twenty-five years.

The shock was brutal, according to Mendez. "Everything goes through your mind. Back then I was either fifty-three or fifty-four years old, and I'm thinking what am I going to do now?"

$ $ $

California's unemployment rate was already 12 percent, one of the worst in the nation. Taking into account those who had given up looking or settled for a part-time job, more than one in five was out of work. NUMMI would be the state's biggest plant closure in years.

But Fremont, California, was no Flint, Michigan. Unlike the cratered birthplace of GM an hour north of Detroit, Fremont was across the bay from the one of the most booming job markets in the country. The city of 200,000 people was the largest suburb in the region—a diverse mix of whites, Asian Americans, and Hispanics—with a median household income of $100,000. Only about 10 percent of the NUMMI workers actually lived in Fremont. Many commuted from Oakland or the Central Valley.

"The Bay Area's got 3.5 million jobs," said Stephen Levy of the Center for Continuing Study of the California Economy. "I mean it's terrible for the families. But it's small relative to what happened in Tracy or Stockton or Modesto when they were building a gazillion homes a year and all of a sudden they were building none and nobody went to Lowe's or Home Depot and their sales taxes crumbled and the cities were running enormous deficits. It's horrible, but it's not a macroeconomic event."

The bigger problem was what NUMMI's closing represented: the tail end of a long structural shift in the state and the nation's economy. California once had a thriving automobile industry, and NUMMI was its last remaining plant. Silicon Valley's industry demanded high-tech skills that many assembly line workers didn't have.

With millions of dollars from the federal stimulus package, the Obama administration acted quickly, providing the workers with trade adjustment assistance and job training, especially in the clean energy sector, which was local and expected to boom.

Just one week after Toyota announced it was closing NUMMI, Energy secretary Steven Chu came to Fremont to deliver some hopeful news. A solar panel startup named Solyndra was receiving a $535 million loan guarantee from the Recovery Act to build a new 300,000-square-foot factory less than a mile from the plant.

Solyndra manufactured cylindrical solar panels that could be arranged in racks and installed easily on flat commercial rooftops (think factories and big box stores like Target and Best Buy). The company came out of nowhere in 2008 but had already attracted nearly $1 billion in private investment from major venture capital firms and funds tied to Wal-Mart's Walton family, Virgin's Richard Branson, and the oil and banking billionaire George Kaiser. Its solar assemblies had been installed at hundreds of sites around the world, primarily in Europe.

Many believed that Solyndra had invented a revolutionary product in the clean-tech sector. With polysilicon prices at more than $400 per kilogram, technologies that used alternative materials, such as Solyndra's, seemed on the verge of growth. By designing solar cells on a round surface, Solyndra panels could absorb more sunlight and didn't have to be tilted throughout the day like traditional solar panels. The United States alone had about 30 billion square feet of unused commercial roof space. And the company already had a backlog of more than $2 billion in orders. What Solyndra needed most was space to bring production up to scale.

The groundbreaking for Solyndra's Fab 2 facility was attended by Chu and California governor Arnold Schwarzenegger. One after another, they took the podium at the construction site, a Caterpillar vehicle draped with an American flag behind them. Schwarzenegger called it a turnaround for a city still stinging with the news of NUMMI's closure. Today at last was a celebration, the governor said, a celebration of job creation, Obama's stimulus package, and "saying hasta la vista to global warming." Solyndra CEO Chris Gronet waxed poetic, painting a scene twenty years into the future when they could stand in front of their families and say that they didn't stand by and do nothing about the environment. "We will make a difference one solar cell at a time, one tube at a time, one module at a time, one panel at a time, one megawatt installation at a time, one gigawatt factory at a time," he said. "We believe what we do here today will someday change our world for the better for generations to come."

The Solyndra loan guarantee was the first of many Department of Energy investments to come, designed to build a new green economy and, in Chu's words, "begin a new industrial revolution." The money would create 3,000 construction jobs and 1,000 more at Solyndra when the plant opened.

But what nobody mentioned that day was that inside the Obama administration, staff members at the Department of Energy and the White House Office of Management and Budget (OMB) were having their doubts about Solyndra's financial sustainability and feeling pressured to rush the final review. To political aides at the White House, the Recovery Act's first loan guarantee had tremendous public relations value and they wanted Vice President Biden to announce it at the factory's groundbreaking. September 4 seemed like an ideal day for the event.

"It's the same day the unemployment numbers come out, and we'd want to use this as an example where the Recovery Act is helping create new high tech jobs," a special assistant to Rahm Emanuel wrote in an e-mail.[11]

But in the weeks leading up to the announcement, OMB staffers pushed back.

"I would prefer that this announcement be postponed," one staffer wrote. "This is the first loan guarantee and we should have full review with all hands on deck to make sure we get it right."

With the groundbreaking just five days away, a senior OMB official took up the issue with Biden's domestic policy adviser, Terrell McSweeny: "We have ended up with a situation of having to do rushed approvals on a couple of occasions (and we are worried about Solyndra at the end of the week). We would prefer to have sufficient time to do our due diligence reviews and have the approval set the date for the announcement rather than the other way around."

It was not the first time staff members had raised their voices about Solyndra.

Solyndra had applied for the loan guarantee in December 2006 under a program authorized by the Energy Policy Act of 2005. Under the Bush administration, a technical review was completed in 2007, with Solyndra scoring 88 out of 100. While the project appeared to have merit, there were a number of concerns raised during further review as the Department of Energy's credit committee met to consider Solyndra's application in January 2009. The company's technology was "immature" compared to other solar technologies. Solyndra's prices were higher than the projected market prices. And an independent market analysis addressing the company's long-term prospects had yet to be conducted. In conclusion, the committee remanded the project to the loan program office for further study.

The next day, Lachlan Seward, a member of the committee, sent an e-mail to department staff: "After canvassing the committee it was the unanimous decision not to engage in further discussions with Solyndra at this time."

But six days after Obama's inauguration, the Department of Energy moved forward on the Solyndra deal. The new administration was eager to show progress on a program that had not made a single loan guarantee during the Bush administration. Making an announcement of at least a conditional commitment within sixty days of inauguration, according to Secretary Chu's stimulus adviser, would show that "the department is moving to address the urgent challenges in the economy."

As the deadline approached in March 2009, with plans for Obama to announce the Solyndra award in California, OMB staff expressed concerns about the process.

"If you guys think this is a bad idea, I need to unwind the WW QUICKLY," the vice president's chief of staff, Ron Klain, wrote, using an abbreviation for the West Wing.

Amid the discussions, one OMB staff member wrote, "This deal is NOT ready for prime time."

Then, in August 2009, a credit-rating agency hired to review the Solyndra came back with a troubling financial model, showing that the project would run out of cash in September 2011.

However high up these concerns appear to have reached, they didn't douse the enthusiasm on September 4, 2009, as the image of Vice President Biden beamed up on a giant video screen at the construction site for Solyndra's groundbreaking. Speaking via satellite, Biden applauded the company's innovations and dappled his speech with sun-themed quotations from Galileo and others.

"These jobs are going to be permanent jobs," Biden told the audience. "These are the jobs of the future. These are the green jobs.

These are the jobs that won't be exported. These are the jobs that are going to define the twenty-first century and the jobs that are going to allow America to compete and to lead like we did in the twentieth century."

After the speechmaking, the dignitaries grabbed their golden shovels and dug into a prearranged pile of soft tan dirt.

$ $ $

It was around this time that I got a call from Ed Neufeldt, the laid-off RV worker from Elkhart who had introduced Obama in the speech that launched the stimulus. Neufeldt had gotten a part-time job stocking the bread aisles at local supermarkets. It wasn't much, maybe $120 to $150 a week, but it felt good to be working again. But the main reason for his call was that he had some real exciting news. He had also been hired by an electric car company and was going to walk to Washington to promote green jobs.

"People have got to stop and look and think about how many people are without jobs," he told me. "Do you know how much we're in debt? Do you know how much money we pay for oil a day? This was in the paper—it's $1 billion a day. If we could just cut that in half, look how much money we could save in a year's time, if we had energy-efficient and electric cars and hybrid vehicles. We need to start doing things here instead of overseas."

"Look," he continued. "Obama—I disagree with some of his policies. But green jobs for America, who could disagree with that?"

TEN

JOBS, JOBS, JOBS

You know what work is—if you're
old enough to read this you know what
work is, although you may not do it.
Forget you. This is about waiting,
shifting from one foot to another.
—Philip Levine, "What Work Is"

EVER SINCE PRESIDENT OBAMA'S VISIT, the economic development
offices in Elkhart County had been buzzing with phone calls and
pitches from idea men. One company talked about solar panels. Another wanted to work with the landfill to turn tires into gas. A persistent salesman called the city again and again about a small unit that he
promised would replace every furnace or air conditioner in the world.
But when officials asked to see one, they never heard from him again.
Few ideas seemed serious or substantive. And little in the area's mood
or prospects seemed to change. Unemployment had gone down
slightly but still hovered around 17 percent.

After losing their home, the Gonyons moved into the Timber-
brook Mobile Home Park, a tree-shaded development laid out like a
misshapen sun, with a main circle shooting off into various dead-end
streets. The family rented a white, single-wide trailer at the end of
one next to the railroad tracks. With the move-in special for families
facing foreclosure, they paid $499 a month. It included three bed-
rooms, a narrow kitchen, and a small living area. Their oldest daughter had moved out, leaving three adults, six children, and two more

kids every other weekend. Terry and Desiree slept in the front bedroom, Desiree's mother had the back, and two daughters shared the last bedroom. The toddler slept with Desiree's mother while the next youngest slept with Terry and Desiree. The middle children, a boy and a girl, shared a walk-in closet. Rumors about children sleeping in closets prompted a visit from child welfare shortly after they moved in. But when the social worker saw that it was big enough to fit two toddler beds in addition to their clothes, she deemed it sufficient.

"I just basically told her it's either here or the homeless shelter," Terry said. "What would you rather have?"

Work was tight for Terry as it had been for Ed Neufeldt. The RV business had picked up a little. Navistar International, the commercial truck and engine maker, had purchased Monaco RV out of bankruptcy, including the factory in Wakarusa, rehiring several hundred workers. But the parking lot remained fairly empty. Neufeldt bet that just one in ten of his former coworkers was really back to work. Some of his buddies had been out so long they were now losing their homes. Neufeldt made do on his bread route, driving to the supermarkets in the morning and then again in the afternoon.

As Elkhart slogged through the bottom of the recession, there came an entrepreneur from California whom one local writer called "the Don Quixote of volts and vehicles."[1] The man's name was Wil Cashen and he had just started a company called the Electric Motors Corporation, which would design and engineer electric drive train systems that could be installed in light-duty pickup trucks to convert them into plug-in hybrids. Cashen had local roots. He had graduated from high school in nearby Mishawaka and set up shop in the old DeMartini RV dealership in Wakarusa, down the street from the Monaco plant, where more than a thousand had lost their jobs the year before. The company had applied for more than $300 million in federal grants and loans from the Department of Energy. It promised hundreds of jobs in the first year and about 1,600 by 2012.

At the company's ribbon-cutting in May 2009, Governor Mitch Daniels came up from Indianapolis to offer $4.6 million in tax credits and up to $200,000 in training grants if the company could meet its job targets. Cashen, wearing a mustard-colored shirt, a black suit, designer glasses, and a flat cap, held up a black-and-white photograph of a Studebaker electric automobile. He noted that northern Indiana had come full circle. Studebaker had manufactured electric vehicles in nearby South Bend in the early 1900s. More than a century later, his company would do the same. Electric Motors would partner with Gulf Stream Coach in nearby Nappanee to mass-produce the hybrid electric pickups. They would soon develop a prototype called the EMC Flash using a Ford F-150. It would get forty miles per gallon, and the company said its research indicated strongly that such an improvement would translate to nearly 200,000 sales in the first year.

"Years from now when somebody's child says, 'Daddy, what's this big recession of 2008–09 and how did we get out of it?'" Governor Daniels told the crowd, "those of us here today will say, 'Well, it all started on a day in May in Wakarusa.'"[2]

Cashen left an impression on nearly everyone he met. In addition to his trademark flat cap, he had a well-groomed composition of facial hair that consisted of a goatee, a soul patch, and pencil-thin L-shaped sideburns that connected to a Fu Manchu mustache. His confidence was contagious, and his brain seemed to contain a Wal-Mart of ideas. A conversation might start with the state of General Motors, veer to offshore drilling and the DeLorean sports car, and end with the life story of Nikola Tesla, an early visionary in commercial electricity. The first time I talked to Cashen, he warned me that his cell phone might ring two hundred times while we were talking.

Cashen, fifty-eight, grew up in Mishawaka, the son of a man who made Uniroyal fuel cells and a mother who worked at Nyloncraft, another automotive supplier. He joined the air force and quickly got in good with his base commander over their shared love of Porsches. When orders came for Cashen to deploy to Southeast Asia, he said, the commander tore them up and reassigned him to work on aircraft on a base in New Mexico. After college, he moved to Germany to work on racing teams, then to California to build sports cars. It was there, he said, in the early 1980s that he got involved with designing automotive electronics, trying to use new Apple personal computers to develop data acquisition tools for automobile manufacturing. He sold his business in the mid-1990s and retired to Malibu, where he built replicas of Porsche Spyders for movies and television shows and for celebrities like Jay Leno.

"Electric Motors Corporation was something I had been thinking about for a long time," Cashen told me. But the recession and the attention Obama was putting on electric vehicles called him home to Indiana. "When I came here, there were people really in real bad trouble, people who hadn't been in bad trouble at all, people who had worked real hard all their lives," he said.

After hearing Neufeldt speak at Electric Motors' ribbon-cutting, Cashen offered him a job as spokesman for Green Jobs for America, an organization promoting the benefits of electric vehicles and renewable energy around the country. Initially, the company was going to fly him to different cities, but it didn't have enough money. So Neufeldt suggested he walk to Washington. Neufeldt was a lifelong runner who meticulously tracked his mileage, estimating that he had run 33,000 miles in the last forty years. Cashen thought he was crazy. But a doctor checked Neufeldt out and said his lungs and heart were in good condition. Neufeldt would be followed by a motor home with solar panels on top so he could sleep at night in between walking and talking at shopping malls along the way. They even had a map drawn up. Neufeldt would start in Elkhart, walk south to Kokomo and Indianapolis, then east through Dayton, Columbus, Zanesville, and Wheeling. When he reached Pittsburgh, he would turn southeast, stopping in Somerset, Cumberland, and Hagerstown before ending his journey in the nation's capital. Meanwhile, Cashen continued to wow the community. He hired the local librarian as vice president of government affairs and delivered speeches at the city's Rotary and Lion's clubs. Thousands of people applied for jobs. In July, he hosted a "green summit" and christened the new headquarters with a bottle of champagne. In one of the funnier and perhaps more symbolic moments, Cashen struggled to smash the bottle against the building's columns several times, ultimately kneeling to break the bottle on the curb. Larry Thompson, the mayor of Nappanee, picked up the broken neck of the bottle, saying that he wanted to preserve it as a memento from that historic day.[3] It was as if the future of Elkhart and its surrounding towns rested on Cashen and Electric Motors. "It was a time where everybody was being let go. Monaco had closed. People obviously were looking for hope and this was a sign of it," said Dorinda Heiden-Guss, president of the Economic Development Corporation of Elkhart County. "People wanted to believe in his vision."

In August, word spread that President Obama was coming back to Elkhart. Specifically, he was going to Wakarusa to announce $2.4 billion in grants for advanced battery and electric vehicle manufacturing. In the diners and downtown stores, buzz swirled about Electric Motors. Cashen called Gulf Stream and had them bring over some motor homes. He hung a sign outside the building welcoming Obama. Wakarusa town leaders even had T-shirts with the company's logo made for the occasion.

But the big announcement, a surprise to local leaders who weren't invited, was for Navistar, the company that moved into the old Monaco RV plant down the road. Navistar received $39 million to build 400 electric delivery trucks.

"A few months ago, folks thought that these factories might be closed for good," Obama told the audience on the plant floor. "But now they're coming back to life."

Despite the excitement over Navistar, everyone in the Elkhart area kept coming back to Electric Motors. Where was its slice of the stimulus pie? "I was all excited. I thought they were coming to meet with us," Cashen said. But he vowed to press on. After all, there was still the pending application for a $70 million loan from the Energy Department. "I decided at that point we needed to be focused on the truck," he said. "We had to take the truck and get it on the road." Cashen constantly reassured the public that Electric Motors would be successful with or without the stimulus money.

On September 5, Electric Motors unveiled the EMC Flash at Green Jobs for America: An Entertainment and Education Exposition. The event showcased live bands throughout the day, leading up to a performance by The Byrds, the 1960s group known for the song "Turn! Turn! Turn!" At the appointed hour, the crowd circled around the truck on the showroom floor. Lights flashed and crews lifted the cover over the silver pickup. Cashen received a long round of applause and Mayor Thompson of Nappanee bestowed upon him a key to the city.

"The hope you have brought us," the mayor said, "can never be expressed in any key to the city."[4]

$ $ $

Hope. It had been a long time since people felt it.

Two days before the Electric Motors expo, Vice President Biden appeared at the Brookings Institution, a Washington think tank, to deliver a report card on the first two hundred days of the Recovery Act.

"In the first two hundred days, we were about necessity," Biden said. "The next two hundred days will be about possibilities."

Because of the Recovery Act, the administration was getting ready to guarantee loans for solar, wind, and geothermal projects. The new smart grid was coming. Rural areas would be wired with broadband so that ranchers could expand the market for their cattle, adults could take college courses online, and clinics could consult with specialists hundreds of miles away. America would be connected to a network of bullet trains exceeding 150 miles per hour and in some cases 240 miles per hour. One day soon, electric cars would get the equivalent of 200 miles per gallon and doctors would be able to access their patients' medical records on a computer instead of rifling through a file as thick as a phonebook.

Then, as he concluded the speech, Biden talked of the difference in what he had heard on the campaign trail and what he was hearing now from local officials, business people, union workers, and farmers.

"The most oft-heard remark," he said, "as we'd go by and in their towns . . . they'd say, 'Well, that used to be. That used to be. This used to be a steel mill. This town used to be the ceramic capital of America. This factory used to—used to employ 1,200 people. This company used to have their headquarters here.' The 'used to' was the most oft-heard phrase over the past two years when I was speaking to local officials. But because of the investments we're beginning to make and investments that's generating and some confidence that's beginning to build, I'm now hearing a different refrain—literally, not figuratively. Not everywhere. But I'm beginning to hear the refrain: 'This is going to be.' 'This is going to be a factory that makes super-efficient windows. This is going to be a place where we make batteries and drive trains for electric cars and get 220 miles equivalent to a gallon. This is going to be the hub of a new smart grid, harvesting energy from the Great Plains to light up the cities of the Midwest.'"

The significance of the speech was largely overlooked in the national press at the time. But by drawing the comparison between "used to be" and "going to be," Biden had eloquently cast the Recovery Act as the pivot point between America's industrial past and America's industrial future.

Soon after, the White House Council of Economic Advisers, in its first report to Congress on the stimulus, estimated that the plan had already created or saved more than a million jobs. The job market was still back breaking and heart breaking, having shed 3 million jobs since the plan was passed. But here, at last, was hope.

$ $ $

The reality was far more severe. The fall of 2009 saw the passing of two psychological milestones: 10,000 points on the Dow Jones Industrial Average and 10 percent unemployment. The jobless rate was at its worst since 1983. Counting those who had given up looking or settled for part-time work, the real unemployment rate was 17.5 percent. The average length of unemployment was now twenty-seven weeks. With the typical worker spending more than four months searching, it was now harder to find a job than at any other time since record-keeping began after World War II.

While any economist will tell you that the unemployment rate usually lags behind the stock market, the disconnect helped cement the idea that Obama's recovery plans benefited Wall Street while leaving Main Street behind. In addition, it sparked fears that America was headed for a jobless recovery, or even worse, a double-dip recession. Jobless recoveries, in which the economy expands while employment remains flat or continues to dip, followed the last two recessions in 1990–91 and in 2001, when the unemployment rate didn't return to normal for almost five years. A double-dip recession, shaped like a W, would surely leave the public with no other conclusion than that the administration's efforts had failed.

Calls for a second stimulus package (actually the third if you count the rebate checks issued by President Bush in 2008) grew increasingly louder. The debate generally divided on partisan lines with liberal Democrats on one side and conservatives and fiscal hawks on the other. The advocates for more included Warren Buffett, the labor unions, and Nobel Prize–winner and *New York Times* columnist Paul Krugman. But moderate Democrats, including advisers in the White House and crucial votes in Congress, took a wait-and-see approach. They noted that only 40 percent of the stimulus was out the door and that the engine would run through 2010 and 2011. Until unemployment breached 10 percent, Obama himself had maintained publicly that the Recovery Act should be given time to work.

But if anyone needed a more poignant illustration of how hard times endured, the scene at a Detroit convention center that October provided it. The city had opened the doors to distribute applications for a stimulus program to avoid foreclosure and prevent homelessness. With only 3,500 spots available, a crowd of 35,000 residents mobbed the Cobo Center downtown. People pushed and shoved. Fights broke out and some fainted. Others were nearly trampled, spurred on by personal desperation and the rumors of $3,000 stimulus checks.[5]

Even as the stimulus began to boost the economy, it was clear that the heels of the recession were dug in far deeper than the administration would admit. Making matters worse, some of the tax credits and safety net provisions from the stimulus were set to run out. If Congress failed to extend unemployment insurance, more than a million people would lose their benefits by the end of the year. Democrats moved to stop that from happening, but some Republicans in the Senate blocked it, yielding only when the parties agreed to expand tax breaks favoring home builders and big businesses. Those provisions cost nearly ten times as much as the unemployment extension. In November, Congress passed the $24 billion mini-stimulus with ease. It provided an additional fourteen weeks of jobless benefits for all workers and twenty weeks in states with high unemployment. With the extension in the Recovery Act, it was now possible to receive unemployment checks for up to ninety-nine weeks, nearly two years. With the first-time home buyer credit set to expire at the end of November,

Congress renewed the tax break through April. The credit was reduced from $8,000 to $6,500 but expanded to include any family, not just first-time home buyers, that earned less than $225,000 a year and had lived in their previous home for more than five years. Pushed by the business lobby, the bill also included a provision allowing companies to get immediate cash by using recent losses to recoup taxes paid in previous years. Under the stimulus, the program was available only to small businesses; now it was open to anyone.

Suddenly, Washington was a bazaar of stimulus ideas. In October, Obama had proposed sending a $250 check to all 57 million seniors, veterans, and people with disabilities who receive Social Security or other government assistance. The next week, Biden released a report on ways to encourage homeowners to fix up their properties and make them more energy efficient. A few days after that, Obama was back on the stump at a Maryland records warehouse announcing a plan to use bailout money to increase lending to small businesses. Also on the table was a plan to extend the 65 percent COBRA subsidy so that laid-off workers could keep their health insurance. The benefit included in the stimulus was set to expire, meaning anyone who lost their jobs in 2010 wouldn't qualify. All the talk about another stimulus also revived the idea for a jobs tax credit, which had foundered during the debate over the Recovery Act. Now the White House and Congress were developing several proposals to give businesses tax breaks worth thousands of dollars for every new employee.

In November, Obama convened his board of outside economic advisers to seek bold ideas to grow the economy. As in the meeting with his transition team nearly a year before, the president again asked advisers to think beyond the usual stimulus measures. The approaches were indeed innovative, focusing more on long-term incentives for the private sector than on a quick burst of government spending. General Electric CEO Jeffrey Immelt suggested a plan to promote exports in the developing world. John Doerr, the venture capitalist behind Google, Amazon, and now clean energy firms, pitched a program called Cash for Caulkers to encourage people to weatherize their homes. Richard Trumka of the AFL-CIO and Robert Wolf of the UBS investment bank discussed a long-term investment in infrastructure through a new transportation bill or a national infrastructure bank. Construction firms had been complaining that while the stimulus allowed them to retain their crews, they wouldn't begin hiring without more certainty. A national infrastructure bank, proposed by Obama during his presidential campaign, would combine public funding and private investment to finance large, regional projects like airports, rail, and power grid improvements, which are often ignored in the appropriation process. By setting up a merit system overseen by a panel of experts, an infrastructure bank could reform the current practice, in which planners think locally, agencies feel pressure to spread the money thin, and powerful lawmakers subvert professional analysis by doling out earmarks.

House Speaker Nancy Pelosi arranged meetings with economists and in mid-November announced that lawmakers would pass a new jobs bill by Christmas. Republicans seized on the news, suggesting that Democrats, consumed with the health care bill, were only now turning their attention to high unemployment. Pelosi repudiated that, saying, "The issue of jobs, jobs, jobs, jobs has been our mantra—jobs and deficit reduction."

Despite the flurry of ideas, inside the White House, the economic team was deadlocked about how to achieve both.

$ $ $

By now, Christina Romer, the head of the Council of Economic Advisers, had come to terms with the fact that the stimulus was smaller than her models suggested was necessary. At $800 billion, they had gone as high as was politically practical. She had accepted that her initial projections of a stimulus keeping unemployment under 8 percent were optimistic. After clashing heatedly with Larry Summers, she had demanded and earned her place at the table and had gained confidence in asserting her viewpoints.

"I had to throw an elbow or two to make sure I wasn't going to be marginalized," she said. "Anyone who knows Larry knows that he can be frustrating, cocky, and incredibly opinionated. He is also brilliant and you can persuade him with good evidence."

None of her early missteps left Romer with any serious regrets. But the period when the trajectory of the economy clearly showed that more needed to be done, yet the White House failed to act, has troubled her most since leaving Washington.

"My biggest regret was that we didn't do more," she said. "As good as the Recovery Act was, we were going to need more. My regret is that in that fall of 2009, we didn't get a second chunk of some important stimulus actions. The economy needed it and I think that would have made a difference."

The economic team was now meeting roughly twice a week to come up with a plan. Yes, unemployment was 10 percent. But the deficit was expected to be $1.4 trillion this year and $9 trillion over the next decade. How could they stimulate the job market while tackling the deficit? Should they do a jobs tax credit? More aid to struggling states? A discretionary spending freeze? Infrastructure was popular and bipartisan, but the Recovery Act showed that even in the best of possible circumstances, it was painstakingly slow. If they pushed more jobs measures, should they do them incrementally? Or all at once, which could lead to assertions that the administration was trying to ram through a second stimulus, which by now had become Republican shorthand for "tax and spend"?

Watching the economy continue to deteriorate, Romer started agitating for more action. A scholar of the Depression, she was worried about repeating the errors of 1937, when Roosevelt pulled back, sending a recovery back into a recession. To simplify her argument, she used the metaphor of a patient who despite beginning to take medicine saw his symptoms get worse. "Do you decide that the medicine is useless? Do you conclude the antibiotic caused the infection to get worse?" she asked in one speech. "Surely not. You probably conclude that the illness was more serious than you and the doctor thought and are very glad you saw the doctor and started taking the medicine when you did."

"It is as if," she continued, "when you went to the doctor for that strep throat, he discovered you had high blood pressure as well. The antibiotic was great for the infection, but he prescribed other medicine, a better diet, and a good dose of exercise for the blood pressure."

If ever the stars aligned for another large stimulus package, now was the time. The recent bill extending unemployment benefits and the home buyer credit had passed 98 to 0 in the Senate and 403 to 12 in the House. From April when Senator Arlen Specter switched parties until January when Scott Brown won Ted Kennedy's old seat, the Democrats had a filibuster-proof sixty-vote majority—the first time since the 1970s. Every member of Congress regardless of stripe faced pressure from their constituents to do something about the scarcity of jobs.

But Peter Orszag, the budget director, doubted the politics were as favorable as the numbers suggested. The key to getting more stimulus measures passed was moderate senators like Kent Conrad of North Dakota and Mark Warner of Virginia.

"They lacked a storyline on the deficit," Orszag told me. "There was no way they were going to do another round of stimulus. Zero. Dead as a doorknob without some story to tell on out-year deficits."

While the anger of Tea Party forces had yet to manifest itself in a major election, there was rising pressure among moderate Republicans and swing-state Democrats to limit spending. Many stimulus measures that attracted bipartisan support a year earlier were becoming taboo as a result of politics.

Nor could the administration ignore the deficit. While the deficit had more to do with the Bush tax cuts and prescription drug plan than the stimulus package, it was ultimately unsustainable. And it could hinder America's recovery onto a firmer foundation. If the government continued to borrow money, it would compete with private investors, causing interest rates to rise and making it harder for businesses to hire and expand. Moreover, it would force future workers to be reliant on foreign creditors.

Rather than finding common ground, the economic team became mired in endless discussions over stimulus versus deficit. Every time Romer suggested stimulus, Orszag talked about the deficit. And every time Orszag suggested a discretionary spending freeze, Romer warned of repeating 1937.

"Looking back on it now, I think the people who wanted more stimulus made a tactical mistake because they decided that they were going to fight anything involving an out-year deficit reduction," Orszag said. "I believe that the combination of out-year deficit reduction and additional short-term stimulus was not only the right policy mix but was a more auspicious way to get the short-term stimulus. We should have said more forcefully we have to do more of both."

Failing to bridge the divide was Larry Summers, who remained a contentious figure in the administration. The job of National Economic Council director was to coordinate economic policy advice for the president, to be a cohesion builder, a team leader, and an honest broker. That didn't fit with Summers's skill set, some economic advisers felt. Rahm Emanuel, the chief of staff, was exceptional at fast-paced power brokering in Congress and the media, but he lacked the amicability and coolness for slow-moving policy debates. Absent from the Obama administration was a senior statesman who could arbitrate disputes and lead to cloture. So instead of a clean-looking process as in the Bush administration or a chaotic process leading to successful policy as in the Clinton administration, Obama's team suffered from a messy process leading nowhere. Meanwhile, the administration was juggling the health care bill, which occupied much of the advisers' time. There was little appetite for a big spending proposal with health care pending, and the intense focus elsewhere allowed economic advisers to go round and round in endless policy debates. While potentially landmark, health care reform shifted the public debate away from jobs, highlighting partisan differences at a time of potential compromise.

$ $ $

While the White House struggled to create more jobs, it was also having problems counting the ones it already had. At the end of October, the Recovery Accountability and Transparency Board released its first batch of reports from recipients of stimulus money. It was a historic transparency effort. Not only did the White House promise to create and save 3.5 million jobs, it was also going to open the books and prove it. But counting jobs was never going to be as easy as lining up work crews and tapping hardhats. Unlike the Works Progress Administration, in which the government paid the workers directly, the projects were being completed by tens of thousands of construction firms, schools, nonprofits, state agencies, and small businesses.

Nearly two-thirds of the $800 billion was being spent on things like tax cuts, food stamps, unemployment checks, and Medicaid. Those would eventually lead to jobs as families spent more money at the grocery store, health clinic, or shopping mall, but it was nearly impossible to count them. It would also be difficult to count the residual effect among suppliers and in communities where a worker could now afford to take his family out to dinner on Saturday nights. So the Council of Economic Advisers came up with a model accounting for changes in gross domestic product and unemployment statistics. By the end of 2009, they estimated that the Recovery Act was responsible for somewhere between 1.5 million and 2 million jobs. Asked whether the various job numbers would undermine the administration's credibility, White House press secretary Robert Gibbs told reporters, "We're not worried about whatever discrepancy it is you're trying to make into a much bigger story." He may have spoken too soon.

When the Recovery Board posted more than 100,000 stimulus reports on its website, it announced the number of jobs with amazing precision: 640,329. About 325,000 were teachers and support staff who would have been laid off otherwise while 80,000 were in the construction industry, White House officials said. Ed DeSeve, the vice president's administrator for the Recovery Act, said he had been "scrubbing" reports so hard that he had "dishpan hands and my fingers are worn to the nub."[6]

Almost immediately though, reporters and auditors spotted errors. A flu vaccine manufacturer reported receiving a contract for $1.4 billion when it was really $10.4 million. A Colorado call center hired to help with the digital television conversion listed 4,200 jobs. But most of those jobs were five weeks or less.[7] The number should have been 635. The California auditor rapped the state corrections department for reporting 18,000 jobs rather than the 5,000 officers who had received layoff notices before the stimulus came in. A shoe store owner in Kentucky reported saving 9 jobs with just $900 when he actually supplied the Army Corps of Engineers with nine pairs of boots.[8] Some contractors counted part-time work as full time. Head Start preschools reported pay raises as jobs. Others simply listed all of their employees.

There was also a significant degree of undercounting. More than 9,000 projects, including some that were already completed, were listed as not creating any jobs. Chrysler received a $53 million contract to build 3,000 government vehicles but listed zero jobs because it used existing employees to fill the orders. Thousands of recipients didn't file reports at all, many of them blaming technical glitches on the government's website. The Louisiana Department of Social Services, for example, failed to report $65 million in grants. A spokesman told me that the agency had a problem with its registration number and tried for months to resolve the issue with the Recovery Board help desk, the White House, and the IRS. A town clerk in tiny Blue Ridge, Georgia, tried to file a report on rural water loans, but the computer system bounced it back while she was out sick with swine flu. Reports from the entire government of American Samoa were missing; the White House gave them a blanket waiver when the island was struck by a tsunami.

Obama called the data errors "a side issue," but the problems soon became political dynamite that dominated cable television for weeks. Congressman David Obey, an architect of the stimulus package, released a statement calling the inaccuracies "outrageous" and "ludicrous." "Credibility counts in government and stupid mistakes like this undermine it," he said.

The issue boiled over in a congressional hearing in late November, in which Congressman Darrell Issa trotted out the *Oxford English Dictionary* definition of "propaganda" on an overhead screen. Earl Devaney, the head of the Recovery Board and the government's chief stimulus watchdog, agreed that the numbers couldn't be verified. "The data reported was riddled with inaccuracies and contradictions," he testified. In reality, the mistakes on Recovery.gov were minor. All government databases have flaws, and the stimulus reports were fairly clean in comparison, especially when you consider that the data was inputted by thousands of people and posted almost immediately.

"You and the American public are now seeing what agencies have seen internally for years," Devaney said. "And what we are all seeing, at least following this first reporting period, is not particularly pretty. This raw form, unsanitized data may cause embarrassment for some agencies and recipients. But my expectation is that any embarrassment suffered will encourage self-correcting behavior and lead to better reporting in the future."

Obama made light of job-counting errors in his traditional Thanksgiving pardon, saying, "All told, I believe it's fair to say that we have saved or created four turkeys." But it wasn't so easily dismissed. Around the same time, a New Mexico blogger wrote that some of the stimulus reports listed congressional districts that didn't exist, including New Mexico's thirty-fifth. (The state has only three.) His post led to an overplayed but viral gotcha implying that the Obama administration was sending money to fake congressional districts and losing track of the funds, neither of which was true. The money went to real stimulus projects in real congressional districts. It was a simple data error requiring a simple data fix. But that didn't stop Fox News and other conservative media outlets from playing it up.

$ $ $

The reports provided the first inside look at the stimulus package, documenting detailed purchases from lab rats for research projects to business breakfasts at Fuddruckers. One of the biggest winners was the Savannah River nuclear site in Aiken, South Carolina. By November, the cleanup had already created and saved 2,295 jobs. About two-thirds of the jobs were new while the others were jobs that would have been eliminated without the stimulus money. The impact on the local economy was evident. Since the Recovery Act work started, unemployment in Aiken County had dipped from 10.2 percent to 8.5 percent in a matter of months. All the while, the national jobless rate was going in the opposite direction. To put a face on the numbers, the Department of Energy released a video in which several new hires told their stories of unemployment, sometimes fighting back tears as they recounted their struggles to provide for their families and hold on to their homes. The job fairs that summer had been mobbed. And to expand their reach into rural areas, the site managers bought a van and painted it with the Recovery Act logo. Workers hit the road, teaching residents how to create resumes and search for jobs and training.

But as soon as the big money arrived at Savannah River, problems began to surface one after another. In August, workers were draining a nitric acid line to decommission a chemical building. A worker brushed against a drill bit in a draining device, which mechanically failed, spilling about a quart of acid on him and two other workers. He grabbed the drill bit with his gloved hand and pushed it back in to stop the leak, suffering third-degree burns in the process. Another worker had acid splash behind his face shield. The three were taken to a hospital burn center while several others were treated on site. Investigators blamed the contractor, Savannah River Nuclear Solutions, for failing to foresee such hazards and making the accident worse with its poor response planning. Workers didn't have a clear path to evacuate, and emergency wash stations were too far away. All stimulus work at the site was stopped as Savannah River Nuclear Solutions issued a time-out to refocus attention on safety.

Around the same time, the Savannah River citizens advisory board questioned the Department of Energy's selection of low-priority projects while ignoring the site's greatest environmental threat. Left over from the Cold War were forty-nine underground tanks each storing nearly a million gallons of liquid nuclear waste. Built in the 1950s, some of the tanks had leaked over the years, and the infrastructure was aging. So the department shifted about $200 million from Savannah River Nuclear Solutions to another contractor at the site.

Within the Department of Energy, pressure to manage the vast influx of stimulus money led to infighting between the federal managers at the site and the Recovery Act managers in Washington. The problems came to light in September 2009 when a whistleblower filed an anonymous complaint alleging political interference by Congressman Jim Clyburn and misconduct by Cynthia Anderson, who oversaw the nuclear cleanup under the Recovery Act.

The employee told investigators that Anderson had directed contractors to hold job fairs in Clyburn's district, ordered them to hire specific people, and orchestrated a $9 million payment to historically black colleges and universities, long a key issue of Clyburn's, in exchange for something in return. At one meeting, the employee said, they were told to stop holding job fairs in Aiken County and to conduct more in counties represented by Clyburn.

Then, within months of receiving the Recovery Act money, the Energy Department shuffled its supervisors, announcing that it was removing the site manager, Jeff Allison, and assigning him to a new position. Almost immediately, questions arose about whether Allison and others were being moved as retaliation for cooperating in the internal investigation about Anderson and Clyburn. In an e-mail, Allison said the statement about his new assignment was "full of untruths" and that he had been pressured to "go along with this detail and put a positive spin on it to my staff and stakeholders." "This announcement continues to demonstrate the hostile work environment and now retaliation I am undergoing," he wrote.[9]

Allison had managed the site for six and half years and was popular and well respected in the community. While jobs in the federal nuclear complex were often transitory, Allison and his family had made a home in Aiken. The *Aiken Standard*, the local newspaper, bemoaned the sorry state of affairs, noting that Savannah River "has seen more public drama unveiled in the past few months than in more than a half a century before."[10] The pinnacle of the vitriol came when the director of stimulus work at the site claimed that a contracting officer had threatened to shoot him.

The inspector general's office interviewed eighty current and former employees and analyzed more than 150,000 e-mails. The extensive review didn't substantiate the allegation that Anderson had arranged for some of the stimulus money to go to historically black colleges as a quid pro quo. The issues of whether Anderson steered job fairs and directed hiring were inconclusive. "We received testimony which supported aspects of the allegations," the final report said. "However, other witnesses provided contradictory testimony." Some senior managers and contractor officials asserted that they were directed to hold job fairs in certain counties. Other federal and contractor officials disputed that. Some claimed they were told whom to hire while others said there was no such direction. "Witnesses' testimony was conflicting and irreconcilable," the report said. "Perceptions, interpretations, and recollections of these events as well as views on the intent of the individuals involved varied dramatically."

Clyburn told me he was proud of his efforts to secure stimulus money for the cleanup and to ensure that jobs helped communities in economic distress. That was his job as a congressman. "I never asked anybody down at the Savannah River plant to hire anybody. I never asked Cynthia Anderson to do anything. She never asked me to do anything," he said. "Nothing like that ever happened in my presence and nothing like that ever happened at my direction."

What investigators were able to conclude, though, was that the situation at Savannah River was out of hand. It boiled down to "an unusual level of distrust and acrimony," a turf battle between Aiken and Washington as the flood of stimulus money, and the tight deadlines that accompanied it, frayed everyone's nerves. Witnesses got highly personal in interviews and described their colleagues in derogatory terms. They raised issues about racism and reverse discrimination. The inspector general said that the heated atmosphere threatened to undermine the credibility and public confidence in the site's stimulus work.

Some people like Manuel Bettencourt, chairman of the Savannah River citizens advisory board, were skeptical of the report's failure to reach a conclusion on many allegations. "The IG tried to straddle the fence and didn't come out with a strong finding as was warranted," he told me. But Jim Giusti, the Energy Department's spokesman at the site, said the dispute was mostly a matter of personality conflicts and a lack of communication. "A lot of it was pressure to get a plan that had a really good defined schedule and control parts done," he said. "We started off crawling and running at the same time."

$ $ $

In Elkhart, things were not going well for the Electric Motors Corporation. Six months had passed and not a dime of stimulus money had come through. Management was getting frustrated with Cashen and his never-ending stockpot of projects. The planned partnership with Gulf Stream Coach fell apart as Cashen's dreams never came to fruition. Electric Motors scrapped the walk to Washington to promote green jobs, and Neufeldt now spent most of his work hours mopping the showroom floor.

"I always had a dream about running across the United States," Neufeldt told me. "That really kind of disappointed me when that happened because I was just really looking forward to that—and oh man, we told everybody! We even told NBC News."

Cashen bristled when he thought of how the stimulus had played out. Navistar was a large, profitable company while his was a startup. While the stimulus was about American manufacturing jobs, Navistar's plans called for using Modec trucks made in the United Kingdom. "I was bummed. I was like jeez! More than anything, it's been confusing," he said. "All you hear is American, American, American, and all you get out of it is 50 percent is going to a foreign country."

Cashen said all the attention surrounding the stimulus money hurt the startup's ability to garner private investment. By picking winners and losers, he said, the Obama administration created the perception that "if they didn't give them the money, there's something wrong with that company." In the days before Obama's visit, Electric Motors' stock price had doubled in value. Within days, the stock crashed from $16 per share to $1.

But many in Elkhart and the surrounding areas were skeptical. The project appeared to be heavily dependent on stimulus money. Dick Moore, the mayor of Elkhart, said the Obama administration recognized that Navistar was a company with trucks all over the world while Electric Motors was still a concept. "So where did the money go? Instead of going to Electric Motors, it went to Navistar, and the next thing you know, Wil Cashen is put out by his own board," he said. "I don't know whether it was just a dream, an invention, just a concept, but so far there's been nothing that's come out of it. I think everybody has questions, and there don't seem to be any answers."

Citing a loss of focus, the company removed Cashen as CEO, locked up the old RV dealership that had served as its headquarters, and laid off its remaining staff. With only his bread route, Neufeldt was back on unemployment. "I think Wil feels like he let everybody down," he said. "I still think if we had gotten that stimulus money that Navistar got, we could have really done something." With Cashen out, Electric Motors hired a veteran of General Motors to serve as president and moved the company twenty miles south to Plymouth, Indiana. Cashen remained in the area, pursuing various ideas including a training school for electric vehicles. Electric Motors was never heard from again.

$ $ $

As the end of 2009 approached, the White House economic team was still struggling to come up with a plan that would balance jobs and the deficit. Advisers from the Treasury Department were excited about the potential for a new jobs tax credit. But anytime the economic team asked a businessperson, he or she confided that it probably wouldn't affect behavior. Without demand, there would still be little reason to hire more workers.

With the national unemployment rate now over 10 percent, many wondered if a new federal jobs program was necessary. The WPA had put millions to work and the historical pictures lingered in people's minds as a stark contrast to the view of the Recovery Act. More recently, Presidents Nixon and Carter had launched public jobs programs though to a lesser effect. The math seemed simple. For about $50 billion, minus benefits and materials, the administration could hire 3 million people at minimum wage for a year and make a serious dent in the unemployment rate.

The idea gained little traction within the White House. Aside from the cries of socialism it would generate, economic advisers felt it would be far more complicated and costly to implement than advocates envisioned. In a book written when he was at the labor-oriented Economic Policy Institute, Jared Bernstein had favored government jobs programs not only in a downturn but also as a limited way to lift up extremely disadvantaged groups of people. But addressing the think tank's plan in his new role, Bernstein questioned its effect. Did cities and states really have enough shovel-ready projects? Could they create jobs that wouldn't compete with the private sector? Would the projects be more than make-work and actually provide some lasting value?

"There's not a lot of political appetite for direct government job creation," Bernstein told me. "The idea that there should be another WPA or something makes sense on paper, but it's actually quite hard to convince policy makers and even economists that that kind of thing can work today. But we got as close as you could get."

The stimulus package included a $5 billion emergency fund for needy families that could be used to immediately create jobs for the unemployed. But few states were taking advantage of it. Where it was being used, the money had dramatic effect. In Perry County, Tennessee, where an auto parts factory had moved its operations to Mexico, the state used $5 million to create jobs clearing brush for the highway department, painting murals, even baking turnovers at a local pie factory. The work helped cut unemployment from 25 percent in the spring of 2009 to 18 percent by that November. Los Angeles County used $160 million to put together a jobs program intent on employing 10,000 people. But many states balked, fearing that they couldn't afford the requirement to put up 20 percent of the costs. One of them was Louisiana, where one in five residents lived in poverty, the second-highest rate in the nation. "We're in an almost crisis level budget situation," reasoned Sammy Guillory, deputy assistant secretary of Louisiana's Office of Family Support. "We're facing budget cuts and staff reductions every day. So even to start a program is not an option right now."[11]

Despite the assistance provided in the Recovery Act, states remained in fiscal stress. The recession had led to a free fall in tax collections, and states struggled to figure out how to hold on to teachers and maintain Medicaid programs. The stimulus would continue to provide support for another year, but most states would begin planning in early 2010 for the 2011 fiscal year that would start in July. Combined, they faced a budget gap of about $180 billion, a situation that could cost the economy 900,000 jobs, according to the Center on Budget and Policy Priorities.

Unemployed workers also faced a funding cliff. While Congress had extended benefits for up to twenty weeks, it still hadn't renewed the emergency compensation program under the Recovery Act. That meant anyone who had lost their job since July would see their unemployment checks run out at the start of the year. More than one million would be affected if Congress didn't act. Laid-off workers would see their COBRA health insurance increase hundreds of dollars a month if their stimulus subsidy ran out. A year after the bank bailout, small businesses still struggled to get credit.

The pressure was growing. As Obama prepared to embark on a trade mission to Asia, he announced that the White House would host a jobs forum in December to gather ideas from CEOs, small business owners, economists, nonprofits, and labor unions on how to create jobs and spur economic growth. While great for public relations, a jobs forum would do nothing if Obama's economic team couldn't agree on a plan.

In one budget meeting in December, the discussion devolved into another round of what Summers had begun to call "relitigation roulette." The advisers had already agreed that the president would announce a discretionary spending freeze and move forward with plans for a deficit commission. But here they were again arguing the economic merits.

Frustrated, Obama lost his cool. "We can't keep going around in circles here," he scolded them.

Meanwhile, Democratic leaders in the House were laying the planks for a major jobs package. But Senate leaders said it would have to wait. First, they had to move the boulder of a health care bill that they had been straining like Sisyphus with for months. While Obama's push for an overhaul stole attention from the immediate needs of a recession, for the White House economic team it eventually became an icebreaker for moving the talks forward. Romer and Orszag agreed that reining in health care costs was one of the biggest things they could do for the long-term deficit. And by using the reform to reassure deficit hawks, it opened some space for additional jobs measures.

"To the degree that we could fight hard for cost containment in health care," Romer told me, "it helped us to worry less about the deficit and feel more comfortable doing more things on jobs."

$ $ $

The White House jobs summit came to order at 1:31 P.M. on December 3 in the auditorium of the French Second Empire–style Eisenhower Executive Office Building. Labor secretary Hilda Solis opened the conference with brief remarks. Then they played a video about a bakery and a small green technology firm in Allentown, Pennsylvania, where the president would travel the following day. Vice President Biden gave the now customary defense of the Recovery Act, how it had pulled the economy from the brink, and added that the best was yet to come with high-speed rail, broadband, and the Race to the Top education program.

President Obama spoke next noting that despite the progress, businesses were still skittish about hiring. "And so that's the question that we have to ask ourselves today: How do we get businesses to start hiring again?" he said. "I want to hear from CEOs about what's holding back our business investment and how we can increase confidence and spur hiring. And if there are things that we're doing here in Washington that are inhibiting you, then we want to know about it."

After the president's remarks, the summit broke up into six sessions focusing on infrastructure, small businesses, green jobs, exports, public-private partnerships, and training workers for the jobs of the future. The White House had invited about 130 participants ranging from the AARP to Xerox. Guests included the CEOs of Boeing, Disney, FedEx, and AT&T, and the mayors of Detroit, Des Moines, Fresno, and San Antonio. The breakout sessions included a diverse mix of voices. Seated around one conference table might be the CEO of Google, the mayor of Allentown, the head of the plumbers and pipe fitters' union, a Southern California florist, and Joseph Stiglitz, the Nobel-winning economist.

It was a historic series of salons reminiscent of the coffeehouses of the colonial era. For three and a half hours, some of the greatest minds in the country came together to hash out America's greatest problems. One of the more interesting exchanges came in the infrastructure session when Gerard Arpey, the CEO of American Airlines, put forward a plan to modernize America's antiquated air traffic control system. While the government committed to investing in the broader infrastructure, the airlines had been urging for federal help to pay for the avionics that planes need to communicate with the system.

"It takes longer today to fly from New York to Boston than it did in the 1940s," Arpey said.

Dan DiMicco of Nucor steel jumped in. "At some point in time, the government has got to get out of paying for all these things," he said. Airlines should put up their own money for equipment, he added, and if they can't afford it, find a way to pass along costs to passengers.

Obama dropped in on two breakout sessions, clean energy and infrastructure. In the latter, a dozen participants were seated around a wooden oval table in the Secretary of War suite. The chairman of the Norfolk Southern railway was discussing the idea for a national infrastructure bank when the door creaked and in came the commander in chief.

After listening to various views, Obama nodded to the tension between high speed and high return, admitting "the term 'shovel-ready'—let's be honest here—doesn't always live up to its billing."

The attendees didn't shy away from disagreements as in the energy forum when General Wesley Clark, the former presidential candidate and now pitchman for the ethanol industry, made a case for biofuels, and Columbia University economist Jeff Sachs called ethanol a "disaster." Sachs said Cash for Clunkers failed the cost test miserably. And he riled up Leo Gerard of the United Steelworkers when he said short-term strategies weren't sufficient.

"You ought to come where I am," Gerard shot back. "They're pissed off. There's things we can do right now that would start putting people back to work."

Republican arguments about the impact of regulations and the corporate tax rate got their airing. And when it came time for the closing question-and-answer session, participants didn't hold back from responding to Obama's initial challenge: How do we get businesses to start hiring again? Fred Lampropoulos of Merit Medical Systems, a Utah-based medical device manufacturer, raised a common criticism of the administration.

"One of the overriding thoughts in our forum was that there's uncertainty," he said, "that there's such an aggressive legislative agenda that businesspeople don't really know what they ought to do."

Obama didn't dodge or get defensive but rather agreed that it was a legitimate concern. He explained during the transition he had thought heavily about this argument that he should put off big initiatives and wait for the economy to stabilize. "But I think the response is," he continued, "that if we keep on putting off tough decisions about health care, about energy, about education, we'll never get to the point where there's a lot of appetite for that."

Here at last was the cooperative tenor that Americans hoped Obama would bring when they sent him to the Oval Office. To be sure, House Republican leader John Boehner countered with a round-table on the Democrats' "job-killing agenda," and former Speaker Newt Gingrich was holding his own jobs summit in Cincinnati. But for an afternoon, people of varying viewpoints abandoned the partisan Beltway bickering, avoided the echo chamber, and got down to business.

For Christina Romer, it was a week filled with moments of exhilaration. After months at loggerheads, the White House economic team was finally moving forward with a plan. Earlier that week, she was allowed to write her first op-ed in a national newspaper, defending the stimulus package in the *Wall Street Journal* and announcing the administration's strategy on jobs. Now, with the summit, Washington was getting serious about additional stimulus, and a repeat of 1937 seemed ever more unlikely.

That evening brought even more good news. The Labor Department was releasing its monthly employment numbers the next morning, and as usual Romer received an advance copy of the report. Wall Street had been expecting a loss of 130,000 jobs. But the number in front of her was 11,000. After months of staggering job losses, the bleeding had nearly stopped. Normally, the Council of Economic Advisers would type up a memo for the president, explaining the report. But this night called for something different.

Romer's secretary called over to the Oval Office.

"Does the president have a moment for Christina to come by?" the secretary asked.

Romer walked over to the West Wing and showed Obama the Labor Department report. They had done it. Four times Obama hugged her in front of the Christmas tree. Rahm Emanuel, his chief of staff, came in and could tell that it was good news. When told, he gave the president a fist-bump.

"That was the first time when it looked like, God, we could actually be getting to the end of job losses," Romer recalled. "And that was an amazing feeling that the thing that had just been so horrible might be abating."

America appeared to be heading for a V-shaped recovery. In the weeks ahead, the president would deliver a major speech on the economy, calling for more investments in infrastructure, small business, and clean energy, foreshadowing the themes of his State of the Union address. The House would pass a $150 billion Jobs for Main Street bill. Congress would extend unemployment checks and COBRA health insurance by attaching them to a defense bill.

The next day, Obama was off to Allentown, Pennsylvania, a steel city fossilized by Billy Joel as a place where "they're closing all the factories down." "Every child had a pretty good shot," Joel sang, "to get at least as far as their old man got. / But something happened on the way to that place. / They threw an American flag in our face." The lyrics resonated. Here was the president on his crusade to make amends for decades of detrimental policy and revive the American dream for the blue-collar middle class.

The work wasn't over. But standing there next to the Christmas tree, Romer basked in the achievements of the past year and the potential for the year ahead. This was the progress she hoped for at the meeting in Chicago the year before. This was why on election night she danced in the Oakland streets. This was what she came to Washington to do.

"December 3 was about the best day of my life," Romer said. "It was one of those days that is seared in your memory as maybe we've accomplished something and really are going to do something very good for the American people."

PART 3

REINVESTMENT

ELEVEN

THE GREEN ECONOMY

*A generation from now, this solar heater can either be a curiosity, a
museum piece, an example of a road not taken—or it can be just a
small part of one of the greatest and most exciting adventures ever
undertaken by the American people; harnessing the power from the
sun to enrich our lives as we move away from our crippling dependence on foreign oil.*

— President Jimmy Carter upon the installation of solar panels
on the White House in June 1979

THE HEADQUARTERS OF SOLYNDRA is located off Interstate 880 and
its angular black-glass building cuts against the rolling hills behind it.
Combined with the yellow Solyndra logo with the "O" in the shape of
a sun, the factory was filled with an aura that this was a path to a
hopeful future when I visited in the fall of 2010. Solyndra's assembly
line was almost entirely automated. The solar panel began as a rack
of long glass tubes, which were inspected and cleaned by an orange
robot, which passed them to another orange robot to stack in trays.
After that, the tubes were coated with a thin film of copper indium
gallium diselenide (CIGS), a solution that is less efficient but potentially cheaper than crystalline silicon cells, which currently dominate
the solar market.

When that was done, a dishwasher-size robot picked up the tray of
tubes and, guided by a magnetic path in the floor, delivered it to the
next station. As the robot worked, it tooted along like an ice cream

truck playing a carnival calliope song. The music was the technicians' way to alert their coworkers that the otherwise quiet robots were coming their way. During the winter, they programmed them to play Christmas carols.

"Everybody loves the robots," said Dave Miller, a corporate spokesman. "Except the Secret Service. When the president was here, they had to shut them down. They were not a big fan of these things coming at him randomly."

The robot carried the trays to a special green-tinted room, where a laser etched the photovoltaic cells onto the glass tubes. The finished tubes were then transported to a back-end facility, where they were inserted into an outer tube and filled with an "optical coupling agent," which enhanced the sunlight and protected the cells. The tubes were then hermetically sealed and underwent a flash test to ensure the individual energy output of each tube.

Machine operators moved around the factory floor wearing hairnets, hardhats, goggles, lab coats, and blue covers over their shoes. Throughout the process, they monitored thousands of points of performance data, measuring things like coating thickness and wattage, looking for ways to make production more efficient. At one station, two technicians hovered over sixteen computer monitors showing various line graphs and flow charts.

But despite the high-tech appearance, at one stop on the tour, a pair of technicians could be seen trying to fix a jam in one of the machines with a broomstick.

Solyndra was founded in 2005 by Chris Gronet, a veteran of the semiconductor industry who had worked on solar as a student at Stanford University. With expertise in both areas, Gronet came up with the concept for a tubular solar panel and began testing it at the National Renewable Energy Laboratory in Colorado. While the prototype was the size of a thermometer or pencil, the modules were now the size of those long fluorescent lightbulbs found in office ceilings. Each solar panel contained forty tubes spaced about an inch apart so that it looked like a giant grilling rack or the frame for a cot.

After qualifying the design, Solyndra moved to its Fab 1 manufacturing facility in 2006 and started production in 2007. The company expanded quickly. In 2008, Solyndra produced 1.6 megawatts worth of panels. The following year, it had ramped up to 30 megawatts. And by 2010, it was producing 80 megawatts a year. Very early, though, Solyndra realized that its success would come by expanding its assembly line to lower the cost of production. So when Congress authorized the renewable energy loan program in 2005, it was one of the first firms to apply. The first phase of the factory, which would open in late 2010, was expected to provide enough energy to power the equivalent of 24,000 homes a year. Over its lifetime, the government said, the electricity generated could equal that of three or four coal-fired power plants.

Solyndra's panels had been installed on commercial rooftops across the country from a cinema in Livermore, California, to the Anheuser-Busch brewery outside Newark Liberty International Airport in New Jersey. But more than 75 percent of its business was overseas. Its strongest market was in Germany, where generous incentives had spurred the demand for solar.

"Germany really makes no sense for solar," Miller explained. "If you look at where it is latitudewise, it's even with Maine or Nova Scotia. So by creating a favorable feed-in tariff over there, they've created an industry. They've created hundreds of thousands of jobs and become the world leader in solar."

Solar power has been around since ancient times when, according to the Energy Department, Greeks and Romans used mirrors to light torches and positioned houses toward the sun to heat rooms. Modern solar cells were developed in the 1950s at Bell Labs in New Jersey. As recently as the mid-1990s, nearly half the world's solar panels were made in the United States. But by the time the stimulus energy provisions took effect, the United States made up less than 10 percent of the worldwide solar capacity, and much of the production now occurred in China.

"Unfortunately, we kind of trained the rest of the world how to do all this stuff," Miller said. "We always thought America's going to be the innovation capital. Nobody else could figure out how to innovate things. Well, the reality is other countries can. And they've figured out if they subsidize it, the clean-tech industry will come to them."

Solyndra's promise rested on its innovative design. According to the company, the glass tubes could capture not only direct sunlight but also the sun's diffused rays and any light reflected from the roof. That made its model attractive to building owners who were also seeking the tax credit for a cool white roof. Traditional solar panels are flat and have to be tilted on a track throughout the day to capture the maximum sunlight. They also have to be spaced far enough apart to avoid creating shadows that would block the other panels. Tubular panels didn't have to be moved and could be arranged close together. The design also allowed wind to pass through, meaning that the panels didn't have to be bolted to the roof like traditional solar panels.

But much about Solyndra's ability to compete rested on the notion that silicon prices would remain high. At the start of the recession, as a result of generous incentives in Europe, the solar market experienced a shortage of silicon, driving prices as high as $460 per kilogram, according to a congressional research report obtained by Dow Jones Newswires.[1] Suppliers rushed to add capacity, and by the time Biden announced the loan guarantee at the Fab 2 groundbreaking in September 2009, silicon prices had dropped to $50 per kilogram.

Solyndra's potential cost advantage began to deteriorate. From 2008 to 2010, the price of photovoltaic modules dropped by half from $3.50 per watt to $1.75 per watt. Solyndra's modules sold for $3.24 per watt in 2009 but, according to company documents, cost more than $6 a watt to produce. With the larger, more efficient factory, it hoped to drop the price to $2 a watt by 2011 and $1.30 by 2013, but already the solar market was getting ahead of Solyndra.

"You hear dollar per watt, Solyndra's too expensive," Miller said. "But where we can make up a lot of money is in the ability to install these things very fast because you're not penetrating the roof."

Solyndra's new factory had recently been completed when I visited, and inside, workers were busy installing the last of the equipment. Solyndra currently had 1,100 employees. They planned to add another 400 when Fab 2 went online and 1,000 over time.

As we talked about the future, a robot zoomed by playing the theme from *Raiders of the Lost Ark*. Watching the robot leave, I couldn't help but think of Maryo Mendez, the autoworker who lost his job when the NUMMI plant closed. The robot was essentially serving the same role—delivering parts to an assembly line. Many of Solyndra's employees came from the local semiconductor and disk drive industries. Solyndra had hired some of the workers laid off from NUMMI, but it wasn't as easy as one would think. "Unfortunately, the skills don't line up perfectly," Miller said. "A lot of the high-tech equipment involves a different kind of experience."

If that wasn't enough bad news for aging factory workers like Mendez, Solyndra's plans for Fab 2 were to lengthen and centralize its assembly line. The glass tubes would move along a conveyor belt, meaning that many of the cheery robots would soon be out of work as well.

At the end of our tour, we climbed up to Solyndra's roof. Here were dozens of panels lined up like plots in a community garden with narrow paths between them. Solyndra panels were specifically designed for flat commercial rooftops with slopes less than nine degrees. The panels snapped together with clips, and the wiring was already attached, meaning that connecting them was as simple as plugging in an extension cord. For one recent project at a Frito-Lay SunChips factory in Modesto, workers installed 5,600 panels in twenty-three days.

"From my perspective, the clean technology industry is where the growth is," Miller said. Standing on the rooftop overlooking the San Jose hills, Miller looked at all the empty roofs of the factories and warehouses nearby and saw opportunity. "It's totally unused space," he said. "You look at any of these rooftops around here, they can hold anywhere between 700 kilowatts and a megawatt on the roof. You basically build a power plant."

But Solyndra essentially served a niche within a niche. Not only was solar a tiny part of America's energy portfolio, but commercial rooftops were a small part of the solar industry. If all went as planned, Solyndra would mature and find its market, and America would have a new manufacturer employing thousands of people. If it failed, taxpayers could be on the hook for hundreds of billions of dollars.

$ $ $

The effort to connect renewable energy with jobs began after 9/11 with a memo written by political strategist Dan Carol, who called for a "moonshot" on the scale of JFK's Apollo program to end America's dependence on oil. The memo catalyzed a movement among environmentalists, business leaders, and labor unions that led to the founding of the Apollo Alliance in April 2003.[2] Being environmentally conscious has almost always been seen as a cost to doing business. Installing equipment to reduce pollution, slogging through regulatory hearings over endangered species all cut against the bottom line. That money, companies argued, could be better spent hiring workers and building more plants, and the regulatory burdens drove American jobs overseas. By reframing the debate, the progressive founders could argue that clean energy created jobs too: building wind turbines, installing solar panels on roofs, blowing insulation in homes, stringing high-efficiency power lines, and assembling electric cars.

The ur text for the green jobs program was a 216-page economic study prepared by the Perryman Group, a financial research firm in Waco, Texas. The report formed the basis for Apollo's New Energy for America plan, which in 2004 called for a $300 billion federal investment over ten years that would create 3.3 million jobs and add $1.4 trillion to the GDP. The plan incorporated many of America's most pressing issues: national security hinging on foreign oil, the threat of climate change, the loss of manufacturing jobs, the gap between the rich and the poor. Included in Apollo's ten-point plan were hybrid cars, energy-efficient buildings, a modern electrical grid, high-speed rail, and investments in solar and wind. The proposal would pay for itself as increased economic activity from new companies led to greater tax revenue for the Treasury.

While Apollo's ideas began to circulate in Democratic circles, for the most part, the political world paid little attention. "I don't think policy makers by and large took it very seriously," Apollo's executive director Cathy Calfo told me. Efforts to interest the 2004 presidential campaigns failed. Congressman Jay Inslee of the Seattle suburbs sponsored the New Apollo Energy Act of 2005, which never made it out of subcommittee. An energy bill that year did offer subsidies for ethanol and "clean coal" initiatives, but it also invested heavily in oil and gas.

With the Democratic takeover in 2007, Congress passed an energy bill that raised the fuel-economy standards for cars and trucks but also authorized money for weatherization, renewable energy research, and green jobs training. Apollo's successes came instead on the state and local level. One of the central creation stories of the green jobs movement is the Gamesa wind-turbine factory in Pennsylvania. Lured by state incentives, the Spanish company opened plants on the sites of old steel mills, hiring more than a thousand workers, included a number of laid-off steelworkers.

It wasn't until gas prices breached $4 a gallon in the summer of 2008 that the Apollo plan gained much traction. By then, Dan Carol was the content and issues director for the Obama campaign. The McCain-Lieberman campaign came out early with a renewable energy plan that called for many of Apollo's ideas. McCain even alluded to the moon landing in his speech announcing it. The plan was similarly titled the Lexington Project after Lexington, Massachusetts, as in "the shot heard 'round the world." But the name took awhile to register and wasn't playing well, giving Carol some time to push the Apollo plan in the Obama campaign.

After several weeks, Carol's efforts culminated in a meeting with the campaign's chief strategist David Axelrod.

"Carol," Axelrod called over to him. "Stop twitching so much. This tested number one in both the domestic and foreign policy polls."

The Apollo plan proved popular because it stood for energy independence, economic development, the environment, and national security. "It's like Ragu spaghetti sauce," Carol told me. "It's all in there." In early August, Obama unveiled his plan called New Energy for America, the same name Apollo had given to its plan in 2004. Obama's goals were more ambitious. While Apollo's called for 3 million jobs with $300 billion, Obama promised to create 5 million green jobs for half the price.

A few months later, Van Jones, then an obscure civil rights activist from Oakland, published his book, *The Green Collar Economy*, which became a best seller and made "green jobs" a household name. Jones, who became a White House adviser, came to the idea from a social justice perspective. To succeed, a green jobs plan would not only have to cater to the "eco-elite" but become a reality for the poor, who often didn't see themselves in the environmental mirror.

"Rather, they perhaps imagine a few Hollywood celebrities eating tofu, doing yoga, and driving hybrid cars," Jones wrote. "When many ordinary people hear the term 'green' today, they still automatically think the message is probably for a fancy, elite set—and not for themselves. And as long as that remains true, the green movement will remain too anemic politically and too alien culturally to rescue the country."[3]

By providing incentives to create demand, the government could also create a need for workers at a time when most blue-collar workers were still employed. But while the stimulus included many of the ideas outlined in his book, the Great Recession nixed the bootstraps component. Factory workers had moved from the assembly line to the unemployment line and, for a brief moment, green jobs seemed like a refuge.

"A labor shortage is a great opportunity to lean in with job training programs and pull in people who have been chronically poor or left out for racial agenda reasons," Jones told me. "So part of the problem that I have now is that I was imagining a scenario that we no longer live in."

By the time the Recovery Act was being drafted, mainstream progressive groups like the Center for American Progress and several labor unions were also pushing stimulus plans that would encourage green jobs.

The constellation of the Apollo Alliance, Jones, and the other groups provided the seed for conspiracy theories. Glenn Beck, the popular Fox News host, painted the green jobs plan as a subversive attempt to destabilize capitalism and replace it with a socialist revolution. As an umbrella organization, Apollo had connections to many other groups. And Jones supplied material with a colorful past that was easily found on Google. After graduating from Yale Law School, Jones became active in a civil rights group protesting police misconduct. Being arrested at a rally following the Rodney King verdict was a turning point, he told a reporter in 2005. In jail, he met radicals and anarchists and decided he wanted to be a part of it. He had gone in as "a rowdy nationalist," he said, and a few months later, he was a communist.[4] By tying the stimulus bill to socialism, Beck was reviving a tried-and-true attack of the New Deal. After repeating the narrative night after night, all Beck needed to fan the flames on any issue was to remind the audience of Apollo, which "wrote the stimulus package" and Jones, who confessed to being a communist revolutionary. Their names had become shorthand for something deviant.

I visited the headquarters of the Apollo Alliance in downtown San Francisco in the fall of 2010. The office is in an old meatpacking warehouse at the end of a long hallway with a paper sign on the door that reads PLEASE KNOCK. There were no posters of Chairman Mao in the small office overlooking the Caltrain station. The only hint of any communist sympathies that I could see were the red-painted wall in the conference room and red canvas screens used to separate desks (there were blue ones too). Calfo and Kate Gordon, one of Apollo's first staffers, told me that Apollo's appeal as a spoke in a conspiracy is a testament to the support it has among a lot of organizations.

"It ends up being like six degrees of Kevin Bacon," Gordon explained. "I think Apollo has been a big idea that makes a lot of sense to a lot of people. So you can draw a lot of lines to it."

In truth, Apollo was just one of many groups that influenced the stimulus bill. In the same way, Building America's Future, a coalition of governors and mayors, provided a framework for the infrastructure sections. But saying Apollo "wrote" the stimulus was like saying Republicans wrote the stimulus because it included their idea for a $70 billion patch to the alternative minimum tax. Many of the renewable energy ideas had been around for decades. Even Richard Nixon invoked the Apollo mission when talking about energy independence.

With $90 billion dedicated to areas like solar, wind, and the smart grid, the Recovery Act was the largest clean energy bill in history. The stimulus package dramatically changed the scope of the Department of Energy from a minor agency that primarily oversaw the nuclear stockpile and cleanup to a federal venture capital firm steering the path to a new economy.

$ $ $

After an excruciatingly slow start, the Obama administration's weatherization program was finally up and running in 2010, and by August, workers had made more than 200,000 homes more energy efficient. Low-income families reported saving $30 to $50 on their utility bills each month. The funding supported more than 13,000 jobs. But the program was rife with reports of misspending and shoddy work.

In Illinois, inspectors failed to detect a gas leak from a newly installed furnace that could have seriously injured the home's residents. Contractors billed for labor that wasn't done and materials that weren't installed. Fourteen of fifteen homes visited failed inspection. In New Jersey, auditors identified twelve households that were approved for free repairs despite having income of more than $100,000. Agencies bought $1,500 GPS systems and underpaid their workers. The state's system of eligible applicants contained the Social Security numbers of 168 dead people. A nonprofit in Waukesha, Wisconsin, got stimulus money despite having spent weatherization funds on Christmas decorations, gift cards for employees, and a parking ticket. An audit found that one employee's husband received new windows from the agency, charging it $10,000—more than ten times the average cost.[5] West Virginia had to take over one agency's weatherization program after finding "shoddy work, falsified reports, credit card abuses, and missing inventory."[6] An inspection of a Houston nonprofit found that work was so sloppy that contractors had to go back and repair thirty-three of the fifty-three homes reviewed.[7] Investigators in California found untrained workers. And Delaware suspended its entire program for nearly a year after a scathing report documented problems with nearly every aspect of the program, leading the Department of Energy to freeze its funds.

The public will probably hear of more problems in the years to come due to a lack of transparency with the program. States weren't required to get a list of contractors from the nonprofits managing the funds, making it hard to know if an employee passed work to a relative. The addresses of weatherized homes were kept confidential to protect the privacy of residents. But that also meant that reporters couldn't independently check to see if work was done on mansions or was even done at all. One state, Tennessee, refused to provide me with inspection records because I wasn't a state resident, even though the work was paid for with federal tax dollars. And when a resident requested the records herself, the state told her that her request would cost $24,936.74.

I reviewed more than a thousand weatherization inspections from various states. There were lots of problems. But for every story about a botched job allowing dangerous levels of carbon monoxide to enter a home, there was a story of a little old lady able to sleep in a warm bed for the first time in years. An inspection from Berkshire County, Massachusetts, was typical. The contractor had done sloppy caulking, used the wrong size pipe insulation, and left fiberglass sticking out of the molding. "Door installation is a real hack job," the inspector wrote. "This contractor is a former roofer and should return to that profession."

But just as common was the inspection of an old mobile home in Craig, Colorado, that received a new furnace, thermostat, insulation, and repairs to leaking lines on the water heater. The resident was a single mother with two children, and the family had not had heat for the past two years. "The client was extremely grateful for the work done by this agency and was moved to tears as she explained that she and her children were finally warm," the inspector wrote. "And her heating bill was cut in half. Nice job!"

Alan Levin, the owner of Northeast Building Products, a window manufacturer in Philadelphia, told administration officials that he was skeptical about the Recovery Act, thinking all the spending was "mortgaging the future." But after the stimulus sparked new business, he added two shifts and a hundred workers. Weatherization may have even saved a life. In Asheville, North Carolina, Gene Senyak, a seventy-three-year-old writer living on Social Security, told the local newspaper that he had used a propane heater to stay warm when a snowstorm knocked out the power. But his new carbon monoxide monitor warned him of dangerous levels of the odorless gas.[8]

The increase in weatherization work meant that Serious Materials, owner of the Chicago windows factory that staged the historic sit-in could bring another thirty people back to work. Ricky Maclin, who worked on the glass line, got the call in late January 2010.

"I was home and my union president called me, and I was ex-tremely happy," he told me. "As a matter of fact I did a little dance around my house. I don't even know what it was. I probably couldn't duplicate it now. It was just a 'thank you, God' dance."

Maclin, fifty-six with sixteen grandkids, spent about a year on un-employment, waiting for the plant to call and struggling to pay for his condo, car loan, and regular bills. "Naturally, Serious would like to bring back all of the workers because they really don't make money with a plant that size with only a few people in there," he said. "But if the work isn't there, you can't just hire people to just stand around."

The same month Maclin was called back to work, Fox Business re-porter John Stossel cited Serious Materials as a case of so-called crony capitalism. The White House had been giving the company a lot of publicity in the last year. A board member was chosen to introduce Obama at a speech on energy policy. Vice President Biden visited the Chicago factory shortly after the stimulus was signed, saying Serious Materials made "the most energy-efficient windows in the world." And the company had recently qualified for a $500,000 tax credit.

It turned out that Robin Roy, Serious Materials' vice president of policy, was married to Cathy Zoi, the assistant secretary for energy ef-ficiency and renewable energy at the Department of Energy and one of the officials overseeing the weatherization program.[9] Stossel may have implied more of a connection than existed, and the relationship wasn't exactly a secret. Zoi had listed it in her financial disclosure state-ment. The timeline wasn't perfect either. Serious Materials had begun receiving national attention months before Zoi took her post. And the Energy Department said she recused herself from any decisions affect-ing the company. The couple was well known in clean energy circles, having worked at green businesses for years and with Zoi serving as head of the Alliance for Climate Protection, which was founded by Al Gore. The White House's embrace of Serious Materials was more likely an attempt to claim the inspiring story of workers fighting back as its own. But Biden, who worried intensely about the optics of skate-board parks, had himself walked right into the clearing.

Dan Carol, the Apollo founder, predicted to me that there would be numerous stories of supposed conflicts because of the way the stimulus programs were set up to pick specific companies rather than encourage ideas from the ground up.

"I think it's quite possible that some of them will fail and it will be some Obama hedge fund donor and Fox News will have fun with it," he told me. "And it looks really, really bad because of the way that's been set up."

Carol was right. Al Gore along with John Doerr, who served on Obama's board of economic advisers, were repeatedly accused of reaping stimulus money because of their ties to the White House and the Democratic Party. Kleiner Perkins Caufield & Byers, the venture capital firm where they were partners, invested in several companies that received stimulus money, including Altarock Energy (geothermal), Amyris Biotechnologies (biofuels), and Silver Spring Networks (smart meters).

Steve Westly, a venture capitalist and top fund-raiser for Obama, was the subject of a five-thousand-word investigation by the Center for Public Integrity. Four companies backed by his firm had benefited from federal money, including Amyris, which received a stimulus grant, and Tesla Motors, which received a $465 million loan guarantee from another government program.[10]

Then, there was Solyndra. Many stimulus critics pointed to the role of George Kaiser, the billionaire investor who also happened to be a major fund-raiser for Obama. Solyndra's largest shareholder, owning 39 percent of the company, was Argonaut Ventures, an investment firm affiliated with Kaiser's family foundation. Kaiser had visited the White House nearly ten times since the stimulus package was passed. In the days before a conditional commitment for the Solyndra project was made, Kaiser had met with several top economic and policy officials, including senior adviser Pete Rouse, according to White House visitor logs. He later met with Rahm Emanuel and senior adviser Valerie Jarrett. While Solyndra's investors included a number of Republican donors as well, the White House's promotion of Solyndra looked bad when coupled with the extensive ties to Kaiser.

How much influence these connections played in securing stimulus money is unknown. For now it appears more of a correlation than a cause. People who had invested in clean energy supported a president who supported clean energy, just as oil companies had backed President Bush. Whether favoritism played a role in any energy award remains to be seen. At a congressional hearing in March 2011, the Energy Department's inspector general testified that the office had sixty-four open investigations, including "the directing of contracts and grants to friends and family."

$ $ $

On the afternoon of New Year's Eve 2010, Dick Moore, the mayor of Elkhart, received some good, but pressing news. Think, a Norwegian manufacturer of electric cars, had been planning to open its first American factory in the nearby town of Middlebury. But at the eleventh hour, things had fallen through. Now, they had found an alternative in Elkhart, the vacant factory of a RV window and door supplier that had shut down last summer laying off 250 employees. The CEO was already flying in from Norway and had been planning to make the announcement about the Middlebury site with Governor Mitch Daniels on Tuesday. Could Elkhart have an incentives package ready in four days' time?

Led by the city attorney, the staff worked over the holiday weekend, pulling together a deal that would phase in property and real estate taxes over ten years. Think would pay nothing the first year, and the percentage would gradually rise until they paid 100 percent in the eleventh year.

"By Monday," Moore recalled, "we put an incentive package together, announced it to them, and they said, 'Well done, we're coming to Elkhart, Indiana.'"

Think promised to create 415 jobs by 2013, paying $16–$20 an hour, as it ramped up production of the Think City, an electric two-seater designed for urban driving. A few days after the announcement, Think got word that it had qualified for a stimulus tax credit worth $17 million.

Think was already making cars for the European market at a plant in Uusikaupunki, Finland. But so far, there were only about 1,500 on the road. The company would invest $43.5 million in equipment and renovations to the 200,000-square-foot facility on Magnum Drive. If things stayed on schedule, Think would begin assembling cars in early 2011, with plans to produce 2,500 cars a year.

While Ed Neufeldt's dream of walking across America had faded when Electric Motors Corporation flopped, Elkhart County was moving ahead with its dreams of green jobs and electric cars. Navistar, the company that had taken over the old Monaco RV plant in Wakarusa, started production of its electric delivery truck. And in May 2010, the company announced the first electric vehicle built under the Recovery Act had rolled off the assembly line. It had been nine months since President Obama visited the factory to announce the $39 million grant as part of $2.4 billion stimulus program for battery and electric vehicle projects. Now, the plant was whirring again with about forty employees and plans to create 700 jobs including suppliers in the next five years.

Navistar's first customer was FedEx, which planned to test the flat-nosed electric trucks in Los Angeles. The truck's hundred-mile range allowed its drivers to work a full eight-hour shift before recharging, said Deborah Willig of FedEx. And in a job with lots of starting and stopping, the process in which energy flowed backed into the battery was a plus. Dave Meisel of Pacific Gas & Electric, which had also shown interest, said the quiet motor could allow the utility to work longer in neighborhoods with noise restrictions.

Navistar's plans called for four hundred trucks at the Wakarusa factory in the first year. If things kept going its way, Mayor Moore thought, the Elkhart area would not only be known as the RV capital of the world, but also the electric vehicle capital of America.

Think's history mirrored the sad fate of the electric car. The company was founded by a Norwegian named Jan Otto Ringdal as the Personal Independent Vehicle Company, or Pivco, in 1991. It introduced its City Bee model to the San Francisco Bay area in the mid-1990s, and in 1999, Ford acquired a majority stake and changed the name to Th!nk Nordic. Ford produced the car for four years during a development and testing phase, in which it built five hundred vehicles and leased them to drivers in the United States. But for whatever reason, Ford stopped making electric cars and sold the company in 2003. Ringdal revived Think in 2006, and by the time it selected Elkhart, it had raised $160 million in investment from a cast of venture capital firms that included Kleiner Perkins, the firm of John Doerr, and RockPort Capital, which had also invested in Solyndra.

Originally, Think had considered a Freightliner factory in Portland, Oregon. But after the company decided to keep it open and the state scaled back an energy tax credit, Think's allegiances switched to Indiana. Elkhart could provide an eager workforce and, if needed, a supplier network that had been hurting since the crash of the RV market in 2008. More important though, the city was close to Think's largest shareholder and battery manufacturer, Ener1, which was based in Indianapolis and had received $118 million in stimulus money to expand production.

"With the change in the administration, the overall political climate became much more friendly to electric vehicles," Brendan Prebo, Think's spokesman, told me. "I would say that the stimulus package played a pretty significant role in helping us decide that we could actually do this here."

$ $ $

In the 2006 documentary *Who Killed the Electric Car?*, the narrator recounts the sorry history of America's last experiment with electric cars, opening at a cemetery with the sound of bagpipes. Electric cars began appearing on California roads in the mid-1990s after state regulators mandated that a certain percentage of automakers' fleets include zero-emissions vehicles. General Motors unveiled the EV1, followed by the Ford Th!nk and a number of other conversions. In this telling, the electric car offered a fast, smooth ride that everybody loved. So who then would kill the electric car? The movie fingers several culprits: The oil companies, which lobbied to crush the California mandate? The batteries, which were heavy and offered limited range? The Bush administration, which promoted hydrogen fuel cells over electric drive trains? General Motors, which made the car seem like a fantasy out of some future wonderland by running commercials that featured a robotic voice and showed toasters and vacuums flocking to greet this space-age mystery? Or was it the consumers who were simply afraid of the unknowns? As then *Los Angeles Times* auto critic Dan

Neil said in the movie, "GM would sell you a car that ran on pig shit if it sold."

So much had changed only eight years after GM pulled its EV1s off the road. The lead-acid and nickel-metal hydride batteries that weighed as much as 1,200 pounds were replaced with a lithium-ion battery that weighed as little as 400 pounds. In the early 2000s, gas hadn't even eclipsed $2 a gallon yet. Less than a decade later, it was twice that. Toyota had proven the demand with its long waiting list for the Prius hybrid. Government policy had changed too with a 2007 energy bill that increased fuel-efficiency standards and provided $25 billion in loans for automakers to upgrade their plants.

But until the American Recovery and Reinvestment Act passed in 2009, the manufacturing of electric cars and their batteries in the United States was nearly nonexistent. The stimulus package included a number of generous government incentives to encourage the development and sales of electric cars. President Obama set a goal of having one million plug-in hybrids on the road by 2015. When the stimulus passed, the United States had only two factories manufacturing less than 2 percent of the world's advanced batteries. Most were made in Korea and Japan. By 2015, America would have thirty factories making batteries and their components with the capacity to produce 40 percent, according to the Obama administration. The investments would help manufacturers increase the batteries' life from four years to fourteen and cut their cost 70 percent, from $33,000 to $10,000. That would make the electric car more competitive and less of a luxury niche.

By the summer of 2010, construction had started at twenty-six of the thirty factories. It seemed like every week brought another groundbreaking or ribbon-cutting. In June, Dow Kokam, a joint venture between Dow Chemical and a Korean company, broke ground on a factory in Midland, Michigan, with plans to create 800 full-time jobs. A few weeks later, Obama visited Smith Electric, which was renovating a Kansas City jet engine hangar to build electric trucks for Frito-Lay, Staples, and others. In July, he traveled to Holland, Michigan, where Compact Power was breaking ground on a $300 million factory to produce batteries for the Chevy Volt and the electric Ford Focus. In September, it was A123 Systems, which was opening the nation's first factory to mass-produce batteries for electric vehicles in Livonia, Michigan. The company, which manufactured batteries for Black & Decker power tools, was now the supplier for Navistar and Fisker Automotive, and it planned to hire more than 3,000 workers by 2012.

Even Aiken, South Carolina, the home of the Savannah River nuclear site, seemed poised to benefit from these investments. In August 2009, Energy secretary Steven Chu announced that Aiken would be the site of a factory making battery separators. But its hopes were dashed when Celgard, the company based in Charlotte, decided to build its plant supporting more than 200 jobs in Concord, North Carolina. Aiken's leaders were sore at the loss of the factory, but Celgard did use some of the $49 million grant for research at Savannah River National Laboratory.

"We could have put this plant in another country," Mitch Pulwer, Celgard's general manager, told me. "The administration's desire to have an industry here in the U.S. was very influential in our decision. Obviously receiving the grant made it a done deal."

Before the Recovery Act, electric cars sold for $100,000. According to the Obama administration, a three-hundred-mile drive from Chicago to St. Louis was impossible because the closest charging station was in Champaign, Illinois, more than a hundred miles from either city. There were only five hundred electric charging stations nationwide. Now, a new industry was quickly becoming a reality.

By December 2010, two mass-produced electric cars went on sale in America: the Chevy Volt and the Nissan Leaf. The Leaf ran purely on electricity, getting a hundred miles on a single charge. The Volt, a plug-in hybrid, could go forty miles per charge before its gasoline engine kicked in, extending the range to the standard three hundred miles. The Energy Department had pumped in $1.4 billion for Nissan to retool its assembly plant in Smyrna, Tennessee. Through the stimulus, General Motors and its battery maker received nearly $400 million to support the Volt. The starting price for the Leaf was $33,000, while the Volt would sell for about $40,000 before tax credits.

There was no better environment for the electric car to thrive. With more than $2 billion in federal grants, matched by another $2 billion in private investment, the Obama administration was supporting electric cars from the mine to the garage. The Chemetall Foote Corporation, which operates the only U.S. lithium mine, received $28 million to boost production at its plants in Nevada and North Carolina. Honeywell received $27 million to become the first domestic supplier of a conductive salt for lithium batteries. More than $1 billion was spent to open and expand battery factories. Automakers received loans to retool their assembly lines. Customers could receive a $7,500 tax credit for buying an electric car. To assuage fears about battery life, GM offered an eight-year warranty on the Volt's battery. The stimulus provided funding for 20,000 electric charging stations by 2013. In many cities, drivers could get a home charger for free.

No doubt, though, electric cars still faced many challenges, according to the Government Accountability Office. The price of the battery is still too high and the price of gas is still too low. About 40 percent of drivers don't have access to an outlet where they park their vehicles. The transition could trade a dependence on foreign oil for a reliance on foreign lithium, which is mainly located in South America and China. The National Research Council doubted that electric vehicles would have much impact on carbon emissions until 2030. According to its report, the electricity grid might not be able to handle the load if millions of drivers plugged in their cars as soon as they got home from work. It also raised questions about costs. "Although a mile driven on electricity is cheaper than one driven on gasoline, it will likely take several decades before the upfront costs decline enough to be offset by lifetime fuel savings," the council concluded.

Perhaps the biggest obstacle was Americans' association of the car with the freedom of the open road. While most people drive less than forty miles per day on average, consumers want cars that they can also take on summer vacations—and they don't want to have to constantly worry about looking for a charging station.

Electric carmakers and advocates have learned their marketing lesson since the EV1. The key to winning over skeptics was not only to make it sound cool, but to make it sound convenient. How far can it go? A hundred miles. Where can I recharge it? Your home garage in eight hours. How much will I save by trading in the gas pump for the wall socket? According to the Obama administration, a driver commuting thirty-two miles round-trip a day would save more than $600 a year in fuel.

Although electric cars would never make up for the generation-long loss of manufacturing jobs, at least not yet, it was novel to see companies creating jobs in the Rust Belt instead of sending them overseas. Here was a beehive of activity, a manifestation of Vice President Biden's testimony to the changing phrase of "used to be" to "going to be." If Elkhart wanted to be the electric vehicle capital of the America, it had some competition. Powered by a state tax credit for battery makers, Michigan had sixteen advanced battery companies promising to create 62,000 jobs in the next decade. Two of the biggest, Johnson Controls and Compact Power, opened in Holland, a town better known for its tulip festival.

$ $ $

I got a chance to test-drive Elkhart's new jewel, the Think City, in Manhattan in the spring of 2010. The Think City has a body made of hard color-injected plastic, giving the car a matte finish that makes it look more like a giant ski boot than a shiny sedan. There is no gas tank. No internal combustion engine. No catalytic converter. No tailpipe.

The car weighs about 2,300 pounds. The lithium-ion battery takes up 625 pounds and sits underneath the seats. Next to the passenger door is a hatch for the charging port and a big blue adapter cord that plugs into the wall. The Think car gets a hundred miles on a complete charge and costs about a third of the price of gas to fill up—er—charge. It maxes out at seventy miles per hour, which will disappoint many a leadfoot but is fine for driving in Manhattan.

The car was quiet and had no *vroom* sound as it zoomed to fifty miles per hour. A gauge on the dashboard displayed what percentage of the charge was left. As we whizzed up the West Side Highway, the car certainly attracted a lot of attention. At the stoplight near Chelsea Piers, two hefty guys in shirtsleeves craned their necks as they crossed the street on the way back from lunch. On Chambers Street, a student hanging out after school ran over and said, "We read about this yesterday on the AP Spanish test." Near the PATH train station, a woman shouted, "Cute car!"

Dick Moore, the mayor of Elkhart, tested it himself. "Very nice," he told me. "Great response. Quiet of course. A hundred miles on a charge. Runs up to seventy miles per hour. The braking was good. The steering was good. . . . I can't imagine that I won't have that at least for a commuter car once they start building it here in Elkhart, Indiana."

$ $ $

Whether the Think City or any other electric vehicle would be an all-purpose car was years, if not decades, away. For now, there were lingering questions, spread by Rush Limbaugh and others, about whether they should even be called electric cars, or if it was more accurate to call them "coal-fired cars." By plugging the car into a socket, drivers essentially tap into whatever source of power their utility uses. And for a lot of people, that means coal. Burning fossil fuels in a power plant is cleaner and more efficient than in a car, but it still carries the irony of trading one source of greenhouse gas emissions for another. "For plug-ins to realize their full potential," the Government Accountability Office noted, "electricity would need to be generated from lower-emission fuels such as nuclear and renewable energy rather than the fossil fuels—coal and natural gas—used most often to generate electricity today."

The Obama administration's solution for this dilemma was to build up cleaner sources, such as wind and solar. But there was no escaping the reality that the United States got nearly half its electricity from coal. So the stimulus invested in a new technology under development to capture the carbon dioxide emitted from coal plants and store it underground.

The Energy Department gave out $3.4 billion in grants, and sure enough FutureGen, the embattled project pushed by Senator Dick Durbin and others from Illinois, was the biggest winner with $1 billion. The administration also planned to invest $330 million in a retrofit for American Electric Power's Mountaineer Plant in West Virginia that would use chilled ammonia to absorb at least 90 percent of the carbon dioxide in the flue gas and then inject it into saline aquifers a mile and a half beneath the earth's surface. It spent another $350 million outside Odessa, Texas, where a new coal-fired plant would use a technology to capture and treat the carbon dioxide and then pipe it to the Permian Basin oilfields, where it would be used to extract additional oil. In addition to storing the carbon dioxide, the administration dedicated money to convert it into useful products such as cement and fertilizer.

The original plan for FutureGen was to build a new demonstration plant in Mattoon, Illinois, that would turn the coal into a gas, rather than a powder, and remove pollutants before combustion. Mattoon, site of the Lender's Bagels factory and once home of the world's largest bagel, had suffered from the loss of manufacturing jobs in recent decades. But when the Energy Department unveiled FutureGen 2.0 in August 2010, there was a sudden change in plans. Instead of building a new plant, the coal companies that made up the FutureGen Alliance would repower an existing plant in Meredosia, Illinois, some hundred and fifty miles west, using a different technology. As a consolation prize, Mattoon could still have the carbon dioxide injected under its ground after it was transported by pipeline from Meredosia. As nice as that sounded, Mattoon said no thanks. In February 2011, the alliance selected a closer storage site in nearby Morgan County. Construction was expected to begin in late 2012 and be completed by the end of 2015.

$ $ $

On the palette of renewable energy sources, perhaps the most vibrant before the Recovery Act was wind. The United States had recently become the biggest producer of wind in the world. Even though it generated less than 2 percent of the nation's power compared to coal and gas, the rapid growth put the sector on pace to generate 20 percent by 2030, according to the American Wind Energy Association. Even oilman T. Boone Pickens was promoting wind with plans to build a massive wind farm with 2,700 turbines in the Texas Panhandle.

Until the Recovery Act, the government's main instrument for subsidizing renewable energy development came in the form of tax credits. But many renewables firms couldn't use them because, like most startups, they struggled to turn a large enough profit. The solution was to partner with investment banks, such as Lehman Brothers, which would provide financing in exchange for the tax credit, which they could use to offset other earnings. Wind farms were tethered like a power line to the titans of Wall Street. So when the banking system collapsed and credit froze, the clean energy industry came crashing down with it. Many wind farm developers considered halting construction. America's few turbine manufacturers suffered layoffs. Gamesa, the green poster child with more than 1,000 jobs in Pennsylvania, was now down to a few hundred. The industry expected new wind power development to drop as much as 50 percent in 2009.

But under the stimulus, the tax credits were converted to grants, making clean energy projects eligible for a 30 percent rebate. Instead of pulling back, the wind industry reported a record year, installing more than ten gigawatts of capacity and allowing it to maintain its prerecession employment of 85,000 jobs. The Spanish firm Iberdrola received $170 million to build the Streator-Cayuga Ridge wind park in north central Illinois, creating 300 construction jobs and enough energy to power 86,000 homes. The Meadow Lake Wind Farm outside Lafayette, Indiana, received the largest grant at $276 million while the Penascal II project on the Texas Gulf Coast came in second with $223 million. Through the loan guarantee program, the Energy Department supported a $1.3 billion loan to the Shepherds Flat Wind Farm in northern Oregon, which, according to the Obama administration, would be the largest wind farm in the world.

But the grants program proved controversial as journalists at American University's Investigative Reporting Workshop found that more than 80 percent of the first billion dollars for wind farms went to foreign-owned firms. In a follow-up, they reported that overseas manufacturers had built about 1,200 of the 1,800 turbines on wind farms that had received grants. The Gulf Wind project in Sarita, Texas, exemplified the problem. The recipient of one of the largest grants, $178 million, it was built by Babcock & Brown, "a bankrupt Australian company . . . using turbines made by a Japanese company." Examining customs records, the workshop found that the Danish firm Vestas had received seventy-two sections of steel towers from

Vietnam that were destined for Meadow Lake, which was built by a Portuguese company. Using a formula developed by a renewable energy think tank, the reporters estimated that the 1,200 turbines created as many as 6,800 jobs overseas.[11]

The workshop's reports drew outcries from labor supporters in Congress. Led by Senator Chuck Schumer of New York, the lawmakers called for the Obama administration to suspend the program and make it comply with the Buy American provisions that applied to other stimulus projects. "It's a no-brainer that stimulus funds should only go to projects that create jobs in the United States rather than overseas," Schumer said in a statement. "These wind projects have a lot of merit, but the manufacturing should be happening here, not in China." The reports spoke at length about European companies, but everyone focused on China.

Much of the confusion came because the workshop's first report came out the same day that a Chinese company and a group of American investors announced a partnership to seek $450 million in stimulus money to build a wind farm in West Texas. The project never received stimulus money. The companies promised to open a turbine factory in Nevada and struck a deal with the United Steelworkers union that major components would be made in America. But the notion that stimulus wind grants were sending jobs to China stuck and inspired a popular but false Republican ad during the midterm elections.

The Energy Department, the wind industry, and environmental advocates argued that the exact opposite was happening: foreign companies were investing in America. By providing incentives to build wind farms, the government was creating the demand for domestic manufacturing. A typical turbine blade weighs eleven tons and is almost as long as the wingspan of a Boeing 747, making it costly to transport long distances and less likely that firms would outsource jobs, they said. At the time of the Recovery Act, however, there weren't many factories making wind turbines in America. According to the Apollo Alliance, 70 percent of the nation's renewable energy systems and components were made overseas.

Manufacturing tax credits, funded by the stimulus, supported fifty-two new turbine, blade, and tower projects. Siemens built and expanded three plants. Brevini Wind constructed a plant in Muncie, Indiana, to make gearboxes, one of the most labor-intensive parts of a turbine. And in October 2010, Nordex USA opened a turbine factory in Jonesboro, Arkansas, with the help of a $22 million tax credit. To promote long-term growth, the Energy Department also funded two wind research centers at Clemson University in South Carolina and at a state-created testing site in Massachusetts. According to the department's Lawrence Berkeley National Laboratory, the share of turbine equipment costs made in America increased from 50 percent in 2008 to roughly 60 percent in 2009. While job estimates vary, industry and government officials say the stimulus saved tens of thousands of construction jobs and created thousands more in manufacturing.

$ $ $

In addition to Solyndra's factory in Fremont, the federal stimulus package was speeding the development of utility-scale solar arrays in the California desert. In the history of solar, 2010 was shaping up to be a turning point. The second half of the year brought the approval of nearly a dozen solar plants, as companies raced to take advantage of a stimulus program that was scheduled to sunset on New Year's Eve. With every announcement came the requisite superlative that Such-and-Such Solar would build the world's largest solar plant. With the nearest contenders in the 100-megawatt range, any of America's planned installations boasting 200, 300, even 1,000 megawatts could easily stake that claim.

The Ivanpah solar plant, being built by BrightSource Energy in the Mojave Desert, was one of the largest of the Obama administration's investments through the Recovery Act. The Energy Department provided a $1.6 billion loan guarantee for the 400-megawatt plant near the California-Nevada state line. The Ivanpah electric generating system would create a thousand construction jobs and eighty-six jobs for its operation. It would consist of a field of 349,000 mirrors arranged around several totemlike towers as if it were a monument to some ancient sun god. Controlled by software, the mirrors would track the sun and reflect its light to boilers atop the towers to generate steam. BrightSource broke ground in the desert in late October 2010. Once operational, it would be the largest concentrated solar power complex in the world.

In the meantime, the Obama administration also placed bets on two other companies: Abengoa Solar and Abound Solar. Abengoa received a $1.4 billion loan guarantee to build the Solana Generating Station in Gila Bend, Arizona, southwest of Phoenix. The plant would be the first of its kind, using parabolic mirrors to heat a special fluid that would produce steam and also heat molten salt, allowing it to generate electricity even when the sun isn't shining. The need for mirrors encouraged a Spanish company to build a $50 million glass factory outside Phoenix. Abound planned to use its $400 million loan guarantee to expand a solar panel factory in Longmont, Colorado, and build a new one at the site of a vacant Chrysler parts supplier south of the hard-hit auto community of Kokomo, Indiana. Together, the factories would employ about 1,500 workers.

The Recovery Act allowed the United States to claim a Yankees-size cache of solar titles. In Pensacola, Florida, the DeSoto Solar Park would be the largest photovoltaic power plant in North America with 90,000 panels. The plant used a technology that directly converts sunlight to electricity as opposed to a traditional thermal solar plant, which uses the heat to drive a steam turbine. In the San Francisco East Bay area, the Mount Diablo Unified School District used clean energy bonds under the Recovery Act to sign the largest contract for a school district solar power system in the country.

At first, the Recovery Act's solar plans seemed doomed to be stalled by rare desert tortoises, the slow loan guarantee program, and claims to Native American cultural sites. But because of the stimulus, several of the world's largest solar projects are now under construction in America. And on October 5, 2010, the Obama administration announced plans to put solar panels back on the White House roof.

$ $ $

Underlying America's clean energy future—whether it be wind, solar, or electric cars—is a network of high-efficiency power lines, batteries, and sensors known as the smart grid. Without it, Biden's dreams of "harvesting energy from the Great Plains to light up the cities of the Midwest" would never be a reality.

There's a story bandied about by policy makers whenever they talk about the smart grid, and it goes like this: If Alexander Graham Bell were alive today he'd be bewildered by the advances in telecommunications, such as iPhones and BlackBerries. But if Thomas Edison were here, he might even be able to operate today's electricity grid. While the comparison exaggerates the point, the century-old grid lumbers along with antiquated technology. Customers have little idea how much electricity their appliances consume. Energy can't be stored, making renewables reliable only when the sun shines and when the wind blows. Power companies don't know there's a blackout until a customer calls to complain.

With the smart grid, utilities can anticipate overloads and reroute power to prevent blackouts. Armed with usage reports from the Internet, consumers could shut off energy-wasting appliances or choose to use them during off-peak hours to save money. Wind and solar can be captured in one region and stored for use in another. Utilities can provide backup electricity even when the power goes out. The whole shebang, though, was decades and hundreds of billions of dollars away.

The Recovery Act provided $4 billion.[12] So instead of the smart grid, America mostly got smart meters. The digital meters provide real-time information to homeowners and power companies about how much energy was consumed. Through the stimulus, utilities also installed 875 sensors and 700 substation devices that serve as early-warning systems. The Energy Department provided a $350 million loan guarantee for the One Nevada Transmission Line (ON Line), equipped for renewable energy and stretching more than two hundred miles from Las Vegas to Ely. But power companies like Baltimore Gas and Electric and CenterPoint Energy in Houston mostly used their $200 million grants to swap out the old clunkers for smart meters.

By June 2011, stimulus recipients had installed more than 5 million smart meters with plans to reach 18 million by 2013. Smart meters would prove controversial. Cybersecurity experts warned that hackers could tap into the system and pull up a profile of someone's routine. Many consumers saw their electricity bills go up instead of reaping the promised savings. Others fretted that the electromagnetic waves would cause brain tumors.

$ $ $

The last piece of the Recovery Act's contributions to clean energy was a $400 million investment in early stage research known as the Advanced Research Projects Agency-Energy, or ARPA-E. Created under the Bush administration but funded by the stimulus, the initiative was modeled after a defense program that in the 1960s and 1970s pioneered the early development of the Internet.

The ARPA-E projects included a bacteria that acts like a reverse fuel cell converting carbon dioxide to gasoline, new refrigerants to make air conditioners more energy efficient, and a semisolid battery that could cost less than one-eighth of today's batteries. One of the most talked about projects was a technique developed by 1366 Technologies in Lexington, Massachusetts. Today, silicon wafers for solar panels are sawed from cast blocks, wasting large amounts of silicon in the process. The company's breakthrough was to form the thin wafers directly from molten silicon, making sawing unnecessary. If successful, it could reduce the cost of solar panels significantly.

In an Energy Department video about the project, secretary Steven Chu stands on the company's solar-paneled roof and provides a poignant illustration of ARPA-E's mission. "Sure there'll be some failures," he says. "But there'll be some home runs and a few grand slams, and with those grand slams we can really transform our energy choices."

But to critics, the Recovery Act's clean energy programs showed the Obama administration was picking winners and losers instead of letting the free market sort them out. To conservatives, the loan guarantees for solar plants, grants for wind farms, and tax credits for the purchase of electric cars were wasteful subsidies to a sector that had competed and lost to the cheaper, more efficient fuels of oil, gas, and coal. Critics complained that green energy would kill jobs, not create them. Wind and solar plants require few jobs once they're built, while drilling and mining are much more labor intensive. A battery-powered car means no oil changes every three thousand miles for the local mechanic. Smart meters would make the job of reading meters obsolete.

The Obama administration had readily available ammunition. In truth, every form of energy is subsidized. Each year, Congress provided $4 billion in subsidies to oil companies. Exxon, Chevron, ConocoPhillips—these were some of the richest companies in America. Oil and gas was a mature industry while renewable energy was a growing sector that had yet to get up to scale. But despite the obvious hypocrisy, in 2010, the Obama administration failed to fight back against the charge that the government was holding the hands of losing companies for social policy reasons rather than economic ones. It wasn't until April 2011, when gas prices returned to $4 a gallon, that Obama made it a priority to end taxpayer subsidies for oil companies.

Instead, the administration compared renewable energy to the government's investment in the Internet and interstate system. As Biden said in a speech, "Government plants the seeds, the private sector makes them grow, and we launch entire industries." If only it were so easy. Establishing a clean energy economy would prove difficult in a world where China was providing bountiful subsidies for its own solar and wind industries. And the awards to Solyndra and others raised a critical question: was the government merely planting the seeds or was it choosing young trees from the nurseries of venture capital and doing most of the grooming and watering itself?

The Obama administration could have avoided some of the flak if it focused more on encouraging bottom-up regional plans, said Dan Carol, the energy guru behind the Apollo Alliance.

"We had this one-size-fits-all federal programming that you can't roll out at the local level and chop up," he told me. "There was this notion that we had to pick the projects and mechanisms for the transformation of our economy in thirty days rather than saying, 'Hey, we need a trillion dollars of stimulus, now let's figure out the right way to do it.'"

Standing on the roof of Solyndra's headquarters, Miller, the corporate spokesman, was fighting a battle to assure the industry, the media, and the White House that the company's finances were sound and that sales would take off as soon as the new factory started whirring. But executives and the Energy Department would soon come to a disquieting conclusion: Solyndra was indeed running out of cash.

TWELVE

"THE CARROT THAT FEELS
LIKE A STICK"

What happens to a dream deferred?
  Does it dry up
  like a raisin in the sun?
  Or fester like a sore—
  And then run?
  —Langston Hughes, "Harlem"

"READY?" Colleen Sheeron asked her class of antsy third-graders. "Eyes on me."

The number of the day, which she held up on a flash card, was 65,284.

"What's the number in the thousandth place?" she asked. "Can you tell me what this number would be if I had five hundred more? Twenty more?"

Each time, Sheeron waited until every student raised their hands. She snapped her fingers, and the class shouted the answers in unison. *"Five! Sixty-five thousand seven hundred eighty-four! Sixty-five thousand three hundred four!"*

"Follow me," she said as she moved around the room still holding the flash cards. A white 4. A red 80. "Good, I like all these eyes."

She asked questions and snapped her fingers in quick succession. "Can you double this number?" "How many more to a thousand?"

The kids, all wearing blue T-shirts and gray sweatpants, were totally engaged. They are part of a grand experiment in American education from one of the poorest neighborhoods in Wilmington, Delaware. In just three years, their school, the Kuumba Academy, a charter school, went from having 49 percent of the students proficient in math to 87 percent, based on state test scores. Kuumba had closed the achievement gap. There are great charters and great public schools, just as there are awful charters and awful public schools. But by unshackling teachers and principals from bureaucracy and allowing more experimentation, some charters have produced tremendous results where few expected it. If such student achievement could happen at Kuumba, why couldn't it happen throughout the state of Delaware? And if could happen in Delaware, why not across America?

This was the basis of the Obama administration's plan for education reform under the Recovery Act. The package earmarked $100 billion for education. The vast majority of it was dedicated to stopping the bleeding: preventing layoffs of teachers during the Great Recession and making sure that schools could keep their commitments to disadvantaged and special education students. But a special fund of $4 billion called Race to the Top sought to promote the kinds of reforms that had already helped Kuumba achieve success.

The Kuumba Academy is located in the old Security Trust and Safe Deposit Company building, a hulking two-story brownstone that once served a thriving commercial district north of Wilmington's riverfront. Kuumba (pronounced *koo-OOM-bah*) was founded in 2001 as a school focusing on music, dance, drama, and the visual arts. Its name means "creativity" in Swahili and it is one of the seven principles of Nguzo Saba, a set of values associated with the black heritage festival of Kwanzaa that also includes unity, self-determination, collective work and responsibility, cooperative economics, purpose, and faith.

But the school might be said to follow an eighth principle: accountability. Outside every classroom was a laminated bar chart showing how well the class performed on the school's internal fall and winter exams in math and reading. For one first-grade classroom, the chart showed that 73.33 percent of students had met or exceeded their goal on the winter test, known as MAPS.

The same day I visited Kuumba in the spring of 2011, a small group of public school teachers was there to observe instruction. One of them noticed the chart hanging on the wall and turned to his colleagues incredulously.

"You think that would fly in a public school?" he asked jokingly.

Walking Kuumba's hallways and sitting in its classrooms, it was apparent that almost every element of the school was built around an expectation of student achievement. Every classroom posted its "Mathematician of the Week" on the door, and one hallway featured a gallery of photos with students holding signs that said I MADE MY MAPS READING GOAL.

The Kuumba Academy has 253 students. Three of them are Latino, one is white, and one is Asian. The other 248 students are black. Three-quarters of the students are poor enough to receive free or discounted meals.

The charter model has given Kuumba flexibility to experiment. Several years ago, the school began using data from the internal assessments to drive instruction. The data allowed the school to pinpoint the areas students were missing and individualize learning so students could focus on their gaps. Kuumba also won a technology grant to put electronic Smart boards in every classroom.

Through another grant, the school introduced a curriculum known as Singapore Math, which emphasizes building blocks, diagrams, and the recognition of patterns rather than the memorization of rules. It is based on the national math program of Singapore, which has ranked among the top countries in math performance since the mid-1990s. An example of the diagrams was shown in a fifth-grade class where students were learning to multiply fractions and whole numbers, such as $3/12$ of 144. Instead of writing an equation, the students drew a bar representing 144 and then divided it into 12 pieces each worth 12 points. They then circled three boxes and added the 12s to get 36.

Charter schools, which began opening in the early 1990s, are publicly funded but independently run without the restrictions of union contracts or district rules. "The analogy is if you think of a school district as a cruise ship, then Kuumba is the motor boat," said Susan

Harris, director of the Delaware Charter Schools Network. "So if you can turn very quickly in that motor boat, then if Singapore Math didn't work, you haven't invested millions of dollars and thousands of children's lives."

In Sheeron's class, the students learn in a fast-paced, competitive environment that emphasizes activity and tries to ensure that every student sees progress. As class started, Sheeron informed her students that they currently had six points, but Ms. Samra's class was close behind with five.

After warming them up with flash cards, Sheeron led her students through a series of drills called "skip counting." As she jabbed her thumb up or down multiple times, the students added or subtracted in their heads by threes.

"You need to follow me carefully because if you're playing with your book or your fingers or you're looking at your neighbors, you're going to miss it," she said.

The students again answered in unison.

"They do feed off of incentives," she said. "So that's why we celebrate their victories and just make sure it's a very happy, exciting experience because if it's a negative frustrating one, a lot of them just shut down."

Since adopting Singapore Math, the students have shown an excitement over math. "Man, they dreaded math and so did I," Sheeron said. "Now they love math. They're excited to do math. They love the sprints. They love the competition. They're just, they're excited. Their emotion about it is a big difference."

While Kuumba Academy could be classified as one of the isolated pockets of success in the American education system, similar to Harlem Children's Zone or the KIPP schools, many questions linger about whether it offers a wide-scale solution. Sheeron's class had eighteen students. Could it work in a class of thirty-five?

$ $ $

In the world of education, there is a persistent sense of defeatism. Every few years, a president or policy maker or a so-called reformer comes out with a new fad to transform education. And every year, the

United States continues to fall behind other developed countries, African Americans and Latinos in the inner cities continue to lag their white peers in the suburbs, and the government continues to spend increasing amounts of money to fix the nation's schools. The documentary *Waiting for Superman*, which came out in October 2010, just as the administration's Race to the Top program took effect, highlighted this with a stunning montage of promises from presidents past.

The foundation of America's modern education policy is the Elementary and Secondary Education Act of 1965. Signed into law by Lyndon B. Johnson, it aimed to narrow the achievement gap by directing additional funding to school districts with low-income students. Nixon continued by desegregating schools, increasing federal aid, and implementing tests to track student achievement. Ford established special education programs. Carter created the Department of Education and expanded research and testing to promote accountability. Reagan had his A Nation at Risk report, which showed that America's schools were failing and recommended reforms. His successor, George H. W. Bush, called himself the "education president." Clinton pushed for systemic reforms to turn around the worst-performing schools or shut them down.[1]

But the most transformative legislation since LBJ was the No Child Left Behind Act, signed by George W. Bush in 2002. The law required students to take state tests in reading and math to measure how well they were learning the material. Schools had to show progress on test scores every year, and every student had to be proficient by 2014. But if a school failed to meet its targets two years in a row, it would face sanctions. It would be labeled "in need of improvement" and be required to develop a turnaround plan. Students could choose to go to another school in the district. If the school continued to fail, teachers could be fired and the school taken over by the state or a private company.

But seven years after No Child Left Behind, states were nowhere near having every student proficient. In some urban areas, fewer than half the students graduated high school on time. As noted in *Waiting for Superman*, only 18 percent of Alabama eighth graders were considered proficient in math. But because the measuring stick was set by the state, many education departments found a solution: lower standards and make their tests easier.

At the same time, there was a growing chorus of nonprofits and public school leaders advocating reforms, such as recruiting teachers from outside fields, tying teacher pay to student performance, expanding science and math programs, increasing the number of charter schools, making greater use of data, even ending the sacrosanct promise of tenure.

It was against this backdrop that Education secretary Arne Duncan, the reform-minded CEO of the Chicago Public Schools, and his senior adviser, Jon Schnur, went to the Hill during the transition period with a plan for the stimulus bill. Up until this point, Congress had been discussing spending $20 billion to $30 billion through the traditional formulas for special-education students and low-income schools. But the Obama administration wanted to use the Recovery Act to encourage long-sought reforms. Its proposal was to allocate $100 billion to avert teacher layoffs and invest in programs that would reap better results from the system.

But the unprecedented windfall wasn't greeted with a groundswell of enthusiasm in Congress. Some of the bill's architects like Representative David Obey were skeptical. The reforms went against traditional liberal education policy and often sowed conflicts with the teachers' unions when implemented at the local level. In some respects, the ideas were more in line with those of Republicans.

At the heart of the proposal was a $15 billion competitive grant program that Schnur, the founder of a nonprofit promoting teacher quality, had put together called Race to the Top. The idea was based on a bill that Obama had sponsored in the Senate in 2006 and 2007 and on a series of competitions that Duncan had run in Chicago to reward low-performing schools that boosted test scores. Despite the pushback, Obama made clear that the Recovery Act would include at least some money for reform. So congressional leaders agreed to sit down and hammer out the details.

The House bill contained $79 billion in aid to the states, including $15 billion to be used at the discretion of the secretary of Education. But when the state relief fund was slashed during Senate negotiations, Race to the Top was pared back too. In the end, the stimulus included $40 billion to avoid school cutbacks and layoffs, $17 billion for Pell Grants for college, $14 billion to increase the tuition tax credit, $13 billion for low-income school districts, and $12 billion for special education.

An additional $5 billion, down from the proposed $15 billion, was reserved for competitive grants. Of that, a $4.35 billion pool would go to states through Race to the Top while the rest would be awarded to school districts. While the Recovery Act set no new federal education mandates itself, the carrot of a gigantic grant would set off a frenzy of state reform bills that lifted restrictions on charter schools and linked teacher evaluations to student test scores.

$ $ $

One of the more poignant moments in Obama's first address to Congress after the Recovery Act passed was when he told the story of Ty'Sheoma Bethea, an eighth grader from Dillon, South Carolina, who attended a school where some facilities were built in the 1890s. Bethea, fourteen, attended J. V. Martin Junior High School, a mishmash of old buildings and rusting trailers, where some of her classmates had trouble identifying letters of the alphabet.[2] Dillon was poor and rural (but coincidentally the hometown of Federal Reserve chairman Ben Bernanke).

Obama had visited the school and described it as "a place where the ceilings leak, the paint peels off the walls, and they have to stop teaching six times a day because the train barrels by their classroom." Bethea had written a letter to the president and borrowed money from the principal for the stamp. "We are just students," she wrote, "trying to become lawyers, doctors, congressmen like yourself and one day president, so we can make a change to not just the state of South Carolina but also the world. We are not quitters."

Obama had used the school in his call for the stimulus to include funding for twenty-first-century classrooms and science labs. The Senate bill originally allocated $16 billion for school construction and renovations. Dillon was set to receive about $2 million. But Republicans balked at the idea of the federal government building schools, and the money was stripped from the final package. While the attention brought donations of desks and other supplies, the cuts threatened to doom any hopes that the school wouldn't shake when the train went by.

The Recovery Act did include about $1.5 billion in grants and loans that rural communities, Indian reservations, and areas with military bases could use to modernize schools. And states were welcome to spend their $9 billion in general fiscal relief for construction, though few did. The stimulus also created a new class of no-interest bonds, known as Q-scabs, which school districts could issue to finance construction and repairs. But many districts turned down the money either because banks or voters weren't interested. At the end of 2009, only one of sixty-nine eligible school districts in North Carolina had found a buyer for its bonds. "The idea is to stimulate the economy," a state administrator said. "Then it comes to a screeching halt because our people can't find lenders."[3]

$ $ $

By the fall of 2009, the Recovery Act had created or saved about 325,000 education jobs, as a result of the state fiscal relief and funding for special education and low-income schools. After the initial refusal from several southern governors, including Mark Sanford of South Carolina, every state accepted the money. The list of layoffs averted included more than 14,000 teachers in New York City, 1,100 jobs in Las Vegas, and 6,300 in Los Angeles, according to a report by the White House Domestic Policy Council. Peoria, Illinois, hired teachers to reduce class sizes in kindergarten and first and second grade. The principal at the Rothschild Middle School in Columbus, Georgia, hired math teachers to increase individualized attention. The stimulus money helped forestall an "education disaster," Arne Duncan told Congress.

It's hard to say if mayors and school boards could have stomached such massive layoffs politically. But it's not hard to imagine the domino effect that even half the planned cuts would have had. While some economists have argued the teachers would have found private-sector jobs,[4] throwing hundreds of thousands of people onto the unemployment rolls at a time when unemployment was already climbing toward 10 percent makes such an optimistic scenario implausible. More likely, the unemployment rate would have climbed as the newly jobless teachers reined in spending and strained the public health care system. Long term, millions of students might have fallen through the cracks as they muddled through several years of forty-student classrooms. Innovations would probably have been off the table. As one education policy expert told me, "You can't start reform by digging a hole."

After already sustaining $17 billion in cuts to the public education system in the previous two years, the stimulus was a "godsend" for California, Deputy Superintendent Lupita Cortez Alcalá told me. But the $100 billion in stimulus money for education wasn't enough to close the gaping budget holes nationwide. A study by the University of Washington before the stimulus passed estimated that 574,000 K-12 education jobs would be eliminated during the next three school years. Indeed, according to the national Bureau of Labor Statistics, there were more than 300,000 fewer local government education employees in September 2011 than there were three years earlier.

Many states didn't increase education funding at all and merely used the federal stimulus money to free up state funding to plug other holes. Under the rules for the fiscal stabilization money, states only had to maintain education spending at 2006 levels. A survey by the American Association of School Administrators found that rather than use the money for reform, two-thirds of administrators said the funds were either maintaining the status quo or providing a marginal increase. The increase in federal funding also allowed districts to divert up to half of their own special education money for other uses.

While legal, the shell games drew a stern warning from Duncan. In a letter to Pennsylvania governor Ed Rendell, scolding the state senate, Duncan wrote: "If a state has disproportionately reduced its education budget and/or if a state has done nothing more than backfill budget holes with these dollars when the state had other resources available to it, such as a rainy-day fund, the state's competitive position to receive Race to the Top funds and/or other competitive grants may be negatively impacted."

To be sure, states received a series of conflicting directions from the Department of Education. Spend quickly, but wisely, it said. Invest in reforms, but don't do anything that you can't sustain after the money runs out. In the back of the mind of every school budget officer was the so-called funding cliff awaiting districts when the money ran out.

"The federal bill was always a bit schizophrenic in that one of the main purposes was to create and maintain jobs, which was really kind of a status quo kind of thing," Carol Bingham, director of fiscal policy for the California Department of Education, told me. "But then the other was to try to influence some education reforms."

To get their second and third portions of school stabilization money, there were strings attached. States were required to create longitudinal data systems to track student performance and identify their ten worst-performing schools. They also had to submit reams of data on how many graduates go on to college, how teachers are evaluated, and how students scored on state tests versus national exams to show whether the state had weakened standards to comply with No Child Left Behind.

The money was not without criticism and accusations of waste. Some school districts used the money not to hire, but to buy out experienced teachers who were close to retirement. Texas used some of it to fund an already planned pay raise for teachers. Others spent tens of thousands of dollars on motivational speakers and teacher conferences in luxurious locales. In Winston-Salem, North Carolina, according to federal auditors, school officials spent $40,000 on a summer enrichment program that included field trips to the Wet 'n Wild water park and to the movie theater to see *Ice Age* and *Terminator*.

The reports posted on Recovery.gov showed some districts funded summer school, reading coaches, and technology like laptops and Smart boards. Many others used the money for standard professional development workshops for teachers. But according to the Domestic Policy Council, a number of schools made strides toward reforms. Anchorage and Baltimore used the money to design data-driven teacher evaluation systems while Detroit purchased software that would link professional development programs to student achievement. In St. Paul, Minnesota, the funding went toward early intervention programs to help students who were falling behind in literacy and math. And in Lafayette, Indiana, administrators extended the school day in two of their poorest schools.

$ $ $

The Race to the Top program made Arne Duncan the most influential Education secretary in history. With $4 billion, Duncan had far more money at his disposal than the previous eight Education secretaries combined. At six-feet-five-inches tall, the salt-and-pepper-haired Duncan had played professional basketball in Australia and could now be found as a regular at pickup games with President Obama. In a way, it was symbolic of the central role that education played in Obama's plan to transform the American economy.

To the administration, education was a civil rights issue, a pillar of the country's future, and the key to global competitiveness. In decades past, a man could drop out of high school and find work in a factory that would pay enough to buy a home and raise a family. No more. "The nation that out-educates us today is going to out-compete us tomorrow," Obama said in some form or another throughout his first term. The Race to the Top plan wouldn't just shake the apple cart; it would turn it over, toss out the bad ones, and deliver a shiny new Gala or McIntosh to any state that made real reforms. To even compete, states could not have laws that prevented districts from tying teacher evaluations to student performance. And in tough words, Obama and Duncan repeatedly admonished states to repeal laws that cap the number of charter schools if they had any dreams of winning the money. To back it up, Duncan embarked on a "listening and learning tour" around the country. But it wasn't clear *who* was supposed to be doing the listening and learning.

In Race to the Top, state applications would be judged on a 500-point scale. The largest category, worth 138 points, was allotted for states that recruited teachers through alternative paths, assigned the best ones to high-poverty schools, and held them accountable by using student growth to inform decisions regarding pay, promotion, and tenure. Another 70 points would go to states that adopted common core standards and high-quality tests; 50 for intervening to turn around the lowest-achieving schools; 40 for promoting charter schools; and 47 for developing a data system and using it to inform instruction.

"In California, they have 300,000 teachers," Duncan said at a research conference in Washington, DC, before releasing the rules. "If you took the top 10 percent, they have 30,000 of the best teachers in the world. If you took the bottom 10 percent, they have 30,000 teachers that should probably find another profession. Yet no one in California can tell you which teacher is in which category. Something is wrong with that picture."

States scrambled to get their education policies in order as the first-round deadline approached in January 2010. In Tennessee, Duncan warned lawmakers that they would hurt their chance of winning if they didn't lift their enrollment restrictions on charter schools. A few weeks later they did.[5] In another speech, he called out California, New York, and Wisconsin, for their firewalls between student and teacher data. All three took up bills to scrap their laws. By the first deadline, twelve states had enacted legislative reforms, such as raising caps or blocking budget cuts for charter schools or enabling test scores to be linked to teachers. Every state except for Texas and Alaska had signed on to develop common standards.

Mike Petrilli of the Thomas B. Fordham Institute, a conservative education think tank, summed it up best in a blog post titled "The Race to the Top: The Carrot That Feels Like a Stick." In it, he described feeling torn. On the one hand, he cheered the plans to evaluate teachers based on student gains, to replicate excellent charter schools, and to expand alternate paths to teaching. "If even a few states change their policies to be in alignment with the vision articulated here, our country will be the better for it," he wrote. But on the other hand, he said the administration had essentially given the states a checklist to comply with in order to win the money. "This is Washington Knows Best at its worst and runs the risk of seeing states superficially swear allegiance to these reform ideas but implement them half-heartedly down the road," he wrote.[6]

Many school districts were opposed to Race to the Top and refused to sign on to their states' applications. The reforms lacked evidence, they argued, and often created hostility between the school board and the teachers. Until then, one of the best known examples of such reform efforts occurred in Washington, DC, where Michelle Rhee, the thirty-seven-year-old chancellor with little teaching experience set off a firestorm by dismissing principals and closing schools. A situation in Central Falls, Rhode Island, reinforced the conflict in February 2010 when the superintendent fired every high school teacher after years of failing. As a result, many unions discouraged their local chapters from participating.

The opposition made for strange bedfellows, with both the New Jersey Education Association, one of the most powerful teachers' unions, and Governor Rick Perry, soon to be a Republican presidential candidate, fretting over the "strings attached." "The conditions attached to the grant are costly and educationally unsound," NJEA president Barbara Keshishian wrote in the Star-Ledger.[7] "To me and to a lot of education experts and parents across our state, that smacks of a federal takeover of our public schools," Perry said at a press conference in Houston.

As states prepared for Race to the Top, Congressman Jim Clyburn and others were working to "keep faith" with Ty'Sheoma Bethea and find a way to repair her school. Finally, on the eve of the president's State of the Union address, the Department of Agriculture announced that Dillon, South Carolina, would receive a loan through the Recovery Act to replace the crumbling middle school Obama had talked about the year before. Bethea was now living in Atlanta after her mother lost her job at a local ambulance manufacturer.[8] But she could feel proud nonetheless; her letter had worked.

In all, forty states and the District of Columbia competed in the first round of Race to the Top. Sixteen were chosen as finalists. The states would now have to pick a team of five to make their pitch to a panel of reviewers in Washington and answer questions about their proposals.

For its team, Delaware chose Governor Jack Markell, who campaigned on education reform; Lillian Lowery, his secretary of education; Diane Donohue, the head of the teachers' union; Merv Daugherty, the superintendent of the Red Clay Consolidated School

District; and Marvin "Skip" Schoenhals, a bank executive who headed a statewide initiative for education reform. The team spent several evenings brushing up and practicing their responses. They even went down to Washington one Saturday to participate in a dry run.

The moment of truth came on March 16, 2010. In a nondescript room, the quintet sat before the reviewers to present their plan. Donohue noted that the state ranked high in improving fourth- and eighth-grade math scores. Markell discussed how the state was partnering with the University of Delaware to develop an alternative-path science and math program that would produce a hundred teachers by 2014. Schoenhals talked about how the private sector provided loan guarantees for charter schools to make capital improvements.

The state had experienced rapid growth in charter schools like Kuumba, but it wasn't afraid to shut them down if they didn't work. It also had invested in meaningful training programs, such as one in which teachers visited the YMCA, Boys & Girls Club, and other community centers to see where students go after school. They brought books to the centers, and some teachers started volunteering there at night. As far back as 1983, Delaware had developed a data system tracking students. And by 2010, the state could follow students from preschool to graduate school.

"However, it is clunky, which is a technical term for not very user-friendly," Schoenhals told the review panel. "The result is that Delaware is data-rich but not data-driven in our educational system. This plan changes that on multiple levels."

The plan would send data coaches to every school in the state to work with teachers for two years on how to interpret the data and use it in their classrooms. Teachers would get three ninety-minute sessions each month to collaborate with other teachers and learn from one another. Teachers who were not interested in becoming principals could become "teacher leaders," serving in the classroom half the day and as a consultant to other teachers for the rest. Teachers rated "highly effective" would receive bonuses up to $10,000 to transfer to high-needs schools. And the state had recently partnered with Mass Insight, a nonprofit consulting firm, to turn around its lowest-performing schools.

What's more, the plan was sustainable, Markell assured the panel. The state could continue the reforms after Race to the Top ran out by setting aside $8.5 million a year, about 1 percent of its budget. Delaware had time and politics on its side. Markell was recently elected and had at least three more years to carry out his plan. He was the cochairman of the governors' association's Common Core State Standards Initiative; so the state could be seen as a leader in that category. And Donohue and the state teachers' union not only supported the plan but campaigned to ensure that every local union president signed on to the application.

"The fact that we were able to pass some of the boldest policy reforms in the country when it comes to evaluation and school turnarounds while at the same time getting 100 percent buy-in from every superintendent, every charter leader, every school board, every affiliate of our teachers' union demonstrates not only a collective willingness to embrace change, but it also demonstrates the level of trust and respect that we have built up and that is needed to make that change stick," Markell said.

When Arne Duncan announced the winners a couple of weeks later, Delaware placed first. It would ultimately receive $119 million, or roughly $950 per student.

"Delaware has articulated a comprehensive, coherent reform agenda that clearly addresses reforms in the four education areas described in the ARRA, and a clear and credible path to achieving their goals," one of the reviewers wrote in comments on the application.

Only one other state, Tennessee, won in round one. Unlike most stimulus programs, such as the infrastructure funds or even transformative elements like high-speed rail, Race to the Top chose only the best proposals, bucking the Washington tendency to spread the money around to make everyone happy. By setting the bar high, Duncan sent a strong message: if you want your state to win in round two you better implement major reforms and get your unions and districts to the table.

Unlike other programs, such as the rural broadband grants and energy loan guarantees, the Education Department also opened up the review process to public scrutiny. It released applications that won as well as those that didn't. It posted reviewers' comments on the

Internet and uploaded videos of the panel interviews to YouTube. The approach kept the nationwide dialogue on education reform flowing and allowed other states to see what it would take to win.

$ $ $

Delaware was uniquely positioned to win Race to the Top. Many of its ideas were already on paper. The origins of Delaware's success can be traced to an artificial leather product made by DuPont in the 1960s. The material known as Corfam was an utter flop. But an entrepreneur named Bill Budinger found other uses for it on printer rollers and computer chips. Soon, the product became as essential to IBM and other computer companies as film had been for the camera industry. Budinger and his brother sold their company, Rodel Inc., in the 1990s and decided to form a nonprofit dedicated to improving public education.

The Rodel Foundation began by creating what business consultant Jim Collins calls a BHAG, a big hairy audacious goal: Delaware would become the best school system in the nation by 2012. In its first years, the foundation helped increase the supply of charter schools in hopes that parents would see the success and demand more of them. Paul Herdman came on board as president in 2004 after twenty years as a teacher, a state policy maker, a consultant to think tanks, and the vice president of a national education nonprofit. To figure out where the state was in reaching its goal, he gathered the available statistics, producing a devastating report. For every hundred high school freshmen, only sixty-one would graduate on time, and only thirty-six would go on to college in five years. Less than a third of middle and elementary school students were proficient in reading and math, based on the national test. Only 23 percent of kindergarteners were in full-day programs, compared to 60 percent nationally. Delaware ranked twenty-seventh on a national index of teacher quality. And the state had achieved these poor results despite spending more on education per student than all but six other states.

The report intentionally didn't include any recommendations, but it attracted a lot of them from the community. Superintendents, school administrators, the head of the state board of education, and leaders from the business community, the public sector, and higher education signed on to develop a new initiative called Vision 2015.

"Frankly, being the best in the country—Rodel's mission statement—was almost irrelevant," Herdman told me in his office in downtown Wilmington. "Our kids are going to be competing with kids all over the world, and if the U.S. was middle of the pack compared to the rest of the world, if we're here and we're among the best, we're still pretty deep in the deck. The thought was let's shift the framing from the best in the country to the best in the world and put it out ten years from when we started the conversation in 2005."

The initiative received funding from the Broad Foundation, a major player in education reform. But getting everyone to agree on a plan wasn't as easy. Early on, Herdman was warned that the teachers' union would only be an obstacle, that they'd only care about pay raises. But Herdman was a new player in Delaware education and offered a clean slate. He called Howard Weinberg, the executive director of the Delaware State Education Association, and asked him about what he'd been hearing.

"His response was we have eight to nine thousand employees. We have a good relationship with the legislature and the governor's office. We're going to be involved one way or another," Herdman recalled. "So if we're not included in this discussion, we may be in a position where the only thing we can do is block. But if you include us in the discussion, you may be surprised that we can help contribute to the vision."

With the union on board, the task force began meeting to develop the plan. They had an agreement that every stakeholder would feel comfortable with 85 percent of the ideas and put aside the 15 percent they disagreed with. They hired a facilitator who had worked in the Middle East and Northern Ireland. He started by asking everyone to state their vision. They went around the room spouting platitudes: all kids can learn, blah blah blah.

"You're all full of shit," the facilitator told them. "You're all afraid of your own constituents, and if you were willing to disappoint a portion of your constituents to actually reach a higher goal, you would have met that goal ten years ago."

His words hit home. "I think there was kind of a harsh realization that he was right," Herdman said. "It wasn't like putting stickies up on the wall."

The task force got to work developing solutions and even drafted legislation, but it never saw the light of day. No one was willing to take the political risk of putting their names to a statewide package of reforms. So the group decided to work from the ground up, forming a network and getting districts and charter schools to sign on. It wasn't until Markell, who had been on Rodel's advisory board, became governor in 2009 that Vision 2015 gained any traction.

The plan called for developing better data systems to track student progress, establishing a new career path for master teachers, lengthening instruction time, investing more in early education, and using student achievement as a measure of teacher performance.

"The basic gist was here. We had started the conversation four years before Race to the Top," Herdman said. "We had detailed conversations with the Delaware State Education Association, for example, that student performance needed to be tied to teacher evaluations. So it wasn't a mad rush to fill out an application; we had already had that conversation."

$ $ $

Diane Donohue, the president of the teachers' union, was a veteran third-grade teacher in the Indian River School District, which is in the southeastern part of the state. Why did Race to the Top appear so painless in Delaware, I wondered, when the exact same reforms seemed so noxious just over the border in New Jersey or in Washington, DC?

The answer was simple. Several years ago, teachers were given a voice in policy discussions. Treated as partners and the experts that they were, the unions no longer felt like porcupines ready to fire their quills whenever someone treaded on their turf. And with firm deadlines under Race to the Top, education reform could no longer be a far-off goal in the future. Where the timeline exacerbated the tensions in some states, the program accelerated the negotiations in Delaware and other states that had already begun to work on reform.

"The governor made lots of changes to his Race to the Top application based on the input of DSEA [Delaware State Education Association]," Donohue said. "Now that's not to say we got everything we wanted because we absolutely did not get everything we wanted. But what we did get were some things that teachers and educators across the state had been asking for for a very long time."

One of those was additional collaborative planning time for teachers. Under the state's plan, schools would be required to carve out ninety-minute sessions. Teachers had been asked to use data more but had never been trained. So the idea of data coaches was appealing. Most important, though, teachers would be given a seat at the table to develop their evaluation system and define what would constitute sufficient student growth. Teachers had been "screaming" for years for an assessment system that was fair and less haphazard, Donohue said. In exchange, they agreed to some stringent rules. One of the major problems in education is that year after year, across the country, nearly every teacher is rated effective. In Delaware, no educator would be rated effective unless their students showed improvement, partially based on state test scores. To be rated highly effective, teachers would have to demonstrate more than a year of student growth. And those deemed ineffective or needing improvement for two or three years in a row could lose their jobs, even if they had tenure.

In her book *The Death and Life of the Great American School System*, the education historian Diane Ravitch argues that No Child Left Behind had gone astray from accountability for student learning to testing for testing's sake.

"What once was an effort to improve the quality of education turned into an accounting strategy: Measure, then punish or reward," she writes. "The strategy produced fear and obedience among educators; it often generated higher test scores. But it had nothing to do with education."[9]

With Race to the Top, Ravitch has said, Obama was giving Bush a third term for education policy. The program was certainly an extension of No Child Left Behind. But to Donohue, Race to the Top seemed different. It wasn't punitive. And in Delaware at least, students and teachers wouldn't be evaluated on a single test score. Under a new assessment system, they would be judged on growth measured several times throughout the year. Where No Child Left Behind was dictated from on high, Race to the Top required states to go to the feds with a plan and it favored union support. For the first time in a long while, reform wasn't happening to them; it was happening with them.

"This is our opportunity as educators to get our voice at the table," Donohue said. "And if we don't do it now because we get frustrated or we get angry, I'm not sure we'll be asked for our input again."

$ $ $

As senator and former governor Tom Carper noted, Delaware is known for the five Cs: credit cards, corporations, chickens, chemicals, and cars. With Race to the Top, perhaps it would also be known for its classrooms. The state's largest city, Wilmington, reflects this hodge-podge. Its downtown features many glass skyscrapers housing its banking and corporate headquarters. But it also has a number of vacant storefronts and decrepit row homes left over from when DuPont and the Port of Wilmington made the city an industrial powerhouse during the First and Second World Wars. Since then, Wilmington's population has declined dramatically from 112,000 before World War II to about 70,000 in 1980, a number that has held through today. Its last General Motors plant closed down in 2009 only to reopen with the help of an Energy Department loan guarantee to the small electric carmaker, Fisker Automotive.

Notably, Wilmington was also the hometown of Vice President Biden. It was the place where his family had moved when his father hit hard times, where he launched his political career, and where he still went home on the weekends even as the nation's second-in-command. His wife, Jill, had taught in the Brandywine School District and had been a member of the state teachers' union.[10]

Wilmington has no school district of its own. Instead, as a result of desegregation, the city was divided into four slices extending out from the city center to the suburbs and exurbs. In the state's largest district, Christina, students from the inner city are still bussed out to high schools in the suburbs. The Christina School District is believed to be one of the only noncontiguous school districts, save for Hawaii, in the

United States. It is made up of a larger piece that contains the city of Newark and its surrounding areas on the Pennsylvania and Maryland borders and a much smaller piece resembling a crumpled ball of paper that contains Wilmington's most urban neighborhoods.

Christina had the highest dropout rate in the state. It was under "Academic Watch," the second lowest level under No Child Left Behind, and all of its high schools were below target for adequate yearly progress. As a result of a zero-tolerance policy, about one in four students was either suspended or expelled in the 2009–10 school year. The policy led to some unflattering national media attention. In 2009, a fifth-grade girl was suspended for bringing a cake knife to school to serve her classmates a treat as part of her candidacy for student government. A few months later, a six-year-old was suspended and threatened with alternative school for bringing a Cub Scout camping utensil that included a spoon, fork, and knife. As Delaware prepared to spend its Race to the Top money, it picked four schools as part of its plan to turn around persistently low-performing schools. Two of them, Stubbs Elementary and Glasgow High, were in Christina.

Interestingly, one of the most vocal critics of Race to the Top in Delaware was John Young, the president of the Christina school board. After being laid off from a truck-stop chain in 2008, Young went back to college to get his MBA and made a decision to become more active in the community. He came from a family of educators and had a son in third grade in the district. So he decided to run for the school board and won. Pointed and direct, Young was known for needling the majority on the school board by posting videos on his blog, such as the scarecrow from *The Wizard of Oz* singing "If I Only Had a Brain." When the state announced the turnaround schools in August 2010, he wrote, "Unproven Reforms are on the way!!!!!!!!!!"

Young's main opposition to Race to the Top, he told me, was that many of the ideas, such as restructuring schools and giving teachers bonuses, weren't backed up with evidence. The interventions, he said, would destroy communities by causing good teachers to leave and taking away the stability that students need to thrive.

"The unrest at the school tends to fracture the community and fracture the school around it and makes it more difficult for success to occur," Young said. Stubbs Elementary, he noted, had recently replaced its principal and allowed more than 70 percent of teachers to transfer in an effort to get another federal grant.

"I've got a school three blocks down the street from Stubbs," he said. "Bancroft Elementary School. Their test scores are bad. But because they scored a little bit higher, the other school gets $700,000 worth of help and Bancroft gets nothing. And so the child at Bancroft that fits the same profile as the child at Stubbs, but just happens to live on a different side of the street, doesn't get any help?" (Bancroft was later chosen for turnaround funds in September 2011, but Young said he could point to several others that fit the same profile.)

The overriding factor that's overlooked is poverty, Young said: students in families living paycheck to paycheck who have to move frequently for a new job or for a better deal on rent. A good way to counter that, he said, is by allowing them to create bonds with good teachers by having smaller class sizes. Teachers didn't go into the profession for a paycheck; so bonuses will have little effect, he said. What they crave is trust and autonomy.

"If you want to change the culture of a building as far as getting the best teachers, I think you have to start with the best leader," he said. "I would argue strongly that if you gave the five best teachers in the district the ability to pick the principal they wanted to work for, they would go to the worst school in the district and they would do it for free."

To Young, common standards would only handcuff a teacher from adapting to the needs of her classroom. Data can be useful, he said. But did they really need to spend so much money on data coaches? Teachers know from being in the classroom every day who's picking up the lesson and who's not.

"But this too shall pass," he said. One thing the constant tinkering has stimulated is the market for education consultants. Since winning Race to the Top, Young told me, he's been bombarded with e-mails from people pitching reforms in a box. Some have taken to calling it "No Consultant Left Behind."[11] "There's going to be another reform three years from now—guaranteed," Young said. "Because this one's not going to work and they won't take any time to reflect on why it didn't work because somebody will have come up with another silver bullet. There's money in it. This is all money, money, money, money, money, money, money."

$ $ $

With the bar and the stakes set high for round two of Race to the Top, states continued to scramble for reforms. Within days of the announcement that only Delaware and Tennessee made the first cut, lawmakers in Kentucky, Maryland, and Florida moved forward with bills intended to improve their standing in the federal competition. Colorado passed a trailblazing law that required at least 50 percent of a teacher's evaluation to be based on students' academic growth. In New York, legislators more than doubled the number of charter schools allowed under state law. By the time the second-round winners were announced, thirty-two states had passed laws in line with the education reforms promoted by Race to the Top, and thirty-five had adopted common core standards.

Arne Duncan called it a "quiet revolution." "This entire process has moved a nation," he said in a conference call with reporters in July 2010. "We have unleashed an avalanche of education reform activity at the state and at the local level."

The ten winners announced a month later were Massachusetts, New York, Hawaii, Florida, Rhode Island, the District of Columbia, Maryland, Georgia, North Carolina, and Ohio. Many education experts who had handicapped the race were surprised that Colorado and Louisiana didn't make the list. Colorado passed perhaps the most aggressive and politically fraught reform bill in the country. It had recently won a federal grant to build a statewide data system. And it had repeatedly garnered praise from the Obama administration. Louisiana had embraced charter schools after Hurricane Katrina and it had adopted a "value-added" model to measure teacher performance.

In fact, the only winner west of the Mississippi River was Hawaii, which won $75 million even though Duncan had rebuked the state for cutting seventeen school days to save money. While some attributed the results to politics, Colorado and Louisiana seem to have been brought down by reviewers who doubted they would succeed without more buy-in from school boards and teachers' unions.

Race to the Top also confounded California. Despite its challenges, the state had passed controversial education reforms and secured the support of districts representing 1.7 million students.

"To compare the complexity and size of a state like California to, oh I don't know, Delaware—my goodness!—the whole state of Delaware is smaller than some of our cities," Deputy Superintendent Lupita Cortez Alcalá told me. "The race won't be won without California. You can't negate 6.3 million kids."

$ $ $

As the 2010–11 school year began, more of Delaware's plans came into view. The Department of Education would divide the grant in half, keeping $60 million for statewide reforms and distributing the other $60 million to school districts and charters based on federal formulas for low-income students. In the first year, the state would pay for every high school student to take the SAT, regardless of academic ability. One district used the money to institute a SAT prep course during the school day.

The Kuumba Academy received $200,000 from Race to the Top and another $150,000 under a regular stimulus program to reward five top-performing schools. While Kuumba's math scores had improved significantly, its reading scores had gone up only marginally. The charter would use the stimulus money to purchase a reading curriculum that had been successful in Massachusetts. It would also create an after-school program, design individualized improvement plans for every student, and try to increase parental engagement. At Kuumba, parents are required to volunteer thirty hours a year as a condition of enrollment, and students don't receive a report card until their parents have met with the teacher. Under Race to the Top, parents would receive their own report card grading their performance on homework completion and participation in school events.

The Christina School District was also moving forward with its plans to turn around Stubbs Elementary and Glasgow High. The district had four options: shut down the school, turn it into a charter, replace the principal and half the teachers, or remove the principal and change the learning environment. The last method, known as "transformation," had been deemed "reform light" by Mass Insight, the consulting firm that had partnered with the state.[12] But it was the model supported by the state teachers' union, and in the end, Christina decided to go with that one.

Christina superintendent Marcia Lyles unveiled the district's plans for Stubbs and Glasgow at community forums in November 2010. Stubbs was located at Eleventh and Pine on the east side of downtown Wilmington. The neighborhood north of the Christina River was filled with old working-class row homes, many of them boarded up or covered in graffiti. The only nonresidential buildings were churches and liquor stores. Over the river and railroad tracks were a prison, the interstate, a landfill, and the Delaware River. Driving back over the bridge, I noticed a sign that read WELCOME TO WILMINGTON—A PLACE TO BE SOMEBODY.

Stubbs was decorated like a typical elementary school. Banners in the hallway asked WHAT IS YOUR DESTINY? and read, EDUCATION—THE PATH TO YOUR DREAMS. The forum was held in the library and began as many school meetings do with technical difficulties involving the projector. About fifteen parents showed up to fill the fifty seats.

Starting in the 2011–12 school year, Stubbs would turn into an early STEM academy. STEM, which stands for science, technology, engineering, and math, was a popular program being adopted across the United States. Students would participate in a central collaborative project, such as robotics or plant and animal research, while learning their core subjects.

"We're not looking to make aerospace engineers out of our babies at Stubbs," Lyles said. "It's about projects and those things that children love to do around discovery and exploration that we want to get them excited about."

The students' interest in technology was evidenced by the fact that the children immediately ran to the computers upon entering the room. Glasgow would also adopt a STEM program as part of its creation of three academies within the school. The other two would be "business and entrepreneurship" and "humanities and the arts."

Both schools would have to add instructional time either by extending the school day or the school year. At Stubbs, officials planned to add an hour to each day and students needing additional help would attend a two-week "acceleration academy" over the summer. Teachers would be picked not by seniority but by effectiveness. Under another grant program, Stubbs would also be part of a community school initiative modeled after the successful Harlem Children's Zone. Run by a nonprofit social services agency, the program sought to engage parents and students in activities such as concerts, poetry readings, and picnics. It would also provide homework help and work to connect parents and children to other services in the community.

$ $ $

Paul Herdman of the Rodel Foundation marveled about how so much had changed is so little time. Delaware was moving to common core standards. Teacher evaluations were being linked to student achievement. A new testing system would measure growth instead of proficiency. The state was building alternative pipelines for strong teachers and principals. Districts were turning around their lowest-performing schools.

"We've seen more movement in the last eighteen months than I've seen in the last eight years," Herdman said.

Many of the reforms wouldn't be in place until 2012 and 2013, and it may be years after that when we can judge whether Race to the Top was a success or failure. Complicating matters was that despite the government interventions, states were still in financial stress. The plan had been that the stimulus would tide states over until the economy was out of this mess. But nearly two years after the Recovery Act was passed, job growth was low and the recovery was slow.

The housing collapse which got America into the recession in the first place would continue to haunt school districts as they struggled to deal with weakened tax revenue from depressed property values. Many states found themselves staring at the funding cliff. According to the Obama administration, as many as 300,000 teachers and staff, roughly the same number saved with stimulus money, were at risk of losing their jobs in the 2010–11 school year. And things looked just as bad for 2011–12.

Still, with Race to the Top starting to take effect, it seemed that Delaware had everything going for it to prove that education reform worked and to lift up their struggling students.

THIRTEEN

THE SHELLACKING

In the shadow of the steeple I saw my people
By the relief office I seen my people
As they stood there hungry, I stood there asking
Is this land made for you and me?
　　—Woody Guthrie, "This Land Is Your Land"

ED NEUFELDT WAS ON HIS Sunday morning bread route. He'd been at it since 5:30 A.M. and by 9:10, he was at the Save-A-Lot in Goshen, Indiana.

It had been almost two years since he found out the RV factory was shutting down, more than a year since he introduced Obama for his stimulus speech, and about six months since Electric Motors Corporation closed up shop and moved out of town. By now, he was a regular face at the supermarkets of southern Elkhart County.

"How's track going?" he asked one of the teenage clerks as he walked in.

"Good," the teenager responded. "We just had relays. I placed sixth in hurdles."

"Good," Neufeldt said, slapping him on the shoulder.

Neufeldt moved through the aisles at a rapid clip as if he were power walking at a high school track himself. He wore black pants, loafers, a ball cap that read ALL-AMERICAN DAD, and a gray collared shirt with sweat dripping three-quarters of the way down his back. Neufeldt pushed a cart of turquoise-and-maroon-colored crates out from the stockroom past a rack of eyeglasses, a stack of soda bottles, and a trough of frozen food. He grabbed the loaves of bread two at a time by their plastic wraps, placed them on the shelves, and moved the bread from back to front to make the display look orderly.

A customer came over and took a package of hamburger buns from the cart.

"Get it fresh, bud!" Neufeldt greeted him.

Overhead, the 1980s pop song "In a Big Country" played on the speakers. "In a big country, dreams stay with you . . ."

The bread aisles of America's supermarkets have become a world's fair of flavors and styles. There was Famous St. Louis–Style Robust Rye, Indiana Spud Potato Bread, and Lewis Circle Thick-Sliced Texas Toast. But Neufeldt wasn't stocking these. Nor was he stocking the Hartford Farms Eight-Grain Super Premium Bread, the Nickles Country-Style Split-Top Oatmeal Bread, or Aunt Millie's Homestyle Cracked Wheat with Whole Grain. Neufeldt's bread was plain and simple, the bread and butter, so to speak, of kitchen tables. Neufeldt stocked Fluffy bread with the bunny logo. It came in wheat and white, hamburger and hot dog.

Where Neufeldt once made $20 an hour at the RV factory, he now earned $9 an hour driving the bread route about twelve hours a week. He was reimbursed thirty-five cents per mile but no longer had health insurance. He supplemented that by cleaning up a doctor's office at night for $11 an hour. Altogether, Neufeldt made about $250 a week. He had been receiving $376 a week on unemployment, but in late May the state cut him off because of his part-time jobs. I asked Neufeldt what he thought about the stimulus package.

"I don't know," he said. "You can throw a negative outlook on it or a positive outlook on it, but I think we're a lot better off than we were a year ago."

Elkhart had bounced back somewhat. The unemployment rate was now 14 percent. New electric vehicle manufacturers such as Think and Navistar were getting going. And some of the RV factories were hiring again, though Neufeldt said some of his buddies had gone back to similar jobs for half the pay.

As we rumbled past corn and soybean fields in his white Chevy S-10, I noticed three fading lime-green bracelets on Neufeldt's right hand. They read GREEN JOBS FOR AMERICA. Neufeldt started wearing them as a gimmick to go along with his walk to Washington. Then it became a commitment and eventually a mission.

"When the unemployment rate in Elkhart County was below 5 percent, I was going to take this one off," he said. "When Indiana was at 5 percent, I was going to take the other one off. And when the U.S. got there, I was going take this one off and wear a red, white, and blue band for the United States of America. But it never got there."

He paused.

"I was going to paint this truck green," he said. "I'm glad I didn't."

After the bread route, we headed to church, and then back to his home in Wakarusa. The town's name was derived from a Native American word meaning "knee-deep in mud." Every year in April it held a maple syrup festival, which featured an all-you-can-eat pancake and sausage breakfast, an all-you-can-eat barbecue, Amish buggy rides, a parade, and the crowning of a maple syrup queen.

Every so often, as we drove, Neufeldt asked a question out of the blue. He had been watching more and more Fox News and wanted to know what I thought. "You think Obama is a Christian?" he asked. "Were most of the stimulus jobs union?"

"I just hope we're not headed toward socialism," Neufeldt said at one point. "I guess I watch too much Glenn Beck. It just seems like he never has anything good to say. I agree with some of the things, but . . ."

$ $ $

In the year and a half since Elkhart was dubbed "Joblessville, USA," the city had made a number of improvements to spruce up its image. The civic plaza, which once instructed residents on how to file for unemployment benefits, had a new electronic sign that rotated with notices about Pay It Forward Day and the Boy Scouts Pinewood Derby. The city website featured a new promotional video highlighting the city's "big-city style" and "big-city cuisine," such as sushi, a microbrewery, mahi mahi, and martinis. "Behind the shining storefronts and modern facades, you can feel the entrepreneurial spirit that made Elkhart legendary," the video said.

The city had received more stimulus money: $4 million for a water treatment system that would prevent raw sewage from flowing into the river during heavy rainfall,

There was $600,000 to tear down an old foundry and chemical pump company and remediate the land for development, $500,000 to make city hall more energy efficient. Elkhart also used Recovery Act bonds to save money on the renovation of the historic Lerner Theatre downtown.

"It appears when Mr. Obama goes on network television, the word Elkhart comes out of his mouth again and again," Mayor Dick Moore said. "He certainly hasn't forgotten us. I think it would be hard to deny with $40 million coming into our city. I think he's pretty much fulfilled that promise."

But signs of the crisis remained. Flytraps restaurant had reopened, but Casey's, another downtown standby, had closed. Michiana Country RV still had BUYERS SALE NOW painted across the glass of its showroom, closed for more than a year. Hopman Jewelers, which once bore the sign BUYING OLD JEWELRY, had been renamed The Treasure Chest. Now its sign read BUYING OLD JEWELRY, COINS, AND DENTAL GOLD. According to a report published by the U.S. Conference of Mayors, the Elkhart area wouldn't return to prerecession employment until after 2039.

The door that sheriff's deputies had kicked in at the Gonyons's old house on Main Street had been replaced with a new black door. But for Terry and Desiree Gonyon, the economic situation hadn't changed much since they were evicted with their nine children.

"Just life in the trailer park," Terry told me. "We're just kind of weathering out the storm if that's what you want to call it. Things aren't really getting any better, but they aren't really getting any worse either."

"Eh, depends on what aspect you look at," Desiree cut in.

"Yeah, we're not back to where we were before the bottom fell out, but I mean the RV seems to be picking up," said Terry, a home construction contractor. "I've been working off and on and off and on, but even last week, the guys that I normally work for, which were the same people I worked for before the collapse, they told me that their work is starting to fall. It's just up and down still. It's not back to normal by any means."

Terry was excited about the prospect of the electric vehicle industry in Elkhart. He was a lifelong tinkerer with cars and electronics. Despite its modest appearance outside, their mobile home was wired with eight computers that Terry had received from reviewing products and offering tech help online. Even the TV was operated by a computer with enough *Tom and Jerry* files to entertain the kids for three days. Maybe, Terry thought, he'd eventually get a job with Think or Navistar.

The morning shift at the Subway had been steady for Desiree. To help out with money, her mom got a night-shift job at the gas station store that houses the Subway. The store provided Desiree with a perch to observe the area's economy. More people were coming in to buy things. But there were a lot of people who seemed to be milking unemployment, carelessly filling out an application at the store and doing nothing to follow up or show they were serious about wanting the job. One day a guy came in and said he was on his way to Washington to protest with the Tea Party.

Then, leaving the supermarket one day, Desiree saw a lady and three kids standing on the corner with a sign reading ME AND MY KIDS NEED FOOD. Figuring she had probably bought more than she needed anyway, Desiree walked over and gave them a bag of food. The kids' faces lit up as they rummaged through the bag and started eating right away. Just because we're in the situation we're in, Desiree thought, doesn't mean there wasn't someone else who needed our help.

The stimulus had helped the Gonyons somewhat. The children had always qualified for Medicaid and food stamps, but now they received a little bit more.

"One of our plans was to take the year and try to save up money and buy one of these homes that the bank has for sale for like five grand or ten grand, and just buy it outright and then spend whatever we would have in fixing it up," Terry said. "But that didn't work out for us either."

"It seemed every time we turned around one of the vehicles was breaking down or one of the kids was getting sick," Desiree said. "And now we found out I'm pregnant and so that's another thing we've got to deal with."

The news came on Valentine's Day, their anniversary. The baby due in October 2010 would be their tenth child. Things were already crowded and hectic as it was. But what was one more? They already had figured out the sleeping situation, the eating situation, the managing of time and money.

"It wasn't like a big deal, like *what are we going to do?!*" Terry joked. "We've already got this down to a science."

$ $ $

As April 2010 rolled around, Fremont, California, girded for the closing of the NUMMI assembly plant. Efforts to save NUMMI or find an immediate replacement had failed. One idea was to use it to make railcars for the new California high-speed rail line. But that was years away. An electric car startup came and went. Some even floated redeveloping it as the new stadium for the Oakland Athletics. But that too was a pipe dream.

The autoworkers had a union hall across the street from NUMMI and began staging rallies to draw attention. Maryo Mendez, the tug driver who had worked there for nineteen years, had an idea. Years ago, he had gone to a toy show and bought a limited-edition Captain America shield made out of real metal. He had planned to hang it over the fireplace with his wife's approval, but as these things go, the shield mostly remained in its box. Then in 2009, his son had a Halloween parade at school and Mendez happened to find a $20 Captain America costume at the store. So he put together the outfit and dressed up for his son's parade. NUMMI also allowed its employees to dress up for Halloween. So he kept the costume on and went about his job, driving the tug, delivering parts to the assembly line.

"Everybody got a big kick out of it," Mendez said, "me walking around with this suit on and hanging on to the shield."

So when time came to make a statement about NUMMI, Mendez donned his Captain America suit again, grabbed his shield, and stood in the bed of his red, American-made Toyota Tacoma. Naturally, the news photographers flocked to Mendez.

Somebody asked him why he was dressed as Captain America.

"I told 'em I did it because of the red, white, and blue. This is an American plant here and I don't want my plant to close," Mendez recalled.

Mendez posed for pictures, standing in the bed of his pickup, holding a sign that said KEEP NUMMI OPEN with another one in the background that read EVEN I DRIVE A TOYOTA. He bent his right leg so his boot rested on the edge of the truck, his shield off to the side, and gazed into the heavens. The picture went global and became a popular symbol of the NUMMI rallies.

"This will get some attention," Mendez thought. "We'll make something happen and maybe everybody will notice and they won't close the plant."

But it was not so. As closing day came, the last NUMMI car, a red Toyota Corolla, made its way down the assembly line. As the car left each station, another group of employees finished their paperwork and walked out of the plant. The stamping people, the paint shop, the guys who put the tires on. Employees gathered around and cheered and whistled. In went the last engine, the last dashboard, the last taillight, the final bolt.

"Being there at NUMMI at the end, this is the bad part," Mendez said. "Little by little, we kept seeing these people leave, and, you know, you see people crying, and, you know, you see some people happy, or trying to be happy. I was thinking, you know, I've seen a whole lot of people crying and said, eh, you know, maybe I can make some of them laugh."

So Mendez went to his locker and put on his Captain America costume. He stood in front of the last NUMMI car dressed as the comic book hero and held the shield. And then they went out of the building. Across the street, the news media gathered to get workers' reactions. Mendez talked to them for a little while, and then his daughter pulled up in her 1966 Ford Mustang. Mendez told the reporters how the Mustang had been built at the Ford plant in Milipitas, and then they closed that plant. His Toyota truck was built at NUMMI, and now they closed this plant. He jumped into the driver's seat as his daughter put the shield in the back.

Mendez turned around and yelled, "This is the American dream!" And then he drove off. There was no sunset on the horizon—just the midday sun, unemployment, and trying to find another job.

The next day, news broke that Solyndra, the Fremont solar panel manufacturer that promised a thousand jobs, had filed an amendment to its SEC registration statement. The auditing firm Pricewaterhouse-Coopers had reviewed the company's financial statements and came to a troubling conclusion. "The company has suffered recurring losses from operations, negative cash flows since inception and has a net stockholders' deficit that, among other factors, raise substantial doubt about its ability to continue as a going concern," the auditors wrote.

Solyndra had lost $519 million in the past three years. While start-ups often lose money in their first years of operation, the notice cast doubt on the survival of one of the crown jewels of the federal stimulus package.

Then one day in May, Mendez heard on the radio that Tesla Motors, a tiny car company in Palo Alto, was buying the NUMMI plant. Tesla had been making all-electric luxury sedans at a small facility near a horse farm west of El Camino Real. The company was well financed by Silicon Valley venture capital firms, and its chief executive, Elon Musk, had struck gold with his previous venture, PayPal, an online payment system that became ubiquitous in e-commerce. Moreover, Tesla would receive a $465 million federal loan guarantee to retool the plant and create 1,500 jobs. The new car would sell for about $50,000 with a federal tax credit, but unlike other electric cars, it could go three hundred miles on a single charge. But in its seven years of existence, Tesla had sold only about a thousand cars, roughly the same amount that NUMMI had produced in a day.

Tesla would buy the NUMMI plant for the rock-bottom price of $42 million. Toyota would purchase $50 million in company stock and agreed to cooperate on the development of electric vehicles, including Toyota's RAV4 EV. The announcement sounded fishy to Mendez and others. It appeared Toyota was essentially giving money to an-other company to operate NUMMI. But it had gotten rid of 4,700 union workers in the process.

$ $ $

As the year began, the economy appeared to be headed for a V-shaped recovery, but now the turnaround was stalling. The unemployment rate shot back up to 9.8 percent in April 2010 and would hover just un-der double-digits through the fall. And while the economy was creat-ing jobs again, most of those were temporary workers brought in for the 2010 census. A CBS News/*New York Times* poll showed that only 6 percent of people surveyed believed the stimulus had created jobs. As Glenn Beck pointed out, that was lower than the percentage of peo-ple who believed Elvis was alive.

The House's $150 billion jobs bill got nowhere in the Senate. And in March, Congress passed a slimmed-down $18 billion package that centered around a tax credit for businesses that hired unemployed workers. Under the bill known as the Hiring Incentives to Restore Employment (HIRE) Act, such employers would be exempt from the 6.2 percent Social Security tax for the rest of the year. They would re-ceive an additional $1,000 credit for each worker who stayed on for at least a year. While some economists estimated it could create 250,000 jobs, the bill suffered from the same flaw President Jimmy Carter's program had in the 1970s: it would reward many more companies that would have hired people without the incentive. Congress also passed a $10 billion extension of unemployment checks and COBRA health insurance after the bill was held up for several days by Senator Jim Bunning. When asked about it, the Kentucky Republican told re-porters "tough shit" and gave them the middle finger as he entered a Senate elevator. Bunning and later Senator Tom Coburn used their ability to block bills to make a point that such measures should be paid for with cuts from the Recovery Act.

Many other jobs bills died on the vine, as Democrats tried to recast every piece of legislation as an engine of job creation. There was the Small Business and Infrastructure Jobs Tax Act, the Disaster Relief and Summer Jobs Act, the Urban Jobs Act, the Rural Jobs Tax Credit

Act, the Energy Jobs for Veterans Act, the Jobs Momentum Act, the American Jobs Matter Act, the Copper Basin Jobs Act, the Coastal Jobs Creation Act, the Fuel Cell Industrial Vehicle Jobs Act, the Stop Outsourcing and Create American Jobs Act, and the Reciprocal Government Procurement with China Creates American Jobs Act. It was as if every time a member of Congress washed his or her hands, it would create jobs. The water flowing down the sink would create jobs at the wastewater treatment plant. The more soap they used, the quicker they'd have to buy another bar, supporting jobs at the supermarket, the soap factory, and the farmer who supplies the lard. The more they used the sink, the more likely they were to wear out the pipes, meaning more work for the plumber.

By the summer of 2010, the tide was clearly turning away from stimulus toward the deficit. A year after its founding, the Tea Party movement was riding high after conservative anger helped Scott Brown take the Senate seat long held by Ted Kennedy, which had been seen as a liberal lock. Speaking on April 15, the same day he signed another $18 billion unemployment extension, Obama ticked off a number of tax cuts for 95 percent of working families and for those who spent money on new cars, first homes, college expenses, and energy-efficient appliances.

"So I've been a little amused over the last couple of days where people have been having these rallies about taxes," Obama told a crowd of Democratic donors in Miami. "You would think they would be saying thank you."

The president was finally highlighting the tax cuts that had been invisible for so long, and he was finally taking the Tea Party argument head-on. In fact, income taxes were at their lowest level since 1950.[1] But by then, it was too little too late. It seemed that only after losing the Massachusetts Senate election did the Obama administration pay this so-called AstroTurf any attention. To Tea Party supporters like Keli Carender, the Seattle blogger who led one of the first rallies, and Pete Seaha, chairman of the Aiken County Tea Party in South Carolina, Obama's quip smacked of arrogance.

"That's a tax cut?!" Seaha responded when I mentioned the president's remarks. "You could play with words all day long. Let's deal with reality. A tax cut is not $10 a month. A tax cut is something substantial. It's something you're able to hold on to permanently. It's not something you get for twelve months in little bitty increments."

Even Democrats were now getting nervous about spending as they sought to defend their stimulus votes in the run-up to the midterm elections. As Congress recessed for Memorial Day, it failed to pass a safety-net bill, cutting off unemployment checks and CO-BRA subsidies for hundreds of thousands of people. One of them was Ron Bender, a machine operator at the Chicago windows factory who still hadn't been hired back more than a year and a half after the sit-in. He had been getting by. But the cut-off, which lasted through July, threatened to send him over the edge.

"If I don't get called back, then if I don't find anything by then and they don't extend unemployment, it's going to be pretty rough," Bender told me. "It's going to be real, real rough. I may have to get out of my house."

$ $ $

Less than two months after Solyndra's negative audit, Obama visited the new solar panel factory on his way to a fund-raiser for Senator Barbara Boxer. The president's helicopter landed on NUMMI property. Then he was ferried by limousine to Solyndra down the road.

Two days before, one of his senior advisers, Valerie Jarrett, had received an e-mail from Steve Westly, the Silicon Valley venture capitalist who had been a major fund-raiser for the campaign. "A number of us are concerned that the president is visiting Solyndra," Westly confided. "I just want to help protect the president from anything that could result in negative or unfair press. If it's too late to change/postpone the meeting, the president should be careful about unrealistic/optimistic forecasts that could haunt him in the next 18 months if Solyndra hits the wall, files for bankruptcy, etc."

Others sounded the alarm from inside. One budget official wrote, "I am increasingly worried that this visit could prove embarrassing to the Administration in the not too distant future."[2]

Speaking to reporters in advance of the trip, though, Matt Rogers, the Energy secretary's senior adviser, downplayed the auditors' concerns. "The letter that PricewaterhouseCoopers issued is a standard

letter that most companies that have not yet gone public tend to receive," he said. "What it simply says is your company requires more
capital in order to make sure that you are successful over the long term
. . . We're quite comfortable with the ongoing health of the company."

Despite the warning signs, it appeared as if the Obama administration was doing everything it could to bolster Solyndra. The White
House featured the company on its blog and created a video to go
along with the president's visit. Here was a turning point. In light of
the negative audit, the administration could have pulled back. But instead it doubled down, for it had staked not only the taxpayers' money
on Solyndra, but also the reputation of the stimulus and the green
economy—and in some ways, the entire notion of government investment. For better or worse, the Obama administration was now in
business with Solyndra, and the company's fate was intertwined with
the president's as well.

Obama arrived at Solyndra shortly after 9:00 A.M. He repeatedly
shook hands with workers in lab coats and hard hats as he toured the
modern factory. "It's impressive," he said.

After the tour, Obama spoke to a crowd of 250 workers. He talked
about the administration's investments in innovation and about the
ongoing BP oil spill in the Gulf of Mexico, tying the two together to
underscore the need for an energy plan that emphasizes alternative
fuel sources. "We can see the positive impacts right here at Solyndra,"
he said. The year before, the site was an empty lot. Now it was an
enormous factory that employed thousands of construction workers
in building it. He nodded to the closure of the NUMMI plant and how
"it was all the more painful and heartbreaking because the factory
had been held up as an example of how America could lead in manufacturing." But despite the shutdown, he said, a government loan to
Tesla would once again make it "a symbol of promise, an example of
what's possible here in America." In closing, he turned back to the
Solyndra workers.

"Every day that you build this expanded facility, as you fill orders
for solar panels to ship around the world, you're demonstrating that
the promise of clean energy isn't just an article of faith—not anymore," he said. "The future is here."

But the president's pep rally could do nothing about the overwhelming competition in solar coming from China. Under the command economy, the government spent billions of dollars every year subsidizing clean energy development, required grid companies to buy electricity from renewable sources, and blocked foreign companies from supplying parts and materials by establishing domestic preference laws. The United Steelworkers charged that the subsidies violated international agreements, leading the U.S. trade representative to launch an investigation in the fall of 2010.

"The biggest challenge right now is, Are we playing on a level playing field?" Solyndra spokesman Dave Miller told me around the same time. "We're dealing with Chinese competition right now that is highly subsidized. There's some pretty clear evidence that these companies are selling at a loss or at pricing that makes it hard for a U.S. company to compete."

Was China engaged in illegal dumping in an effort to drive out competitors and dominate the solar market? It was a question raised a number of times when it came to America's effort to lay the groundwork for a green economy. Chinese imports of solar panels had increased nearly 1,600 percent from 2006 to 2010, according to members of Congress. But whatever the answer, one thing was clear: China was providing its solar companies with low-cost loans that were multiple times what the Obama administration had offered Solyndra.

The $535 billion loan guarantee through the Recovery Act wasn't enough to overcome Solyndra's challenges. And in June, the company pulled its IPO. A few weeks later, one of Solyndra's founders left to take a job as CEO of another energy company. The following month, Solyndra replaced its CEO Chris Gronet with an executive from Intel. While the company tried to put it in a positive light, the shakeup signaled the struggles that would play out further in the year ahead.

$ $ $

On June 17, 2010, Vice President Biden kicked off Recovery Summer, a series of groundbreakings and other events to bring attention to the progress of stimulus projects. The administration had done a similar publicity tour the summer before called Roadmap to Recovery as a way to signal to the public that the shovel-ready projects were finally beginning. A year later, it was promising that now the Recovery Act would *really* get into gear. More than 10,000 highway projects would be under way. Workers would weatherize 82,000 homes. Utility crews would install a million smart meters.

There was less poetry in Biden's speech this time around—no romantic visions of factories whirring again, no hard-luck towns turning from "used to be" to "going to be." Instead, Biden spoke more modestly: "I think most of the skeptics have come around to the point that all the talk about the Recovery Act being dead on arrival and how it was going to be this great boondoggle and all the fraud and abuse that was going to occur and it wasn't going to have much impact—well, the fact is, the Recovery Act is working."

One project that was producing a lot of jobs was the remediation of the Savannah River nuclear site in Aiken, South Carolina. By the summer of 2010, the blue billboard outside the plant read 39 percent complete and 3,356 jobs created or saved. One of the more prominent milestones of the work thus far was the implosion of the K Reactor cooling tower. Built in 1992 in hopes of restarting production after Three Mile Island and Chernobyl, the concrete tower rose 450 feet. But faced with opposition to nuclear energy, the reactor never went beyond the test phase and the cooling tower was never used.[3] Now with stimulus money, demolition crews drilled 3,860 holes in the tower and stuffed them with nitroglycerin-based explosives. One spring morning, the charges were detonated, unleashing a thunderous clap and several large smoke rings around the strategically placed explosives. The tower collapsed vertically as if it was sinking into the ground, and within seconds, it was nothing but concrete rubble and rebar.

Touring the complex, I could see the stimulus money translate into jobs. Workers were dismantling a heavy-water test reactor, completing a project that wasn't scheduled to be done until 2024. Another group of employees in yellow protective suits installed pumps into the liquid waste tanks that would slurry the ash-colored radioactive sludge so that it could be transported and turned into glass logs for permanent storage. An excavator clawed at a red dirt mound to unearth concrete culverts full of contaminated gloves and tools that had been buried decades ago.

Entering the P Reactor building, which produced nuclear weapons from the 1950s to the 1980s, was like walking into a time capsule. The control room was lined with dusty meters and dials, and at the center was a console with a pistol-grip joystick that the operator used to remove the rods from the reactor. Workers drilled holes through the four-foot-thick concrete floors, where they would pour cement from a hose to fill the building's most contaminated areas and seal the building forever. Listening to the drilling, the project director, Ray Hannah, smiled.

"Good to hear that," he said. "The sound of progress."

At every stop I met a worker who had lost his or her job during the Great Recession only to find employment at Savannah River because of the stimulus package. For Jimmy Hughes, working at the Savannah River Site, was a bit of a homecoming. He had started there when he was twenty years old, but eventually started his own home-building firm. "Then the economy went bad and I guess I about starved to death for a year," he said. A friend told him about the stimulus work at Savannah River, and he got hired on as a first-line manager. "There's been a lot of wasteful spending in Washington, DC," Hughes said. "We need to get a grip on that. We need to be accountable for every dime spent. I know it's a lot of money, but I hope it's going to do some good because at a time like this, we need jobs."

For Kera Woods, a twenty-one-year-old from Aiken, the stimulus provided her with a job she never thought she'd have. She had worked at McDonald's and at a plant making wheel rims for John Deere tractors. Then in the spring of 2009, she entered a training program for minority and low-income people living near hazardous waste sites to work in environmental remediation. Woods applied for a stimulus job and was assigned to shipping and receiving. "I didn't think I would have a good job like I do at the age of twenty-one, that I'd be able to help my family the way I am at this age," she said. "I thought I would still be working fast food or something like that. Honestly. Not out here. I didn't even have any of my family that ever worked out here. You see how big I smiled on my badge? I couldn't believe it."

Then there was Bill Picciano, a father of two from Cleveland, Ohio. Picciano, forty-seven, had worked for a ceramics company for eight years before being transferred to Augusta, Georgia, and laid off in 2005. He found another job at a brick company but was laid off right before Christmas 2006 when the housing market began to decline. After that, he worked for a business that manufactured cutting tools and drill bits. The company went through layoffs as well but kept him on until his contract ran out in March 2009. Picciano found himself back on unemployment.

"Things got a little bleak there," he said sighing. "We were pretty much tapped into everything that we had saved up in the bank and made our last house payment in May. It was the last house payment that we had money left for and we were scrambling to try to figure out how to stay afloat on $277 a week."

Picciano closed his eyes and rubbed his hands over his forehead and scalp.

"We had two children—we were trying to keep them in school and keep them active so that they weren't distracted with what my wife and I were going through," he said. "The stress level was unbelievable. We weren't sure where we were going to go and what were going to do."

Then Picciano got a call from a job placement agency that was hiring for the Savannah River stimulus work. He was hired as a logistics expediter for the transuranic waste project. Every day, Picciano checked the jobs board, and in the summer of 2010, he found a permanent spot as an associate engineer helping to build a plant disassembling weapons at the site. Since getting the full-time job, Picciano's family was catching up on lost time. They recently had gone to Hilton Head for the weekend, something they hadn't done in two years.

"What do I think of it?" Picciano asked of the stimulus. "It was a godsend—at least for me it was. It got us back on track."

$ $ $

In the 2008 presidential election, 61 percent of Aiken County voters cast their ballots for John McCain, compared to 37 percent for

Obama. But despite the area's deep-red leanings, many local leaders had come to support the stimulus. Its impact was evident wherever one went, said David Jameson, president of the Greater Aiken Chamber of Commerce.

The same day I visited with Jameson, the *Aiken Standard* reported on its front page that Aiken County had the lowest unemployment rate in the state.[4] Almost every other county in South Carolina tracked the national unemployment rate, continuing to rise through the end of 2009 and then tapering off. But Aiken County saw its jobless rate drop as soon as stimulus money kicked in at the Savannah River Site in June 2009. A year later, it had dropped from 10.2 percent to 8.2 percent.

"It's had a tremendous impact on Aiken's economy," Jameson said. Other cities may have seen three thousand jobs, "but they were ten here and seventy-five there and ninety here and a hundred over there, and they don't see or feel the synergy. But ours are all located in one place, and so I think that makes it a little bit clearer about why we're having an impact."

When the recession hit, Aiken's hotel tax collections plummeted almost 20 percent overnight, city manager Roger LeDuc said. But when the stimulus package went into effect, it not only bounced back but increased 5 to 10 percent over the levels before the recession. Contract workers from out of town had filled up nearly all of the county's rental properties, hotels, apartments, and long-term stays. They shopped at the grocery store, filled their cars at the gas station, and ate out at restaurants every once in a while, some of them every night.

At Carolina Bar-B-Que outside the plant entrance, workers lined up to the door during the lunch hour and it was hard to find a seat. The buffet line offered an all-you-can-eat smorgasbord of chopped pork, hash and rice, macaroni and cheese, hush puppies, fried okra, green beans, baked beans, sweet potatoes, coleslaw, potato salad, peach cobbler, banana pudding, and lemonade. The couple behind me said they had never seen the place like this.

Across the street at Momma Bear's Bar & Grill, cars and pickups filled the gravel parking lot in the early evening. The place was smoky and decorated with beer posters and neon signs. In the front were a plastic Christmas tree and a jukebox playing hard rock. There were three pool tables in a wood-paneled backroom. And at the center was a wooden horseshoe bar, around which sat several sunburned plant workers with sunglass tan lines.

Janice Coleman, the proprietor and eponymous Momma Bear, told me she'd seen extra business because of all the new people at the plant. Sometimes they'd get sixty people, and two Thursdays ago, it was so busy people had to park in the back lot.

"I'd probably say it's increased probably 20 to 30 percent from what it was," she said.

Not everyone in Momma Bear's was a fan of the federal stimulus package, though. One of them was Vance Fleming, a laid-off truck driver who sat at the end of the bar nursing what appeared to be whiskey but what he insisted was 7-Up. Fleming, sixty-two, had grown up around the Savannah River Site after his father, whom he claimed built the first bomb shelter in the United States, moved the family to Aiken to work on the nuclear plant. "People around here, they work hard, but the stimulus package ain't done shit," Fleming said. "They're darn happy to have a job. But it's temporary. They know it's bullshit. They're just doing it to feed their families. They know it's a failure. They're worried what they're going to do next."

"The thing you've got to realize about a plant of this magnitude," said his friend, who had worked in the nuclear industry for twenty years, "when the money comes in everybody's employed."

When I asked the friend his name, he replied, "We don't get into that." But Vance kept calling him Jim.

Fleming wore a yellow T-shirt, a black baseball cap, and had a grayish brown mustache. He was a born chatterer, he said, just like his father, and had a fondness for phrases like "that's a fact jack and you can write that down." Fleming said he lost his job as a truck driver delivering MRIs and CAT scanners around the country.

"Everybody thinks this darn stimulus package is a crock of shit," he said. "Where is it going? I can't get a job. It ain't nothing but damn numbers. It's a numbers game for someone writing a damn report."

"Let's get a little realistic," his friend said. "You think anybody out there is going to bitch? No one is ever going to ever say anything bad about the Savannah River Site as long as it is going to the local economy. Nobody bites the hand that feeds them."

Though many in Aiken had rallied around the stimulus, dissent was alive and well. In fact, Aiken County had not one, but two active Tea Party chapters.

$ $ $

In late July 2010, the economists Alan Blinder and Mark Zandi released the first report that tried to assess how the Great Recession came to an end. Though it wasn't official yet, the National Bureau of Economic Research would announce a few months later that the recession that started in December 2007 had ended in June 2009. That was on paper, of course, as many struggling families didn't feel a thing. Blinder was a Princeton professor and former vice chairman of the Fed while Zandi had consulted for both congressional Democrats and the presidential campaign of John McCain. The pair concluded that the combination of the bank bailout, stress tests, Federal Reserve policy, and the American Recovery and Reinvestment Act likely averted a second Great Depression. Without them, the economy might have lost another 8.5 million jobs, bringing the unemployment rate to 16.5 percent.

"The Great Recession gave way to recovery as quickly as it did largely because of the unprecedented responses by monetary and fiscal policymakers," Blinder and Zandi wrote. "If policymakers had not reacted as aggressively or as quickly as they did, the financial system might still be unsettled, the economy might still be shrinking, and the costs to U.S. taxpayers would have been vastly greater."

While the bailout and Fed actions made a larger impact, they said, the stimulus prevented unemployment from reaching 12 percent and brought the recession to an end months earlier than expected. "We do not believe it a coincidence that the turnaround from recession to recovery occurred last summer, just as the ARRA was providing its maximum economic benefit," the economists wrote.

A few weeks earlier, the White House Council of Economic Advisers reported that the Recovery Act had created or saved 2.5 million to 3.6 million jobs. The estimate was higher than those of private firms, which forecasted about 2 million jobs, but close to the nonpartisan Congressional Budget Office which gave a range of 1.4 million to 3.4 million jobs. While the economy was technically in a recovery, few people would describe it as such.

Meanwhile, Senators Tom Coburn and John McCain were readying their third report on stimulus waste. The listed projects were just as comical and controversial as the first two hundred projects. Released in August, it included $713,000 for researchers to develop a joke-telling machine, $90,000 for a sidewalk that led to a ditch, and $762,000 for computer software that could lead to a YouTube–like website for interactive dance.

The Recovery Accountability and Transparency Board, charged with stimulus oversight, would ultimately receive more than 7,500 complaints, leading to over 1,500 investigations. But of the hundreds of thousands of recipients, only about two hundred cases had resulted in criminal convictions, as of the fall of 2011. One of the first cases to reach prosecutors was the case of Peter and Robbie Scott, a businessman and his nephew, who were indicted in July 2010 for allegedly submitting fraudulent bids and surety bonds for a Sacramento water meter project. According to the prosecution, their company Advantage Demolition and Engineering won $3.5 million in contracts based on paperwork signed by an attorney who didn't exist. In September 2011, Peter Scott pleaded guilty to fraud. The case against his nephew was ongoing as of this writing. Caught up in the stimulus dragnet were garden-variety hucksters and thieves: a man cashing a $250 Social Security check intended for his dead father,[5] a group of people claiming unemployment benefits despite having jobs, an Indianapolis man accused of stealing stimulus checks from ninety-four of his disabled clients as part of a scheme that had been going on for years.[6]

While not necessarily illegal, a lot of controversy surrounded contractors that outsourced work to firms in other countries. In Ohio, for example, investigators found that the company managing the appliance rebate program hired a call center in El Salvador. The Harris County METRO system in Houston violated Buy America rules when it used stimulus money and other federal funds to purchase light-rail vehicles assembled in Spain, according to the Federal Transit

Administration. Charlie Dent, a Republican congressman from Allen-town, Pennsylvania, complained that Staten Island shipping terminal, financed with stimulus bonds, would benefit a Peruvian cement pro-ducer at the expense of domestic plants in the Lehigh Valley. But the initial worries that the Recovery Act would be another Katrina or Iraq, that as much as $55 billion would be lost to fraud, hadn't come true.

"A year and a half in, I'm not seeing the amount of fraud that I imagined I would have and I think it has a lot to do with trans-parency," Earl Devaney, head of the Recovery Accountability and Transparency (RAT) board, told me at a government auditors' confer-ence in San Antonio. "Given the amount of money out there, I don't see anything unusual. I just see some usual administrative mistakes, sloppiness in giving the money out. Nothing big had happened really. To my knowledge, there haven't been any big losses. The American public will have to make the judgment about whether that bridge was the right bridge to build or that road was the right road to build. That's not our business. But we really haven't seen any major fraud cases. I don't know. I'm looking at it and I don't see it."

With that, Devaney balled his fist and knocked on the wooden table.

$ $ $

That summer, the U.S. Chamber of Commerce hung four banners from its beaux arts style building across the park from the White House. They read J-O-B-S, an unmistakable missive from America's business lobby that the administration's policies were hurting rather than helping the jobs situation. The Obama administration mainly blamed Greece and the European debt crisis for the slowdown. But hanging in the air was uncertainty about what direction the economy, and the White House, was going.

"Given that there wasn't going to be more dollars flowing, we could have better emphasized the so-called softer side of things both by boosting business confidence and by reassuring corporate leaders that we weren't about to do something crazy," Peter Orszag, who was budget director at the time, told me. "I think there was the perception . . . the fear that something really problematic could be done that caused more caution among corporate leaders than would have been desirable."

Business groups claimed the uncertainty was only made worse by the major reforms pushed by the White House. A comprehensive energy bill, seen by environmentalists as the absolutely essential "phase two" for the green economy, fell apart in late July as Senator Majority Leader Harry Reid tried to turn the attention to immigration and as Republicans succeeded in painting cap-and-trade as a burdensome tax on business. Construction firms that had added temporary workers for the Recovery Act were reluctant to staff up permanently without a multiyear transportation bill. While the landmark health care and financial reforms had now passed, there was tremendous confusion about how the rules would be written and what the laws would actually do. Whatever the reason, companies and corporations had $1.8 trillion in cash sitting on the sidelines.

After signing a $34 billion measure to extend unemployment through November, Obama called on Congress to pass more jobs proposals to support the slow-moving recovery. In so many stimulus programs, from renewable energy to tax cuts, it seemed the Obama administration was always a year late in countering criticism and promoting the benefits. So it was with the state fiscal relief that saved hundreds of thousands of teachers' jobs. Instead of big press conferences focusing on teachers, the administration put their eggs in the infrastructure basket. It wasn't until August 2010, when Congress was about to pass an extension of the education jobs fund, that Obama introduced America to Shannon Lewis, a special education teacher in Romney, West Virginia, who lost her job for lack of funding but could get it back with government help.

In a rare session during their summer vacation, lawmakers returned to Washington to pass a $26 billion bill to avert teacher layoffs and extend the increased Medicaid funding under the stimulus for another six months. After the White House beat back an effort by Representative David Obey to cut Race to the Top funding, Congress paid for the bill by limiting a tax break for corporations that have operations overseas and trimming stimulus money for food stamps, broadband, and renewable energy loans.

The following month at Milwaukee Laborfest, Obama called for a $50 billion infrastructure plan to repave roads, rehabilitate airport runways, modernize the air traffic control system, and invest in twenty-first-century infrastructure like high-speed rail. Later that week in Cleveland—where Republican leader John Boehner had unveiled the GOP's economic plan to cut taxes, spending, and regulations—Obama proposed an extension of the research and development tax credit and a tax break for businesses to write off all of their capital investments in 2011. Then at the end September, Congress finally passed a $42 billion bill to increase lending and provide tax cuts to small businesses, a plan Obama had been calling for since February. But again the administration was too late to steer public opinion back in its favor. Perhaps if it had seriously pushed these measures in the fall of 2009 instead of the fall of 2010, they wouldn't have looked like mere feel-good entreaties to win votes in the midterm elections. Late-night TV host Jay Leno made an observant joke when he said, "The White House announced today that the stimulus package saved three million jobs. But they said there are still more jobs that need to be saved: President Obama's, Joe Biden's, Harry Reid's, Nancy Pelosi's."

The campaigns for November were in high gear all summer. Obama and Biden crisscrossed the country to raise money for vulnerable Democrats, often pairing the fund-raising dinners with an event to promote the Recovery Act. The president sought to emphasize an emotional connection on kitchen-table issues with a series of back-yard conversations with families in Columbus, Albuquerque, and Des Moines. He also sharpened his stump speech, retooling the "ditch" metaphor that President Bush had used in 2008 to warn about over-correcting with too much government stimulus. In Obama's version, the Republicans drove the car into the ditch. Then, as Democrats got into the mud to push the car out, the Republicans stood on the side-lines drinking Slurpees, criticizing them for not pushing fast enough or hard enough. Finally, Democrats got the car out of the ditch, and the Republicans had the nerve to ask for the keys back.

"Have you noticed when you want to go forward, what do you do with your car?" he would ask a cheering crowd. "You put it in D.

When you want to go backwards, what do you do? You put it in R. That's not a coincidence."

But the Democrats' most effective strategy to strike Republicans and defend the Recovery Act was an online gallery put together by the Democratic Congressional Campaign Committee called the "Hypocrisy Hall of Fame." The group compiled a list of 128 House Republicans who voted against the stimulus but later took credit or requested money for a project in their district. It included House minority whip Eric Cantor, GOP budget leader Paul Ryan, and future presidential candidate Michele Bachmann. Some even attended ribbon cuttings. The hostility from the White House boiled over when Obama all but called out Representative Pete Hoekstra at a groundbreaking for a battery plant in Holland, Michigan.

Many Republicans defended their actions by saying that while they opposed the overarching policy, once passed they were going to ensure that their constituents' tax dollars stayed in their district. "Senator Phil Gramm, who is about as fiscally conservative as anyone who has ever served here, said that if the U.S. Senate decided to build a cheese factory on the moon, he would have voted against it. But if it passed, he would sure make sure that the parts for it were built in Texas," Senator George LeMieux told the *St. Petersburg Times*. "I believe the same thing."[7]

In public, the administration expressed confidence in a Democratic victory, but in reality it was starting to prepare for the consequences if Congress changed hands. In one of his regular conference calls to governors and state officials, Vice President Biden urged participants to use their education money soon. "The message was simply spend this money quickly because they were afraid that it would be taken away," California stimulus czar Rick Rice told me.

The months before the midterm elections saw an exodus of several officials who had been central to putting together the stimulus package. First out the door was budget director Peter Orszag in July, followed by Christina Romer, chairwoman of the Council of Economic Advisers, in September. There were growing rumors, which turned out to be true, that chief of staff Rahm Emanuel was going to run for mayor of Chicago. Then came Larry Summers, the president's top economist, who announced he would leave at the end of the year.

Depending on how you looked at it, they were leaving after epically saving the economy from a second Great Depression or they were resigning after the stimulus failed to live up to expectations. In truth, the economic team was exhausted. The long hours of meetings and negotiations month after month were straining their already fraught relationships, especially between Orszag and Summers, who after butting egos repeatedly over how to handle the deficit were barely getting along now. The mission was changing from bold policy to end a historic recession to more mundane calculations of how to reduce the deficit while eking out some stimulus. And no one wanted to be there for the bruising post-election reckoning should the Republicans win.

$ $ $

About six weeks before the election, Obama sat down for a town hall meeting hosted by CNBC at the Newseum in Washington, DC. It was a powerful and insightful glimpse into the moods and mindsets of American voters. The first question came from a chief financial officer for a veterans' service organization.

"I'm one of your middle-class Americans," the woman, Velma Hart, said. "And quite frankly, I'm exhausted. I'm exhausted of defending you, defending your administration, defending the mantle of change that I voted for and deeply disappointed with where we are right now. I have been told that I voted for a man who said he was going to change things in a meaningful way for the middle class. I'm one of those people, and I'm waiting, sir. I'm waiting."

The next question from the audience came from Ted Brassfield, a thirty-year-old law school graduate struggling to find a job and pay his student loans. "Like a lot of people in my generation, I was really inspired by you," he said. "I really want to know, is the American dream dead for me?"

Americans were coming to terms with a new reality, an intransigent economy with effects that would linger for years. In selling the stimulus, Obama had warned of such a doomsday: unemployment in the double digits, a nation losing the competitive edge that had served as its foundation, a generation sapped of its potential and promise. In spite of the stimulus, the scenario seemed to be here.

Terry and Desiree Gonyon struggled with this at their home in Elkhart, as their kids ran back and forth through the trailer playing and yelling in the background.

"I know they passed all kinds of legislation or other stuff, but I don't think it's helped anybody," Terry said.

"What you also got understand too, Terry, when this all happened, Obama wasn't even elected," Desiree said.

"It doesn't matter."

"But the problem didn't start with him. That's what everybody keeps saying, 'Oh, Obama's not doing that, Obama's not doing this.' He wasn't in office when this all started."

"But that's how politics works," Terry said. "It all started back with Ronald Reagan. He's the one who opened up the housing market and then Clinton widened it more."

"Each president can only do so many things."

"But still," Terry said. "If you're going to make a program to where you're going to say government stimulus, you need to stimulate the right people. If you're going to stimulate the banks to pay off their brokers, their supporters, and everybody else, and screw the little people—the little people like us are the ones that give those people money by taking out loans and paying exorbitant interest rates. We've made those people that money, but yet when we get in trouble, they don't bail us out."

Terry and Desiree were typical of many voters. All they really knew was that whatever was happening in Washington wasn't helping them. Fed up with both Republicans and Democrats, they were equally intrigued by the Tea Party movement and by Michael Moore's call at the end of *Capitalism: A Love Story* for workers to protest against rule by the rich.

Ed Neufeldt was also coming to terms with his new reality working three jobs that together paid less than the one he lost at the RV plant. In addition to the bread route and cleaning the doctor's office, he was working again for Wil Cashen, who had started a new business artfully named the Electric Motors and Vehicles Corporation. Ever since he was chosen to introduce Obama, Neufeldt had been a supporter. But now he was losing faith.

"I'm convinced that none of this is because of the Obama stimulus," he told me.

In September, Neufeldt heard that Glenn Beck was going to be in Indiana. So he took off work, and he and his wife drove about fifty miles east to the rally in Angola. The speakers were inspiring, he said, and Beck understood what was really going on in this country.

"I don't want to be down on President Obama on everything," Neufeldt said. "I still like the man, but I've just been down on some of the decisions he's made. If Republicans take back the Senate and the House and Congress, maybe he'll move a little bit to the right and maybe he'll start making decisions to get our country going again. I hope so."

On November 2, voters went to the polls. The Democrats held on to the Senate. But the Republicans regained control of the House, picking up sixty-three seats in one of the biggest GOP victories in history.

FOURTEEN

CONNECTING THE COUNTRY

*When I took office, only high-energy physicists had ever heard of
what is called the World Wide Web . . . Now even my cat has its
own Web page.*

—President Bill Clinton, 1996

IN THE DAYS AFTER "the shellacking," much about Obama's policy
agenda was in doubt. Through the Recovery Act, the Obama administration had paid a hefty down payment on a twenty-first century
economy built around renewable energy, broadband, electronic medical records, education reform, and high-speed rail. But efforts to
move beyond that cornerstone with major bills on energy, education,
and infrastructure had gone nowhere. Much of Obama's political capital had been eroded by the stimulus, and he had staked whatever little
was left on health care reform, which took longer than any of his advisers expected. By tying up his staff and betting all his chips on a bill
whose importance might not be realized for a generation, Obama had
frittered away any chance at energy, education, and infrastructure
bills, which might have been easier to pass and would have helped the
economy more in the short term. Now aides wondered how much
they could accomplish with a divided Congress and an opposing party
driven by what it saw as a mandate to cut spending. Not only had
Democrats been defeated in the House, but America had six additional Republican governors, who would now control the purse
strings on billions of dollars in stimulus projects.

Voters had indeed sent a strong message, Obama acknowledged. But he understood it to mean that he should focus more on the economy and jobs. Yes, the United States had to get its long-term debt and deficits under control, but that didn't mean it shouldn't make investments to remain competitive in the global economy.

Central to that was a plan to bring high-speed Internet to rural America, much in the way that Roosevelt had electrified the heartland during the New Deal. Few programs captured Obama's ambitions as well as broadband. Wrapped up in the technical details was the vision of expanding health care, higher education, and business opportunities to a population that had long been left behind. In his 2011 State of the Union address, Obama used the word "Internet" six times as he spoke about how innovation could lead to an economic revolution. It was the most since President Bill Clinton, who also used the word six times in 2000 when he promoted a program connecting classrooms to the web and in 1997, the first State of the Union broadcast live on the Internet.[1] Just weeks before the midterm elections, the administration had unveiled the winners of broadband funding, some of the final projects to be announced under the Recovery Act.

The United States ranked fifteenth in the world in broadband penetration at the end of 2010, behind the Netherlands and South Korea, according to the international Organization for Economic Cooperation and Development. Even Romania had faster Internet speeds on average, the consulting firm Akamai reported.

Nationally, only 60 percent of Americans had access to high-speed Internet at home, according to the Commerce Department. There were vast divides. Sixty-eight percent of whites used broadband, compared with 50 percent of African Americans and 45 percent of Hispanics. Among college graduates, the rate of adoption was 84 percent; for people who hadn't finished high school, it was 30 percent. People with a family income higher than $150,000 were three times more likely to have broadband at home than those making less than $15,000.

The biggest reasons people didn't use high-speed Internet were because they felt they didn't need it or because it was too expensive. But in rural areas, lack of availability was cited 9 percent of the time, compared with 1 percent for urban areas. States in the South lagged the furthest behind. Roughly 50 percent of Mississippi households had broadband compared with 75 percent in Connecticut.

High-speed Internet was quickly becoming a necessity akin to electricity and plumbing. No longer could farmers survive in isolation. To compete in the global marketplace, they needed real-time access to crop prices and weather information. But lack of broadband wasn't just a problem in rural areas. Some inner-city neighborhoods were just as off the grid as rural Montana when it came to having high-speed Internet at home. In urban areas, many residents relied on computers at the public library to write school papers, look up health information, or search for a job. And libraries were having trouble keeping up. According to the American Library Association, nearly 60 percent of libraries lacked sufficient Internet speeds to meet demand during peak hours.

In the halls of Congress, there were many factions competing to shape the stimulus broadband program. There was a rural contingent pushing for a focus on unserved and underserved areas. And there was an urban constituency advocating for public computing centers for the poor. Another group wanted the stimulus money to finally fund a public safety network to fix the communications problems that had been exposed during 9/11. The stakes were high, as the tug-of-war would determine how the money would be divided and even which agency would manage it. Senator Jay Rockefeller, chairman of the Commerce, Science, and Transportation Committee, wanted the program to be run by the National Telecommunications and Information Administration (NTIA), the technology branch of the Commerce Department. But Senator Tom Harkin, who headed the Agriculture Committee, insisted that at least some money be reserved for the Department of Agriculture, which ran the only current government broadband program and was most in tune to the needs of rural residents.

The Recovery Act ultimately included $7.2 billion for broadband grants and loans. To satisfy the competing interests, $2.5 billion was allocated to the Rural Utilities Service to connect homes and businesses while $4.7 billion was given to the NTIA for infrastructure projects and anchor institutions, such as hospitals and schools. Of that, $200 million would have to go to public computer centers set up at community colleges and libraries, and another $250 million would be spent to encourage broadband adoption. In doling out broadband stimulus money, though, the government faced a problem. It didn't know where service existed and where it didn't because there was no national map. Information was scattered across the various telecommunications authorities in every state. Private providers knew their coverage area but considered it sensitive business data. So Congress dedicated $350 million to help yet another agency, the Federal Communications Commission, develop a map, detailing the Internet speeds for every community in the United States. The map wouldn't be ready until 2011, so the grant and loan reviewers would have to make do without it.

The Rural Utilities Service traces its history back to the New Deal when Roosevelt created the Rural Electrification Administration to string power lines to the farms and ranches that hadn't been served by private utilities. In little more than a decade, rural America went from having less than 20 percent of farmsteads with electricity to more than 90 percent.[2] Then, in 1949, the agency's mission expanded to include rural telephone service. By the time the Recovery Act passed, it was also handling loans to promote broadband. But the Rural Utilities Service program had only a small operation that had been troubled with waste and mismanagement. In recent years, the program had wired wealthy suburban enclaves and communities within thirty miles of major cities, defining "rural" only as a community with fewer than 20,000 people. Now, the federal government would be spending twenty-four times the amount of money. It would have to coordinate across three separate agencies. And it would have to do it without a national map directing them to what areas were most in need.

$ $ $

The broadband program was part of a major investment in technology through the Recovery Act. The stimulus had provided about $100 billion to spur advances in energy, transportation, health, and telecommunications. And according to the White House, those investments had pulled $286 billion in private capital off the sidelines. With $7 billion for broadband, the administration planned to connect 2 million rural households and more than 25,000 community institutions to high-speed service. Another $4 billion would be spent on the smart grid. And with more than $20 billion for health information technology, the stimulus was accelerating the transition from paper to electronic medical records.

"More than ever, America needs to innovate," Vice President Biden said in August 2010, as he released a report indicating the stimulus was helping the country do just that. "Our investments in innovation are creating jobs, creating new industries, making existing industries more competitive, and in the process, they're driving down the cost of new technologies that are so badly needed, and are helping our nation reset our place and reassert our place as the world's center of innovation and entrepreneurs."

More than twenty-five years after the first personal computer, you could still walk into any doctor's office and find shelves filled with folders overflowing with charts, medical histories, and test results. Surveys published in the *New England Journal of Medicine* found that only 17 percent of physicians and 9 percent of hospitals had even a basic electronic records system. The Recovery Act provided a number of incentives to get doctors and hospitals to adopt computerized systems. Doctors could receive up to $44,000 under Medicare and up to $64,000 under Medicaid, while hospitals were eligible for at least $2 million. The new systems would alert doctors if a drug could cause a harmful interaction with medicine the patient was already taking. Patients would no longer have to drop off prescriptions scrawled by hand as doctors could automatically send the information to the pharmacy. The White House estimated that such an advance could avert 10 million medication errors by 2013. In rural areas, telemedicine would allow patients to connect with specialists remotely, saving them a long drive, or even flight, for routine visits. With upgraded Internet, patients could go to a local clinic where a doctor could talk to them and monitor their conditions via equipment that works like a video phone.

The health IT program also designated fifteen "beacon communities" in Tulsa, Buffalo, and elsewhere to demonstrate how electronic records could improve the quality of health care. In Tulsa, which the White House said had the highest rate of cardiovascular disease deaths in the country, a $12 million grant would help 1,600 physicians monitor diabetic and obese patients as they moved from one care setting to another. The Geisinger Clinic in Danville, Pennsylvania, would create a medical home to improve care for patients with pulmonary disease and congestive heart failure while the Southern Piedmont Community Care Plan in Concord, North Carolina, would focus on patients with high blood pressure and children with asthma.

State health networks received grants to build electronic exchanges to improve information sharing between hospitals and outpatient clinics. Ivy Tech Community College in Indiana, Otero Junior College in rural Colorado, and dozens of other colleges and workforce boards received millions of dollars to train students in health IT. The White House estimated that the digital transition would create tens of thousands of jobs in the next few years as doctors and hospitals relied on help desks and IT professionals to get used to the software.

To gain nationwide acceptance of electronic health records, the government had to ensure that such systems would prevent errors and protect patient privacy. Some medical studies found that computer systems only marginally improved care. And medical groups warned that the rush to develop and adopt new systems would contribute to errors: a Boca Raton gynecologist failed to inform his patient about a bad Pap smear for four years in part because an early electronic records system defaulted to an old test result. According to the *Palm Beach Post,* the woman developed cancer and had to have her uterus and ovaries removed.[3]

Obama had set a goal for all medical records to be computerized by 2014. But in developing the necessary rules, health IT ended up being one of the slowest stimulus programs. The bonus payments didn't kick in until 2011, and the vast majority of the money was expected to be spent after that. While the economic impact of electronic health records remains to be seen, the percentage of doctors using them increased, but only to 29 percent by the spring of 2011.[4] The push has also been a boon for medical software and information services companies as venture capital funding increased nearly 20 percent in 2010, according to Dow Jones VentureSource.[5]

$ $ $

By the time Vice President Biden announced the first broadband projects at a metal fabrication plant in the Appalachian foothills town of Dawsonville, Georgia, the government agencies in charge of the program were swamped with requests for funding. For the $4 billion available in the first round, the NTIA and the Rural Utilities Service received 2,200 applications requesting $28 billion. Ironically, the government's own servers couldn't handle the traffic, and some applicants had to submit documents by snail mail. Major telecom companies, such as AT&T, Verizon, and Comcast, avoided the program largely because of rules that would restrict their ability to manage traffic on their networks. The policy, known as "net neutrality," requires that all content and applications be treated equally in an effort to prevent the Internet from becoming a class system where certain users got priority over everyone else.

The requests for broadband money came from state and local governments, Indian tribes, nonprofits, industry, libraries, community colleges, hospitals, and police and fire departments. Filled with technical details, the applications could easily run five hundred pages or more. To wade through the overwhelming response, the agencies hired consulting firms and relied on volunteers, whom they refused to name, raising questions about whether they had any conflicts of interest. Compared with Race to the Top, the broadband program was far less transparent. The agencies refused to release the full applications. While the NTIA did create a database with two- to three-page summaries, the Rural Utilities Service decided to post one-paragraph summaries in an 846-page PDF, which would have been extremely difficult for people in rural areas to open.

The broadband program also faced heavy criticism over what qualified as "broadband." The rules set a low bar: a download speed of 768 kilobits per second, which would barely allow users to watch videos or open photos sent over e-mail. Basic service in a city was twice that, and the forefront of the industry was already moving toward lightning speeds of 50 to 100 megabits, even a gigabit, per second. The term "unserved" was defined as an area where at least 90 percent of households lacked access to broadband while "underserved" was defined as a place where no fixed or mobile provider offered speeds of at least 3 megabits per second or where fewer than half of the homes had access.

Areas classified as "remote," defined as more than fifty miles from a city, could receive 100 percent grant funding while others had to rely partially on loans or put up some of their own funding. This preference ruffled Senator Rockefeller, who noted at a hearing that few areas of West Virginia would qualify despite their lack of access. Urban members of Congress complained the rules for "underserved" excluded poor neighborhoods in the inner cities.

The quantity and complexity of the applications led to significant delays in announcing winners. To streamline the process, the agencies decided to consolidate the final rounds. The Dawsonville project run by the North Georgia Network Cooperative won $33.5 million to create a 260-mile fiber-optic ring connecting schools, universities, hospitals, and government facilities in Appalachian communities. The administration compared the project to President Kennedy's Appalachian Regional Commission, which helped create a textile and manufacturing base in the region. With those mills and factories now closed, better broadband could bring new economic development to the area, the White House said.

Addressing complaints from Congress, the second round removed the requirement for unserved and underserved areas, eliminated the remote designation, cut down on paperwork, and added categories for rural libraries, satellite networks, and public computer centers. In a rolling series of announcements throughout the summer of 2010, the NTIA and Rural Utilities Service distributed billions of dollars to hundreds of projects across the country. Some of the biggest included a $124 million award to the West Kentucky Rural Telephone Cooperative to bring fiber-optic lines to more than 21,000 homes; a $126 million grant to lay 2,400 miles of new fiber and build a high-speed network across West Virginia, including at every K-12 school; and a $101 million project by the Rural Telephone Service Company that would create 400 jobs in an area of western Kansas that was 99.5 percent unserved or underserved.

In addition to rural areas, the Recovery Act was bringing broadband to Native American reservations. The Navajo Nation received fiber-optic cable and new microwave towers to connect forty-nine community centers across an area where more than 60 percent of residents lacked telephone service. High-speed Internet would arrive at homes on the Coeur d'Alene Reservation in northern Idaho and the Tohono O'odham Reservation in the Sonoran Desert of Arizona.

The stimulus program also provided money to construct interoperable public safety wireless networks in Charlotte, San Francisco, and New Jersey. The high-speed networks could stream real-time video from emergency scenes to police and fire stations, allow paramedics to upload medical images from ambulances to hospitals, and allow firefighters to download floor plans of burning buildings on their way to a blaze. Urban areas also benefited with public computing centers in South Los Angeles, Boston, and the Coppin Heights/ Rosemont neighborhood in Baltimore. Philadelphia received $6.4 million to build forty-eight computer labs in recreation centers, homeless shelters, and public housing projects.

The broadband program was also playing a significant role in Obama's plan to modernize classrooms. The awards were expected to bring high-speed Internet to 3,300 rural schools, which served more than a million students, about 40 percent of whom qualified for free or reduced-priced lunch programs. More than $29 million went to fund computer training, desktop computers, and free Internet access for 33,000 low-income sixth graders in New York City and Los Angeles. A $100 million grant was designated for rural school districts in Colorado.

By expanding broadband, the stimulus wasn't just intended to bridge the digital divide but an economic divide as well. With new skills and a better understanding of the benefits of the Internet, neglected communities would have new opportunities through distance learning programs and access to faraway jobs. A grant to the University of Massachusetts, for example, sought to promote awareness and increase computer literacy among low-income Cambodian residents in Lowell. A nonprofit called Boat People SOS received money to provide training to limited-English speakers who had been affected by Hurricane Katrina and the BP oil spill. The Deaf Action Center of Louisiana received $1.4 million to use video conferencing to provide sign language translation at hospitals, courts, schools, and shelters.

But perhaps the most ambitious broadband project was a plan by the Vermont Telephone Company to bring wireless to nearly every unserved home, business, and community institution in the state. If successful, the Green Mountain State would be the first in the nation with universal coverage. Under the name VTel Wireless, the company received an $82 million grant and a $35 million loan to potentially serve 130,000 people. The project known as Wireless Open World (WOW) would rely on 4G LTE, considered the fastest wireless available, and it would directly support at least 1,800 jobs upfront. For its current customers in eastern Vermont, VTel would extend fiber capable of speeds up to one gigabit per second.

VTel's plans also harkened back to the Great Depression, providing a symbolic link between past and present. Part of the project included the creation of a "rural broadband farm forum" modeled after U.S. and Canadian radio farm forums of the 1940s. In the early days of radio, a number of organizations would gather small groups of rural neighbors to listen to a broadcast and then discuss matters such as grain prices, the role of women, and the future for rural youth. In a similar fashion, VTel would scout the back roads of Vermont, organizing small forums to help people find jobs online, start small businesses, and use the Internet more effectively in schools. Such a plan combining new broadband build-out with community awareness programs proved effective in Michigan, Texas, and Kentucky, according to researchers at Michigan State University.[6]

"This is an extremely aggressive effort to get 4G out throughout areas that are unserved currently in Vermont," Rural Utilities Service administrator Jonathan Adelstein declared. "They've got a very effective cost model to serve rural America that is going to work, I think, and transform the nature of broadband in the state of Vermont."

Vermont Telephone was a small rural company serving just fourteen towns and villages around Springfield in east central Vermont. It was a family-owned company that had been around since 1890. A live receptionist still answered the phone on the first or second ring, and a request to speak to the president was met with the response, "Hold on, let me transfer you." The president, Michel Guite, had been a vice president and equities analyst in telecommunications at the Salomon Brothers investment firm before purchasing VTel. Over the last decade, the company had been buying up wireless spectrum, becoming one of the largest owners of FCC licenses in Vermont, New Hampshire, and upstate New York.

VTel's plan to extend broadband to virtually every unserved resident fit nicely with the state's own plans. The previous governor, Jim Douglas, had pledged in 2007 to bring 100 percent coverage to Vermont by 2010. But the financial crisis shattered that plan and weakened many of Vermont's telecom companies, not to mention the state budget. The largest provider, FairPoint Communications, which had purchased Verizon's operations in northern New England in 2008, filed for bankruptcy in 2009. The next governor, Peter Shumlin, took office in 2011 and vowed to bring universal access by 2013. That also happened be the deadline for VTel to complete its stimulus project.

$ $ $

In the villages of rural Vermont, not having the Internet is unexceptional. The town of Granville in the Green Mountain National Forest didn't have indoor plumbing in its clerk's office until April 2011. Along with the villages in Vermont's Northeast Kingdom, it was one of the last communities to get electricity in the United States in the mid-1960s. When residents had one at all, Vermont had one of the slowest Internet connections in the country, according to Speed Matters, a project by the Communications Workers of America union.

"The problem in Vermont in early 2009 wasn't that there were vast areas of the state that didn't have any broadband," Christopher Campbell, executive director of the Vermont Telecommunications Authority, explained to me. "The problem was that we had a lot of smallish and widely scattered areas that had no broadband. It was more like a Swiss cheese pattern."

One of those holes was a community named Halifax in the far southeast corner of the state near the border with Massachusetts. Settled as bounty land to reward soldiers who fought in the French and Indian War, Halifax saw its population peak in 1810. The decline in agriculture wiped out the dairy and sheep farms, and by the 1960s, the census showed only 268 people. But as hippies and retirees discovered Vermont in the following decades, the population has risen to about eight hundred full-time residents. It was where the novelist Saul Bellow spent his summers in the 1970s and 1980s.[7] A half hour outside Brattleboro and two and a half hours from Boston, it was more recently a pass-through on the way to the ski resorts at Stratton and Mount Snow.

Earl B. Holtz, a retired electrical engineer who moved to Halifax in 2009, told me a story about a woman who was driving up and down his road with a cell phone out the window and laptop perched on the passenger seat. The Massachusetts resident, who had a summer home in Halifax, was desperately trying to find a place where she could get both her phone and computer to work at the same time. Holtz had one of the few homes where this was possible; so he invited the woman to park in his driveway while she worked. One of the few hotspots was the Jacksonville General Store about five miles north. It wasn't uncommon to find people sitting in their cars outside the public library, the glow of their laptop lighting up the night as they tried to take advantage of the faster Internet.

Holtz was chairman of the Halifax broadband committee. Many Vermont select boards have such committees, but a number of them have disbanded out of frustration. Holtz had a white beard and mustache and lived in a geodesic dome. Through a telephoto lens, you could see the communications tower miles away on Mount Olga that makes his home a rarity in Halifax. A so-called flatlander, Holtz spent most of his life in Connecticut, where he made postage meters for Pitney Bowes. He and his wife bought the land in 1995 and eventually retired there. Holtz was one of the last homes in town reached with FairPoint DSL service. The only options for everyone else were dial-up and satellite.

"Most people would love to have it but don't," he said.

The broadband committee had been trying to get Internet providers interested in serving Halifax. But several concluded it was economically infeasible. Now, Halifax was on a map of communities VTel was planning to serve with the stimulus project.

Holtz gave me a tour of Halifax in his pickup. The town had only two paved roads, Branch Road and Brook Road. At their intersection was a set of white clapboard buildings, including the community hall, the Baptist church, the historical society, and the Guiding Star Grange, a fraternal order for farmers. Another crossroads in an old unpaved part of town has an older church and the solitary chimney of a demolished hotel back from when a stagecoach used to run between there and Jacksonville. The town's website was updated so infrequently that to find out what was going on, residents had to drive down to the three bulletin boards posted at the town hall, school, and post office. It did, however, become critical when Hurricane Irene washed away parts of Route 112 through town and made several roads impassable. The town used the website to inform residents of hazards and how to get help.

Holtz's truck rumbled over washboard roads that always seemed to be rising or descending or bending. Thick maples lined the roads from when the old farmers planted them to have better access to the sap. Many properties still had sugar houses where the sap was boiled to make maple syrup. The farmers' fields have since been sold off for hay or are filled with high grass and yellow buttercups.

"It's all up and down, sparsely populated," Holtz said. "Sometimes the road ends up going through a farmer's yard."

The population of Halifax is divided between transplants who moved out to the country and people whose families have lived there for generations. The houses are a mix of new wooden cabins, small cottages, and mobile homes. According to the census, the median household income was $36,000, and 16 percent of the population lives in poverty.

As we headed down Stowe Mountain Road, Holtz told me about a woman who lived nearby who upgraded her satellite Internet service so that the neighbors' children could use it for school. We continued driving past the Green River dam and a red covered bridge with a sign that said TWO DOLLAR FINE TO DRIVE ON THIS BRIDGE FASTER THAN A WALK.

After a while, we reached a custom glass-blowing shop called Vitri-Forms Inc. Started in the 1960s in Brattleboro, the shop made specialized scientific equipment such as laser tubes and chromatography columns to test water and soil. When the lease was terminated in the late 1990s, the family decided to build the shop at their home in the country rather than renovating a new space in town. The business manager, Lisa Stagner, explained that the company relies on the Internet to communicate with customers, research particular jobs, and send pictures of products. After years of battling dial-up, the family got fed up with promises of faster service and signed up with Hughes-Net for satellite service.

"We've been told for years from various phone companies that it would be coming, it would be coming," Stagner said. But then one time a repairman came to the house and told them the system was so old that he couldn't figure out how they even had phone service. "There was a pretty good chance we weren't getting broadband if they didn't know how we were getting phone," she said.

Halifax had few businesses outside the self-employed writers, researchers, and hobbyists who worked from home. In addition to the glass shop, there was a bed and breakfast, a vineyard, and Abbott's Glen Clothing Optional Inn. But throughout Vermont, in conversations about broadband, proponents often brought up the notion of the "weekend CEO." The state was close enough to New York and Boston that a number of business executives had second homes there that they visited a few times a year during ski season, the summer, or to look at the fall foliage. If the villages had better broadband, the theory went, those executives might come up more frequently or even open up a satellite office bringing new jobs to remote areas that had few.

Next to Holtz's geodesic dome was the Honora Winery, a two-hundred-acre vineyard that specialized in cold-weather varieties such as Sabrevois, St. Croix, and Frontenac. Honora also imported from California the more traditional Merlot, Cabernet, and Chardonnay grapes, which they distilled at the winery and sold at a tasting room across from the general store in Jacksonville. There, I met Brad York and Lorraine Muha, who ran the tasting room and organized special events like weddings at the winery.

"It's a mess," Muha said when I asked about what it was like trying to run a business with the current Internet service. "The heat is a problem, the snow is a problem—"

"The wind is a problem," York said, finishing her sentence.

The owner of Honora Winery was Patricia Farrington, who was born in White Plains, New York, and operated bars, restaurants, and other businesses from her home in Stamford, Connecticut. She used to ski in the area as a kid, and she and her husband decided to move out there in the early 2000s. They started by planting a few vines in 2004 as a hobby. But it quickly expanded to 10,000 vines by 2006, and they now produce 400 to 500 cases of wine a year.

"It's a really interesting thing to operate a business with limited access to broadband, cell service, anything," she said.

To manage, Farrington bought two Internet packages, FairPoint DSL and HughesNet satellite service, and had her IT guys set it up so they would automatically switch back and forth when one or the other is down. They even put a public-safety radio tower on their property because the Halifax fire department couldn't get calls if the emergency was on the other side of the hill. In June 2011, the winery's Internet had recently been down for seven days straight. That made it a challenge as brides from New York City were sending final counts on guests and coordinating the vendors.

Honora was a rare example of a new business bringing jobs to the community. Farrington had hired young people from Providence and upstate New York and prevented a couple from moving after they had lost their inn during the recession. But she worried that without broadband, newcomers would leave. If America could build broadband networks in the war zone of Iraq or in remote locations in Afghanistan, why not in Vermont?

"There are third-world countries right now that have better access than we do, and we're two and half hours from Boston," Farrington said. "These communities need an economy. You need to have businesses. You can't have everyone be over sixty."

The week I was there, the Halifax School PTA was holding its annual picnic. While the school had a T1 line that provided decent speeds during school hours, many students were without when they went home at night. As they ate hot dogs and pasta salad, parents told horror stories of school projects and papers that took forever.

"It's grueling," said Holly Fox, who has a daughter in eighth grade and a son in sixth. "It definitely adds on to homework time. Sometimes my daughter is working on the Internet for four to five hours trying to Google something. Or it takes five minutes for a picture to download and then you find out it's not the right one."

Fox worked as a dental hygienist in Brattleboro and struggled with classes where she had to download medical journal articles for term papers. With dial-up, she couldn't get her continuing education credits at home and had to travel hours to classes in Burlington or Boston.

Fed up with dial-up, Lisa Noyes recently upgraded to satellite, which cost about $70 per month. But even with that, Noyes and her family were limited in how much they could use per day. A business package like the one needed by Honora had cost more than $100 a month. VTel planned to offer basic Internet service for $10 a month and advanced service for about $35.

Earl Holtz shared the frustration. As I got out of his pickup, I noticed two bumper stickers that read IMPEACH OBAMA and I'LL KEEP MY GUNS, FREEDOM, AND MONEY. YOU KEEP THE "CHANGE." A "conservative by nature," Holtz felt differently about the role of government when it came to broadband.

"Businesses should either sink or swim on their ability to perform for their stockholders," he said. "The broadband issue, I'm between a rock and a hard place on. You can't always win every conversation. I think that in the case of Vermont, it's probably the only way it's going to happen. Is broadband important? I think it's as important as electrification. Even being a libertarian, there are certain things the federal government can help out on."

$ $ $

Shortly after VTel received its stimulus award, Senator Bernie Sanders organized a town meeting at Vermont Technical College in Randolph Center with Michel Guite and Jonathan Adelstein, the Rural Utilities Service administrator. The white-maned senator leaned on the podium with the sleeves of his blue button-down shirt rolled up to his elbows.

"The issue that we are discussing may not be the sexiest issue in the world, but it's an issue of huge consequence," Sanders told the audience of three hundred people. "If this project does what I hope and expect it will do, within three years, every home, every office in the state of Vermont will have good-quality broadband at an affordable price, and that is nothing to sneeze at."[8]

After the requisite speeches, Sanders called Michel Guite up to the microphone.

"I want to put Dr. Guite on the record," Sanders said. "There's a television camera. Look into it."

Did he promise to bring universal broadband coverage to every single unserved community in the state of the Vermont?

"Yes."

One after another, members of the audience told of shoddy service and promises broken by previous providers. Many in the audience were skeptical of VTel. How good would the wireless be given the obstacles of hilly terrain, foliage, and snowstorms? VTel didn't plan to build many new towers. But the current towers failed to provide cell phone service to many areas. One woman told of how with satellite she can download updates to her computer only between 2:00 A.M. and 6:00 A.M. and how FairPoint was in the area but wouldn't serve the ten people on her hill. Did "everybody" really mean everybody?

"When we say everybody," Guite said, "we mean pretty much functionally everybody, but life is complicated."

"Oh, come now!" someone shouted, as others in the audience groaned.

Many people who attended the meeting had signed up to get service from another company called EC Fiber. The partnership of twenty-three communities planned to build a municipally owned network that would string fiber to the homes instead of relying on wireless. But the financing for the project collapsed when Lehman Brothers went under in 2008. Loredo Sola, chairman of EC Fiber, told me that he thought the stimulus would be the saving grace. It was shovel-ready and a perfect example of a project that had stalled due to the frozen credit market.

"We were feeling cautiously optimistic," Sola said.

But EC Fiber didn't get any funding under the Recovery Act. Neither did FairPoint, the largest incumbent in the area. FairPoint, which had protested stimulus projects in Maine and New Hampshire,[9] was also bringing high-speed service to many of the communities covered by VTel. Here was a private company that had just come out of bankruptcy having to compete with another company getting more than $100 million in government funding.

"This is not a good scenario for the long-term stability of phone service in Vermont," Sola said. "This is not a level playing field."

$ $ $

Accusations that the stimulus money was duplicating existing broadband service tailed the program from its beginning. An economic study commissioned by the National Cable & Telecommunications Association, the cable industry's trade group, concluded that the agency was continuing its poor record under the stimulus. Released in April 2011, the report by Navigant Economics focused on three of the largest projects in Montana, Minnesota, and Kansas. Combined, they had received $232 million in federal support. But more than 85 percent of homes in those areas were already served by companies providing DSL, cable, or wireless at adequate speeds and affordable rates, the researchers found. When that was factored in, that left only 5,200 unserved homes, raising the cost of bringing broadband to more than $30,000 per home.

The rules of the Recovery Act gave recipients significant leeway in establishing unserved and underserved. At least 75 percent of the project had to be in a geographic area where fewer than half the homes had broadband access. But that final 25 percent could be in an area where everyone's Internet was lightning fast. While the vast majority of the *area* had to be underserved, there was nothing to say where the *customers* had to be distributed. The result, the report concluded, was that the stimulus was subsidizing competitors to overbuild existing networks.

In the Big Sky Country outside Bozeman, Montana, near Yellowstone National Park, the stimulus was funding a $64 million project by

Montana Opticom to bring fiber to the premises of 9,000 households across 150 square miles. The only problem, according to the cable association, was that only 136 homes met the Rural Utilities Service's definition of being unserved. Four companies operated in the area, and two offered service at 1.5 megabits per second to nearly all the homes for less than $40 a month.

The same thing occurred along Lake Superior in northeast Minnesota, the researchers said. There, a public initiative similar to EC Fiber called the Lake County Fiber Network received $66 million in grants and loans to bring fiber to nearly 12,000 homes across 2,675 square miles. But much of the area was uninhabited, and most of the homes were in communities that already had cable or DSL.

Then there was the project in northwest Kansas around the Old West town of Hays. The Rural Telephone Service Company, a subsidiary of Nex-Tech, won a $101 million project to cover 4,200 square miles. Only 8 of those miles were located in the city of Hays. But nearly half of the homes were, said Gary Shorman, president of Eagle Communications, one of the competitors.

"Companies that have taken [the] financial risk of serving rural markets and serving them well, it's unrealistic to expect us to continue to do so if we have to face large government competition," Shorman testified at a congressional hearing in February 2011. "Eagle is happy to face competition from other providers, but we cannot effectively compete with a government-backed favorite."

In the conservative narrative, the broadband stimulus program was repeating a mistake of the New Deal. As the columnist Amity Shlaes documented in her alternative history of the Great Depression, *The Forgotten Man*, similar accusations were levied against Roosevelt's plan to electrify the South. The Tennessee Valley Authority's plan to build hydroelectric dams caused great concern for Wendell Willkie of the Commonwealth & Southern Corporation, who warned that the TVA would supplant the utility's investments, making it impossible to compete.[10]

Frequently, the Government Accountability Office (GAO) found, companies submitted inaccurate information to claim they were already serving a proposed area. When a Rural Utilities Service field representative asked one company to verify the number of its sub-scribers in an area, the company quickly withdrew the complaint. Ad-vertised rates and speeds didn't always reflect the reality on the ground.

But with incomplete data, even in the national broadband map fi-nally released in 2011, it was difficult to rule out every complaint. The GAO did find several instances in which a stimulus project overlapped service from an existing provider. To make it worthwhile economi-cally, the Rural Utilities Service allowed this so that companies would have an incentive to extend coverage to remote areas. As a result, ap-plicants gerrymandered their proposed service area by piecing to-gether census blocks like Legos until they had a map that met the stimulus criteria. Under such a practice, Los Angeles could be made into a rural area.

$ $ $

The broadband program was a fertile testing ground for the debate over the government's role in the economy. By the spring of 2011, about 75 percent of projects had started, creating roughly 3,000 jobs, according to project reports submitted to Recovery.gov. VTel Wireless had contracted with two engineering firms. It had hired a project manager and requested bids for the wireless equipment. The com-pany estimated that it had created 10 jobs.

"The impact of the VTel stimulus award has been huge in terms of shrinking the number of remaining pockets of unserved areas," Campbell of the Vermont Telecommunications Authority told me. "We really do believe at this point that the notion of 100 percent avail-ability by the end of 2013 is achievable."

On the same day as the congressional hearing on broadband, a couple of hours after Gary Shorman testified that the stimulus was hurting his business, President Obama traveled to the Upper Penin-sula of Michigan to announce his national wireless initiative. The pro-posal would build off the Recovery Act investments to bring high-speed Internet to 98 percent of Americans within five years. Sim-ilar to the VTel plan in Vermont, the nationwide initiative would use 4G networks to provide access to hard-to-reach rural areas.

Speaking at Northern Michigan University in Marquette, Obama drew from the American narrative he had laid down in *The Audacity of Hope*. The government had built the transcontinental railroad, brought electricity to rural areas, and constructed the Interstate Highway System, transforming the nation and providing the backbone for a stronger economy. Now, America was in need of a broadband network.

"For our families and our businesses, high-speed wireless service—that's the next train station," Obama told the crowd. "It's the next off-ramp. It's how we'll spark new innovation, new investment, new jobs."

But to get there, Obama would have to overcome a political and economic environment that had changed substantially since he introduced America to his vision on that warm November night in Chicago's Grant Park.

FIFTEEN

SPUTNIK MOMENT?

The people who have been longest without work, are gradually be-
ing forced into the class of unemployables—rusty tools, abandoned,
not worth using any more. . . . And so they go on—the gaunt,
ragged legion of the industrially damned. Bewildered apathetic,
many of them terrifyingly patient.

—Lorena Hickok, as quoted by David Kennedy, *Freedom from Fear*

THE BATTLE CRY OF the Republicans was first sounded in October 2010 at the statehouse in Trenton, New Jersey. Governor Chris Christie, a conservative who had won the office a year before, announced that he would kill one of the biggest public works projects in America: a $9 billion transit tunnel under the Hudson River to Manhattan. Anyone who has ridden an overcrowded NJ Transit train during the rush-hour commute can tell you how much another tunnel is needed. The ARC Tunnel (which stood for access to the region's core) would have been the first new rail tunnel between New York and New Jersey since 1910, would have alleviated congestion that has quadrupled in the past twenty years, and would have created 6,000 construction jobs.

The project was funded with $3 billion from the federal Department of Transportation, $3 billion from the Port Authority of New York and New Jersey, and $2.7 billion in other money, including $130 million from the economic stimulus package. But Christie said the plan left New Jersey taxpayers on the hook for potential cost overruns expected to amount to $2 billion to $5 billion. That left him with no choice, he said, but to accept a recommendation from a study committee to shut the project down.

"Bottom line is this: New Jersey has gone for too long and for too many decades ordering things that they can't pay for," Christie explained at a press conference announcing his decision. "I simply cannot responsibly allow this to go forward."

The fate of the tunnel was bemoaned day after day by *New York Times* columnists from the left and the right. "We are no longer the nation that used to amaze the world with its visionary projects," declared Princeton economist Paul Krugman.[1] "Why are important projects now unaffordable?" asked conservative writer David Brooks.[2] To many, it was a sign that America was moving into an age of austerity, where it no longer built grand icons of public works, where the old motto "Trenton Makes, the World Takes," had become exactly the opposite.

Immediately upon taking office, the new Republican majority in the House sought to rescind all unobligated stimulus funds. In an ironic twist of fate, the sponsor of the bill was Representative Sean Duffy, who won the Wisconsin seat given up by David Obey, who had fought so hard to get the Recovery Act passed. More than 98 percent of the stimulus money had already been committed to projects. But if passed, the rescission bill would have curbed Obama's most ambitious projects for renewable energy, electronic health records, and high-speed rail. In reality, it was mainly a symbolic gesture. Such a bill stood no a chance in the Senate, where the Democrats still held a majority. With split chambers and the parties at loggerheads, the Republican Senate leader Mitch McConnell told the *National Journal* that "the single most important thing we want to achieve is for President Obama to be a one-term president."[3] It was a stark change in tone from two years before when McConnell called on the Senate to rise above "the politics of division."

Yet the biggest political threat the White House faced in trying to carry out the Recovery Act was not in Congress, but in the mansions and offices of America's newly elected Republican governors. The cast may have been new, but it was essentially a repeat of the spring of 2009, when Mark Sanford, Sarah Palin, and other governors tried to reject the stimulus money on the front end. In Wisconsin, Governor Scott Walker, the former Milwaukee county executive, returned a $23 million grant to bring fiber broadband connections to more than four hundred schools and libraries.[4]

In Ohio, education reform advocates worried that the state would lose its Race to the Top funding after Governor John Kasich, a former congressman and Fox News host, promised to scrap his predecessor's formula for distributing money to schools. Ohio had won the $400 million grant by three points over New Jersey, where rather than encouraging cooperation, Race to the Top seemed only to further divide the key players. The state's education commissioner, Bret Schundler, was fired by Governor Christie after the application was docked five points for omitting a minor detail. Schundler in turn accused Christie of torpedoing the extraordinary accord he had reached with the state teachers' union, which he himself had battled for years. In Maryland, state lawmakers nearly jeopardized Race to the Top funding when a committee voted against a state plan to tie 50 percent of teachers' evaluations to student achievement. Despite being in line for hundreds of thousands of dollars, dozens of school districts in Ohio, Massachusetts, and Florida pulled out of Race to the Top when the reform plans became more clear.[5]

Even in Delaware, the state where education reform seemed most plausible, plans were thrown into chaos. Led by John Young, the Christina school board voted to nullify the district's decision to reassign nineteen teachers as part of its plan to turn around Stubbs Elementary and Glasgow High, two of its lowest-performing schools. Board members were angered by the district's process of determining which teachers would be moved, which consisted of a twenty-minute interview. Reading a speech from the public-comment podium, Young condemned the reform movement. "The introduction of massive staff and leadership change may make the adults feel productive, but it does very little for our students," he declared. The following day, the state Department of Education froze the funds promised to Christina.

Under pressure, the school board eventually reversed its decision, allowing the Race to the Top reforms to go forward. But facing the first full year of implementation, every state except Georgia amended their blueprints to delay or scale back part of their plans.[6]

The most significant pushback to the Recovery Act, though, came when Governors Walker, Kasich, and Rick Scott of Florida rejected $2.5 billion in stimulus money for high-speed rail. By killing the bullet trains in Ohio, Wisconsin, and Florida, the trio caused a major setback for Obama's national rail plan. The return of money after months, and sometimes years, of planning forced Transportation secretary Ray LaHood into a game of Whac-A-Mole as he scrambled to redistribute the money to other rail lines.

$ $ $

In the months leading up to the midterm elections, Keli Carender, the young Seattle woman who held one of the first Tea Party protests, told me that many people had misunderstood the movement's mission as an internal struggle in the Republican Party. But the goal wasn't just to move Republicans to the right, it was to move the entire spectrum of what was acceptable for fiscal policy.

"It's not shrinking it; it's more like shifting it," she said. "If you read back over leftist literature, that's what they talked about in the sixties, changing the range, but making it more to the left. The Tea Party movement's main goal, I think, is to change the range back."

With the sweeping GOP victory, the Tea Party's goal seemed not only to be working in Congress, but to be affecting Obama as well. The president had repeatedly vowed to end the high-income tax cuts passed during the Bush administration. But when push came to shove, Obama was trapped. With the Bush tax cuts, extended unemployment benefits, and several stimulus provisions set to expire at the end of 2010, Obama could either make a deal with Republicans or risk economic hardship for everyone should the middle-class tax cuts expire as well. The president agonized in public over his struggle to end the Bush tax cuts.

"The issue is, How do I persuade the Republicans in the Senate who are currently blocking that position?" he said. "I have not been able to budge them."

Two million unemployed workers would lose their checks if Obama stuck to his guns. And with a substantial Republican majority set to take over the House in January 2011, there would have been little traction for an extension of stimulus provisions for renewable energy, public transit, and low-income families. The approaching deadline resulted in a swift compromise. Congress passed a two-year extension that would keep income taxes at a lower rate for couples earning more than $250,000 a year. In exchange, it enacted a thirteen-month extension of unemployment benefits and a $110 billion payroll tax cut that would lower workers' Social Security taxes by up to $2,000. The final bill cost $858 billion, more than the Recovery Act. But wrapped inside the tax deal were a series of measures that would keep parts of the Recovery Act going through 2011. Wind and solar farms would continue receiving lucrative grants instead of the more restrictive tax credits for producing renewable energy. Parents with kids in college could keep taking the American Opportunity Tax Credit for tuition expenses. Low-income families qualifying for earned income and child tax credits would receive expanded assistance. And bus and train riders could continue claiming double the usual amount for their transit passes. In all, the extension of the Bush tax cuts included nearly $250 billion in additional stimulus.

Facing resistance among progressive Democrats, the White House trotted out nearly every administration official to sell the package as a good deal for the middle class. They released a report detailing how the framework would affect hypothetical families in Iowa, Florida, Ohio, Wisconsin, and Colorado—all swing states for the 2012 election. Even former president Bill Clinton made a cameo in the White House press room, taking the mic for an extended question-and-answer session to express his support. In one exchange Clinton mentioned a recent trip to Hong Kong and began to talk about its "stimulus" before recognizing his error. "Well," he said, "I guess we're not supposed to use that word anymore."

In the midst of this new climate, Obama unveiled his plan to "win the future." Speaking before Congress at his State of the Union in January 2011, he laid out a series of new investments that would put the country on a firmer path to recovery. He drew on history and spoke of the need to look ahead, even in tough times.

"We know what it takes to compete for the jobs and industries of our time," the president said. "We need to out-innovate, out-educate, and out-build the rest of the world."

In the speech and in the weeks that followed, Obama called for $53 billion for high-speed rail and proposed his wireless initiative to bring broadband to 98 percent of the country. By 2035, he said, 80 percent of the nation's power should come from "clean" energy, including nuclear, clean coal, and natural gas. To get there, he would increase funding for renewables in the budget and launch an initiative to make solar competitive with fossil fuels. He called for a rewrite of the No Child Left Behind law modeled after the reforms promoted in Race to the Top. And he reiterated his pledge to put one million hybrid and electric vehicles on the road by 2015.

Obama recalled a time when workers could find a good job at their local factory that would give them a decent middle-class life, when the only competition was their neighbors, and when everyone had a shot. But the world was different now as technology and globalization had eroded American manufacturing in a single generation. Obama alluded to Thomas Edison and the Wright Brothers, the transcontinental railroad and the Interstate Highway System. And he frequently alluded to China. The sleeping dragon was a popular bogeyman for both the right and left. Anti-spending groups had released a TV commercial showing Chinese students learning about the fall of the American empire with banners of Chairman Mao on the wall. Obama invoked China as an opponent racing to educate and innovate to prepare itself for the jobs of the future.

America, he said, was facing a new "Sputnik moment." Political leaders frequently had used the phrase "Sputnik moment" to throw down a challenge in education, technology, and renewable energy. It was the founding metaphor of the Apollo Alliance. Obama had used the phrase two years earlier in a speech at the National Academy of Sciences. And in the months leading up to the State of the Union, the administration had tested the phrase in a number of settings. One of the first was a speech by Energy secretary Steven Chu, who declared in November that China's clean-energy endeavors marked a new "Sputnik moment" for America. At a community college in Winston-

Salem, North Carolina, Obama talked to laid-off mill workers now in a biotechnology class and declared, "Our generation's Sputnik moment is back."

While the messaging may have been sharper, the "win the future" platform was nothing new. Obama essentially said the exact same things in his State of the Union the year before, in his address to Congress the year before that, on the campaign trail, and as a senator in *The Audacity of Hope*. Two years later so much of the hope America had for the stimulus remained unfulfilled. Soon enough, "win the future" would fade into a distant memory as the debt and deficit would dominate the rest of his term.

In a nod to the new reality, Obama vowed in the State of the Union to achieve all his goals within the confines of a spending freeze while also cutting the corporate tax rates, eliminating regulations, and working with Republicans to reduce the deficit. Where he had once urged his economic team to think "bolder" when it came to the stimulus package, he was now calling on Congress to "think bigger" when it came to cutting red tape.

"The administration pivoted to deficit reduction before the economy was ready for that," Biden's economic adviser, Jared Bernstein, later recalled. "The politics moved us away from a jobs agenda too soon, and the president has been fighting to get back there."

After the speech, Obama was on his way to Manitowoc, Wisconsin. One stop on the trip was an energy-efficient lighting firm, which also happened to have a partnership with Solyndra, the embattled solar company. Biden was going to Indiana to visit Ener1, the company making batteries for Elkhart's all-electric Think car. So much had changed since the stimulus passed. The year before, as the economy appeared to be charging out of the Great Recession, Obama triumphantly took off to visit a factory in Allentown. Now the recovery had slowed to crawl, and the company had closed the factory down.

$ $ $

Allentown Metal Works was a century-old complex that employed some of the only steelworkers left in a region that was once home to Bethlehem Steel. The metal fabricator had hoped that the stimulus package's investments in bridges and other public works would bring new business. But it never happened. Now, after years of debt and other problems, Allentown Metal Works decided to shut its doors.[7]

Internal and external forces were eroding the Recovery Act's achievements. Already, despite the historic investments in renewable energy, China had surpassed the United States in wind power capacity, according to the Global Wind Energy Council. America's claim to the fastest supercomputer in the world was short lived. The stimulus had funded a $20 million upgrade to the Jaguar computing system at Oak Ridge National Laboratory. But by the fall of 2010, it had been surpassed by China. By the summer of 2011, Japan had the top spot, knocking America down to third.[8]

The Department of Homeland Security headquarters, heralded as the largest federal building project since the Pentagon, got a kick-start under the Recovery Act. But in its 2012 budget request, the Obama administration proposed delaying the second phase of the project, the construction of the Federal Emergency Management Agency headquarters, to focus on day-to-day security operations. Republican lawmakers tried to cut funding even further, meaning that the Coast Guard might have a new building, but workers would have no roads to get there.

Consumers were slow to embrace the electric car. The boasts that the new vehicles could get the equivalent of 230, even 367, miles per gallon were tempered by the government's official ratings which put the Nissan Leaf at 99 miles per gallon and the Chevy Volt at 93 when running on electricity only. The rating also reduced the Leaf's range from the advertised 100 miles to an estimated 73 miles per charge. Thanks to the stimulus money for fuel-efficient fleets, nearly one in four of the hybrids that Ford and General Motors sold in 2009 and 2010 had been purchased by the government, according to a Bloomberg analysis.[9] By the first half of 2011, fewer than seven thousand Leafs and Volts had been sold in the United States.

A report by congressional researchers in March 2011 concluded that the cost of batteries, anxiety over vehicle range, and more efficient internal combustion engines could make it difficult to achieve Obama's goal of putting a million electric vehicles on the road by 2015.

While the $2.4 billion in stimulus money had increased battery manufacturing in the United States, the report noted that South Korea and China had announced plans to invest more than five times that amount over the next decade. Still, the Department of Energy in its own report said the Recovery Act and other government policies had gone a long way toward making a million vehicles achievable. The administration proposed a number of new incentives, including spending more money on research and development, turning the $7,500 tax credit into an immediate rebate à la Cash for Clunkers, and giving grants to communities that become early adopters. And in May, the administration announced that agencies would purchase more than a hundred electric vehicles from Chevrolet, Nissan, and Think as part of a government transition to alternative fuels.

$ $ $

Solyndra was now producing its signature cylindrical solar panels at its brand new state-of-the-art plant in Fremont, California, a project that had been completed thanks to the stimulus. But the company's financial condition had continued to weaken. In November 2010, just one day after the midterm elections, the company disclosed that it would shut down its older factory. After promising to create 1,000 jobs with stimulus money, Solyndra said it was scaling back its expansion plans in the short term and would instead eliminate more than 150 jobs.

In an effort to infuse the company with additional cash, the Department of Energy negotiated with two of Solyndra's investors to restructure the terms of the loan guarantee. The investors, including the firm tied to Kaiser, agreed to provide Solyndra with $75 million in capital with the option of another $75 million later. But in exchange, the department would give the investors priority over the U.S. government to recover money should the company go bankrupt.

In a January 31, 2011 e-mail with the subject line "Solyndra optics," an employee at the White House Office of Management and Budget (OMB) questioned whether it was worth it to give the company a lifeline. "Given the PR and policy attention Solyndra has received since 2009, the optics of a Solyndra default will be bad whenever it occurs," the staffer wrote. "While the company *may* avoid default with a restructuring, there is also a good chance it will not." Then in underlined text, the e-mail continued, "If Solyndra defaults down the road, the optics will arguably be worse later than they would be today," noting that the timing would likely coincide with the 2012 presidential campaign. "At that point, additional funds have been put at risk, recoveries *may* be lower, and questions will be asked as to why the Administration made a bad investment, not just once . . . but twice."

Still, the Department of Energy decided to press forward. Officials made the case that by securing additional capital it was protecting the taxpayer's investment by allowing the company to stay in business and execute its strategic plan. At the end of February, the government and the investors signed the restructuring deal.

The narrative raised red flags among Republicans: A prominent investor in Solyndra raises significant cash for the Obama campaign. The president then delivers a huge loan guarantee to Solyndra as part of his first major package. Obama and Biden provide publicity. But the company struggles in the free market. A negative audit. The withdrawal of the stock offering. The stepping down of the CEO. And now a plant closure and layoff. Taking the reins of Congress, they would seek to make Solyndra the emblematic boondoggle of the Recovery Act.

In February 2011, the House Energy and Commerce Committee announced that it had launched an investigation into Solyndra's loan guarantee. "I am concerned that the DOE is providing loans and loan guarantees to firms that aren't capable of competing in the global market, even with government subsidies," Florida congressman Cliff Stearns said in requesting documents from OMB. "I also question the competence and judgment of companies such as Solyndra that receive government support and still struggle financially."

An audit by Department of Energy investigators found that managers of the loan guarantee program couldn't always document how decisions were made, instead relying on "professional judgment" and informal deliberations. Of the eighteen loan guarantees and conditional commitments that had been made, three projects had no information in the department's official electronic system, and twelve had only limited data. The sloppy recordkeeping left the department "open to criticism that it may have exposed the taxpayers to unacceptable risks," investigators wrote. Meanwhile, the Government Accountability Office reported that the Energy Department had "treated applicants inconsistently, favoring some and disadvantaging others." Some projects, including Solyndra's new factory,[10] had received conditional loan guarantees before external reviews were completed. That allowed them to save significant money on the front end while other applicants had to pay for such reviews. Testifying at a hearing in March 2011, Inspector General Gregory Friedman said, "In summary, massive funding, high expectations, and inadequate infrastructure resulted, at times, and I stress at times, in less than optimal performance."

This lack of documentation complicated Stearns's investigation. After months of pressing for documents, he said, OMB had produced only eight e-mails. In June, the Energy and Commerce subcommittee on investigations called the office's deputy director, Jeffrey Zients, to testify. But Zients didn't show up. The dispute came to a head the following month when the subcommittee used its power to issue a rare subpoena for the Solyndra documents. "If OMB has nothing to hide," Stearns said, "they should have turned the documents over four months ago."

Maryo Mendez, the autoworker who lost his job when the NUMMI plant closed in Fremont, was still looking for work. He had been filling out applications, going to job fairs, and driving to the plants to drop off his resume and talk to the managers. He even considered going back to his old work in plastics manufacturing. But when he showed up at two companies that said online they were hiring, the buildings were boarded up and bore signs that they had closed.

The family had cut back on vacations and going out to eat. No more summer camp or soccer leagues or baseball. His daughter who had just graduated high school might have to put off college for a year. Mendez was now fifty-five. He had been out of work for nearly sixteen months. With $450 a week in unemployment benefits, the family was able to stay afloat on their mortgage and other bills by drawing on their life savings, every so often closing CDs and transferring the money into checking. They were $10,000 in the hole for the year by July 2011. Health insurance was due to run out in October. Mendez was now considering drawing on his NUMMI pension years before he ever expected he'd have to. He had hoped to get a job with Tesla, which had taken over the NUMMI plant, to build electric cars or with another company working in clean energy. But he was growing skeptical. Only a few people he knew had found such jobs, and some of them had already been laid off. The NUMMI plant was practically empty. Were people ready for an all-electric car or solar panels on their roofs?

"All these green technology things that are going on, it seems like it's not taking off," he said.

He was right. In September, Solyndra filed for bankruptcy, shutting down production and laying off all 1,200 employees.

In court documents, Solyndra's chief financial officer, W. G. Stover, said, "The combination of general business conditions and an oversupply of solar panels dramatically reduced solar panel pricing worldwide." Foreign manufacturers had expanded operations thanks to low-interest government loans, forcing Solyndra to cut its prices to remain competitive. In addition, European countries including Germany had scaled back their solar incentives, reducing demand. The Department of Energy also blamed the changing economics of the solar industry, citing the substantial subsidies provided by China.

But there were other reasons. Solyndra didn't sell its panels directly to flat-roofed warehouses and box stores, but instead yielded control to resellers to market its products. There were cheaper alternatives to Solyndra's technology, and the company's panels had little utility outside the commercial niche. Several analysts began to wonder if Solyndra had expanded too fast. In our interview the year before, Dave Miller, the corporate spokesman, had told me that Solyndra might have been profitable sooner if it had stayed small. But it might also have died a slow death without the capital to expand capacity and get up to scale.

The fallout was nuclear for the Obama administration. The House Energy and Commerce Committee raised new questions about the loan guarantee, and journalists began looking closer at the ties to Kaiser. Many critics said the administration should have seen this coming. By early 2009, silicon prices were plummeting and had been for the better part of a year.

Making matters worse, Solyndra's new CEO, Brian Harrison, met with Democrats on the Energy committee in mid-July 2011 to assure them that Solyndra's prospects were bright and that the company wasn't in danger. In a letter to the committee, Harrison said revenues were projected to double in 2011 and that the stimulus project was on track to meet its job creation commitments. But according to the committee, around the same time, Solyndra was preparing to restate its financial projections to reflect the difficult market. Solyndra again met with its investors and the Department of Energy to try to restructure the loan guarantee. But this time, the department decided against it, and the next day Solyndra ceased operations.

On September 8, two days after Solyndra filed for bankruptcy, FBI agents raided Solyndra's headquarters and the homes of its top executives. The agency was looking for evidence that the company had misrepresented its financial condition when it submitted documents to the Energy Department to secure the government loan guarantee.[11]

The Obama administration had placed their bet on Solyndra and lost miserably. Now it was blowing up into a true scandal. Solyndra was a company that seemed to be a model for a new era of American manufacturing through green technology. It had an innovative product that was performing well in Europe. It had the backing of prominent private investors and the glowing reviews of outside analysts. And while other U.S. solar companies had built plants in Asia, Solyndra was expanding in America. This is what the administration had dreamed of when it designed the stimulus to lay the groundwork for the green economy. But blinded by their desire to create a success story, administration officials ignored the warning signs and failed to realize how much the future of government investment in renewable energy depended on the success of a single company.

$ $ $

In Aiken, South Carolina, the stimulus money for the nuclear cleanup at the Savannah River Site had a tremendous impact on the local economy, according to an April 2011 report by the University of South Carolina Aiken. With about half the funding spent, the Recovery Act had resulted in about $525 million in additional output for the region. The work at the plant and the spending it generated in the community was responsible for a total of 4,600 jobs, the research team concluded.

"ARRA-funded projects have been instrumental in ensuring the economic stability of the local economy," the report concluded. "Without the ARRA funding, local economic growth and development would have been hindered due to the severity of the economic and financial condition currently being experienced."

But as the funding began to run dry in 2011, local leaders faced a new dilemma: what to do with 3,000 workers who would lose their jobs when the stimulus money ran out. After the initial drop from the Recovery Act, Aiken County's unemployment rate had leveled off at about 8 to 8.5 percent. Would the region now face a delayed recession?

The stimulus workers knew from the get-go that their jobs were temporary. But area officials had hoped to hold on to the new residents after the money was gone. Perhaps many of the newly trained nuclear workers would slide in easily as new reactors at Plant Vogtle outside Augusta and V.C. Summer near Columbia went online. A report commissioned by the Savannah River Site community organization in late 2009 found that the regional nuclear industry would need 6,100 new employees by 2014 and nearly 10,000 in the next decade. But the timing was a couple of years off from when the stimulus projects ended and when the new reactors would start operations. Then the nuclear meltdown at the Fukushima plant following the earthquake and tsunami in Japan cast doubt on America's nuclear renaissance.

In late 2010, Savannah River Nuclear Solutions announced that it would lay off 1,400 workers, including 800 whose jobs had been saved by the stimulus. At the same time, Recovery Act projects were ending on a rolling basis from the summer of 2010 through December 2012. As their work finished, the stimulus hires went on their way. Realizing that his projects were coming to an end, former home builder Jimmy

Hughes used his new connections to find a job with the contractor URS in Oak Ridge, Tennessee. Bill Picciano was hired on full time by Savannah River Nuclear Solutions and was enjoying the newfound stability. Jagadish Memula, an engineer who had been hired for the liquid waste project, was hopeful about his prospects but remained worried about the layoffs. "I'm very much concerned," he said. "But the outside market is getting much, much better so I don't have that much fear as when I started here."

On June 29, 2011, two of the largest stimulus projects at the Savannah River Site came to an end. At a ceremony, workers in hardhats and hazard vests buried a time capsule with the Recovery Act logo and sealed the P and the R reactor buildings for good.

"The Recovery Act enabled us to accomplish a remarkable feat," said David Moody, manager of the Savannah River operations office. "In just two years, we successfully and safely delivered a fitting end to these relics that led our nation to a Cold War victory. For that we are proud."

$ $ $

More and more, the long-term effects of the Great Recession were laid bare. After beginning to fall, the unemployment rate crept back up over 9 percent in the spring of 2011. The private sector was slow to hire, and much of the job growth was canceled out by government layoffs. More than 6 million people, nearly half of all the unemployed, had been out of work for more than six months. For those fifty-five and older, the average length of unemployment was more than a year. Overall, only 58 percent of the population was employed, the lowest level since 1983. Amid such dire statistics, the recession spawned a new term, the "99ers," those jobless individuals who had been on unemployment for ninety-nine weeks, had exhausted all the extensions of their benefits, and were now left to fend for themselves with no money coming in.

A survey of the unemployed by Rutgers University's John J. Heldrich Center for Workforce Development found a discouraged and pessimistic group coming to the realization that they might never work again. Nearly two-thirds of the unemployed they surveyed had been looking for jobs for more than a year. More than a third had been looking for more than two years. Titled "The Shattered American Dream," the report found that those who had found work often went back to lower wages, part-time hours, fewer benefits, a new field, or a move to a new city or town. Their futures looked grim.

"We are witnessing the birth of a new class—the involuntarily retired," the report concluded.

> Many of those over age 50 believe they will not work again at a full-time "real" job commensurate with their education and training. More than one-quarter say they expect to retire earlier than they want, which has long-term consequences for themselves and society. Many will file for Social Security as soon as they are eligible, despite the fact that they would receive greater benefits if they were able to delay retiring for a few years.
>
> One of the casualties of the Great Recession has been a core American principle since the foundation of the nation—that if people work hard and play by the rules, they can get ahead. Now, the majority of the unemployed do not believe that simple hard work will guarantee success. They feel powerless, and voice little confidence in the government's ability to help them.

The recession had also left its mark on recent college graduates, according to another report by the Heldrich Center. The survey showed that in just a few years, there had been a big change in the ability of graduates to find a job. Although 90 percent of those who graduated in 2006 or 2007 had found work, only 56 percent of 2010 graduates had jobs. The median starting salary for them was $27,000, compared with $30,000 for those entering the job market before the recession. The new graduates were loaded with student debt. Nearly half received some financial support from their parents. In summarizing the mood, the authors referred back to their previous report about how the unemployed felt about the American dream.

"Now it is those who should have the most reason for optimism— young graduates of four-year colleges—who are expressing doubt in another cornerstone of that dream—that each generation can work its way up and have more prosperity than the one that came before it," they wrote. "The vast majority expects their generation will not do better than the one that came before them. They do not even expect to do as well."

The Great Recession and its timid recovery were producing not only a class of older workers abandoned by employers but also a generation of younger workers starting their careers without the skills or experience of their peers of the past.

$ $ $

In July 2011, an unusual sight appeared on Nappannee Street in Elkhart County. Posted in the parking lot in front of plants 2, 3, and 4 of the truck maker Utilimaster, not far from where Monaco Coach had laid off 1,400 just three years before, was a sign that stated the following:

23 NEW OPENINGS

MANY 3RD SHIFT ASSEMBLY

PAINTERS PAINTERS PAINTERS

APPLY WITHIN 8–3

"That's something I haven't seen in three years," said Ed Neufeldt, the RV worker who lost his job when Monaco closed.

It was a roadside oddity in Elkhart County. At the height of the recession, the only business advertising that they were hiring was the Flavor Freeze ice cream stand. While the county was still 20,000 jobs below its peak in the summer of 2006, it had gained 8,000 since its low point in the spring of 2009. Remarkably, the jobless rate which had peaked at 20.3 percent had fallen to 10.2 percent by June 2011. If the American economy had done the same, the nation would be back to full employment. But the apparent turnaround in Elkhart County also masked a large number who had settled for part-time work, moved out of the area, or given up looking after being unemployed for more than two years.

Terry and Desiree Gonyon, the couple with nine kids who lost their home to foreclosure, had also noticed the turn in the want ads.

"If you look in the paper now for jobs, there's actually jobs posted, whereas before it was always people looking for work, you know, looking to mow lawns or whatever," Desiree said.

"Yeah, I was sitting in the break room at Wal-Mart the other night and somebody just happened to have the newspaper and I opened it up to the jobs section and there was actually jobs posted there for like factory stuff," Terry added. "You start at ten bucks an hour; so the hourly rate has really declined like five bucks an hour. So they're hiring. You just have to take less."

Much had changed for the Gonyons. Baby Gabriel was now crawling and pulling himself to a standing position by holding on to the futon. The trailer park had kicked them out for having too many kids, and they were now renting a four-bedroom World War I–era home just three blocks from their old house in Elkhart. Residential construction work remained dry for Terry. It seemed like he was spending more money on gas driving around looking for work than he was making on the few jobs he found. Some of the jobs were late in paying or didn't pay at all, forcing Terry to put liens on the houses he worked on. The Gonyons were falling behind on bills. And Terry had missed enough child support payments that the state attorneys were threatening him with jail.

So in January, he closed his home remodeling business and took a job unloading trucks at the Wal-Mart in Osceola. After the baby was born, Desiree left her job at a discount tobacco store, but in February she joined Terry at the Wal-Mart stocking grocery shelves. They each made about $7.50 an hour. When I visited, Desiree was waiting to hear on a promotion to bakery manager, which would bump her up to $9 an hour. While the pay was low compared with what construction offered when times were good, working at Wal-Mart was far more predictable in the current economy.

"They always had the thing about being an Indian and a chief, and you know, I always liked being the chief, you know the boss, but sometimes it's nice to just be the Indian, you know. You show up, you get paid," Terry said. "It's a lot less stress on me. It's a lot less stress on my wife. The bills are all paid. It used to be that we would fight a lot. We fought about money and other stuff, typical married couple stuff.

When there's no money there, we don't get along. She's needing stuff for the kids and I don't have it. This way, we both know we're working. We both go to Wal-Mart. We know we've got so much money to deal with."

Terry and Desiree had caught up on bills, and with a little spare money in their pockets, they could take the family camping and go to the 4-H Fair this year. On an earlier visit, I had asked the kids what they wanted to be when they grew up. "A spaceman," one said. "A racecar driver," said another. "I want to work at McDonald's," said a third, "so I can eat all the cheeseburgers."

"I just hope they do better than us," Desiree acknowledged. "I mean, I don't want to say that I hope they become president of the United States or a lawyer or a doctor. I just want them to do better than us. I want them to follow their dreams. I just want them to be happy in whatever they do. I don't want them to live paycheck to paycheck. I want them to be able to, you know, go on vacation to Rome or, you know, do whatever they want when they want it and not have to rely on 'I don't have money' or 'I've got to rob Peter to pay Paul.' I just want them to do better than us."

At that, the toddler, Haylee, walked in with only a shirt on.

"Where's your pants?" Desiree asked.

"I peed in them," Haylee admitted quietly.

"You peed in them?"

"Yeah."

And so Desiree was off to put out another fire.

$ $ $

Things in Elkhart seemed to be improving. The stores were busier and the parking lots at the RV plants were full or close to it. The economy was certainly getting better, but Terry and Desiree thought little of it was because of the stimulus package.

"Last time I talked to you there were some electric car companies that came into the area that were looking really promising," Terry said. "Most of those have gone by the wayside. I was hoping something like that would take off."

Navistar, which reopened the old Monaco plant and received stimulus money for its new electric truck, had hired about forty employees and assembled only seventy-eight vehicles by early 2011. While several companies had shown interest in the delivery truck, Navistar's general manager, Shane Terblanche, was hesitant when asked by a local reporter about the promise of four hundred trucks in the first year. "I'm not as fixated on the four hundred," he told the *Elkhart Truth.* "We would like to deploy as many vehicles as we possibly can, based on the willingness of fleet customers to step up to the plate and the ability of the supplier base to meet our needs."[12]

Think, the Norwegian electric car company, had rallied into 2011 with plans to start production at its North American facility in Elkhart earlier than expected. But in April, assembly work suddenly stopped as they waited for parts to arrive from Europe. Then in June, Think's parent company filed for bankruptcy. The decision left the Elkhart plant teetering toward extinction until the American subsidiary was purchased by a Russian entrepreneur, who promised to restart production in early 2012. The Elkhart plant had hired only eleven employees thus far. In late July 2011, there were two pickups and a motorcycle out front and foot-high weeds were growing in the cracks in the parking lot.

"They have not achieved anywhere near the employment that we had hoped for," Mayor Dick Moore told me. "By 2014, about eighteen months from now, they should be at about 415 people. That was our hope."

The city itself had purchased a baby-blue Think car, which they used for the zoning department and proudly parked in front of the municipal building. But Elkhart's dream of becoming the electric car capital of the world was greatly in doubt, or at least deferred until things picked up.

"I built that up in my mind as what happened with the RV industry," Moore said. "All of those things produced trained employees. So if Think had 415 employees in that shop building electric cars and someone else was into building electric cars, why not come to Elkhart? You've got a trained workforce."

"The fact that this hasn't moved very quickly, that doesn't bode well for that idea," he said.

Elkhart was visibly different from when I first visited. The Michiana Country RV showroom, which had been closed since early 2009, had reopened as a Coachmen factory outlet and was filled with tent campers and towable trailers. The Treasure Chest was once again named Hopman Jewelers, and instead of advertising that it was buying old jewelry or gold teeth, it now simply said DIAMOND CENTER and BUYING GOLD. At the funeral home that Ed Neufeldt and other laid-off RV workers had remodeled into a shelter, a mother pushed a stroller and walked with four boys all under ten, their shirts off in the summer heat. All around town were painted elk statues, an art project benefiting a child abuse prevention program.

The downtown appeared at first to have revived with salons, galleries, and even a cupcake shop. The Lerner Theatre had been restored to its neoclassical beauty, thanks in part to stimulus bonds. Its grand opening featured a production of *Fiddler on the Roof*, and in August, the 1970s funk band War was passing through for its Why Can't We Be Friends? tour, which included a prime rib buffet before the show. But just past the theater was a different scene. Main Street was a strip of dirt with backhoes, bulldozers, and piles of pipe. It was part of a city revitalization project to replace the sewers and improve the streetscape. Bordering it, though, were two stretches of vacant storefronts. Flytraps restaurant was out of business again. And Casey's was now the Moore for Mayor election team headquarters. When we met, Moore was in campaign mode, ticking off the achievements during his term that had made Elkhart a "cleaner, safer, and quieter city." In his opinion, the stimulus had a lot to do with Elkhart's recovery.

"As a mayor, I can't say enough about the Recovery Act," Moore said. "Barack maybe never got enough credit for what he'd done. The president gets a lot of blame for what he didn't get done. But this wasn't a new idea. Every time we've had—even during the Depression—every one of these cycles that we've had, the only money that we had that was available was public money, and what did we do? Invest the public's money in what the public owned. If we hadn't had it, would Elkhart or anywhere else in this country be as well off as they are today? I don't think so. I don't think so."

Ed Neufeldt wasn't sure what to think. He was back down to two part-time jobs, driving the bread route in the morning and cleaning the doctor's office at night. His sons-in-law, who had also lost their RV jobs, went back to work, one for Monaco and another for Open Range RV. One of his daughters was now a home health aide while another who had worked in the RV industry was studying to be a nurse.

"We had a group of about sixteen that went to the Faith Mission that all lost their jobs, and all but two of them are back to work," he said. "Four or five of them went back to Monaco. A lot of the other RV workers like me, it seems they found a way."

Neufeldt didn't think any of it had to do with the stimulus package. Still, there remained something about Obama that he just kind of liked. If Obama just changed his views on abortion, he might even vote for him. But even if the president was elected out, he didn't think anyone else could get the country out of the mess it was in.

"I'm kind of a flip-flopper," Neufeldt said. "I think they criticize him too much because of how he tries to help the poor. I know I flip back and forth, but I'll hear a story about how poor people are and I'll say they need to tax the rich. Then I'll hear that if you tax the rich, then they won't hire the poor. I don't know."

The embodiment of this conflict was a picture frame sitting next to the kitchen table at his home in Wakarusa. On one side was Ed shaking hands with Obama after introducing him for the speech that launched the stimulus. On the other was his wife, Marianne, arm in arm with Glenn Beck at the rally they went to in Angola.

Driving past the Monaco plant, Neufeldt pointed out the new RVs and electric trucks sitting on the lot. On his wrist, he still wore the Green Jobs for America bracelets he had vowed to take off when the unemployment rate reached 5 percent again.

$ $ $

The promise of green jobs remained elusive. Early on, the Recovery Act had created a frenzy of interest in such work. One employment center manager in Minnesota told me that the office had been flooded by laid-off workers seeking green jobs, not because they knew what they were, but because they had heard they were more stable. Obama had pledged to create 5 million green jobs in the next decade. His Council of Economic Advisers estimated that the stimulus had resulted in 225,000 clean energy jobs by the fall of 2010 and would be responsible for 600,000 more by the end of 2012.

But for many who hoped that renewable energy would provide a new foundation as the stimulus ended, green jobs remained a far-off dream. According to data gathered by the labor-oriented BlueGreen Alliance and the Economic Policy Institute, about 3,600 workers had graduated from green jobs training funded by the Labor Department. But by the fall of 2010, only 466 had found new jobs at the end of the program.[13]

Even inside the administration, Obama's advisers were raising doubts about how the programs were being run—that in an effort to get money out the door, the Energy Department was subsidizing projects that would have been done anyway or weren't economically feasible save for the government support. In late October 2010, top environmental adviser Carol Browner, Larry Summers, and the vice president's chief of staff, Ron Klain, wrote a memo to the president. The memo noted that the multiple energy grant and loan programs in the stimulus raised questions about project sponsors double-dipping on government subsidies. The result shifted the risk onto the taxpayers, leaving the sponsors with "little skin in the game." To illustrate, Obama's advisers brought up the Shepherds Flat project in Oregon that when built would be the largest wind farm in the world. After taking advantage of stimulus-funded grants and loan guarantees, accelerated depreciation, and state incentives, the government subsidy amounted to more than 65 percent of the $2 billion project. Meanwhile, the sponsors, General Electric and Caithness Energy, had equity of just 11 percent of the project's costs. To justify the environmental benefits, the carbon dioxide reductions would have to be valued at nearly $130 a ton, more than six times the standard used by the government.

"This project would likely move without the loan guarantee," the advisers wrote. "GE signaled through Hill staff that it considered going to the private market for financing out of frustration with the review process."

With Solyndra's demise in September 2011, the internal memo seemed all the more prescient. How much of a role could the government really play in building an industry? It was a question debated early in Obama's term from Sand Hill Road to Pennsylvania Avenue.

In one e-mail, released in October, Brad Jones of Redpoint Ventures, which had invested in Solyndra, told Summers that the spending on clean energy was "haphazard." "The government is just not well equipped to decide which companies should get the money and how much," he wrote at the end of 2009. "One of our solar companies with revenue of less than $100 million (and not yet profitable) received a government loan of $580 million; while that is good for us, I can't imagine it's a good way for the government to use taxpayer money."

"I relate well to your view that gov is a crappy vc [venture capitalist] and if u were closer to it you'd feel more strongly," Summers replied. "But suppose we think there are all kinds of externalities to renewable investments. What should we do?"

What should they do? It was not an easy question to answer. Abandon clean-tech and the government could risk ceding a generation of jobs to China. But while many economists say the sector will continue to be a growth area, it will be hard to drive it on loan guarantees alone. Without a renewable energy standard, a price on carbon emissions, or a subsidized price for solar and wind, the green economy might as well be Emerald City.

The disintegration of the energy bill in the summer of 2010 already seemed like distant history. But without it, the Recovery Act investments looked like bridge supports sitting in a river waiting for the deck to be installed. With gas prices rising toward $4 a gallon again in the wake of the Arab Spring protests, Obama renewed his calls for a clean energy package. Speaking at Georgetown University, he said, "We cannot keep going from shock when gas prices go up to trance when they go back down." He announced a goal to cut oil imports by a third and released an outline for a national energy policy. But consumed with a potential government shutdown and a debate over the debt ceiling, the pressure to act faded again as gas prices receded to $3.50 a gallon. Without a comprehensive energy plan, American Electric Power pulled the plug on one of the Recovery Act's most prominent projects: a carbon capture and storage initiative at its Mountaineer coal plant in West Virginia. It was almost symbolic of the challenges that the plans to put solar panels back on the White House roof by the spring had yet to materialize.[14]

"I think we lost the opportunity of the century," Van Jones told me. "The Recovery Act was Act 1 in at least a two-act play."

In August 2011, the Congressional Budget Office estimated the cost of the American Recovery and Reinvestment Act would be about $825 billion. Including the various extensions of stimulus provisions, the federal government had now spent well over a trillion dollars, not including the interest. But two and half years after the stimulus passed, after dramatic drops in jobs losses and a steady decline in the unemployment rate, the economy seemed to be stuck. It seemed as if every time Obama drew a line in the sand in the jobs versus deficit debate, the tide rose up and washed it away.

SIXTEEN

MAGIC BULLETS

Engine, engine, number nine,
Going down Chicago line.
If the train goes off the track,
Do you want your money back?
—Children's rhyme

ON MAY 10, 1893, the Empire State Express No. 999, a new steam locomotive operated by engineer Charles Hogan, passed through Batavia, New York, on its way to Buffalo at a speed of 112.5 miles per hour, eclipsing the record for the fastest train in the world.[1] For decades after that, America was the model with its Zephyrs and its world-famous 20th Century Limited. The trains inspired a number of songs and a rivalry of sorts between regions, with Hank Williams crooning about the Pan American, "the beauty of the southlands." But with the Interstate Highway System and the advent of modern airline service, along with strict new regulations, America turned away from trains. Many U.S. passenger routes now take just as long, or even longer, than they did back then.

"Railroads were always the pride of America, and stitched us together," President Obama told a group of reporters shortly after the stimulus passed. "Now Japan, China, all of Europe have high-speed rail systems that put ours to shame."

In reporting this book, I frequently traveled back and forth on the Amtrak train from my home in New York to interviews in Washington, DC. Those three-hour rides along the Atlantic coast gave me a firsthand look at the wretched shape of passenger rail in the United States. At times, it felt like I was living America's infrastructure problems. There was the time the train stalled somewhere outside Wilmington, where we waited without air conditioning for the conductor to recharge the electrical system. There was the time they had to replace the engine in Philadelphia—yes, the engine—delaying the trip about half an hour. And then there was the time I barely made an appointment with a top Recovery Act official as the train crawled along at an aggravating 15 miles per hour between Baltimore and Washington due to signal malfunctions.

The Acela Express, which travels from Boston to the nation's capital, is the only train in America that qualifies as high-speed rail. For two short sections in Rhode Island and Massachusetts, it runs at 150 miles per hour. Trains in Europe and Asia can reach nearly twice that speed. More realistically, the Acela averages a pokey 75 miles per hour, which many drivers hit cruising down Interstate 95. Take the Northeast Regional line instead—only thirty minutes longer and half the cost—and you make odd stops in small towns like Aberdeen, Maryland, or the Jersey trio of Iselin, New Brunswick, and Princeton Junction, each only ten minutes apart. But rail is far worse outside the Northeast. One morning while visiting St. Cloud, Minnesota, I stopped at the Amtrak station and found a dozen passengers waiting in the predawn darkness. The once-daily eastbound train to Minneapolis and Chicago arrives at 5:14 A.M. while the westbound train to Fargo comes in at 12:40 A.M. The trip to Chicago lasts more than ten hours, longer than it takes to drive. And the train can often be two hours late, as the station agent announced to frustrated groans the morning I was there.

So perhaps the most visionary aspect of the Recovery Act was a plan to create a network of high-speed trains across the country. Inserted during final negotiations by the White House, the $8 billion down payment would essentially spur a new form of transportation in America. Despite its manifold problems, Amtrak was seeing record ridership in recent years as passengers sought to avoid the congestion of the highways and skies. There was something appealing about leaving from downtown and arriving in the center of another town, something romantic about looking out at the countryside, and something gratifying about avoiding the hassles of airport security, cramped seats, and endless fees.

$ $ $

In 1964, with the United States in the heat of the civil rights movement, the Warren Commission report, and the Gulf of Tonkin incident, Japan unveiled its Shinkansen bullet train from Tokyo to Osaka, the first high-speed rail line in the world. The announcement of trains going 130 miles per hour set off a frenzy of activity in the United States with the passage of a new transportation act the following year.

Ken Simonson, the construction industry economist, remembers hearing about high-speed rail while working at the U.S. Department of Transportation the summer after graduating from college in 1969. "It was called the Office of High-Speed Ground Transportation and they already had bookshelves full of consultant studies on building high-speed rail in the Northeast Corridor and elsewhere," he said. "So then twenty years later when I was at the ATA [American Trucking Associations], I had this episode that I got into as a lobbyist, and now another twenty years later, here we are talking about high-speed rail and the same corridors."

The French unveiled their high-speed rail service, the Train à Grande Vitesse or TGV, going 162 miles per hour, in 1981. And again America was interested in high-speed rail. Congress funded a number of high-speed rail studies in the 1980s and promoted the development of magnetic levitation, or maglev, trains, which use magnets instead of electricity to suspend the train above a guideway and achieve substantially faster speeds. In 1989, a Senate advisory committee recommended a $750 million program to design a maglev train, and a Department of Energy study called for a 2,000-mile network built along interstate highways.[2] It was enough that Gilbert Carmichael, then head of the Federal Railroad Administration, predicted in a 1991 book that "in this decade, we will have two or three high-speed rail corridors and one or two maglev systems."[3]

But discouraged by the costs and other challenges, federal interest faded once again. Over the years, states have launched their own high-speed rail projects. California approved a bill in 1982 to build a route between San Diego and Los Angeles, but the project died after a series of protests. In 1991, the Lone Star State approved the "Texas Triangle," a private franchise to connect Dallas, Houston, and San Antonio by rail. But the project faced intense lobbying by the airlines and failed to secure financing. Florida voters approved high-speed rail in 2000 but overturned it a few years later amid concerns over cost.

As a result, by the time the stimulus became law, America was decades behind. Japan and France had trains running at nearly 200 miles per hour. Test trains had reached more than 350 miles per hour. High-speed networks had been developed in Germany, Spain, Italy, Russia, and China. Even Turkey, Morocco, and Vietnam had plans for bullet trains. America had Amtrak.

"In the absence of a decisive outcome to this debate over whether the level of passenger rail service should be determined by the market or by federal transportation policy, Congress has generally provided Amtrak enough funding to survive, but not enough to make significant improvements in its service, or to maintain all of its infrastructure in a state of good repair," the nonpartisan Congressional Research Service reported in 2009.

High-speed rail is a totally different breed of transportation than the hulking Amtrak trains to which Americans are accustomed. The European and Asian trains resemble bottlenose dolphins whereas Amtrak trains are closer on the genetic line to their iron horse ancestors. Bullet trains are lighter and run on straight, electrified routes that are separated from road and pedestrian crossings. Amtrak shares curvy tracks with private freight companies, which dictate traffic and often force passenger trains to wait or slow down. The United States uses diesel-electric trains that are made heavy to withstand crashes. High-speed rail focuses on crash avoidance using advanced technology to automatically react to dangers ahead. In Europe, high-speed rail is defined as 125 miles per hour. In America, the standard is 90 miles per hour.

$ $ $

Obama and Biden, along with Transportation secretary Ray LaHood, laid out their vision for high-speed rail on April 16, 2009, designating ten corridors across the country from the Pacific Northwest to the Gulf Coast, California to the cities of New England. Drawn out on a map, one could envision at some time in the future being able to zip across America without ever getting into a car or an airplane.

"With [a] high-speed rail system, we're going to be able to pull people off the road, lowering our dependence on foreign oil, lowering the bill for our gas in our gas tanks," said Biden, an avid train rider who seemed to take personal ownership over the project. "It's about time we took those railways and made them the national treasures they should be. They're the best way to reconnect and connect communities to each other to move us all forward in the twenty-first century."

The plan called for upgrading existing lines to increase speeds from 70 miles per hour to more than 100 miles per hour. The next step would be to build new systems, such as in California, where voters had approved a train running up to 220 miles per hour. Taking the microphone, Obama alluded to the Interstate Highway System and the Transcontinental Railroad. He said high-speed rail would be a "faster, cheaper, and easier" solution to congested roads and airports. It would create jobs that couldn't be outsourced, revive withering cities, and reduce pollution.

"Imagine whisking through towns at speeds over 100 miles an hour, walking only a few steps to public transportation, and ending up just blocks from your destination," Obama said. "Imagine what a great project that would be to rebuild America."

As with past efforts, the commitment unleashed a frenzy of activity. LaHood embarked on a fact-finding mission to Europe. Biden talked up high-speed rail at his home train station in Wilmington and at a roundtable with governors at the White House. "The money is there and all of a sudden it's like build a better mousetrap," he said at a meeting in Denver. State officials formed strategic partnerships in the West and Midwest. When applications were turned in, the Department of Transportation had received 250 requests totaling $57 billion, more than seven times the money that was available. Even areas like Wichita that hadn't had passenger rail for years were included in proposals.

The project was so central to Obama's vision that he followed up his 2010 State of the Union address with a trip the next day to Tampa, where he and Biden announced the winners of the high-speed rail grants. That afternoon, before three thousand people at the University of Tampa arena, he announced $1.25 billion for America's first high-speed rail line between Tampa and Orlando.

"I'm excited," Obama said amid thunderous applause. "I'm going to come back down here and ride it. Joe and I—you all have a date. When that thing is all set up, we'll come down here and check it out."

The Florida project, which would eventually extend to Miami, would include 84 miles of new track connecting Orlando International Airport to Disney World to downtown Tampa. It would be completed by 2014 with trains reaching 168 miles per hour. The other big winner was California, which received $2.25 billion to purchase right-of-way, complete environmental reviews, and construct track between San Francisco and Los Angeles. When completed in 2020, the train would cut the six-hour drive down to two hours and forty minutes.

The Midwest received $1.1 billion to improve existing tracks so that trains could reach 110 miles per hour. Wisconsin was awarded $810 million to extend passenger rail service from Milwaukee to Madison. In Ohio, $400 million would jump-start the long talked about "3C Corridor" connecting Cleveland, Columbus, and Cincinnati. And there were other projects, such as upgrades between Seattle and Portland; New York and Buffalo; and Charlotte and Washington, DC.

America's newfound commitment to high-speed rail sparked interest among foreign train manufacturers. Ever since the cachet of the Pullman sleeper car began to decline in the 1950s, train manufacturing had mostly been done by foreign companies. The Acela was designed and built by Bombardier, a Canadian firm, and Alstom from France. But now more than thirty manufacturers had agreed to open or expand U.S. plants if they won contracts. The Spanish manufacturer Talgo announced plans to open a factory in Milwaukee. Siemens, the German conglomerate, said it had purchased land to expand its Sacramento plant in hopes of capturing the California and

Florida business. And a group of investors in Ohio bought the assets of a defunct manufacturer and formed a new American firm named US Railcar. An investment in high-speed rail in just four cities—Los Angeles, Chicago, Orlando, and Albany—could produce up to 150,000 long-term jobs, according to an economic impact study by Siemens and the U.S. Conference of Mayors.

"This is an absolute game-changer for American transportation," LaHood wrote on his blog when the awards were announced. "And I assure you that one day, not too many years from now, ours will be the go-to network, the world's model for high-speed rail."

$ $ $

Rod Diridon has been involved in transportation for so long that he already has a train station named after him in San Jose. His office, just a couple of miles away at the federally funded Mineta Transportation Institute, is a testament to a life spent building things and planning to build things. Every memento is organized in its place: first, the medals; then, the collection of hardhats; the model railroad trains; the gavels; the mugs; the paperweights and railroad spikes; the wall of awards, plaques, and certificates; the framed trolley posters; and finally, on the far wall, the bookcase full of transportation studies. Most prominent among the congeries, though, is the model of the French TGV. Diridon was there for the inauguration of the TGV as part of a California contingent studying technology breakthroughs around the world.

"We came home and we were all so enthused about what the French were doing," he recalled. "Shortly thereafter, we encouraged the state to create a high-speed-rail commission and they did in the late '80s and another one in the early '90s, and each one of those study commissions indicated that California was perfect for a high-speed rail program."

Now, as a board member of the California High-Speed Rail Authority, he was playing a central role in bringing bullet trains to the United States. Voters had approved a $9.95 billion bond package for the rail line in 2008, just a few months before the passage of the Recovery Act. An animated video produced by the rail authority showed the blue-and-yellow train picking up passengers at a modern station in Anaheim, whooshing through Los Angeles and Burbank apart from the highway traffic, gliding through the foothills north of Palmdale past windmills and farmland, coasting by Gilroy (the garlic capital of the world), and ending in the high-tech corridor of San Jose and San Francisco with glittering skyscrapers growing alongside the rail line. Building the whole route would require about $43 billion in federal, state, and private money. And there were plans to extend the train to San Diego and Sacramento.

The vision was grand and poetic, which made it immediately suspect. In the modern environment, infrastructure meant boondoggle. When Americans thought of public works, they were less apt to think of the Hoover Dam and the Brooklyn Bridge and more likely to think of the Bay Bridge and the Big Dig. Plans were scrutinized and doubted. Some concerns were exaggerated; others were serious and struck at the core of the planners' assumptions.

A scathing report released by the state auditor in April 2010 concluded that the business plan was wildly optimistic and lacked critical details. Getting right to the point, it was titled "High-Speed Rail Authority: It Risks Delays or an Incomplete System Because of Inadequate Planning, Weak Oversight, and Lax Contract Management." The authority had predicted about $17 billion to $19 billion in federal funding, but so far it had secured only about one-eighth of that, the auditor noted. Unlike highways and airports, high-speed rail had no dedicated funding source and would have to compete against other federal budget priorities such as health care and national defense. Since California voters approved the bonds, planners had already increased the initial estimate of $34 billion to $43 billion after accounting for inflation. The price of a one-way ticket from San Francisco to Los Angeles had nearly doubled to $105.

Critics had long been skeptical of the high-speed rail authority's ridership projections, and in July 2010, an assessment by the Institute of Transportation Studies at the University of California, Berkeley supported those suspicions. The authority had estimated that about 88 million to 117 million passengers annually would use the train by 2030. But the Berkeley researchers said the model was flawed, making the forecasts unreliable. A sample of long-distance travelers, for example, wasn't representative enough, and the methodology inflated the importance of frequent service, they said.

"This means the forecast of ridership is unlikely to be very close to the ridership that would actually materialize if the system were built," Samer Madanat, the study's principal investigator said in a statement announcing the report. "As such, it is not possible to predict whether the proposed high-speed rail system in California will experience healthy profits or severe revenue shortfalls."

The reports only fueled an ongoing onslaught of "not in my backyard" opposition from some in the peninsula cities of Palo Alto, Atherton, and Menlo Park. The affluent towns had grown up around the railroad, and residents worried that more tracks would come too close to their homes and alter the character of their communities. A faster train seemed like it would create more noise and more vibrations. And what about the elevated rails that would be an eyesore dividing the community? Because the San Francisco–to–San Jose corridor was narrow and had dozens of road crossings, the train would either have to be built above or below ground to maintain speed. The opponents wanted the rail authority to change the route or consider more expensive tunnels or trenches. Their concerns led to several lawsuits that tangled up the project but were mostly thrown out. And several city councils passed "no confidence" resolutions against the project. To illustrate what the aerial viaducts might look like, the city of Burlingame built two fifty-nine-foot poles connected with an orange net. The apparatus was quickly deemed unsafe and taken down after the point was made.[4]

Outside the Silicon Valley, the freight line Union Pacific objected to sharing its right-of-way with the high-speed train. There were eminent domain concerns in Southern California, creating challenges for how engineers would get the train into Los Angeles Union Station. Legislators sought to force European rail operators to reveal what roles they played in transporting Jews during the Holocaust. There were even concerns about a thousand-year-old redwood tree standing just ten feet from the rail line.[5] For better or worse, building high-speed rail in America was not going to be without some controversy.

$ $ $

A fundamental argument I heard again and again was that Americans would come to embrace high-speed rail as soon as they saw a bullet train up and running. This almost-platitude makes it all the more perplexing why the U.S. Department of Transportation repeated the flaw of other stimulus infrastructure projects and spread the money out like peanut butter. In all, thirty-one states had received high-speed rail money in some form or another. Iowa, for example, received $17 million to install track switches in the Ottumwa district.

Congressional auditors had trouble figuring out why the department funded certain projects because the documented rationales were "typically vague." "For example," the auditors wrote, "we found several instances in which, without documentation, it was difficult to determine the reasons why some projects were selected and others were not." In addition, more than half the $8 billion didn't actually go toward high-speed rail but instead went to fixing up Amtrak lines and extending conventional train service. California and Florida were the only states eligible for service above 150 miles per hour. But federal officials picked projects with low technical review scores to achieve regional balance. The approach baffled green advocates like Dan Carol, the former Obama campaign strategist.

"When you hand out $100 million to the state of Oregon or the state of Washington to do high-speed rail and split up $8 billion instead of awarding it to two people to actually build a fucking system, nobody goes anywhere, so everyone's short cash of the project they want to do," Carol said. "The feds split the baby because they think they're doing good politics, but in fact it leaves everybody a little short."

California's system alone was projected to cost $43 billion, five times the amount allocated for the entire program in the stimulus package. The Northeast Corridor, which made the most sense for high-speed rail, was virtually shut out of the stimulus grants. Before the awards were announced, the urban-planning coalition America 2050 had ranked the best routes for high-speed rail. Five of the top six city pairs were in the Northeast Corridor, including New York to Washington and Boston to New York. But the Northeast hadn't had a comprehensive environmental review in more than thirty years and technically wasn't a designated high-speed-rail corridor in the administration's strategic plan. As a result, it received just $112 million in the initial round to complete engineering work for a new Baltimore tunnel, build a new station at Baltimore-Washington International Airport, and upgrade other tracks in New Jersey and Rhode Island.

"To maintain public support for a continued federal commitment to high-speed rail, the initial investments must be viewed as a success," America 2050 warned in its report. "For this to be true, they need to fund projects in corridors with the appropriate density, economic activity, and existing travel markets to support strong ridership on these new services." Other top routes included between Los Angeles and San Francisco, Dallas and Houston, and Chicago and Detroit.

The Florida corridor, from Tampa to Orlando to Miami, was ranked one hundredth. Tampa to Orlando by itself wasn't even considered. The route made little sense. Studies have shown for years that the routes with the best chance of success range between 100 and 600 miles. The line between Tampa and Orlando was 84 miles. The train would shave about thirty minutes off the ninety-minute drive. And once riders arrived at their destinations, they would have little access beyond the station because neither city had extensive public transit. Yet with the earliest completion date, this was supposed to be the flagship project, America's first taste of high-speed rail under Obama's plan.

Early on, the administration faced criticism when short-term infrastructure projects took longer than the public expected. Now the administration and Congress seemed to be making the opposite mistake: sacrificing the quality of long-term infrastructure investments in favor of speed. By setting short deadlines and picking projects of low national importance, officials risked shaking confidence in the entire vision. Given the high cost and typical subsidies associated with high-speed rail around the world, many critics questioned whether such an investment even made sense in America.

"Compared to the United States," congressional researchers reported, "countries with HSR [high-speed rail] have higher population densities, smaller land areas, lower per capita levels of car ownership, higher gas prices, lower levels of car use (measured both by number of trips per day and average distance per trip), and higher levels of public transportation availability and use."

These arguments were presented front and center in the midterm gubernatorial elections across the country. In Ohio, Republicans mocked the train with a video splicing talk of the 3C plan with clips from the silent film *The Great Train Robbery*.[6] The 3C train, promoted by Governor Ted Strickland, would max out at 79 miles per hour. But it was estimated to average just 39 miles an hour over the entire route. "Shhhh . . . don't tell anyone but I'm driving twice as fast on 71 to Columbus as Strickland's slow speed rail," a Republican state senator joked on Twitter. "Even my soccer mom mobile can far exceed slow rail speeds."[7] State transportation officials later revised estimates to about 50 miles per hour, but that seemed unlikely with multiple stops and freight trains dominating the route.[8] John Kasich, the Republican candidate for governor, vowed that if he were elected, the train would be dead.

A similar debate played out in Wisconsin, where Republican Scott Walker made high-speed rail central to his campaign by setting up the website NoTrain.com. The $810 million for the Milwaukee-to-Madison line would be better spent on repaving crumbling roads, he said. After Transportation secretary Ray LaHood visited Wisconsin to release the first $47 million, Walker posted a letter to Obama on his website.

"I am drawing a line in the sand, Mr. President: No matter how much money you and Governor Doyle try to spend before the end of the year, I will put a stop to this boondoggle the day I take office," he wrote. "Governor Doyle and Secretary LaHood say we can't stop the train. I say, just watch us."

The Democrats used the trains themselves. Just a week before the midterm elections, the Department of Transportation revealed new high-speed rail projects funded by the federal budget. It included $900 million more for California, $800 million for the Tampa-to-Orlando line, $230 million to connect Iowa City and Chicago, and $160 million for upgrades between Detroit and Chicago. But the administration didn't announce it until days after members of Congress had a chance to hold their own press conferences touting the funding.

Work had already begun on high-speed rail, as Florida crews began drilling to survey the rock along the route[9] and as Illinois began construction in the Mississippi River city of Alton in September 2010. Amtrak unveiled a $117 billion plan to cut the travel time between Boston and Washington, DC, down to three hours by 2040. But with Republican election night victories in Ohio, Wisconsin, and Florida, Obama's vision for high-speed rail was beginning to fog.

$ $ $

Walker and Kasich made good on their promises. At his first news conference after the election, Kasich declared, "Passenger rail is not in Ohio's future."[10] A few days later, he sent letters to President Obama and Governor Strickland announcing his intent to terminate the project and asking the governor to cancel all contracts related to the rail line. The outgoing Wisconsin governor had already suspended work on the Madison-to-Milwaukee line, and LaHood told Walker that he would wind down the state's funding unless he changed his mind. Despite protests from train supporters and labor groups, Walker stuck to his guns.

Their decisions to kill the trains had economic consequences as well. Talgo, the Spanish railcar manufacturer, was now scaling back its plans to bring 125 jobs to a shuttered automotive plant in Milwaukee. Without new orders, it might even leave Wisconsin when its current work ended in 2012. The Ohio venture US Railcar curtailed its manufacturing plans after a company backed by Carl Icahn pulled out of the deal, citing "current market conditions."

LaHood moved quickly to redirect the money, sending $600 million to California, $340 million to Florida, and $160 million to Washington State. In an op-ed published in the *Orlando Sentinel*, he acknowledged the setbacks but noted that building the Interstate Highway System wasn't easy either. "When we look to America's past, it can be easy to forget that America was never predestined to have the world's best highways," he wrote. "Progress only became possible because generations before us dreamed big and built big— because they imagined, invested, and sacrificed for the infrastructure on which we rely to this day. . . . If we work together, a national high-speed-rail network can and will be our generation's legacy."

Florida now had $2.4 billion in federal funding, more than 90 percent of the money it needed to complete the project. If the state couldn't come up with the rest, private firms from across the world indicated they would cover it, as they clambered to get in on America's first high-speed rail line.[11] The federal Department of Transportation promised that contractors would be responsible for cost overruns and operating expenses, further eliminating the Sunshine State's financial risk.

But Rick Scott, a former hospital executive who became governor in 2011, wasn't convinced. The project would likely cost billions more by the time it was completed, he reasoned, and ridership estimates were overly optimistic, leaving Florida taxpayers on the hook for annual operating subsidies. In truth, many bullet trains around the world are self-sustaining if you don't include the infrastructure costs. Highways also require billions of dollars every year in federal funding and gas taxes. Airlines would have a much tougher time turning a profit if they had to supply their own runways, air traffic control, and security. Like it or not, every mode of passenger transportation is substantially supported by taxpayers. But even LaHood, a prolific blogger and speechmaker, failed to hammer this point.

On February 16, nearly two years to the day that the Recovery Act was signed, Scott rejected the money for high-speed rail and killed one of the marquee projects of the federal stimulus package. Democrats and Republicans in the Florida congressional delegation worked with the Department of Transportation to try to salvage the line. Two state senators sued the governor in the Florida Supreme Court. But nothing worked, and by March 2011, it became clear that the train was dead.

The U.S. Public Interest Research Group responded by releasing a video featuring an actor from the AMC series *Mad Men* in a scene set in 1965, shortly after Japan unveiled its Shinkansen. An adman with a half-filled tumbler walks through various concepts for marketing high-speed trains: a woman confused by "all the knobs, levers, and gizmos" of a car. A complicated piece involving a scalpel and an aorta.

"Why are you worrying about this?" a smoking adman in a bowtie responds. "Look, trains make sense. They're efficient. They're convenient. They're good for jobs. Hell, I would rather take a train than fly or drive anywhere. We don't need to sell trains."

If only it were so easy.

"I don't get it," Vice President Biden told a crowd at a fund-raiser in downtown Tampa a few weeks after Scott's decision. "You had the chance. You were the best-situated of all the states in the country . . . Even if you were doubtful, I don't understand how in this economy in Florida, you could walk away from 24,000 high-paying jobs."

The Department of Transportation again scrambled to reallocate the money. In May, at dual press conferences in New York and Detroit, LaHood announced $2 billion for twenty-two projects in fifteen states. The plan finally included significant funding for the Northeast Corridor: about $800 million to ease delays in and out of Manhattan and to upgrade segments so trains could run up to 160 miles per hour in those areas. The Midwest received $400 million for faster tracks from Chicago to St. Louis and Detroit. And $300 million more went to California to extend track from Fresno north to the wye junction near Chowchilla.

"Who says America isn't ready for high-speed rail?" LaHood asked on his blog. "From coast-to-coast, America is abuzz today with the news that the high-speed train is just around the bend."

But with huge chunks of Obama's network now dismantled, all eyes turned toward California.

$ $ $

While high-speed rail faced significant hurdles in the Bay Area and Los Angeles, the cities of the San Joaquin Valley—Bakersfield, Fresno, and Merced—generally embraced the project. Historically poor and mostly rural, the area had come to be referred to as the new Appalachia after congressional researchers compared its woes to the mining regions of West Virginia and Kentucky. Even before the recession, unemployment was in the high single digits. Now, into 2011, the Merced area had 21 percent unemployment. The Bakersfield area was at 17 percent. Fresno had 18 percent.

The train would dramatically change the flat landscape of the San Joaquin Valley. With elevated tracks and stations absorbing several downtown blocks, the rail line would become a central and defining aspect of daily life. It would make its communities, which had been experiencing a housing boom before the recession, even more convenient for people commuting to the coast. Most important, the train held the promise of more than 135,000 jobs. While other areas of California exhibited entrenched opposition, there was excitement in the Central Valley.

Under the Recovery Act, the state had to begin construction by September 2012. Realizing the project's success hinged on getting a stake in the ground, federal railroad officials made their funding contingent on the high-speed rail authority building the first segment in the San Joaquin Valley. So at its meeting to decide where construction would begin, the board voted unanimously on a 65-mile stretch connecting Borden, an unincorporated ghost town, to Corcoran, a small city best known for the prison that's home to Charles Manson. The high-speed rail authority wouldn't even run trains on it until it connected to a major urban center. Critics quickly dubbed it the "train to nowhere."

"It defies logic and common sense to have the train start and stop in remote areas that have no hope of attaining the ridership needed to justify the cost of the project," Democratic congressman Dennis Cardoza wrote to LaHood. He added in a statement, "For the HSR authority to choose this route is to significantly undermine the public's trust, marks a gross misuse of taxpayer funds, and will alienate significant supporters of the project, including in Southern California and the Bay Area."

Additional funding extended the first section north toward Merced and south to Bakersfield, but the route would be no more than a test track until more money became available. Federal and state officials tried to justify the project by noting that the first miles of interstate were built in Missouri. The Central Valley offered the cheapest and best chance to build long, connected sections of track that would one day allow speeds of 220 miles per hour. To get true high-speed rail, Roelof van Ark, the authority's chief executive, reasoned, California would need to first build the backbone. Sending the money elsewhere risked having it soaked up by existing rail lines and achieving only marginal improvements.

Federal rules required each segment to have "independent utility" even if the route was never finished. In a scenario the authority spokeswoman described to me as "Plan Z," the new tracks would be connected to an existing freight line for use by Amtrak's San Joaquin line. But by choosing the sparsely populated Central Valley for the first phase, officials risked building a train line that would never be used for high-speed rail. As Michael Cooper of the *New York Times* wrote, "President Obama's efforts to bring bullet trains to America have gone from the 'Yes We Can' optimism of his campaign slogan to the less certain 'I think I can, I think I can' of a certain storybook train engine."[12]

By July 2011, Ron Diridon seemed slightly frustrated but hopeful nonetheless. He was loath to criticize the administration's decision to spread the money far and wide.

"First of all, when those funds were passed out, it was before the Tea Party took control," Diridon said. "In retrospect, it would have been better to put the money into a few projects that could get going. But no one could have predicted the ultraconservative control in the House that has now jeopardized high-speed rail for the nation."

Diridon said he initially opposed the idea of starting the California rail line far from urban areas that already had proven ridership. But he has since realized that it was a "brilliant decision." Not only were they building on the path of least resistance, but the San Joaquin segment had set up a competition for whether the high-speed rail line would first go to Silicon Valley or to Los Angeles. "Now you have the major communities in the north and south demanding that they settle those differences immediately so that they can win the first extensions," Diridon told me. In addition, as the longest corridor became a reality, he said, it would open the door for private investors bidding to link the system to the population centers where they could turn a profit. Despite what had happened in Ohio, Wisconsin, and Florida, Diridon's vision of an American high-speed rail network was very much alive.

But every time California high-speed rail seemed closer to reality, something else would come up that made it seem further away. In May 2011, the state legislative analyst estimated that the $43 billion project was more likely to cost $67 billion and advised legislators to reconsider the decision to start in the Central Valley. Sure enough, when the high-speed rail authority released its new business plan in November, the cost estimate had more than doubled to $98 billion, and the project wasn't expected to be complete until 2033. The news prompted talk of killing the project or shelving it for better times. Many wondered if California would ever finish its high-speed rail line.

$ $ $

Leaving New York's Penn Station at 6:00 A.M., you are immediately confronted with the fossils of a bygone industrial world. The sun breaks over the abandoned redbrick factories of Harrison and Jersey City. The streets where trucks once loaded and unloaded are now torn up with crabgrass and weeds growing from the cracks. The metal bay doors are rusted or covered in graffiti or both. You reach Trenton, where the sign that says TRENTON MAKES, THE WORLD TAKES now seems as kitschy as a neon motel sign on Route 66. The montage of rusting hulks continues through the once dominant port cities of Philadelphia and Wilmington and on past the boarded up row homes of Baltimore. It continues until you arrive at Washington's Union Station, virtually on the doorstep of the Capitol. It is a diorama of economic neglect.

In many ways, it is what the Recovery Act was about: not only changing the course of the biggest recession since the 1930s, but also reversing the trajectory of a generational American decline. While the Recovery Act certainly prevented the unemployment rate from reaching 12 percent, when most of it was gone, the car was still stuck in the mud at 9 percent. Responding to one of these dismal reports, Vice President Biden's former economic adviser Jared Bernstein wrote on his blog, "First Impression of the Jobs Report . . . YUK . . . You want my second impression? Double YUK." Later he added, "You never want to freak out over one month's numbers in this biz, but when a monthly result reflects other stuff going on in the economy— in this case, slowing growth—you want to give that monthly number a little more weight."

To address fears of a new recession, President Obama unveiled the America Jobs Act in September 2011 in a speech before a joint session of Congress. The $450 billion package featured substantial tax cuts, a large infrastructure investment, and targeted spending to save teachers' jobs. On its surface, it sounded like a miniature trailer attached to the bumper of the Recovery Act. Though only two and a half years had passed since Obama signed the stimulus package, it was a far different time. Unlike the stimulus, the American Jobs Act focused on a few sets of programs, many of which were acceptable to both Republicans and Democrats. There was no mention of renewable energy, health IT, or high-speed rail. The administration appeared to have adapted some lessons from the stimulus: don't announce job numbers, bring your own bill to Congress, and highlight the people whose jobs will be saved instead of the projects that will start some time in the future.

There will always be Monday-morning quarterbacks pontificating about what the president should have done during the Great Recession. But an alternative that one former White House adviser offered me seemed worth sharing. In his scenario, the stimulus package was broken up into two bills. The first focused entirely on emergency provisions: rushing money to states and cities, helping the poor and unemployed, and cutting taxes for the middle class. Then, instead of claiming credit for infrastructure projects that hadn't started yet, the president could burnish his reputation as someone who cut taxes and saved the jobs of teachers and cops. Meanwhile, his aides could have been working on a serious investment package. Having headed off the criticisms that overwhelmed the Recovery Act, there would still be an appetite for such a package with unemployment high in the summer and fall of 2009.

Instead, the American Recovery and Reinvestment Act became a Rorschach test of amorphous programs, on which critics of all stripes could project their dissatisfaction with government and politics in general. In trying to address nearly every American challenge from education to energy, it absorbed the controversies and battles over how to deal with those challenges. "I've always heard that the definition of a giraffe is a racehorse that was assembled by committee," one Democratic congressional aide told me. "Sometimes, that's what you end up with when you have a lot of voices working on it."

The Recovery Act failed to live up to its promise not because it was too small or because Keynesian economics is obsolete, but because it was poorly designed. Even advocates for a bigger stimulus need to acknowledge that their argument is really one about design and presentation. The swing votes in Congress wouldn't stomach a stimulus over a trillion dollars. So the questions are, Could the administration have sold the stimulus differently or could Congress have designed a more effective stimulus, leaving room for a second longer-term recovery bill in the fall of 2009?

During the transition, Obama could have given a speech in which he said, "My economic advisers have considered packages of $400 billion, $600 billion, and $800 billion, but their research shows that to fully get our country back to strength, we need a package of $1.2 trillion. I recognize the political difficulties of doing that, but I promised to be up front and tell you what the facts are, no matter how uncomfortable they may be."

The incoming administration could have led more from the outset to ensure the bill was quicker, more targeted, and written with Republican support. The president and his aides could have tackled criticism head-on instead of letting it fester. They could have taken advantage of a rare supermajority in Congress to deal with jobs and deficits before the political winds shifted.

In explaining the stagnant economy, President Obama has said that the recovery was trammeled by the European debt crisis, rising gas prices, and the impact of the Japanese earthquake on the supply chain. But if the Recovery Act had been designed to generate more thrust on the front end, the American economy might have been in stronger shape to withstand these headwinds. Others have said that businesses are scared stiff with uncertainty and a lack of confidence. It might not be this way if the president and congressional leaders had focused on long-term infrastructure and energy bills instead of health care reform in 2009 and 2010. Health care was one of the few growing sectors during the Great Recession. And by setting Congress down on one of the most divisive policy paths, the administration was left with an atmosphere in which everything the president proposed, including ideas that Republicans supported in the past, were now considered radical and corrosive.

The administration vastly underestimated the political danger the stimulus package would have. In this new environment, even disaster relief was treated as a form of liberal spending. Emergencies had always been held up as a hallmark of when government spending can do a lot of good. Republicans frequently pointed to the collapse of the Minnesota bridge, which was rebuilt in a little more than a year, as an example of an efficient infrastructure project. Even Herbert Hoover had burnished his reputation by bringing relief to the victims of the Great Mississippi Flood of 1927. But as the victims of Hurricane Irene and the Texas wildfires struggled to get back on their feet, Congress searched for ways to offset the cost of the recovery.

The stimulus money wasn't enough to transform American infrastructure, the education system, or the energy sector. But it was just enough for Republicans to be able to say, "We tried that already." Despite the historic investments in the Recovery Act, such landmark bills now seem further off than when Bush was in office. Left with only a down payment on his major initiatives, Obama now faces a tough election and may end up like many of the homeowners who ran out of money during the Great Recession.

On the fiftieth anniversary of President Kennedy's "moon shot" speech, Vice President Biden delivered a speech at the John F. Kennedy Presidential Library and Museum in Boston. He stood at the podium, as luncheon guests clinked their forks and plates in the background, and tried to recapture the inspiration and vision of the former president's historic challenge.

"I want you to imagine the benefits to the first country that develops smart anti-cancer therapies that kill cancer cells and leave healthy cells untouched," he said. "Imagine the first country that makes solar power as cheap as fossil fuels and builds the first building that literally can be able to reproduce all the energy it consumes . . . Imagine the first country that creates that car battery that is even lighter and cheaper than the new lithium batteries we are now producing—able to store enough energy in one charge to have an automobile go one thousand miles.

"Folks, the one thing I'm absolutely convinced of . . . if President Kennedy were standing here today . . . that's what he'd imagine, that's what he'd envision, and that's what he would challenge all of America to repair to—to accomplish all of those goals I mentioned and more, for they're literally within our grasp . . . For it would have been beyond his comprehension that the United States of America would fail to invest in these visionary notions."

Rising with frustration, Biden took aim at the political gridlock. After winding up, his voice lowered. He recited a passage from Ralph Waldo Emerson comparing society to a wave. "The wave moves onward, but the water of which it is composed does not," Emerson had said. America's character had not changed. But what had was an occasional lack of boldness and lack of resolve. "We've become too incremental, in my view, in everything we do," Biden said. Then he finished his speech and walked out of the room.

It was rare testimony from an administration that always spoke of visionary promises and bold reforms. In this new era, audacity had met reality. Riding on the Amtrak line, looking out at the vestiges of America's industrial past, I could see the consequences of the government's inability to address its challenges. I could see it in the factory closings and layoffs that have left their mark on Elkhart, Aiken, and Fremont. The nation might never see such an extraordinary and flawed endeavor as the American Recovery and Reinvestment Act again. But through my travels, in the homes of unemployed workers and struggling families, I could see something else, a certain resilience that however difficult it became, they would continue to look ahead and go about their business trying to make it in America.

NOTES

INTRODUCTION

1. Nick Taylor, *American-Made: The Enduring Legacy of the WPA* (New York: Bantam Books, 2008), 166–168.

2. The costs of the Public Works Administration and the Works Progress Administration are from David Kennedy, *Freedom from Fear: The American People in Depression and War, 1929–1945* (New York: Oxford University Press, 1999). The historical figures on the federal budget come from "The Budget of the U.S. Government for Fiscal Year 2010, Historical Tables," 21, http://www.gpoaccess.gov/usbudget/fy10/pdf/hist.pdf.

PART 1: RECESSION

CHAPTER 1: FILE YOUR UNEMPLOYMENT ELECTRONICALLY

1. Dave Stephens, "Tearful Robber Targets Eatery," *South Bend Tribune*, February 5, 2009.

CHAPTER 2: THE DITCH

1. Lawrence Summers, "Wake Up to the Dangers of a Deepening Crisis," *Financial Times*, November 25, 2007.

2. Vivien Lou Chen and Michael McKee, "Summers Says U.S. Faces 'Serious' Economic, Financial Stress," *Bloomberg*, March 7, 2008.

3. Joe Biden, *Promises to Keep* (New York: Random House, 2007), 219.

4. Ibid., 65.

5. Nicholas Johnson, Elizabeth Hudgins, and Jeremy Koulish, "Facing Deficits, Many States Are Imposing Cuts That Hurt Vulnerable Residents," Center on Budget and Policy Priorities, last updated November 12, 2008, http://www.cbpp.org/cms/index.cfm?fa=archivePage&id=3-13-08sfp.htm.

6. Barack Obama, *The Audacity of Hope* (New York: Random House, 2006), 180–188.

7. Ibid., 202–203.

8. Andrea Mitchell, "The Details on Today's Meeting," NBC's *First Read* blog, November 10, 2008.

9. *This Week*, ABC News, November 9, 2008.

10. Ryan Lizza, "Inside the Crisis," *New Yorker,* October 12, 2009.

11. Liz Sidoti, "Obama Vows to Help States Weather Economic Woes," Associated Press, December 3, 2008.

12. Ceci Connolly, "States Want $176 Billion Slice of Stimulus," *Washington Post,* December 2, 2008.

13. *Meet the Press*, NBC News, December 7, 2008.

14. Jim Kuhnhenn, "Obama Proposed Economic Jolt Could Reach $850 Billion over Two Years, Dwarfing Earlier Action," Associated Press, December 17, 2008.

CHAPTER 3: LET'S MAKE A DEAL

1. Manuel Roig-Franzia and Paul Kane, "Two Moderate GOP Senators Give Big Voice to Little Maine," *Washington Post*, February 16, 2009.

2. Karen Tumulty and Jay Newton-Small, "How Maine's GOP Senators Are Key to Obama's Agenda," *Time*, February 12, 2009.

3. Carl Hulse and Jeff Zeleny, "Stimulus Offers Glimpse of Obama's Battle Plan," *New York Times*, February 13, 2009.

4. Jared Bernstein, *Crunch: Why Do I Feel So Squeezed? (And Other Unsolved Economic Mysteries)* (San Francisco: Berrett-Koehler Publishers, 2008), 24.

5. Eric Pianin, "David Obey: I Leave More Discontented Than I Started," *Fiscal Times*, July 16, 2010.

6. "Porn Kings to D.C.—Help Us Through Hard Times," TMZ.com, January 7, 2009.

7. Beth Fouhy, "Poll Finds High Hopes for Obama, Economic Plans," Associated Press, January 16, 2009.

8. Laura Meckler, "Obama, Stimulus Proposals Enjoy Broad Backing in Bill," *Wall Street Journal*, January 15, 2009.

9. Liz Sidoti and David Espo, "Obama Tells GOP He'll Consider Changes on Eve of Big House Vote on $825B Stimulus Plan," Associated Press, January 27, 2009.

10. *State of the Union*, CNN, February 1, 2009.

11. *Today*, NBC, February 2, 2009.

12. David Lightman, "Stimulus Still Expected to Pass but Not Without Complications," McClatchy Newspapers, February 4, 2009.

13. Tumulty and Newton-Small, "How Maine's GOP Senators."

14. Shailagh Murray and Lori Montgomery, "Bipartisan Deal Eases Way for Stimulus Bill in Senate," *Washington Post*, February 7, 2009.

CHAPTER 4: FOLLOW THE MONEY

1. Marla Dickerson, "Stimulus Plan Gives a Boost to Clean Energy," *Los Angeles Times*, February 18, 2009.

2. Julie Hirschfeld Davis, "The Influence Game: Hospices Win $134M in Stimulus," Associated Press, January 28, 2009.

3. Dan McNichol, *The Roads That Built America: The Incredible Story of the U.S. Interstate System* (New York: Sterling Publishing, 2006), 22.

4. Christopher Weaver, "Recovery.gov Falling Short of Expectations So Far," ProPublica, April 1, 2009.

5. Alec MacGillis, "Tracking Stimulus Spending May Not Be as Easy as Promised," *Washington Post*, May 21, 2009.

6. Brian Boyer and Olga Pierce, "Lobbyists Skirt Disclosures on Stimulus Lobbying," ProPublica, May 15, 2009.

7. Brett J. Blackledge, "Stimulus Watch: No-Bid Contracts Mean Higher Costs," Associated Press, July 17, 2009.

8. The CACI material was found by ProPublica intern David Epstein for a story we wrote: Michael Grabell and David Epstein, "For Some Stimulus Contractors, a Blemished Past," ProPublica, May 21, 2009.

9. James Rosen, "Clyburn Says Leadership Job Is Getting Harder," McClatchy Newspapers, May 10, 2010.

10. Mary Beth Reed et al., *Savannah River Site at Fifty* (Washington: U.S. Government Printing Office, 2002), 526.

11. Ibid., 184.

12. Ibid., 57.

CHAPTER 5: NO, THANK YOU

1. *Squawk Box*, CNBC, February 19, 2009.

2. Jenny Sanford, *Staying True* (New York: Ballantine Books, 2010), 40–41.

3. Mark Sanford, *The Trust Committed to Me* (Washington: U.S. Term Limits Foundation, 2000), 28.

4. Ibid., 4–5.

5. Mark Sanford, "Don't Bail Out My State," *Wall Street Journal*, November 15, 2008.

6. *Fox News Sunday*, February 22, 2009.

7. "S.C. Governor Evokes Zimbabwe in Arguments Against Stimulus," CNN.com, March 11, 2009.

8. Sarah Palin, *America by Heart: Reflections on Family, Faith, and Flag* (New York: Harper, 2010), 76.

9. Sarah Palin, *Going Rogue: An American Life* (New York: HarperCollins, 2009), 357–363.

10. Joe Biesk, "Tax Deadline Brings Out Thousands of Protestors," Associated Press, April 15, 2009.

11. KTVU-TV, Oakland, April 15, 2009.

12. Kate Zernike, *Boiling Mad: Inside Tea Party America* (New York: Times Books, 2010), 40.

13. Frank Graham, "Housing Authority Board Rejects Stimulus Funds," *North Platte Bulletin*, April 1, 2009.

14. Marie Rossiter, "Warren County to Obama: Keep Your 'Filthy Money,'" *Dayton Daily News*, April 22, 2009.

15. Bruce Smith, "SC Gov Still Facing Protests, Criticism on Anti-Stimulus Stance as Legislature Takes Furlough," Associated Press, April 6, 2009.

16. *Morning Joe*, MSNBC, April 8, 2009.

17. "Exclusive: Read E-mails Between Sanford, Woman," *State*, June 25, 2009. http://www.thestate.com/2009/06/25/839350/exclusive-read-e-mails-between.html.

18. Palin, *Going Rogue*, 377.

PART 2: RECOVERY?

CHAPTER 6: SHOVEL-READY

1. *The Situation Room*, CNN, February 9, 2009.

2. *Fox News Sunday*, Fox News, February 15, 2009.

3. Michael M. Phillips, "Shovels Are There, but the Readiness May Not Be," *Wall Street Journal*, March 17, 2009.

4. Nick Taylor, *American-Made: The Enduring Legacy of the WPA* (New York: Bantam Books, 2008), 117–118.

5. Carol D. Leonnig, "Murtha's Earmarks Keep Airport Aloft," *Washington Post*, April 19, 2009.

6. Brett J. Blackledge and Matt Apuzzo, "Bad Bridges Passed Up for Stimulus Cash," Associated Press, July 31, 2009.

7. Brad Heath, "Analysis: Road Stimulus Money Is Unwisely Distributed," *USA Today*, September 25, 2009.

8. Eileen Sullivan and Matt Apuzzo, "Secret Process Benefits Pet Projects," Associated Press, August 26, 2009.

9. *This Week*, ABC News, July 5, 2009.

10. *Good Morning America*, ABC News, July 7, 2009.

11. Ibid., July 9, 2009.

12. Sara Murray, "Slowing Job Losses Put Economy on Firmer Footing," *Wall Street Journal*, August 8, 2009.

CHAPTER 7: RECOVERY INACTION

1. Van Jones, *The Green Collar Economy: How One Solution Can Fix Our Two Biggest Problems* (New York: HarperOne, 2008), 16.

2. Don Lee, "Stimulus in Need of Some Prodding," *Los Angeles Times*, July 20, 2009.

3. "VP Biden Makes Stop to Raise Money for Driehaus," WLWT-TV, March 15, 2010.

4. John Lockwood, "Not Enough Stimulus for the Mall," *Washington Post*, May 3, 2009.

5. Christine MacDonald, "Bing Vows to Recover Demolition Expenses," *Detroit News*, January 18, 2010.

CHAPTER 8: ONE MAN'S WASTE

1. "The Mysterious Lake," *Knickerbocker* 19 (1842): 158–159.

2. Mark Hohmeister, "Lake Jackson Ecopassage Advances at a Turtle's Pace," *Tallahassee Democrat*, January 10, 2009.

3. Steven Friederich, "State Grant Still in Hand," *Daily World*, July 1, 2009.

4. John Maynard Keynes, *The General Theory of Employment, Interest and Money* (Palgrave Macmillan, 1936; reprinted New York: Classic Books America, 2009), 107–110.

5. Jason Scott Smith, *Building New Deal Liberalism: The Political Economy of Public Works, 1933–1956* (New York: Cambridge University Press, 2006), 136–137.

6. Geoff Earle, "Sex Study Stimulus," *New York Post*, August 24, 2009.

7. Joseph Abrams, "Stimulus Bill Funds Go to Art House Showing 'Pervert' Revues, Underground Pornography," *Fox News*, July 31, 2009.

8. PolitiFact checked this out and found that on January 21, 2010, after the report was issued, the martini bar owner withdrew his application "after it was discovered that the company had liens placed against it by the IRS and the state for failing to pay a little more than $8,000 in taxes." Rob Farley, "McConnell Says $100,000 in Stimulus Funds Were Used for a Martini Bar and Brazilian Steakhouse," PolitiFact, February 19, 2010.

CHAPTER 9: CASH FOR CLUNKERS

1. Alan S. Blinder, "A Modest Proposal: Eco-Friendly Stimulus," *New York Times*, July 27, 2008.

2. Steven Rattner, *Overhaul: An Insider's Account of the Obama Administration's Emergency Rescue of the Auto Industry* (New York: Houghton Mifflin, 2010), 140.

3. Robert Channick, "Car Rebate Could Be a Jackpot," *Chicago Tribune*, July 24, 2009.

4. Dan Strumpf, "Clunkers Program Draws Car Buyers in First Days," Associated Press, July 28, 2009.

5. Neil King Jr. and Andrew Grossman, "New Cash Steered to Clunkers," *Wall Street Journal*, August 1, 2009.

6. Matthew L. Wald, "In Congress, a Jump-Start for Clunkers," *New York Times,* August 1, 2009.

7. Gregory Korte, "Rebate-Inspired Shoppers Not in a Water Heater Mood," *USA Today*, November 16, 2010.

8. Tom Krisher, "Car Dealers Fight Slow Sales After End of Clunkers," Associated Press, September 13, 2009.

9. Peter Whoriskey, "A Post-Clunkers Slump," *Washington Post*, October 2, 2009.

10. Ted Bridis, "Clunker Data Show Pickup-for-Pickup Trades," Associated Press, November 5, 2009.

11. The e-mails were released by Republicans on the House Energy and Commerce Committee or summarized in committee reports written in preparation for congressional hearings. Most of the e-mails did not list the senders or recipients, and the reports referred to them with generic titles.

CHAPTER 10: JOBS, JOBS, JOBS

1. Richard Lieb, "Wil Cashen Is Still Trying to Grab the Brass Ring," *Elkhart Truth*, November 14, 2010.

2. Marilyn Odendahl, "Hybrid Vehicle Venture Energizes Two Towns," *Elkhart Truth,* May 15, 2009.

3. Marilyn Odendahl, "Electric Motors Corp. at the Center of Local Green Summit," *Eklhart Truth,* July 24, 2009.

4. Audrie Garrison, "1,600 Jobs and a Flash? EMC Shows Off Its Hybrid Truck," *Elkhart Truth,* September 6, 2009.

5. Corey Williams, "Thousands Mob Detroit Center in Hopes of Free Cash," Associated Press, October 8, 2009.

6. Matthew Jaffe, "Obama Admin Slashed 60,000 Jobs from Recent Stimulus Report," ABC News, November 16, 2009.

7. Brett J. Blackledge and Matt Apuzzo, "Stimulus Jobs Overstated by Thousands," Associated Press, October 29, 2009.

8. Louise Radnofsky, "In Battle for Stimulus Jobs, Shoe Store Owner Tells War Story," *Wall Street Journal,* November 2, 2009.

9. Mike Gellatly, "Allison Out of Top Position at SRS," *Aiken Standard,* September 29, 2009.

10. "Troubles at SRS Require Answers," *Aiken Standard,* October 1, 2009.

11. Some reporting on the emergency fund for needy families was done by Christopher Flavelle and Emily Witt for our story: Michael Grabell, Christopher Flavelle, and Emily Witt, "States Ignoring Stimulus Welfare Fund," ProPublica, September 7, 2009.

PART 3: REINVESTMENT

CHAPTER 11: THE GREEN ECONOMY

1. Ryan Tracy, "Solyndra Faced Headwinds Before Loan Guarantee—Report," Dow Jones Newswires, Sept. 27, 2011.

2. Jay Inslee and Bracken Hendricks, *Apollo's Fire: Igniting America's Clean Energy Economy* (Washington: Island Press, 2007), 223–24.

3. Jones, *Green Collar Economy,* 100–1.

4. Eliza Strickland, "The New Face of Environmentalism," *East Bay Express,* Nov. 2, 2005.

5. Ben Poston and Dave Umhoefer, "La Casa Violations Put Contracts at Risk," *Milwaukee Journal Sentinel,* April 11, 2010.

6. Eric Eyre and Alison Knezevich, "Agency Fights for Weatherization Program," *Charleston Gazette,* April 14, 2010.

7. Mark Lisheron, "Shoddy Workmanship Found in $22 Million Federal

Stimulus Contract to Improve the Homes of the Poor," Texas Watchdog, May 13, 2010.

8. Dale Neal, "Weatherization Project Saves a Life in W. Asheville," *Asheville Citizen-Times*, Jan. 18, 2010.

9. *Stossel*, Fox Business Network, Jan. 14, 2010.

10. Ronnie Greene and Matthew Mosk, "Green Bundler with the Golden Touch," Center for Public Integrity, March 30, 2011.

11. Russ Choma, "Renewable Energy Money Still Going Abroad, Despite Criticism from Congress," Investigative Reporting Workshop, February 8, 2010.

12. The Recovery Act also increased the borrowing authority for the Bonneville Power Administration and the Western Area Power Administration by $3.25 billion each. The federal agencies borrowed several hundred millions dollars for high-voltage transmission lines.

CHAPTER 12: "THE CARROT THAT FEELS LIKE A STICK"

1. "Federal Education Policy and the States, 1941–2009," States' Impact on Federal Education Policy Project, http://nysa32.nysed.gov/edpolicy/research/res_essay_contents.shtml.

2. Howard Witt, "Sick School Dreams of Aid," *Chicago Tribune*, February 12, 2009.

3. Christopher Flavelle, "Schools Have Trouble Tapping Stimulus Funds," ProPublica, December 24, 2009.

4. Timothy Conley and Bill Dupor, "The American Recovery and Reinvestment Act: Public Sector Jobs Saved, Private Sector Jobs Forestalled," updated May 17, 2011, http://web.econ.ohio-state.edu/dupor/arra10_may11.pdf.

5. Libby Quaid, "States to Compete for Extra Stimulus Dollars," Associated Press, July 24, 2009.

6. Mike Petrilli, "The Race to the Top: The Carrot That Feels Like a Stick," Flypaper blog, July 23, 2009.

7. Barbara Keshishian, "New Jersey Loses in 'Race to the Top,'" *Star-Ledger*, January 17, 2010.

8. Eli Saslow, "A Vision Unfilled: Three People Symbolizing Administration's Goals Are Still Waiting for Change," *Washington Post*, January 26, 2010.

9. Diane Ravitch, *The Death and Life of the Great American School System* (New York: Basic Books, 2010), 16.

10. Jennifer Price, "Biden to Teachers: Change the System," *News Journal*, February 28, 2009.

11. Andrew Brownstein, "Is the Stimulus Really 'No Consultant Left Behind,'" Hechinger Report, February 12, 2011.

12. Nichole Dobo, "Four Delaware Schools Chosen to Undergo Full Restructuring," *News Journal*, September 1, 2010.

CHAPTER 13: THE SHELLACKING

1. Dennis Cauchon, "Tax Bills in 2009 at Lowest Level Since 1950," *USA Today*, May 11, 2010.

2. The e-mails were released by Democrats on the House Energy and Commerce Committee.

3. Mary Beth Reed et al., *Savannah River Site at Fifty* (Washington: U.S. Government Printing Office, 2002), 517–519.

4. Rob Novit, "Aiken County Unemployment Rate Lowest in South Carolina," *Aiken Standard*, June 18, 2010.

5. Michael Cooper, "Few Cases of Fraud Involving Stimulus Money Have Been Detected, Officials Say," *New York Times*, September 18, 2009.

6. Joy Leiker, "Reports: Man Stole Disabled Victims' Stimulus Checks in New Castle," *Star Press*, July 8, 2010.

7. Alex Leary, "LeMieux Says Stimulus Like 'Cheese Factory on the Moon,'" *St. Petersburg Times*, March 14, 2010.

CHAPTER 14: CONNECTING THE COUNTRY

1. Brad Borevitz, "State of the Union," OneTwoThree.net, accessed June 28, 2011, http://stateoftheunion.onetwothree.net/.

2. David M. Kennedy, *Freedom from Fear: The American People in Depression and War, 1929–1945* (New York: Oxford University Press, 1999), 252.

3. Stacey Singer, "E-Records Can Fail, Doctor Warns," *Palm Beach Post*, June 6, 2010.

4. Eric Engleman, "More Physicians Adopting Electronic Health Records, U.S. Reports," Bloomberg, April 26, 2011.

5. Nicole Lewis, "Healthcare Software Venture Funding Jumps 19%," *InformationWeek*, January 31, 2011.

6. Peter Svensson, "Stimulus Money for Rural Broadband Will Connect Some Homes, but Questions Arise Over Wisdom," Associated Press, February 19, 2009.

7. Benjamin Taylor, ed., *Saul Bellow: Letters* (New York: Viking, 2010).

8. "Broadband Town Meeting," produced by Kenric A. Kite (Orca Media: 2010), http://www.cctv.org/watch-tv/programs/senator-bernie-sanders-town-meeting-broadband.

9. Denis Paiste, "UNH Broadband Plan Challenged," *Union Leader*, May 23, 2010.

10. Amity Shlaes, *The Forgotten Man: A New History of The Great Depression* (New York: Harper Perennial, 2007), 173–88.

CHAPTER 15: SPUTNIK MOMENT?

1. Paul Krugman, "The End of the Tunnel," *New York Times*, October 8, 2010.

2. David Brooks, "The Paralysis of the State," *New York Times*, October 12, 2010.

3. Major Garrett, "Top GOP Priority: Make Obama a One-Term President," *National Journal*, October 23, 2010.

4. Rick Barrett, "State Giving Back $23 Million for Web," *Milwaukee Journal Sentinel*, February 15, 2011.

5. Sean Cavanagh, "States Press Race to Top Blueprints," *Education Week*, December 8, 2010.

6. Michele McNeil, "More Race to Top Winners Push Back Promises," *Education Week*, July 13, 2011.

7. Spencer Soper, "Factory Held Up as a Symbol of Hope to Close in One Week," *Morning Call*, January 8, 2011.

8. "Japan Reclaims Top Ranking on Latest TOP500 List of World's Supercomputers," TOP500 Supercomputing Sites, June 16, 2011, http://top500.org/lists/2011/06/press-release.

9. Angela Greiling Keane and Jeff Greene, "Obama Bolsters U.S. Hybrid Automobile Sales in Waning Consumer Market," Bloomberg, November 23, 2010.

10. Ronnie Greene and Matthew Mosk, "Skipping Safeguards, Officials Rushed Benefit to a Politically-Connected Energy Company," *iWatch News*, May 24, 2011.

11. Seth Stern and Jim Snyder, "Solyndra Said to Be Investigated by FBI for Possible Accounting Fraud," Bloomberg, Sept. 30, 2011.

12. Marilyn Odendahl, "Is eStar Gaining Traction?" *Elkhart Truth*, February 9, 2011.

13. Amy Rigby, "Work Scarce for Obama's Green Job Training Grads," ABC News, May 4, 2011.

14. Mark S. Smith, "Promises, Promises: WH Solar Panels Are No-Shows," Associated Press, June 21, 2011.

CHAPTER 16: MAGIC BULLETS

1. "Great Speed on the Central," *New York Times*, May 12, 1893.

2. Joseph Vranich, *Supertrains: Solutions to America's Transportation Gridlock* (New York: St. Martin's Press, 1991), 18–19.

3. Ibid., 22.

4. Mike Rosenberg, "Burlingame Takes Down Fake Railroad After It Proves Too Dangerous," *San Mateo County Times*, October 18, 2010.

5. Doug Ray, "In Palo Alto, a Historic Tree Stands in the Path of High-Speed Rail," *Peninsula Press*, November 19, 2010.

6. John Michael Spinelli, "'Great Train Robbery' Video by Ohio House Republicans Mocks Strickland 3C Train Plan as 'Wasteful,'" Examiner.com, April 15, 2010.

7. Aaron Marshall, "Train Speed Remains Focus of Passenger Rail Critics," *Plain Dealer*, April 3, 2010.

8. James Nash, "Railroads Weren't In on New 3C Rail Study," *Columbus Dispatch*, October 24, 2010.

9. Grayson Kamm, "Florida High Speed Rail Work on Tampa-Orlando Train Line Begins Today in I-4 Median," WTSP-TV, July 19, 2010.

10. Sonu Wasu, "Kasich Says No Passenger Rail for Ohio," WDTN-TV, November 3, 2010.

11. "Stranger on a Train," *Orlando Sentinel*, December 17, 2010.

12. Michael Cooper, "Administration Pitches Big Rail Projects," *New York Times*, February 9, 2011.

CREDITS

ACKNOWLEDGMENTS

This book could not have been completed without the help of hundreds of middle-class workers, White House advisers, policy experts, economists, state and local government officials, lawmakers, and congressional aides (named and unnamed in the text), who took the time to tell me their stories and provided valuable insight to inform my reporting. I would especially like to thank the Neufeldts, the Gonyons, and the Mendezes for inviting me into their homes and their lives over the past three years. May God keep your spirits high and guide you to better days ahead.

My agents Glen Hartley and Lynn Chu of Writers' Representatives helped me shape my idea into a proposal, worked hard to get it into the world, and advocated for me every step of the way. My editor, Clive Priddle, provided brilliant advice on structuring the narrative. He offered encouragement and feedback when I needed it—and left me alone when I needed to be left alone. To the team at PublicAffairs—Melissa Raymond, Christine Marra, Gray Cutler, and Jaime Leifer—thank you for your wise suggestions and the professional attention you gave to this book. Jane Raese designed the interior, Donna Riggs wrote the index, and Sandy Chapman proofread.

A world of thanks to Andrea Bernstein at WNYC, who first approached ProPublica about working on a project about the stimulus package. The stories I did at ProPublica led to my obsession with the stimulus and my desire to write this book. Thank you to the editors Paul Steiger, Dick Tofel, Steve Engelberg, and Tom Detzel for throwing me into the subject and trusting that I would find my way. It is wonderful to do journalism at a place that gives reporters the time and resources to dig deep. Jennifer LaFleur, my colleague at ProPublica and the *Dallas Morning News,* taught me everything I know about analyzing data. And several ProPublica interns—Christopher Weaver,

David Epstein, and Christopher Flavelle—aided some of my early reporting on the stimulus.

Recognizing that every moment in life affects one's path, I'd like to thank my grade school teachers Mrs. Walsh and Mrs. Guido, who allowed me to write stories during class when I should have been learning the cursive for an uppercase Q. I'd also like to thank Willard Spiegelman at the *Southwest Review* for nominating a poem of mine for the *Best American Poetry* anthology, and the poets David Wagoner and David Lehman for selecting it. It was through that anthology that I met my agent and started the ball rolling on this book. To three people who have no idea how much they helped me—David McCullough, Susan Orlean, and David M. Kennedy—thank you for providing the inspiration and beauty of language to help me through the toughest periods of writers' block.

To my daughter Lola, who was born in the middle of Chapter 5, thank you for not being such a fussy baby. Without your cooperation and ability to sleep through the night, I might still very well be on Chapter 5. To my mother, there are no words to describe the sacrifices you made for my brothers and me.

And most important, to my wife Laura: Thank you for holding our lives together as I wrote this book. Without your support, it never could have been done. Without you by my side, none of this would be worth it.

INDEX

© Lars Klove

MICHAEL GRABELL has been a reporter at ProPublica since 2008, producing stories for *USA Today*, Salon, NPR, MSNBC.com, and the CBS Evening News. Before joining ProPublica, he was a reporter at *The Dallas Morning News*. He has twice been a finalist for the Livingston Award for Young Journalists. He lives in Brooklyn, New York.

PublicAffairs is a publishing house founded in 1997. It is a tribute to the standards, values, and flair of three persons who have served as mentors to countless reporters, writers, editors, and book people of all kinds, including me.

I. F. Stone, proprietor of *I. F. Stone's Weekly*, combined a commitment to the First Amendment with entrepreneurial zeal and reporting skill and became one of the great independent journalists in American history. At the age of eighty, Izzy published *The Trial of Socrates*, which was a national bestseller. He wrote the book after he taught himself ancient Greek.

Benjamin C. Bradlee was for nearly thirty years the charismatic editorial leader of *The Washington Post*. It was Ben who gave the *Post* the range and courage to pursue such historic issues as Watergate. He supported his reporters with a tenacity that made them fearless, and it is no accident that so many became authors of influential, best-selling books.

Robert L. Bernstein, the chief executive of Random House for more than a quarter century, guided one of the nation's premier publishing houses. Bob was personally responsible for many books of political dissent and argument that challenged tyranny around the globe. He is also the founder and was the longtime chair of Human Rights Watch, one of the most respected human rights organizations in the world.

.   .   .

For fifty years, the banner of Public Affairs Press was carried by its owner, Morris B. Schnapper, who published Gandhi, Nasser, Toynbee, Truman, and about 1,500 other authors. In 1983 Schnapper was described by *The Washington Post* as "a redoubtable gadfly." His legacy will endure in the books to come.

Peter Osnos, *Founder and Editor-at-Large*